Additional Praise for *America 1933*

"In vivid detail, [Golay] conveys the suffering and poverty that over-whelmed Americans as they coped with the greatest economic crisis the nation had ever faced. . . . In his portrait of day-to-day life in the first year of FDR's first term, Golay puts this sobering reality back at center stage, where it belongs."

—*The Washington Post*

"Golay's elegantly written book gives a granular account of [Eleanor Roosevelt's] three-year mission, focusing on its most intense portion, from July 1933 to September 1934."

—*The Boston Globe*

"[A] masterful re-creation."

—*The Miami Herald*

"Provides an intimate glimpse into the afflicted heartland as Hickok criss-crossed the nation. . . . An invaluable contribution to the scholarship of the era."

—*Booklist*

"A moving and memorable account of the impact of the Great Depression."

—*Minneapolis Star Tribune*

"[A] highly detailed, richly referenced portrait."

—*Concord Monitor*

"Golay ably captures Hickok's roadwork and personality."

—*Library Journal*

ALSO BY MICHAEL GOLAY

To Gettysburg and Beyond:
The Parallel Lives of Joshua Chamberlain and Edward Porter Alexander

A Ruined Land: The End of the Civil War

The Tide of the Empire: America's March to the Pacific

Critical Companion to William Faulkner: A Literary Reference to His
Life and Work (coauthor)

AMERICA
1933

Simon & Schuster Paperbacks | *New York London Toronto Sydney New Delhi*

The Great Depression,
Lorena Hickok, Eleanor Roosevelt,
and the Shaping of the New Deal

MICHAEL GOLAY

Simon & Schuster Paperbacks
An Imprint of Simon & Schuster, Inc.
1230 Avenue of the Americas
New York, NY 10020

First Simon & Schuster trade paperback edition January 2016

SIMON & SCHUSTER PAPERBACKS and colophon are trademarks of Simon & Schuster, Inc.

Photo insert credits: Franklin Delano Roosevelt Presidential Library: 1, 2, 3, 4, 5, 6, 7, 8, 9, 10, 15, 19, 20, 23, 27, 28, 29, 30; Library of Congress, Prints & Photographs Division: 11, 12, 13, 14, 16, 17, 18, 21, 22, 24, 25, 26.

For information about special discounts for bulk purchases, please contact Simon & Schuster Special Sales at 1-866-506-1949 or business@simonandschuster.com.

The Simon & Schuster Speakers Bureau can bring authors to your live event. For more information or to book an event contact the Simon & Schuster Speakers Bureau at 1-866-248-3049 or visit our website at www.simonspeakers.com.

Designed by Jill Putorti

Manufactured in the United States of America

10 9 8 7 6 5 4 3 2 1

The Library of Congress has cataloged the hardcover edition as follows:

Golay, Michael.
    America 1933 : the Great Depression, Lorena Hickok, Eleanor Roosevelt, and the shaping of the New Deal / by Michael Golay.
        p. cm.
1. Hickok, Lorena A. 2. Investigative reporting—United States—History—20th century. 3. United States—History—1933-1945. 4. Depressions—1929—United States. 5. United States—Economic conditions—1918—1945. 6. United States—Social conditions—1918—1945. I. Title.
    PN4874.H477G65 2013
    973.917092—dc23
    [B]

ISBN 978-1-4391-9601-4
ISBN 978-1-4391-9602-1 (pbk)
ISBN 978-1-4391-9603-8 (ebook)

To my mother, born in 1931

How were we caught? What, what is it that has happened? What is it has been happening that we are living the way we are?

—JAMES AGEE AND WALKER EVANS,
LET US NOW PRAISE FAMOUS MEN

I feared that men would no longer remember well what had really happened.

—MATTHEW JOSEPHSON, *INFIDEL IN THE TEMPLE*

CONTENTS

Preface   xiii

Prologue: Muffled Figures, Bitter Winds   1

1. View to a New Deal   9

2. Part of the Story   40

3. Coal Country   65

4. Strandees   91

5. The Ghosts of Wall Street   119

6. America's Siberia   148

7. "The Richest Village in the World"   174

8. The Stricken South   200

9. Empire of Misery   229

Epilogue: Prospects   261

Notes   269

Index   303

PREFACE

They were gaunt years, 1933 and 1934, the hardest of times during the decade-long era of the Great Depression. Americans approached the catastrophe in different ways and with varying degrees of desperation. This book sets out to describe how ordinary Americans—"one third of a nation," in Franklin Delano Roosevelt's phrase—experienced the Depression's icy grip. The organizing principle is a series of nine on-the-road investigative assignments Lorena Hickok, a former Associated Press writer, carried out for Harry Hopkins, who headed the first national welfare program in U.S. history. Hopkins instructed Hickok to report on how people were riding out the crisis in cities and small towns and on the farms, and to assess the workings and effects of the New Deal ameliorative programs President Roosevelt and Congress rushed into existence during the Hundred Days of the spring of 1933. She would cover thousands of miles by train, bus, airplane, and automobile. Her reports, sprawling, immediate, atmospheric, and packed with significant detail, brought the ordeal of the Great Depression vividly to life for Hopkins—and for the President, too.

In an introduction for a book she never came to write, Hickok called her work for Hopkins's Federal Emergency Relief Administration "a three-year odyssey through Everyman's land—and no man's land." She completed the most intense of the journeys between July 1933 and September

1934. The FERA assignment took her to nearly every part of the United States—from Houlton, Maine, to Miami; from Washington, D.C., to San Francisco; from Philadelphia to Bottineau, North Dakota; from Tupelo, Mississippi, to Phoenix. In more than one hundred reports to Hopkins and in a flurry of letters to her intimate friend Eleanor Roosevelt, Hickok produced a comprehensive account of the lives and times of Americans upon the edge of the abyss. She had an astonishing capacity for work. Active, efficient, a quick study, she interviewed people from all walks of life: industrialists and bankers, social workers, politicians and newspapermen, laid-off mill workers, postal clerks, waitresses and bellhops, union organizers, disinherited farmers, migrant fieldhands, out-of-work musicians, and stockbrokers without portfolio. "I think I probably talked with more people on relief than anyone else in the world ever did," Hickok would recall. This book retraces a number of her journeys and draws on her reports and letters; on a trove of American journalism (newspapers big and small, breezy new weekly magazines such as *Time* and *Business Week*, and *The New Republic, Harpers, The Atlantic Monthly, The Nation,* and other thoughtful periodicals); and on the incomparable American Guide series of the Federal Writers' Project, researched and written from the mid-1930s on for Hopkins's Works Progress Administration.[1]

The book recalls Americans' grim encounter with job loss, poverty, self-doubt, and despair. It pursues, too, a theme of response: from the New Deal in Washington, from union organizers in the coal patches of eastern Kentucky, from committed writers. Taken together, Hickok and the other journalists and writers who appear in these pages shaped a vivid and unsparing portrait of these hard times. "One man is always representative when he gives honest testimony about what he has felt and observed," the literary critic Malcolm Cowley wrote of the 1930s generation. "Scholars working from the record can be more dispassionate, but also, not having taken part in events, they can go subtly wrong."[2] In absorbing Hickok's reports and in reading Cowley, Edmund Wilson, Matthew Josephson, and many others, one witnesses what they witnessed, comes to experience their era as they experienced it, and learns to admire stricken Americans for their pluck, compassion, and endurance.

Some economic historians now argue that, along with misery and deprivation, the gray decade of the 1930s saw gains in infrastructure, technology, productivity, and education that would power the astonishing run of U.S. growth and prosperity of the post–World War II years.* Mechanical cotton pickers, giant steam shovels, high-performance transport aircraft, heavier trucks, synthetic fabrics, television ("seeing by radio," developed by 1929 but delayed for nearly two decades by depression and war) would change irrevocably the pace, texture, and quality of American life. As in our own time, though, advances were bought dear, at a painful, sometimes intolerable, social cost. Much of the suffering seemed avoidable; and one finds little to exalt in Americans' sacrifice, except perhaps their stoicism. Hickok wrote gloomily of what she called "a stranded generation," miners, unskilled industrial workers, farmers and others displaced by machinery and more efficient processes and by requisites for sophisticated skills and advanced education, people for whom no place could be found in a changing economy. Unattached, orphaned and 40 years old, cast adrift from the only profession she had ever known, Hickok used to wonder whether she would end up a strandee too.[3]

As early as 1933, investment began to pick up and manufacturing to revive. Incomes rose for those fortunate enough to be in work. By 1934 the economy had begun to grow again; adjusted for inflation, the gross domestic product would regain 1929 levels by 1936. Yet high levels of unemployment persisted—the jobless rate would not drop below 14 percent at any time during the 1930s. Millions of jobs lost between 1929 and 1933 would never return, a preoccupation of the New Dealers, some of whom believed underconsumption and mass unemployment had become a permanent feature of American life.[4] What would the future hold for the strandees? Figuratively, and perhaps literally too, their descendants are among the 40 million Americans stranded in poverty today.

As noted, this book is based on archival sources and journalism of the period. It would not have been possible without the assistance of archivists and librarians. My thanks go to the staff of the Phillips Exeter Academy Library in Exeter, New Hampshire, to the archivists at the Franklin Delano Roosevelt Presidential Library in Hyde Park, New York,

---

* See Alexander J. Field, *A Great Leap Forward: 1930s Depression and U.S. Economic Growth* (2011).

and to librarians in cities and towns from Houlton, Maine, to Moultrie, Georgia, from Logan, West Virginia, to Bismarck, North Dakota. I want to thank my wife, Julie Quinn, for her patient attention to the many drafts of the work in progress; thanks, too, to my agent, Scott Waxman, to Emily Loose, my editor at the Free Press, and, later, Alice Mayhew at Simon & Schuster, and finally to my History Department colleagues and the students of Phillips Exeter, past and present, who have made me a clearer thinker and a better writer.

Michael Golay
Old Lyme, Connecticut
January 14, 2012

MUFFLED FIGURES, BITTER WINDS

Their paths crossed briefly during the autumn political season of 1928, two women approaching the middle years and distinguished in their different ways. Lorena Hickok, a rising reporter for the Associated Press, managed to land a first formal interview with Eleanor Roosevelt on November 7, the day after Franklin Delano Roosevelt won election as governor of New York. She filed a fulsome profile of Mrs. Roosevelt, perhaps an echo of her sob sister days on W. R. Hearst's *New York Mirror.* "I failed to get much news out of her," Hickok would confess long afterward, "but I was so impressed with her graciousness and her charm that I ended my story with this sentence: 'The new mistress of the Executive Mansion in Albany is a very great lady.'" An editor struck out the line. Hickok and Mrs. Roosevelt met from time to time over the next four years, though nothing much came of the encounters, mainly owing to Hickok's aversion to what she called "women's page stuff."[1] But the Hickok-Roosevelt intimacy would ripen in the glare of presidential politics and in the consuming national tragedy of the Great Depression. Their partnership would make it possible, in eighteen months spanning 1933 and 1934, for Hickok to assemble as powerful a documentary record as we have of the hardest of American times.

As 1932 opened, a new national political campaign appeared on the horizon. By then Hickok, thirty-nine, was an Associated Press veteran, a skilled and resourceful reporter with the armor-plated façade of a woman who makes her way alone in a man's world. She played poker, smoked cigars and sometimes a pipe, liked her liquor hard, and regarded herself as "one of the boys." Ungainly when in motion but with plenty of "attack," she moved at speed from story to story. People noticed Hickok. She was "a big girl," in colleague Ishbel Ross's words, "in a casual raincoat with a wide tailored hat, translucent blue eyes, and a mouth vivid with lipstick." She went about in drab olive skirts and blouses, accenting them with bright silk scarves. Driven by her own private Furies, Hickok felt a compulsion to prove herself over and over again. "Every time I go out on a story I'm scared stiff," she once said. Still, she relished the role of caffeine-fueled, deadline-driven news hawk: crime, mayhem, and disaster mostly, with the occasional political assignment for variety. By her own valuation "just about the top gal reporter in the country," the ambitious, determined Hickok had worked hard to earn the trust of her editors. She learned the craft on midsize newspapers in Milwaukee and Minneapolis, moving to New York in the mid-1920s and apprenticing as a Hearst sobbie before catching on with the AP's New York City Bureau in August 1928.[2]

Over the years, Hickok assembled a gaudy collection of clips. She outhustled the competition with a dramatically detailed story built on an interview with a survivor of the wreck of the steamer *Vestris* in a near-hurricane off the Virginia Capes in November 1928, a coup that earned her the first female byline to appear on the front page of *The New York Times*. Passenger Paul Dana awoke the morning of November 12 to find the sea at the level of the porthole of his starboard cabin. The order to abandon ship came just before noon. From a lifeboat, Dana watched the *Vestris* slip below the surface. "She went down silently," he told Hickok, "with just a little puff of steam." The waves dashed Dana's lifeboat into pieces, and he and another survivor passed the night clinging to a broken spar. Not long after dawn a freighter appeared in the mist a mile or so off. "I tore off my shirt and waved it wildly in the air," Dana recounted. Among the few to be rescued, he recovered under a doctor's prescription of two shots of whiskey and an alcohol rub. At least 110 passengers and crew drowned in the *Vestris* disaster.[3]

In November 1930 Hickok interviewed a relic from an earlier great depression, Jacob Coxey, whose ragged army of five hundred men had marched to Washington in 1894 to demand congressional action to create jobs. Congress ignored Coxey, and when he tried to deliver a harangue from the steps of the Capitol the police arrested him for walking on the grass. Nearly a half-century's reflection on the rebuff led him to say to Hickok, "The American people are still dumb as beetles."[4]

The calamitous year of 1932 would pass into history unmourned. In-dustrial production continued a long, steep decline from late in 1929, banks failed, farm income sank, 12 million men and women were with-out work, and hundreds of thousands of people lacked adequate nourish-ment and shelter. The United States had endured nothing to approach the catastrophic scale of the Great Depression since the Civil War. In the Marxist philosopher Sidney Hook's grim accounting, "The lives of millions of useful people were being slowly but surely destroyed."[5] The physical wounds were gross, if not often mortal: stunted, underfed chil-dren; men and women in the full tide of life who wore the peevish, wiz-ened, and defeated expression of the aged and infirm; young men who hadn't worked in years; the middle-aged cast adrift, stranded with scant hope of ever working again; young women forced to ply the ancient trade of the streets; old people abandoned, derelict.

The Depression arrived at different times in different places. Hickok, for one, hardly saw the crisis coming. The Big Story, whatever happened to break on a given day, preoccupied her; she barely noticed the 10 per-cent salary cut the struggling wire service imposed on bureau staffers. The lengthening lines of the Depression's victims formed a distant, dim backdrop. "They were not really people at all," she wrote. "They had no faces. They were just 'the unemployed.' Muffled figures, backs curved to the wind, selling apples on the street." Within a few months, she would look back in wonder at all she had missed. Observing the debacle up close, she would write with sympathy and insight about the cascading effects of deprivation on ordinary Americans. "I came out of that experience with a sense of guilt for my own ignorance and former lack of interest that I shall carry with me for the rest of my life," she would say.[6]

In Hickok's New York City, three-quarters of a million people were jobless on December 31, 1932. Yet New Yorkers lived in the moment, buoyed with hope for the new national leadership and (not inconsequentially) in anticipation of an end to the Dry Era. Thousands spilled into the streets on a mild New Year's Eve after a day in which the temperature soared to a record 61 degrees. A great din erupted on Broadway that night, *The New York Times* reported; New Year's celebrations were said to be the wettest since the coming of Prohibition in 1920, and the speakeasies and nightclubs were packed. "Liquor flowed freely and at moderate prices," *The Times* went on, Prohibition agents keeping a respectful distance. Some four thousand people crowded into St. Patrick's Cathedral for a watch-night service; the rector, Monsignor Michael J. Lavelle, asked the parish to swear off profanity in 1933. At midnight, with Times Square filled curb to curb, the white ball at the top of the flagpole of *The Times* building slid slowly down. "It was manifestly a relief that 1932 had reeled from the stage forever," the newspaper noted. Only two persons died at Bellevue Hospital that night from the effects of poison liquor. Perhaps this augured well. *The Times* expressed cautious hope for the return of prosperity in 1933—a caution born not of cynicism but of the chastening effect of bitter experience.[7]

How desperate were Americans as the Depression deepened? Recent scholarship suggests their sufferings were broader and deeper and more widespread than previously had been believed.[8] The tally of the unemployed passed 10 million early in 1932—20 percent of the workforce—and rose throughout the year. By March 1933, 13 million Americans would be jobless, fully 25 percent of the laboring population. As many as a third of working people were reduced to short time. The U.S. Steel Corporation's Homestead, Pennsylvania, plant, with 5,235 men on the payroll in 1929, employed 424 full time in March 1932. Statewide, Pennsylvanians' wages fell by more than half between 1929 and 1932; officials estimated a third of them had no income at all. Industrial production had fallen 50 percent from its 1929 level.[9]

How desperate? The city of Chicago, with 700,000 people out of work, owed $20 million in back pay to 14,000 public school teachers. In California, with perhaps the highest standard of living the world had ever known, personal income dropped 29 percent from 1929 to 1933. Nationally, railroad operating revenues were down 50 percent since 1929, and 750,000 rail workers had been let go. The money supply withered;

between August 1929 and March 1933, the amount of printed currency in circulation decreased by a third. Early in 1933 a national survey put the estimate of the homeless in the United States at 1.5 million, many of them living without light, heat, or water in ramshackle communities knocked together out of wooden boxes, metal cans, cardboard, and tar paper and derisively known as Hoovervilles. Given the relentless numbers, optimism such as that of the New Year's Eve revelers in Times Square tended to be fleeting. Suicides were up 25 percent from 1929.[10]

Where could Americans turn for help? In New York City, drawing on municipal funds, the city's Welfare Bureau provided a weekly dole in 1932 of $2.39 per couple and $6.60 for people with children, supporting ninety thousand families—a quarter of the total in need. Private agencies, overwhelmed, found it impossible to make up the difference. *The Times*'s Neediest Cases Fund, with a balance of $249,311.91 on December 31, 1932, provided relief for four hundred families, but it turned down another hundred "attested as desperately needy through no fault of their own." Those unfortunates were sent back to the private charities that had referred them to the newspaper in the first place. The New York office of President Hoover's Emergency Committee on Unemployment furiously solicited donations to the private agencies. "All the personnel were hustling about or shouting nervously into telephones. It was as busy as Wall Street in the old days," recalled New Yorker Matthew Josephson, a thirty-three-year-old former stockbroker. Busy, but not effectual: the city was frayed, out at elbows, submissive. Josephson evoked rows of empty storefronts, buildings with peeling paint, prostitutes soliciting passersby from the recessed doorways of moribund shops along Broadway, threadbare men idling in the parks and public squares.[11]

Across the United States, the relief load in cities doubled and then tripled in 1932, while relief budgets increased only 20 to 30 percent. A third of the nation's private charities were shut down by the end of 1932 because there were no resources left to share out. "One got used to seeing older men and women scrounging in garbage cans for their next meal," Malcolm Cowley, a rising literary critic, would write. In the West Virginia coalfields, social workers with the American Friends Service Committee weighed children to determine which ones would be fed out of the meager stocks available. A child had to be 10 percent underweight to be eligible; in one school, the AFSC found that 99 of 100 students qualified. Estimates of the "floating population"—itinerants, people living rough—reached 1.5 million, including 165,000 boys and 100,000 girls younger than twenty-one.[12]

The causes of the Great Depression were many and complex. They included overexpansion of industry during the booming 1920s, a dangerously uneven distribution of wealth, declining consumer purchasing power, structural deficiencies in the banking and credit system, and a long-standing slump in agriculture and in ailing industries such as textiles, coal, and railroads. Government mismanagement exacerbated the downturn of 1930–31. The Hoover administration's high tariffs and tax increases and the Federal Reserve's deflationary tightening of credit made matters worse. So did President Hoover's stubborn adherence to the gold standard, which some economic historians say transformed an ordinary downturn into a decade-long economic catastrophe.[13]

The Depression came to rural America early, in the aftermath of the Great War. Prices dropped as demand for American agricultural products slumped with the armistice and farmers responded instinctively, increasing their holdings and putting more land under the plow, usually assuming a heavier burden of debt in the process. Overproduction pushed down prices inexorably; by the spring of 1933 they had fallen to 50 percent of 1918 levels. Along the Middle Border, in Minnesota, Iowa, the Dakotas, Kansas, and Nebraska, the market price of a bushel of wheat, $1.03 in 1929, plummeted to 38 cents in 1932. In the Appalachian mountain districts, flush times in the mines were a faint memory, and an atmosphere of desperation overspread the coal patches of Pennsylvania, West Virginia, and Kentucky. Seventy percent of U.S. coal miners were out of work in 1932–33. Textiles, an industry as ruthlessly exploitative as coal, had been debilitated for a decade and more. In eastern Pennsylvania, half the women workers in textiles earned less than $6.58 for a work week that could stretch out to sixty hours.[14]

For Matthew Josephson, hard times arrived with the Great Crash in October 1929. Bred to the money trade, he left Wall Street after two years in a brokerage firm in the mid-1920s. He had failed to rise high in the house. "My duties were but to help distribute the stocks manipulated by the Big

Fish to a public of small fry, and to keep them trading," he wrote. Big and small, they all wanted something for nothing, or anyhow very little, and with the pressures of work Josephson's health broke down: "One side of my head throbbed continually, and I was losing my hearing in one ear." He quit, turned to freelance writing (journalism, popular biographies of Zola and Rousseau), invested an inheritance from his father, and soon saw the value of his portfolio double. Then, over a few frenzied weeks in the autumn of 1929, his notional fortune vanished, along with more than $50,000 in real money he had sacrificed to the whims of the Great Bull Market.[15]

Clever, able to improvise, and facile with words, Josephson fared better than many. Deploying the remains of his capital, he joined a growing exodus from the city, settling his family on a former tobacco farm in Sherman, Connecticut. For the first time in a quarter-century, America's farm population actually increased in the early 1930s. (A New York City realtor named E. A. Strout reported that 70 percent of his firm's farm sales involved "city or former city people.") In the spring of 1932 a casual acquaintance turned up in Josephson's dooryard: Montgomery Schuyler, a middle-aged out-of-work engineer, the son of the Episcopal bishop of St. Louis. He had known Thorstein Veblen and had worked in the Soviet Union during the intoxicating years after the 1917 Revolution. Now he asked Josephson if he could do farm chores for food and lodging. Josephson offered him shelter in an old corn crib on the place.[16]

The Depression came to the writer Gerald P. Johnson's middle-class Baltimore neighborhood in 1931. His neighbors, a mix of professionals, artisans, and skilled workers, accepted their fate with gloomy resignation tinged with unearned optimism. He wrote, "We are persuaded that we are going to have to sweat for the next six months, but we do not believe for a moment that the hard times are going to continue for the next six years." Even as he prepared his article for publication in February 1932, home foreclosures were on the increase; within a year, they would swell to a thousand a day in cities and large towns, engulfing neighborhoods such as his. That said, Johnson found the people on his street less innocent now and more critical of the ethos of big business. Of the leaders and institutions that had ruled the American imagination before the Great Crash, he went on, "the whole pantheon of their ideas has been pulled down. We now know that they are not magicians. When it comes to a real crisis they are as helpless as the rest of us"—and as bewildered too.[17]

Herbert Hoover, an exemplar of the ruling business class, had done more than any of his predecessors to deploy the power and resources of the federal government in a time of economic crisis. He endorsed a $1 billion program for public works.* His Reconstruction Finance Corporation won congressional authorization to disburse $500 million to bail out the nation's overextended banks. And he sent $300 million to the states for relief. But a $10 billion public works program would have put only half the jobless to work. Five thousand banks would fail by the end of his term. In the fall of 1932 only one in every four jobless men received any relief at all. Then too, Hoover could not comprehend why the Depression continued to deepen or what more he and his Republican supporters in Congress might do to reverse the slide. Highly intelligent, an administrator of demonstrated competence, a man with authentic humanitarian credentials, the president, for all his assets and abilities, remained trapped in conventional patterns of thinking: the market would right itself eventually; it would be dangerous to intervene further; too much government interference with the natural laws of economics would delay the inevitable recovery, or even make things worse.

By early 1933 Hoover's energies were spent, his morale broken. On the last day of the old year, the Democratic president-in-waiting cleared out his office in the Executive Mansion in Albany. Franklin Roosevelt and his wife hosted a dinner for the cabinet and spent half an hour or so at the inaugural ball for the new governor, Herbert Lehman. His outlook optimistic, his disposition sunny, Roosevelt waxed expansive with the press as the final hours of his governorship ticked away. "I have signed the mail and everything is cleared up," he told reporters. "I have left Herbert a few pencils, an old pen, half a card of matches and some rubber bands. Everything else is mine and I am taking it away." Then he left for his home, Hyde Park, 1,100 acres of plowland, pasture, and woodlot on a bluff overlooking the Hudson River, to wait out the wintry last weeks of Hoover's ruined presidency.[18]

---

* There are various ways to measure the relative value of a dollar. By one cost-of-living calculation, $1 billion in 1932 would be the equivalent of $16.5 billion today.

1

VIEW TO A NEW DEAL

June 1932–June 1933

Lorena Hickok drew two prime assignments from the Associated Press in New York in the summer of 1932. She would be among a dozen reporters covering Franklin Delano Roosevelt while the Democratic National Convention met in Chicago, and one of three AP reporters—and the only woman—attached to the nominee's presidential campaign. As the summer advanced, though, Hickok found herself drawn more to the candidate's wife than to the candidate himself. By autumn, the presumptive first lady would become her full-time beat.[1]

By custom, presidential candidates kept to the wings until the national party convention completed its business, and even then the winner would lie low until the party sent official notification of the nomination some weeks later. Roosevelt, his wife, two of their sons, and members of his brain trust monitored developments in Chicago from the governor's study in the Executive Mansion in Albany. Roosevelt had gathered pledges from hundreds of delegates, but party rules required him to reach a two-thirds threshold to win the nomination. With his forces entering the convention around a hundred delegates short, the two-thirds rule gave his main rivals, 1928 nominee Al Smith, Texas congressman John Nance Garner, and Virginia governor Harry Byrd, a chance to stop his momentum and pick off his delegates.

Roosevelt may have been mindful of the two-thirds rule as he burnished his reputation for opacity in the months leading up to the convention. So enigmatic was he that his opponents, and even some of his friends, complained they could never be certain where he stood on a given issue. At one moment he would pledge unprecedented expansion of government power to attack the Depression and restore prosperity; at another he would promise economy in government and a balanced federal budget. Some of his pronouncements were visionary; others, such as his notion that joblessness might be dealt with by resettling city people on farms, cast a backward glance to an irrecoverable America. Roosevelt straddled the Prohibition issue too, at one point suggesting the federal government should allow the individual states to decide the question.[2]

The influential political commentator Walter Lippmann confessed he found the candidate difficult to read and limited in political understanding. "Mr. Roosevelt is a highly impressionable person, without a firm grasp of public affairs and without very strong conviction," Lippmann wrote. "He is a pleasant man who, without any very important qualifications for the office, would very much like to be president." Still, Roosevelt had been clear enough in articulating his broad political philosophy: unrestrained capitalism had failed, and the national government's resources must be used to repair the damage and rebuild the shattered economy. And he promised to be creative and improvisational. He had told graduates of Oglethorpe University in Atlanta in May, "The country needs—and, unless I mistake its temper, the country demands—bold, persistent experimentation. It is common sense to take a method and try it. If it fails, admit it frankly and try another. But above all, try something."[3]

The Democratic National Convention opened in hot, airless Chicago Stadium on June 27. The radio in FDR's Albany study crackled and droned, the candidate tracking events up to the minute via a direct long-distance wire to Louis Howe, his political mastermind, operating from a suite on the seventeenth floor of the Congress Hotel in Chicago. Organizational matters, platform debates, and nominating speeches for Roosevelt and his rivals consumed the convention's first three days. On the first ballot, recorded just before daybreak on July 1, Roosevelt collected 666 of the 770 votes needed to win the nomination. He kept a careful tally as he chain-smoked in an armchair next to the radio. The key was to maintain an aura of invincibility. With James Farley and his lieutenants working the convention floor, FDR picked up eleven votes on the second ballot, while Smith lost six. Imperturbable on a sofa opposite the governor, Mrs. Roosevelt knitted away at a sweater for the near-invalid, gnomelike Howe, with whom she had enjoyed a long, beneficial association. Roosevelt gained a net of nine votes on the third ballot, and Garner began to contemplate releasing his delegates to the front-runner, a move that might send others to Roosevelt and break the deadlock. The convention adjourned at breakfast time. The delegates, jaded, blue-chinned, reeking of tobacco, sweat, and liquor, strung out from lack of sleep, scattered to their hotels. They would return to settle the business at 8:30 in the evening.[4]

Hickok and the rest of the Albany press pool had passed the night in a garage behind the Executive Mansion, their improvised newsroom equipped with a radio, telephones, and a telegraph link. Toward midnight Mrs. Roosevelt looked in briefly, then ordered coffee and sandwiches for the reporters. Early on July 1, Hickok and a colleague, Elton Fay, the AP's Albany Bureau chief, encountered Mrs. Roosevelt on the lawn; she waved them onto a screened side porch with an invitation to breakfast. She struck Hickok as distracted, pensive. The nomination remained in the balance, Hickok knew, with Howe and his operatives in high anxiety as Garner weighed his options, but she sensed something more. As they moved off, she turned to Fay and said, "That woman is terribly unhappy about something." A dozen hours later, on the fourth ballot, the Chicago convention awarded the Democratic nomination to Franklin Delano Roosevelt and second place on the ticket to Jack Garner. Next day, breaking precedent, Roosevelt flew from Albany to Chicago— a long, turbulent voyage into fierce headwinds—to claim the nomination in person. In his acceptance speech, he pledged "a new deal" for Americans, coining the happy phrase that would define an era.[5]

Roosevelt regarded the nine-hour flight to Chicago as a stunt, even though America's pioneering airlines were transporting more than half a million passengers a year by 1932. The railroads were the candidate's preferred mode of travel, and he chose them for the most important initiative of the campaign, a late-summer tour of the western half of the country. The seven-car special steamed out of Albany just before midnight on September

11, Roosevelt in his private car, *Pioneer*, with a son, James, and a daughter, Anna Dall, in the entourage. (Mrs. Roosevelt stayed behind to settle their two younger sons into boarding school at Groton in Massachusetts and would board in Arizona on the return.) Press secretary Marvin McIntyre, brain trust chief Raymond Moley, twenty-four reporters, among them Lorena Hickok, and twelve photographers were berthed in three Pullman cars. The three-week trip would cover 8,900 miles and traverse twenty-one states. Roosevelt called it a "look, listen and learn" tour, but he also planned to deliver major speeches on the farm crisis, railroads, electric power, industrial policy, and the tariff. The special raced through the Midwest, stopping only for an equipment change in Indianapolis, where FDR confined himself to a wave in the direction of a delegation of Indiana Democrats gathered under the soot-blackened train shed. Serious campaigning commenced west of the Mississippi. He seemed most to enjoy the prairie town whistle-stops, where he found the crowds large and enthusiastic. Amateur bands struck up "Happy Days Are Here Again," and the paraplegic Roosevelt would appear on the rear platform in shirtsleeves, supporting himself on a set of upright bars upon which loudspeakers were rigged, "cheery and chatty with all comers" in the September dust and heat.[6]

The governor delivered the farm speech early in the sun-blasted afternoon of September 14 on the grounds of the Kansas State Capitol in Topeka against a backdrop of acute crisis and intermittent violence in the countryside. America's 6.3 million farms, most of them of a hundred acres or fewer, supported fully a third of the nation's population of 123 million. "We have poverty, we have want in the midst of abundance," Roosevelt told the crowd in what *Time* magazine called his "bland, cultured voice"; with agricultural prices at historic lows, "the farmer misses not only the things that make life tolerable but those that make decent living possible." The Kansans were noncommittal, wrote Hickok. "They did not applaud. They just stood there in the broiling sun, listening." Roosevelt went on to propose national planning for agriculture, vast forestation projects on surplus land, reduced taxes, federal credits to banks that rallied to help farmers avert foreclosure, and tariff adjustments favoring farmers. Short on specifics, the speech nevertheless received passable reviews, although *The Nation* found Roosevelt nebulous and observed that Topeka "seems to confirm what his adversaries have charged—that he has a confused mind which has not thought things through, and therefore has no clear remedies to suggest." But by consensus, Roosevelt at least avoided any major blunder with the farm speech.[7]

It wasn't clear, though, how the address would play in the Middle Border. In mid-August 1,500 farmers in western Iowa had launched a strike that aimed to force processors and distributors to pay higher prices for their milk, corn, and hogs. Picketers established a cordon along the eastern approaches to Sioux City, where they spoke defiantly of the Boston Tea Party and renamed Highway 20 "Bunker Hill 20." Iowa country people were approaching the end of their endurance. Reporting for *Scribner's Magazine,* Josephine Herbst, a native of Sioux City, interviewed a striker who collected a pittance selling cucumbers out of his kitchen garden. "No one had money and he would even take an old pair of shoes," she wrote. "Other day he took a corset. He didn't know what he could do with it, but he took it." Another striker resolved that with hogs at 2 cents a pound he'd experiment to see how big he could grow one. "I got some 600 pounds right now, eating their heads off," he told Herbst. He had plenty of corn—he couldn't get a price for corn either—and figured the hogs might as well consume it.[8]

The strikers halted milk trucks, spilled the contents into the road, roughed up uncooperative drivers—and reduced the flow of milk into Sioux City by 90 percent. Prepared for violence, they armed themselves with billies and old shotguns. "The first day the deputies drove through, the boys scattered through the corn," an old man with a white moustache and fluffy white hair told Herbst. "They wouldn't do that so easily now. Look how tall that corn grows. It's as good to fire from as to hide in." The insurgents were big weather-beaten men in loose denim, faded blue shirts, and slouch hats, and to Herbst they carried themselves with an air of desperate dignity, as though they had retreated to the last ditch. With breezy cynicism, *Time* called them a scruffy lot, "shiftless, debt-ridden, many of them with no underwear beneath their ragged blue overalls." (This prompted a tart rejoinder from Iowan F. B. Taylor, who wrote, "Where on earth do you get the idea that Iowa farmers are shiftless? They not only have shirts but generally keep them on.") In early September the strike spread south to Council Bluffs, opposite Omaha, Nebraska. The sheriff, a veteran of the World War named Percy Lainson, mobilized a hundred citizens at $3.50 a day and armed them with baseball bats and pick handles. The strikers' lines held against a night assault with tear gas bombs that yielded sixty arrests. Farmers in the Sioux City area eventually won concessions, gaining a price rise of a couple of cents a quart. In Council Bluffs, farmers and the authorities fought to a drawn battle, so that one could hardly tell whether farmers unable to sell or city folk unable to buy were the worse off.[9]

The Democratic presidential special rushed west at a steady sixty miles an hour. In the baggage car, the reporters skimmed the local newspapers, played cards, smoked, and tapped out stories to be filed at the next stop. The train carried FDR from Topeka to Denver overnight, arriving in the Colorado capital on the morning of September 15. Crowds lined the downtown pavements three and four deep as the governor motored slowly to the Brown Palace Hotel. In a brief speech there FDR, who would direct the most active, interventionist federal administration in the nation's history, promised a return to the minimalist governing principles of Thomas Jefferson. After midnight the special bore north and west for Cheyenne and Laramie, then due west to Salt Lake City for a twenty-four-hour layover on September 17–18. In a speech before a crowd of eight thousand in the Mormon Tabernacle and a much larger audience listening to stations of the NBC and CBS radio networks, the candidate addressed the troubles of America's sickly railroads, again emphasizing the importance of national planning.[10]

In Seattle seventy-five thousand people cheered FDR's motorcade and another thirty thousand, equally divided between the city's auditorium and an adjacent loudspeaker-equipped baseball park, heard his call for tariff restructuring to spur world trade. The special moved on to Portland for the utilities speech on September 21, then finally to San Francisco for a two-day stop. There, at a Commonwealth Club luncheon on the 23rd, FDR delivered what historian Kenneth Davis would call "the least characteristically Rooseveltian" speech of the entire campaign, a somber address to two thousand Bay Area businessmen. Doleful, drained of his natural optimism, the speech emphasized the tension between aspirations for equality and the protection of property, a preoccupation that dated to the era of the Founders. Conflict between two sets of rights, two contrasting definitions of liberty, two notions of individualism, Roosevelt suggested, had intensified as unfettered capitalism fostered vast concentrations of wealth and power that, used irresponsibly, led to the colossal economic collapse of 1929–30 and brought misery to every part of the land.[11]

The time had come, Roosevelt told the Commonwealth Club, for "a reappraisal of values." The economy had matured; the boom times were gone, probably for good. Equality of opportunity no longer existed in America. New economic realities had hobbled the Titan and his day was over. Roosevelt stopped short of calling for a new economic order, though he argued for every man's "right to make a comfortable living" and to provide for his dependents and for sickness and old age.[12]

"Our task now is not discovery or exploitation of natural resources, or necessarily producing more goods," Roosevelt said. "It is the soberer, less dramatic business of administering resources and plants already in hand, of . . . meeting the problem of underconsumption, of . . . distributing wealth and products more equitably, of adapting existing economic organizations to the service of the people. The day of enlightened administration has come."[13]

The San Francisco business elite responded politely, and at times with applause. Still, according to James Hagerty in *The New York Times*, "silence followed some of the most striking passages in the governor's discussion of economic problems and remedies." Hagerty wondered whether the audience fully comprehended the drift of Roosevelt's thinking. A. A. Berle, an economist, Columbia Law School professor, and member of FDR's brain trust, had written the first draft of the speech in New York City, forwarding it via airmail to overtake Raymond Moley aboard the campaign train. The speech reflected the bleak views of some New Dealers: the United States had entered a postindustrial era of overproduction, underconsumption, and high structural unemployment. It would powerfully shape the thinking of key Roosevelt advisors and heavily influence policymaking in the early New Deal.[14]

The campaign train jogged southward to the Republican bastion of Los Angeles on September 24, where a crowd of 200,000 lined the route of FDR's motorcade from Central Station to the Biltmore Hotel. A delegation of thirty men in tattered clothing greeted him with a banner that read, "Welcome to Roosevelt from the Forgotten Men." Mayor John Porter, a

Republican, snubbed the candidate at the depot, then evidently had second thoughts after FDR called briefly at City Hall. Porter ran, panting, to catch up as the motorcade sped away. Roosevelt addressed an enthusiastic gathering of twenty-five thousand at the Hollywood Bowl that evening, walking slowly to the podium on the arm of son Jimmy. *Time* assessed the far western stages of the long trip this way: "If September crowds and applause mean November votes, the Pacific Coast was in the bag." Finally, just after midnight on the 25th, the special turned east for Williams, Arizona, south of the Grand Canyon. Eleanor Roosevelt joined the entourage there.[15]

Admiring her intelligence and poise, Lorena Hickok had long wanted to know Mrs. Roosevelt better. "But she always kept me at arm's length—and her arms were very long," Hickok recalled. Now the long hurtle through the lonely wastes of the West presented an opportunity for a closer engagement. It began inauspiciously, with a complaint from Hickok that Mrs. Roosevelt had given the press pack the slip—that is, except for the *Chicago Tribune*'s John Boettinger—when she left the train at Williams for an overnight stay with a friend, Isabella Greenway; they were girls at school together, and Greenway had been a bridesmaid at Eleanor's wedding. Boettinger, a junior member of the press corps, had penetrated the circle of two of the Roosevelt children, Jimmy and Anna, and so cadged an invitation to join the excursion. ER assured Hickok the visit was purely social and therefore no harm done, but the next exclusive invitation, a tour of a cattle ranch, went to Hickok. "The story didn't amount to much," Hickok wrote later. "I saw some cowboys roping steers and trying to stay on bucking broncos, and I ate some barbecued beef." Afterward, though, Mrs. Roosevelt came to sit with her alone for a time and spoke of personal matters, the beginning, perhaps, of an *amitié* that would ripen over time.[16]

Mrs. Roosevelt left the special at Colorado Springs for an early Christmas shopping trip, the subject of an Associated Press dispatch by Hickok. The brief article noted that ER maintained more than three hundred names on her Christmas list, but it was first thing in the morning, few shops had opened, and she made off with only three Indian dolls and three bracelets, gifts for her three grandchildren. The caravan moved on, east and north through Kansas and Nebraska, the mountains receding in the campaign special's wake. The train paused at Waterloo, Nebraska, for a Roosevelt appearance at the 1,200-acre farm of Gus Sumnick: a chicken dinner on trestle tables set up on the lawn and a brief speech in which Sumnick announced in German-accented English that since 1929 Hoover farm policies had cost him $75,000 to $85,000 in receipts for his corn and hogs. Mobile and energetic, Mrs. Roosevelt ranged over the Sumnick farm as though to the manner born, nimbly surmounting barbed-wire fences while Hickok trailed along, wheezing and drenched in sweat.[17]

After a brief stopover in Milwaukee, a crowd estimated at 200,000 turned out for a torchlight parade in Chicago's Loop on the night of September 30, a "wild, roaring welcome" for Roosevelt, the *Tribune* reported under John Boettinger's byline. *The New York Times*'s Hagerty judged it "one of the greatest demonstrations ever accorded a candidate." Next day the Roosevelts took in game 3 of the Yankees–Cubs World Series at Wrigley Field. Babe Ruth and Lou Gehrig each hit two home runs, and the Yankees won 7–5; they would complete the four-game sweep with a 13–6 win at Wrigley the next day. After a last stop in Detroit, where FDR vowed modestly to abolish poverty, they were home at last in Albany on October 3.[18]

Hickok had taken on the Eleanor Roosevelt beat by default, and in mid-October her editor, W. W. Chapin, made it official. "She's all yours now, Hickok," he told her. "Have fun!" In an extraordinary lapse of journalistic standards, she promised Louis Howe she would file nothing important without showing him the copy in advance.* In turn, Mrs. Roosevelt granted Hickok exclusive access. ER had been skeptical at first, protesting she wouldn't make good copy, but she opened up to Hickok almost at once. In one interview, Mrs. Roosevelt, who turned forty-eight on October 11, said, "I'm a middle-aged woman. It's good to be middle-aged. Things don't matter so much. You don't take it so hard when things happen to you that you don't like." Hickok turned over the comment in her mind. Roosevelt's long-ago affair with Lucy Mercer had devastated ER, changed her—and her marriage—forever. The remark seemed to Hickok to explain a lot.[19]

---

*In fairness, Hickok's close-ups with Eleanor Roosevelt are of greater historical importance than her work with the Associated Press, as is the investigative assignment she carried out for the Federal Emergency Relief Administration after she left the AP.

Hickok continued to compromise her journalism as her intimacy with Eleanor Roosevelt grew. In an early note to "Dear Mrs. Roosevelt," she sounded less like a news hawk than a press secretary. "About those reporters and cameramen," Hickok wrote before ER boarded a train for Boston, "if there are any at the station I can probably get rid of them without any hard feelings if I tell them you'll see them when you get back from Cambridge. Would that be too awfully bad? Anyway, I'll do whatever you say." And she signed the note "Hicky."[20]

Mrs. Roosevelt played an offstage role in the 1932 presidential campaign. Early in their acquaintance, her lack of style had taken Hickok aback. She favored frumpy dresses and hair nets, and, according to Hickok, "Somebody remarked that her hats looked as though she had rushed in and bought them while the bus waited for the traffic light to change." Nor did she have much of a presence in front of a crowd, in spite of her queenly carriage. "She was not a good speaker," Hickok wrote. "Her voice would become shrill . . . and she hated making speeches." All the same, Mrs. Roosevelt set out in late October on a five-day vote-getting swing for New York's lieutenant governor, Herbert Lehman. Typically working past midnight, she kept to a punishing schedule of meetings, interviews, correspondence, and telephone conversations. The journalist filed admiring stories. "She is never hurried," Hickok wrote in an October 30 dispatch, "apparently never harassed, and is seldom, her secretary says, even slightly irritable." Mrs. Roosevelt retained a degree of anonymity too. When she entered the busy dining room of a Massena hotel, reported Hickok, nobody looked up.[21]

By the end of October the Roosevelt campaign had relaxed, all but certain of the election result. Mrs. Roosevelt had given a great deal of thought to what an FDR victory would mean for her—and for the country. Late on the rain-swept night of November 6, election eve, she drove from Hyde Park to New York City with Hickok in the passenger seat. "Of course Franklin will do his best if elected," she said, giving voice to her musings. "He is strong and resourceful. And he really cares about people. The federal government will have to take steps. But will it be enough? *Can* it be enough? The responsibility he will have to take is something I hate to think about." She hosted an Election Day buffet at the family's town house at 49 East Sixty-fifth Street before moving on with her husband to Democratic National Committee headquarters at the Biltmore Hotel to monitor the returns. By midnight the big board in the Biltmore's ballroom told an astounding tale. FDR had captured 57 percent of the vote and carried forty-two of the forty-eight states, and the Democrats gained heavy majorities in the House and Senate.[22]

Hickok filed a three-part profile of Mrs. Roosevelt with Bill Chapin in the New York Bureau on November 9, 10, and 11, the harvest of several weeks' reporting. The articles emphasized ER's "strict and conventional" though privileged childhood, her physical stamina, her fondness for children and animals, her frugality (she bought her dresses off the rack), and the perfection with which she played the traditional part of the great man's wife. Hickok presented an idealized portrait, perhaps, but also a revelatory one, for ER briefly drew aside the veil to show a profound ambivalence about leaving behind the rich, rewarding private life she painstakingly had built for herself. "If I wanted to be selfish," she told Hickok for the record, "I could wish that he had not been elected. . . . I never wanted to be a president's wife, and I don't want it now."[23]

A crowd of John Hansel's neighbors in Doylestown, Bucks County, Pennsylvania, turned out for the sheriff's sale in early January 1933. The auctioneer called first for bids on Hansel's plow horse; someone offered a nickel. Bids for a Holstein bull and three hogs topped out at a nickel. "Tough-muscled farm boys circulated to make sure that no outsider thought the hogs were worth more than 5 cents, or two calves worth more than 4 cents," *Time* magazine reported. The sale netted $4.18 for Hansel's creditors. But nobody took anything off the place, and the neighbors collected $25 for Hansel and his three motherless children.[24]

In Logan County, Iowa, dozens of rustics pushed into the county treasurer's office to discourage the sale of some two thousand properties on the block for delinquent taxes. "None was bid on, none bought," according to *Time*. In LeMars in Plymouth County, a center of Iowa unrest, eight hundred farmers, their leaders twirling a rope, rallied on the courthouse steps to save the John A. Johnson place. Herbert S. Martin, a lawyer for the New York Life Insurance Company, the mortgage holder, offered $30,000 for Johnson's 320-acre farm—$13,000 less than the balance on the mortgage. "Lynch him!" the mob howled. Martin raced to the Western Union office to wire a plea to headquarters for permission to increase the bid: "RUSH ANSWER MY NECK AT RISK." And at a foreclosure sale in Bowling Green, Ohio, in early February, Wallace Cramp's neighbors bought his stock and implements for $14 and deeded them back to him.[25]

Fears of a rural uprising spread during the first weeks of 1933. "The biggest and finest crop of revolution you ever saw is sprouting all over the country right now," John A. Simpson, president of the National Farmers Union, told the U.S. Senate Agriculture Committee. The head of the American Farm Bureau Federation, Edward A. O'Neal III, seconded Simpson: "Unless something is done for the American farmer we'll have revolution in the countryside in less than twelve months." In Bismarck, North Dakota, a state legislature debated secession for the first time since 1861. State Senator William Martin, eighty-three years old, proposed that North Dakota and thirty-nine other states separate from a union dominated by Wall Street, the six New England states, and New York and New Jersey. The editors of The Nation regarded the potential for revolution as far-fetched, though they acknowledged that two elements were already in place: defiance of the law and apathy and contempt for the government.[26]

Prices continued to plunge in February, intensifying farmer anger: cotton to 5.5 cents a pound (the average before the Great War was 12.4 cents); corn to 19.4 cents a bushel (prewar, 64.2 cents), wheat to 32.3 cents a bushel (prewar, 88.4 cents), hogs to 2.9 cents a pound (prewar, 7.2 cents). When the veteran journalist Oswald Garrison Villard toured the middle parts of the country by bus and train for The Nation early in the new year, he found a lone island of prosperity in Eau Claire, Wisconsin. "Everywhere else I went there were the same stories of blasted homes, ruined banks, wrecked existences; men and women who have seen the labors and savings of a lifetime go to nothing as if overnight," Villard wrote. "A terrible feeling of fear and insecurity has come over the great rural stretches." He met no one who would tell him things were getting better. Trains ran virtually empty; the highways were long deserted ribbons of gravel or concrete. Villard met a farmer who had made a good crop of corn in 1932, but he had burned it for furnace fuel because it would cost more to ship to market than he expected to receive for it.[27]

Private and public, responses to the farm crisis failed to match its urgency. The Prudential Insurance Company announced an indefinite suspension of foreclosures on $209 million worth of mortgages on thirty-seven thousand U.S. and Canadian farms. A number of smaller insurance companies moved to suspend foreclosures in Iowa, the most heavily farm-mortgaged state in the country. But while these palliatives eased farmer anxieties, they delivered yet another shock to the financial system, especially to small banks and insurers. With hundreds of thousands of defaulters, millions of skittish depositors, and fatally weakened banks, the states finally began to act. Its signature auto industry moribund, Michigan declared an eight-day bank holiday in mid-February, closing 550 banks. The action extended and deepened the nationwide financial crisis as state after state followed Michigan's example.[28]

Ill-judged loans, questionable, careless, or inept practices, bad luck, and panicked depositors withdrawing their little all led to a renewed rush of bank failures (nearly four hundred in the first two months of the new year alone), and proliferating bank holidays in turn led to a virtual collapse of the credit system in the winter of 1933. Businesses couldn't pay wages, buy materials, or borrow money. Individual depositors couldn't draw on their assets. The former stockbroker Matthew Josephson found himself down to a last $10 in cash to support his family of six. "The land of the almighty dollar had run out of dollars," he remembered. Even sound banks buckled under the demand for withdrawals. By early March all the banks in thirty-two states had closed, most were closed in six others, withdrawals were severely restricted in ten states and the District of Columbia, and the New York Stock Exchange and the Chicago Board of Trade had suspended operations.[29]

Meanwhile, Roosevelt set out on a pre-inaugural vacation, a dozen days at his trim white-frame cottage on the lower north slope of Pine Mountain in Warm Springs, Georgia, and another dozen fishing and basking in the sun off the Florida coast aboard Vincent Astor's yacht *Nourmahal*. In New York City, Hickok and Eleanor Roosevelt were much together, either at the Roosevelt town house or in Hickok's midtown apartment at 10 Mitchell Place, a living room with an alcove for a bed, a dressing room, a kitchen, and a small balcony. By now the friendship had become charged with tremendous emotional power. The extent to which a physical relationship advanced is a matter of conjecture; there can be no certainty, only more or less informed speculation: some historians suggest one thing, others another.* It's clear, though, that the emotional intimacy ran deep.[30]

ER had revealed to Hickok details about her miserable childhood, ravaged by an adored father's alcoholism. Born into privilege in New York City in 1884, Anna Eleanor Roosevelt grew up plain, awkward, and solemn, so unprepossessing a child that her mother called her "Granny." Her father, Elliott Roosevelt, a drunk, an opium addict, and a misfit, held an exalted place in his daughter's memory all the same. She could not have seen much of him, yet she embalmed him in her memory as loving and nurturing, a dazzling figure who fired her imagination. He died when she was nine, and the family kept her away from his funeral.[31]

She spoke, too, about finding the love letters that betrayed Franklin's affair with Lucy Mercer, and about the physical and emotional distance that opened out between the Roosevelts as they dealt with middle age in their varying ways. The marriage survived the Mercer affair but only just, and in a profoundly altered form. In the assessment of Blanche Wiesen Cook, ER's biographer, the Roosevelts were "endlessly embattled but irrevocably united . . . in a marriage of remarkable and labyrinthine complexity." They liked and were affectionate with one another. They were both devoted to large and intimate circles of family and friends. But in essential ways they lived apart. Eleanor developed personal and professional interests quite distinct from Franklin's, including close friendships with women with emotional and physical preferences for their own sex. That said, the Roosevelts shared a powerful commitment to service through politics. After all, it had been Eleanor in alliance with Louis Howe who insisted her husband continue his political career after polio felled him in 1921.[32]

For her part, Hickok spoke about her own harrowing childhood with

---

*Their correspondence is warm, intimate, and inconclusive. Hickok later destroyed an indeterminate number of letters between the two.

a monster of a father (some sources say she told ER he had raped her) and of the sudden, shattering end to her live-in arrangement with a young woman in Minneapolis. Born over a creamery in East Troy, Wisconsin, in March 1893, she was the first child of Addison Hickok, a butter maker, and his wife, Anna. Her mother's people were prosperous farmers in the Heart Prairie region. She evidently married down, for Lorena memorialized her father as ill-starred, coarse-grained, and sadistic in his ungovernable rages. Anna Hickok couldn't, or wouldn't, stand up to him, not when he horsewhipped Lorena's collie pup, nor when he dashed out her cat's brains on the side of the barn, nor yet when, to break the little girl of the vile habit of chewing her nails, he forced her fingers into her mouth and with his large, powerful hands clamped her jaws shut until the tears streamed down her cheeks.[33]

As a rule, the memoir form is to be approached with caution.* In Hickok's attempt, detailed but incomplete and unpublished, there is scant evidence of a working over of material for literary effect; the language is plain, the descriptions precise and matter-of-fact, the anecdotes, most of them, raw and unadorned. She recalls that she was slow to talk, so slow it occasioned comment in the family. She was awkward, shy, conscious of her lack of charm, uneasy in her own skin. Her sisters, Ruby and Myrtle, with their golden curls, were the adorable ones. Lorena preferred animals to people. In her own pitiless evaluation, she was "aloof, inarticulate, defiant . . . and thoroughly disagreeable" as a child. She lists *Uncle Tom's Cabin* as the first book she read on her own and Theodore Roosevelt as her childhood hero. When she first met Eleanor Roosevelt, Hickok remembered, what most interested her was the fact that she was TR's niece.[34]

The Hickoks migrated to South Dakota in the fall of 1903 after an interlude in Elgin, Illinois, where her father failed at running a barbershop. Now he tried traveling sales; his daughter remembered him as a forbidding if faintly ludicrous figure in his drummer's tan suit, stiff white shirt, and brown bowler hat. The family drifted from one town to the next, Milbank first, an overgrown village on the Milwaukee Railroad a dozen miles west of the Minnesota line. Fresh surroundings did noth-

---

*Hickok's is undated, but circumstantial evidence suggests 1949 or thereabouts.

ing to sweeten her father's disposition. In her recollection, she impassively accepted the beatings he delivered regularly. She had always feared him, but in early adolescence fear turned to loathing. "My hatred of my father made me dislike and distrust all men," she would say. She became increasingly self-conscious about her height and weight. She took pride in her singing voice, though; low for a child, it would mature into a rich contralto. Despite encouragement, she refused to sing in public; music became her secret language. "Music has run through me . . . a kind of soundless music, vibrating behind my vocal cords," she wrote. Outwardly, she remained remote, wary, and taciturn.[35]

From Milbank the family moved down the Milwaukee line to Summit and then to Bowdle. Anna Hickok died in Bowdle midway through Lorena's thirteenth year, and the widower arranged for a housekeeper to move in and look after the girls. Soon it became clear she was more than a housekeeper, and in due course Addison Hickok married her. By the autumn of 1907 her stepmother had let Lorena know she wanted her out of the house. Now fourteen and—though she couldn't know it yet—wholly on her own, she found a temporary home as a hired girl with an Irish family in Bowdle. They treated her considerately, but the arrangement didn't last. Over the next two years, she shifted from one family to another in Bowdle and nearby towns. Some employers were kindly, others cruel. More than once she was fired. She moved as far afield as Aberdeen, finding work as a scullery maid in a boardinghouse there. "I lived at the kitchen sink," she recalled. But it wasn't the drudgery that threatened to crush her spirit. "I could not have put it into words at that time, but I think now that what I really wanted was self-respect," she would write. "Lonely as I was, I did not expect love or affection from anyone." Somehow during those years she managed to attend school intermittently. She even found a way, briefly, to overcome her paralyzing shyness and sing in a Methodist church choir.[36]

Hickok caught a last glimpse of her father, conspicuous in his tan suit and brown derby, on the train from Aberdeen to Bowdle. She avoided an encounter. She was fifteen and soon would leave Dakota for the semblance of a normal life with kin in Battle Creek, Michigan. She enrolled in the high school there in September 1909, earned mostly *A*s, conceived a schoolgirl crush on her (female) English teacher, graduated with the Class of 1912, made unsuccessful attempts at college, and went to work as a police beat reporter for the *Battle Creek Journal* for $7 a week. Years later word reached Hickok that her father had taken his own life. Her sister Ruby wired her for help with the burial expenses.

"Send him to the glue factory," she replied.[37]

The Michigan experience prepared Hickok for her first significant job, reporting for *The Milwaukee Sentinel*. By March 1917 she had migrated to Minneapolis. Her stay was brief; full of illusions, she left for New York City in hopes of catching on with a news organization that would send her to Russia to report on the October Revolution. Instead, she spent six nerve-wracking weeks on the *New York Tribune*. She wasn't ready for the stresses of big city journalism; the *Tribune* fired her, and in July 1918 she returned to Minnesota.[38]

The *Tribune* of Minneapolis took Hickok on, assigning her at first to the nightside rewrite desk and then appointing her Sunday editor, a demanding job that took her away from daily reporting.[39] She kept her hand in by working the Minnesota college football beat, covering the Golden Gophers for a full season, traveling with the team and meeting the football legends Knute Rockne and Red Grange along the way. For a change, her personal affairs turned satisfactory too. She met Ella Morse in 1918, and soon they were living together. The two hardly could have been less alike: Hickok a scuffler, broad, mannish, careless of her appearance; Morse an heiress, a Wellesley College dropout, dreamy, petite, and elegantly turned out. For several years they shared a three-room suite in the Leamington Hotel—a "Boston marriage," in the euphemism of the era. Morse inherited $750,000, a fortune in those days, on her father's death in 1926, and in August that year the couple moved to San Francisco, where Hickok hoped "to write." It didn't go well. She missed the excitement and instant gratification of the news, and anyhow her talents proved ill-suited to the long form. Mercurial, chronically afflicted with the blue devils, she tried Morse's patience, and finally Morse decided she'd had enough. She rekindled a friendship with an old Minneapolis acquaintance, a man named Roy Dickinson, and they decided to elope. Hickok turned east again, to give New York a second try, landing a job

on the women's pages of William Randolph Hearst's *Daily Mirror*. By the
end of the decade she had moved beyond the soft stuff and established
herself as one of the stars of the AP's New York Bureau.

With FDR vacationing, Hickok and Mrs. Roosevelt regularly dined out
and attended concerts and lectures. They were spending the chilly evening of February 15 together (dinner at an Armenian restaurant, an ER
speech to film executives at the Warner Club), when a young anarchist
named Giuseppe Zangara stepped out of a Miami crowd and fired five
shots toward the president-elect's open car as it drew up to the bandstand
in Bay Front Park. An agitated butler delivered news of the assassination
attempt to Mrs. Roosevelt when she returned home. A call to Miami
went unanswered; finally, at 10:40 p.m., Roosevelt came through on the
long-distance wire and spoke briefly with his wife. "He's all right," she
announced. "He's not the least bit excited." Zangara had missed Roosevelt, but five others were wounded, one mortally—Anton Cermak, the
mayor of Chicago. Zangara himself would die in the electric chair on
March 20.[40]

The next day, a calm, fatalistic Eleanor Roosevelt delivered a scheduled speech before a Farm-and-Home Week crowd of three thousand at
Cornell University in Ithaca, New York. "If they want to get you, they
can," she said, "and so the only thing you can do is just go along and not
think about such things any more than you have to." That weekend she
and Hickok traveled by car to the Groton School, a quick trip to reassure
the two Roosevelt younger sons. By now the tensions growing out of her
friendship with ER were threatening to wreck Hickok's career. She knew
a great deal about the private troubles of the two rackety adult Roosevelt
children, and anything about the first-family-in-waiting graded as news.
Like so many Depression-era men, though perhaps for different reasons,
their son Elliott had abandoned his family and struck out for the West.
Hickok refused to provide details or even confirmation when her AP colleagues pressed her for information. When daughter Anna Roosevelt Dall
left her unsatisfactory stockbroker husband (and later took up with John
Boettinger, the Chicago newspaperman), she kept that confidence too.[41]

Before she and ER left for the trip to Massachusetts, Hickok laid out the rules of engagement for Bill Chapin in the AP's New York newsroom. "I believe the understanding is I don't have to put out anything unless a really good story breaks," she wrote him. "About the only good stories I can think of are: an automobile accident, attempted kidnapping of her, or something of that sort: or a folo from her should anything happen to the governor or her family. . . . She understands that, if anything of the sort happened, I would of course have to get on it." The bureau, she emphasized, should make no effort to get in touch with her over the weekend through officials at the school.[42]

Professional pressures intensified for Hickok: love versus duty. ER acknowledged the conflict and its traumatic effects. "When you haven't the feeling of responsibility to the AP you have a happier time with me," she wrote her. Hickok continued to file soft stories about Mrs. Roosevelt: features on Major, a German shepherd with the security corps; Meggie, a Scottish terrier (ornamental detail: Meggie disliked baths); and Dot the saddle horse. She did offer occasional insights into ER's mood, her apprehensions about her new role, and her determination to preserve her privacy. "I have realized all along," she told Hickok for the record, "that I shall have to give up a good many things on March 4. Some of them do not matter. Some of them mean a good deal to me." She trusted Hickok, and Hickok never failed her. In return, ER continued to grant Hickok extraordinary access, and late on the blustery, overcast afternoon of March 2 she boarded President-elect Roosevelt's Baltimore & Ohio special in company with Mrs. Roosevelt, bound for Washington and the inauguration.[43]

An atmosphere of gloom enveloped the Hoover White House, palpable to the Roosevelts when they paid a ceremonial call on the outgoing president on the afternoon of March 3. Snappish and fault-finding, Hoover had even turned on the staff, to Eleanor Roosevelt an unforgivable lapse of *noblesse oblige.* "We were told afterwards how difficult it had been for him to say good-morning or smile at the people of his household," she wrote later. Hoover's relations with the president-elect were frigid. Since early February he had been pressing FDR for joint action to deal with the banking crisis—more precisely, for Roosevelt to lend his name and landslide-victory prestige to Hoover's policies. Hoover's advisors urged the president to declare a national bank holiday, but he refused to act on his own. Reasoning that Hoover offered him responsibility without power, FDR declined to go along. In their last brief encounters, a petulant, resentful Hoover found it difficult to look his successor in the eye.[44]

The departing president sought, too, to extract a promise from Roosevelt to keep the United States on the gold standard. Hoover maintained an unshakable faith in gold, "the mechanism," say the economists Barry Eichengreen and Peter Temin, "that turned an ordinary business downturn into the Great Depression." In practice, the gold standard's deflationary pressures meant wage reductions, an insufficiency of money in the hands of consumers, and tight credit. FDR would effectively abandon the gold standard in early June, three months into his administration.[45]

As Hoover importuned Roosevelt, the political press prepared a detailed to-do list for FDR's first weeks in office. Nobody knew quite what to expect of him. The literary critic Malcolm Cowley recalled that Roosevelt had delivered twenty-seven major speeches during the campaign, more or less outlining the leading features of the New Deal. "But the suggestions were expressed vaguely, so as to hearten the radicals without frightening the conservatives," he wrote. *The Nation*, a left-leaning weekly, proffered detailed advice: "He must be prepared to render emergency relief to the millions in actual physical distress. He must be prepared to create jobs for the millions who are able to work," to inflate the money supply, and to "correct the appalling maldistribution of wealth which makes millionaires of a few and paupers of a majority." A growing number of commentators, among them Walter Lippmann, believed Roosevelt would need to claim unprecedented executive authority. "The situation is critical, Franklin," Lippmann had told the president-elect at Warm Springs in early February. "You may have no alternative but to assume dictatorial powers." Lippmann regarded FDR as "a kind of amiable boy scout," so perhaps he could be trusted to dictate judiciously. As usual, *The Nation* offered a dissenting view: "Do we need a dictator? Emphatically not!" The country needed a better, wiser leader in the White House, and the latest dictator to bully his way onto the scene, Adolf Hitler, already had shown how abruptly and savagely individual rights and liberties could be mauled. Anyhow, *The Nation* went on, "nothing in Mr. Roosevelt's record warrants the belief that everything he recommends will be completely wise." *The New Republic* echoed *The Nation*: "The extent to which the hopes of a large part of the entire world are centered upon [FDR] is a pathetic reminder of how desperately the people are seeking a Messiah, some mystic and powerful savior who will put everything right." *The Nation, The New Republic,* and others joined in calling for a massive public works program to provide jobs, direct federal relief to millions, and redistribute income.[46]

Late on the evening of March 3, FDR sent a final draft of his inaugural speech to his wife for her comments. ER read it aloud to Hickok, who probably also knew of the late-night phone calls from Hoover to Roosevelt, last-ditch efforts to persuade him to collaborate on banking policy. That night in the presidential suite of the Mayflower Hotel opportunity beckoned for the scoop of a lifetime. "There I was, right in the middle of what was the biggest story in the world," Hickok wrote afterward. "And I did nothing about it. . . . Scoops and my career did not seem important that night, even to me. That night, Lorena Hickok ceased to be a newspaper reporter." Later, when she took her troubles to Louis Howe, himself a former journalist, he showed scant sympathy. "A reporter," he told her stiffly, "should never get too close to the news source."[47]

On Inauguration Day, March 4, 1933, a Saturday, Franklin Delano Roosevelt took the oath of office outside the Capitol. Skies were leaden, with cold gusts of wind sweeping over the crowd. He was the sunny Roosevelt at first: "Let me assert my firm belief that the only thing we have to fear is fear itself." But toward the end he hinted that a suspension of the Constitution might be required—"a temporary departure from [the] normal balance of public procedure," he put it delicately. If there were delays, if the legislature or the courts were dilatory, he would act: "I shall ask the Congress for the one remaining instrument to meet the crisis— broad executive power to wage a war against the emergency, as great as the power that would be given me if we were in fact invaded by a foreign foe." And then it was over. The applause swelled, Roosevelt waved, threw back his head, and smiled his famous smile, and a jubilant crowd of 500,000 gathered along the curbs for the Inaugural Parade.[48]

Hickok arranged a final exclusive interview with Eleanor Roosevelt before responsibility for coverage of the first lady passed to the Associated

Press bureau in Washington, the first White House interview ever granted a reporter. They met on Inauguration Day afternoon in Mrs. Roosevelt's second-floor sitting room in the private quarters, a high-ceilinged chamber with tall windows and a long view southward toward the Washington Monument. As so often had been the case, their conversation was personal as well as professional. For the inaugural ceremony ER had worn a sapphire ring, a gift from Hickok. Both women knew they soon would part. The radiator thumped and wailed but failed to take the chill off the room. ER sounded troubled by the facile talk of dictatorship and perhaps by the martial imagery and authoritarian implications of parts of the inaugural speech. In the Election Eve drive to New York City with Hickok, she had expressed the fear that Americans, desperate and bereft, would be prepared to give up too much for a sense of safety and security. "The responsibility he will have to take is something I hate to think about," she had said then. Now, during the interview, Hickok asked for her impressions of the inauguration.[49]

"It was very, very solemn and a little terrifying," Mrs. Roosevelt said. "The crowds were so tremendous, and you felt that they would do *anything*—if only someone would tell them what to do. . . . One has the feeling of going it blindly, because we're in a tremendous stream, and none of us knows where we're going to land."[50]

Hickok left Washington the day after the inauguration, the parting with Eleanor Roosevelt infinitely painful, to return to her apartment in Mitchell Place and the New York Bureau. From the White House ER wrote, "I felt a little as though a part of me was leaving to-night, you have grown so much a part of my life that it is empty without you even though I'm busy every minute." Resistant to the changes that were sweeping over her, the first lady managed to evade the Secret Service detail early in the evening and see her two youngest boys to Union Station for the return trip to Groton, her "first assertion of independence" as the president's wife. But as she, and Hickok, soon would learn, life as she had known it had changed forever.[51]

The constraints were powerful. Mrs. Roosevelt's days were crowded with commitments public and private, a gladiatorial social and personal schedule that would severely strain her relationship with Hickok. She outlined a marathon March 6 in a letter to Hickok. She arose at 7:15, walked Meggie the terrier, received word of Anton Cermak's death from FDR's private secretary, unpacked and moved furniture, accompanied the president to the funeral of Senator Thomas J. Walsh, moved furniture, attended a luncheon for a delegation of governors and their wives, moved furniture, attended a National Women's Press Association tea, had tea with her mother-in-law, dined with her old friend Isabella Greenway, put through a long-distance call to Hickok, and retired to bed after midnight.[52]

By background and temperament superbly equipped for the role, Eleanor Roosevelt served that spring as Hickok's emotional anchor, confidante, job counselor, and medical advisor—and as a prop to her self-esteem. "I want to put my arms around you, I ache to hold you close," she wrote Hickok on her birthday, three days after the inauguration. "Your ring is a great comfort, I look at it & think she does love me, or I wouldn't be wearing it!" She fussed over Hickok's health; her friend was overweight (200 pounds, but only 5 feet 8 inches tall), a heavy smoker, diabetic, and her teeth gave her a lot of trouble. "Stick to your diet, lose twenty pounds more & you'll forget you are forty & please go see the doctor next week," she wrote. Powerful forces were acting upon Hickok, as ER knew: "I felt I had brought you . . . almost more heartache than you could bear."[53]

Hickok and Kent Cooper, the AP's general manager, had fallen out over a conflict of interest involving the first lady ("keeping a confidence," she put it), and bridging the divide between the personal and the professional had become all but impossible for her. She sensed that her life had come upon the turn, and she would cry herself to sleep with grief over the slow-motion dissolution of her reporting career. Journalism was her living and also her identity, the vocation that brought her in from the margins, gave her a sense of self-worth, provided companionship and bonhomie (if rarely intimacy) in a lonely world. "I do understand your joy and pride in your job, and I have deep respect for it," ER wrote her in early April. "I know I'd glory in the newspapermen." But Hickok realized her time with the AP was nearly up, and with ER's encouragement she began to cast about for freelance magazine work. In 1933, though, writers were as likely to turn up in the soup kitchens as members of any other profession, probably more so. Resourceful, self-sufficient Lorena Hickok now acknowledged the AP paycheck to be a fragile stay, all that separated her from millions of decent, willing, and perfectly capable Americans set adrift without a livelihood or any prospect of it.[54]

Hickok would receive her last AP assignment in May 1933. The bureau had fitfully covered the scandal enfolding financier Charles E. Mitchell, the chairman of National City Bank, the country's largest. At hearings in February in Washington, Chief Counsel Ferdinand Pecora and the Senate Committee on Banking and Currency had roughed up Mitchell, certainly a soft target in hard times, with charges that his extensive securities speculations helped materially to bring about the 1929 stock market crash. Mitchell's extravagant compensation ($3.5 million over three years), antic management practices, and high living (his nickname: "Sunshine Charley") made him easy to caricature. With Mitchell's tax evasion trial opening on May 11 in New York City, Chapin turned to Hickok. "We had an early story on Mitchell," he told her, "but it will never win the Pulitzer Prize so you start your own running at earliest possible moment." Hickok dutifully turned up at the Federal Building on Varick Street every day and worked hard on the story, but if Chapin meant to give her an opportunity to reclaim her place as "just about the top gal reporter in the country," the offer came too late.[55]

Mrs. Roosevelt knew that Harry Hopkins, the just-appointed head of the newly created Federal Emergency Relief Administration, was on the scout for an experienced investigator to travel the country and report to him in detail how ordinary Americans were experiencing the Great Depression. She strongly recommended Hickok to him, and by mid-June she had ventured the irrevocable step, leaving the AP just ahead of Charley Mitchell's surprise June 22 acquittal.[56]

"Poor Hick," Eleanor wrote her, "I know how you hate to leave Bill and the life. I do hope there will be enough interest in the next few years to compensate."[57]

With his offer to Harry Hopkins to head the Federal Emergency Relief Administration, President Roosevelt laid down two imperatives: rush help to people in need and avoid entanglements with politicians. An Iowa-born social worker who had directed Governor Roosevelt's innovative welfare operation in New York State, Hopkins joined the administration on May 22, 1933, the eightieth day of the unprecedented detonation of government activism known as the Hundred Days. When Hopkins reached his tenth-floor headquarters in the dilapidated yellow-brick Walker-Johnson Building an hour after the swearing-in at the White House, the staff hadn't turned up and the movers were manhandling an oversized desk from the hallway into his uncarpeted office. Ignoring the dust, disorder, and peeling paint, he started spending right away. Within two hours telegram flimsies were sailing out of Hopkins's dingy room, authorizing more than $5 million in relief to desperate Americans in eight stricken states—the first installment of the $500 million in aid Congress had approved ten days earlier.[58]

Bureaucratically speaking, Hopkins had moved with astonishing speed. "The half-billion dollars for direct relief to the States won't last a month if Harry L. Hopkins maintains the pace he set yesterday," *The Washington Post* reported. That day, May 22, as many as 16 million Americans subsisted on what social workers called "the dole," and millions more were suffering because no help had reached them. Hopkins calculated it ultimately might be necessary for the relief program to sustain 50 million people. While he deplored the expense, he said, "We will not forget that there are a lot of people to be taken care of, and that the government is going to keep people from going hungry."[59]

County "poor boards," vitiated by patronage and political feuding, continued to act according to the old Poor Law principles of the Age of Elizabeth, dealing with destitute Americans as though they were paupers in sixteenth-century England. Conventional social worker thinking held that cash grants encouraged sloth and dependency. The theory, as Matthew Josephson explained it in *The New Republic*, "is still that of charitably helping 'bums' and weaklings over the rough places rather than masses cut down by a kind of economic massacre." A nobler vision inspired Hopkins: relief wasn't charity, Roosevelt had said in a memorable 1931 speech, it was a social duty. FERA would help anyone in need—not only the jobless but the underemployed too, men (and women) whose earnings were barely sufficient to sustain life. *Time* magazine would call Hopkins "the greatest disburser of cash in the nation's history." His approach cut against the grain of three centuries of

American social practice, challenging the sink-or-swim tradition of rugged individualism and self-help. Sharp and shrewd, he expected, perhaps even courted, resistance to the scale and speed of the relief effort.[60]

"I'm not going to last six months here, so I'll do as I please," he said.[61]

Forty-three years old in 1933, Hopkins was the son of a harness maker father with a gambler's instincts and an austere and principled Methodist mother with teetotaler convictions and an impulse for good works. He inherited a raffish streak and "champagne appetites" from the one, an ambition to put the world right from the other. The elder Hopkins was unpredictable and shiftless, a glad-hander with a roguish charm. A skilled enough bowler to supplement an erratic income by betting game to game, he won $500 one night and showed the windfall to the boy on the understanding he wouldn't mention it to his mother. "She would have made Dad give it away to church missions," Hopkins recalled. New Dealers would remark upon how comfortably Sunday School pieties and a taste for low living coexisted in Hopkins.[62]

A 1920s social work colleague recalled Hopkins as "an ulcerous type," lath-thin, sharp-featured, edgy. "He was intense, seeming to be in a perpetual ferment," Dr. Jacob Goldberg wrote, "a chain-smoker and black coffee drinker." He kept late hours and was a bit of a taverner. Careless of his appearance, he had been known to wear the same shirt three or four days in a row. Like his father, he developed an affinity for a regular flutter—in his case, the $2 window at the racetrack. (Hopkins's friend and biographer Robert Sherwood reported that he used to conduct important FERA staff conferences in his car as it sped to and from the Maryland tracks closest to the capital.) With a presidential brief to establish the nation's first public welfare agency, Hopkins prepared to venture into the unknown. "It was almost as if the Aztecs had been asked suddenly to build an aeroplane," he said later. He was in a perpetual lather, he did not waste a moment, and he gave his staff the impression they were "fighting a holy war against want." He seemed to regard money, his own as well as the government's, as an article to be spent as quickly as possible. Hopkins spent it on relief, though, not on administration. He had taken a salary cut to come to Washington, and FERA employed only 121 staffers at headquarters, at a modest monthly payroll of $22,000.[63]

Candidate Roosevelt had promised action, and in the spring of 1933 President Roosevelt delivered. Hopkins submitted a draft federal relief program in a late December letter to FDR, and in mid-March he joined the new labor secretary, Frances Perkins, and William Hodson, a senior New York City relief official, in drawing up the formal proposal that would establish FERA. The new administration addressed the banking crisis first; FDR declared a four-day national bank holiday on March 5, the day after the inauguration. In some quarters, anyway, the shutdown really did evoke a holiday feeling, especially after Roosevelt addressed the nation in the first of his soon-to-be-famous Fireside Chats. "In this hour of universal misfortune people were not only unaccountably cheerful, they were positively kind," Josephson remembered. "The voice of the new president came over the radio, very clear, very calm, telling what was happening and why." A few days later, hastily adopted emergency legislation extended Hoover-era federal aid to banks, with new provisions for close government supervision of faltering banks.[64]

The president took the first steps, too, toward bringing the experiment of Prohibition to an unlamented end, signing legislation that amended the Volstead Act to allow the sale of "nonintoxicating" 3.2 beer and light wines. ("Now let's all have a beer," an effervescent FDR said after the signing.) After the banks and, perhaps, beer, Roosevelt's brain trust regarded agriculture as the most pressing of the nation's problems. The Agricultural Adjustment Act, passed in May, asked farmers to voluntarily limit production in seven basic commodities—corn, wheat, rice, hogs, cotton, tobacco, and milk—in return for government subsidies. In theory, this would reduce supply and push up prices, though farm leaders were doubtful. "What we have is overproduction of empty stomachs," John Simpson, the National Farmers Union head, told the Senate Agriculture Committee. Finally, the omnibus National Industrial Recovery Act of mid-June sought to boost recovery through planning; curbs on competition in basic industries; regulation of wages, hours, and child labor; and guarantees of union bargaining rights. Business, consumers, and labor would negotiate voluntary codes governing output, prices, wages, and working conditions, all with the benevolent and expert guidance of the federal government.[65]

Roosevelt had launched the New Deal, but the crisis remained acute.

The Commerce Department announced on May 1 that unemployment had reached an "all time peak" of 16 million, 25 percent of the workforce. By a (probably conservative) *New Republic* calculation, unemployment directly affected 37.5 million men, women, and children. When he arrived in Washington to take up the FERA post, Hopkins asserted that the peak had passed and that the number of jobless would begin to decline. A promising forecast, especially in the context of the hope-stirring hundred-day flurry of executive orders and congressional legislation, but help couldn't come soon enough for those without work—or for Chicago schoolteachers, Iowa farmers, or Pennsylvania loom girls.[66]

In April, Chicago high school students had gone on strike to demand back pay for their teachers, fourteen thousand of whom had received a total of two weeks' salary in cash since June 1932. Ultimately fifty thousand Chicago students and teachers went truant. In Grant Park, according to *Time*, five thousand strikers "burned in effigy a wicked banker who would not buy city tax warrants so teachers could be paid." Marchers from Englewood milled about the home of acting mayor Frank T. Coon, carrying banners with the slogan "Sixty million dollars was paid to the unemployed. What did teachers get?" The school superintendent, William J. Bogan, attributed the unrest to the spring weather and Communist agitators.[67]

Disorder flared anew in LeMars, Plymouth County, Iowa, when men in rough overalls and others who "looked like black-shirted hoodlums" crowded into Charles C. Bradley's courtroom on April 27 to observe the day's foreclosure proceedings. They were yokels, mostly; they wore blue bandanna masks, they were impertinent, and they vibrated with anger. They were about to carry out what one contemporary with a background in early American history called a "miniature Shays's Rebellion." (Daniel Shays, a Revolutionary War veteran, led a violent uprising of farmers and debtors in Massachusetts in 1786–87.) Judge Bradley moved to silence a farmer who demanded to speak. "Next thing he knew," *Time* reported, "Bradley was being yanked off his bench and dragged out to the courthouse lawn." When the mob instructed him to swear he would sign no more foreclosure orders, the sixty-year-old bachelor judge refused. Somebody slapped him; still he refused.[68]

Farmers surged forward, seized Bradley, wrestled him onto the flatbed of a truck, and drove him to a country crossroads a mile outside of town. Rough hands pulled off his trousers. Someone slung one end of a rope over the crosstrees of a telephone pole and looped the other end around the judge's neck. Again the men insisted that Bradley, now blind-folded, vow not to grant any more foreclosure motions. Again he refused. Pray, the farmers advised. "O Lord, I pray thee, do justice to all men," Bradley whispered. Suddenly the crowd's fury seemed to abate. A couple of men dumped a hubcap filled with grease on Bradley's head and left him dazed, half-naked, and filthy along the edge of the road.[69]

The next day, Governor Clyde Herring declared a state of martial law in Plymouth County and sent 250 National Guardsmen to LeMars. Sixty farmers were arrested and held in a stockade on the edge of town for transport to Sioux City for a military trial on charges of contempt of court and conspiracy to hinder the law. In the event, Judge Bradley, a decent man who lived modestly on a salary of $5,000 a year, declined to prosecute or even to identify any of his assailants. With LeMars peaceful again, Governor Herring lifted martial law on May 11.[70]

In Washington, Roosevelt signed the Agricultural Adjustment Act on the 12th, a stroke of the pen with an immediate emollient effect: Jesse Reno, the Iowa frontman for the Farmers' Holiday Association, agreed to call off (or anyway postpone) a farm strike promised for Saturday, May 13, market day. Meeting in Des Moines a week earlier, delegates from eighteen states claiming to represent 15 million farmers had voted to strike unless Congress approved agricultural price supports and the refinancing of farm mortgages at 1.5 percent. The new law contained provisions for emergency mortgage assistance along with the crop reduc-tion and subsidy scheme. It appeared to palliate the farm belt, although an intermittently violent dairy strike continued in Wisconsin, where pickets halted delivery trucks and emptied enough milk into roadside ditches to push Chicago milk prices up a penny a quart.[71]

Factory laborers were restless too. Sweatshops in eastern Pennsylva-nia's Lehigh Valley employed 200,000 men, women, and children in 1933, many of them in conditions of Dickensian squalor. In Northampton in early May, four hundred strikers, including dozens of children ages thir-teen to eighteen, walked the picket lines outside the D&D Shirt Company to protest starvation wages (as little as 3 cents an hour for cutters) and, ominously, "immoral conditions." The "children's strike" in Northampton attracted a high-profile picketer, Cornelia Bryce Pinchot, the flame-haired wife of Pennsylvania's governor Gifford Pinchot. She walked seven circuits around the mill with the strikers, wearing a bright red coat festooned with a white streamer bearing the word "STRIKER." Fifteen-year-old mill hands told the star picketer they worked ten hours a day, six days a week; one girl took home 57 cents for a week's work, another $2.50. "Also," *Time* reported, "they told of 'weekend trips to New York with their bosses,' which, it was understood, were compulsory on pain of losing their jobs." Mrs. Pinchot pledged she would see all the teenagers back in school before she stopped working on their behalf. Then she moved on to Allentown, where she chatted up eighty strikers in front of the Morris Freezer shirt factory and declined Freezer's offer to meet with girls working as strikebreakers, saying she couldn't support two sides at once.[72]

Tall and slender, the daughter of a friend of Theodore Roosevelt's, the vivid, powerfully intelligent, and socially prominent Cornelia Pinchot spoke with candor, held views that shaded toward pink, and campaigned with the aplomb of a veteran politician.

One of the girl strikers asked, "Is it ladylike to picket?"

"Well, it's a matter of *noblesse oblige*," the governor's wife replied. "You are obliged to do it out of consideration for the many others who are suffering from low wages if not for yourselves. Our ancestors fought their revolution. We must fight our economic revolution now."[73]

Cornelia Pinchot's presence doubtless built momentum for a settlement, though it would turn out to be a temporary victory for the mill hands. Strikes at four Allentown factories ended on the evening of May 10 with an agreement with the Amalgamated Clothing Workers of America that included a pay increase and a minimum wage. But in late July some seven hundred workers in Allentown and Northampton would return to the picket lines when management failed to honor agreements raising wages and recognizing the union.[74]

By then Lorena Hickok had quit the Associated Press for the investigative job with Harry Hopkins that would take her into the depths of the Great Depression and give her an unusual if not unique perspective on the suffering of millions of Americans. She accepted Hopkins's offer partly to please Mrs. Roosevelt. But Hopkins would have made a compelling case during the interview, and she could hardly complain about the salary: $5,000 a year plus expenses. "What I want you to do," Hopkins told her, "is to go out around the country and look this thing over. I don't want statistics from you. I don't want the social worker angle. I just want your own reaction, as an ordinary citizen. Go talk with preachers and teachers, businessmen, workers, farmers. Go talk with the unemployed, those who are on relief and those who aren't.

"And when you talk with them," he went on, "don't ever forget that, but for the grace of God, you, I, or any of our friends might be in their shoes. Tell me what you see and hear. All of it. Don't ever pull your punches."[75]

2

PART OF THE STORY

Pennsylvania, July–August 1933

The train eased into Market Street Station, Harrisburg, shortly after sunrise on August 1, the end of the first stage of what would be a draining ten weeks of travel for Lorena Hickok. Lethal heat—a record 100 degrees in New York City on July 31, a 1933 misery index—intensified the ordinary rigors of the trip. Hickok haunted newsstands wherever she went, and she would have absorbed the headlines of the bulldog editions in the night train; the front page of *The New York Times* carried stories about a National Recovery Administration code agreement with grocers, clothiers, and other retailers; NRA counsel Donald Richberg's admonition that "slackers" could lose the right to display the NRA's Blue Eagle;* Mohandas Gandhi's arrest in India on the eve of a renewed campaign of civil disobedience; and Governor Herbert Lehman's call for the death penalty for kidnappers in New York.[1]

There would have been time during the four-hour trip from New York City for reflection on Harry Hopkins's charge to her and time, too, for rereading an anxiety-allaying letter from Eleanor Roosevelt. "I know you are going to do a swell job and please let me share it," ER wrote, "for

---

*The emblem indicated participation in the NRA program. And it wasn't an eagle but a Navajo thunderbird, with lightning bolts in one claw and a cog in the other. Critics noted the Blue Eagle's stylistic kinship with the fascist symbols of Italy and Germany.

I have an interest in what you are doing and then twice as much interest and pride in the way you are doing it." The two had spent the first three weeks of July on a private motoring tour of upstate New York, New England, and the Gaspé region of Quebec, an interlude, something of an idyll, during which newspapering, Hopkins, the Federal Emergency Relief Administration, and the Great Depression all seemed far-off, faint disturbances, like heat lightning on the summer horizon.[2]

Now Hickok confronted the realities of an unfamiliar and challenging assignment. Moving slowly in the early morning heat, she hailed a cab and checked into the Penn-Harris Hotel to freshen up for a call on David Fernsler, the Associated Press bureau chief in the Pennsylvania capital. As of May, Fernsler would tell her, 400,000 families were on relief in the state. He said food prices had shot up in Harrisburg "something like 30 percent," but the amount of assistance hadn't changed. Such aid as the relief board dispensed came in the form of food orders because few functionaries trusted the clients with cash in hand to spend wisely and keep away from the speakeasies. Hickok challenged this notion. "'These people aren't children,' you hear over and over again," she wrote Hopkins. "The vast majority of them have always managed their own affairs, can be trusted with cash—however little they're going to get to live on—and should be." She interviewed a grocer who told her that food orders in his neighborhood topped out at 75 cents a week per person. "He and I sat down and tried to figure out how much you could buy per week for—say, $1.50," she wrote. "We didn't get very far." She discovered that a twelve-pound sack of flour, at 63 cents, would feed a small family for a week, and that, more likely than not, bread would be the family's principal sustenance. There were no public efforts to help with shelter, clothing, or medical expenses. That sort of aid came from private charities, when it came at all.[3]

Fernsler spoke, too, about Pennsylvania politics. One of his journalist colleagues noted that the state legislature seemed more interested in resuming the flow of beer and allowing fishing on Sunday than in relieving unemployment. The New Republic reported that the Pennsylvania State Assembly had "succeeded in killing every piece of social legislation placed before it," including bills for a forty-four-hour work week and a minimum wage for women and children. County agents and a powerful poor board lobby were "fighting for the privilege of distributing patronage," Fernsler went on, and were waging a covert war against FERA's move to take charge of public assistance. Hickok predicted trouble by winter unless the local boards distributed relief more widely. In an encouraging sign, a $20 million bond issue for jobless relief would appear on the ballot in November. Not so encouraging: Word that a Pennsylvania poll tax probably would bar many of the unemployed from voting. Hickok encountered poor board cultural norms, too, that first day. A woman had been deemed "immoral" and denied relief because she boarded with an unmarried couple; occasional work as a hotel maid kept her afloat. There simply were no jobs. *The Harrisburg Telegraph* advertised three openings, all marginal, in the classified section on the afternoon of August 1, against a couple of dozen ads in the "Situations Wanted" section.[4]

Hickok caught an early evening train for Philadelphia, took a room at the Benjamin Franklin Hotel on Chestnut Street, and sorted through her notes and impressions for what would be her first report to Hopkins. The weather continued hot and steamy, with only drugstores and movie theaters available for air-conditioned respite. Had there been time, she might have taken in MGM's *Tugboat Annie*, whose heroine's "raffish, kindly, troubled, brave and energetic" character bore at least a superficial resemblance to her own.* Over the next two days, August 2 and 3, walking the scorching pavements and breathing in the fug of trolleys, subways, and taxis, she interviewed a labor leader, a banker, the heads of two Philadelphia realty boards, officials of the American Friends Service Committee, the city relief director, and the managing editor of the worker-friendly *Philadelphia Daily Record*.[5]

The union leader, David Schick of the Full Fashioned Hosiery Workers of America, briefed Hickok about disturbances during a strike of ten thousand workers in Reading and uprisings elsewhere; altogether, there would be 110 walkouts in Pennsylvania in August 1933. Schick's union had launched an organizing drive in Berks County in June, targeting Reading's Berkshire Knitting Mills, the country's largest textile

---

* The movies were a favorite Depression-era distraction, with audiences averaging 85 million a week during the 1930s.

manufacturer. There had been considerable violence. In the most recent incident, a group of pickets turned sullen when the Blue Eagle appeared in the window of one of the Berkshire shops, a signal to the strikers that the government backed the bosses in spite of a provision in the National Industrial Recovery Act that guaranteed workers the right to organize and bargain collectively. "Someone threw a stone," Schick told her. "Then the mounted police arrived. And the fight was on." According to *Time*, strikers had shut down half the mills in Reading and picketers were spoiling to rough up strikebreakers who tried to rush the lines. When the police set a dead line in front of the shop, "a curly-headed girl stepped defiantly over it and jeered," *Time* reported. "*Thwack* went a police club. Roaring like a monster in pain the crowd surged forward. Mounted police charged. Women and children were trampled. Rocks, bricks and bottles flew." When the forces of order launched tear gas, strikers in gas masks scooped up the smoking bombs and hurled them back into the police lines. Police gunfire wounded two men, and scores were beaten and arrested. Suspecting misuse of the Blue Eagle symbol, Hickok suggested the agency ought to hold off distributing it until the Labor Department could determine whether or not conditions justified a strike.[6]

Hickok liked Schick, even though he appeared to be dyed a fairly deep shade of Red. "He honestly believes a revolution is the only way, and he thinks it is coming," she wrote in one of the long, incident-packed letters she would post to Mrs. Roosevelt several times a week during her travels. To balance the radical's views, she met with a partner in the banking house of Drexel & Co., who told her that the prospect of Hopkins and federal government involvement in relief thoroughly alarmed him. "Now what do you make of that," she wrote. "Madame, I am still a conservative, but gosh, when I talk to some people, like that man! What in the world does he think is going to happen to people who are out of work and can't get jobs? He says private philanthropy can no longer carry them. Yet he doesn't want the government to have anything to do with it. So— what?" Actually, Philadelphians already had experienced "what"; the city abruptly (if temporarily) cut off relief in June 1932, depriving fifty-two thousand destitute families of grocery and milk orders.[7]

People didn't starve *to death* during the month-long suspension, reported Evan Clague, writing in *The Survey* magazine. "They just starve, with the margin by which life persists maintained by the pity of their neighbors and by a sort of scavenging on the community." The Philadelphia Community Council tracked four hundred families, a total of 2,464 persons, who went without assistance for ten to twenty-five days. Around 250 families had children five or younger. Some earned irregular incomes, perhaps $2 to $3 a week. The average income for 128 families came to $4.10 a week. The other 272 households reported no income at all.[8]

One family, the Bakers, emptied out the last of their $2,000 savings account in January 1931. The Beccaras, under the threat of a second eviction, owed $45 to a grocer, $112 to a baker for two years' worth of bread, $150 to a cousin, and $300 on a 6 percent bank loan. They subsisted on a starch-heavy diet of bread, potatoes, and spaghetti. The MacIntyres, a young married couple with an eight-year-old daughter, had earned no steady income for more than a year. They lived on bread and coffee mostly, with a bit of fish occasionally and a quart of milk a week for the little girl. The child was underweight and misshapen from rickets. Clague wrote, "She needs cod liver oil, milk and oranges," items impossible to purchase when relief ran out. As for MacIntyre, a bricklayer by trade, he was probably tubercular.[9]

Why were people not dying of starvation? "The poor are looking after the poor," Clague explained. "Usually it was leftovers, stale bread, meat bones for soup, a bowl of gravy. Sometimes the children are asked in for a meal." Families foraged. Children prowled the Delaware River docks where fruit and vegetables were sorted for the markets; they crept around the waterfront stalls and picked up the discards until the police chased them away. They went into stores to plead with grocers for scraps of food. Grown people begged on the streets and stole milk and groceries from doorsteps. More than a third of the families in the Community Council's study no longer sat down to three meals a day—not even three meager ones.[10]

Of the 400 families, 349 were in arrears with rent or mortgage payments, some by as much as three years. There were evictions, but "on the whole," Clague wrote dryly, "the contribution of the landlords of Philadelphia to unemployment relief in the form of unpaid rent has been very substantial." Hickok met a landlord who finally had been forced to apply for relief because the tenants in the two houses he owned had fallen years behind with the rent. (The poor board turned him down.) Nor did matters improve when relief payments resumed. Abandoned buildings, squatters, ramshackle dwellings: Hickok toured a twenty-block-long district of bandbox houses along the Schuylkill River flats, three-story buildings, one room to a floor, a mixed population of poor blacks and whites, virtually everyone down and all but out. There was no sanitation. The heat intensified the stench rising from outhouses in the backyards. The bandboxes rarely were connected to the gas and electric grids, and many lacked running water. Hickok interviewed a black family of four, a married couple and their married daughter and her husband. All were jobless; they survived on a $1.50-a-week grocery order. The women supplemented the paltry relief payment with maid work, when they could find it, at 10 to 15 cents a day.[11]

Hickok would take particular note of the ravaging of the middle class, especially in Philadelphia and other large cities. Families moved frequently, often every six months or so, as they tried to stay a step ahead of the landlord and other creditors. And invariably they descended with each move into less desirable, more crowded neighborhoods. "You have the spectacle of a family with half grown children having started in a comfortable, detached house in the suburbs now living in one room in the slums—a room alive with bed bugs," she wrote Hopkins. "The effect on the children is terrible, too." People desperately needed clothes and shoes as well, especially with a new school year about to open. In many places the Red Cross, having used up the last stocks of finished garments, gave out only cloth, with buttons and thread not included. Hickok looked on one afternoon as a man resoled his family's shoes with pieces of automobile tire.[12]

The sights, sounds, smells, and voices left Hickok emotionally overwrought, physically spent, and, strange to say, exhilarated. "Tonight I feel like a great big sponge all filled with water," she wrote Eleanor Roosevelt. "I seem to have lost all my individuality and (to use another figure of speech!) have become a kind of wax record for the recording of other people's ideas and complaints and hopes. And it is the most interesting thing that has happened to me in my life." She had scant time to recruit her strength, though, for she entrained on August 4 for the Lehigh Valley manufacturing town of Northampton, where several hundred men and women were struggling to recover from the spring-time textile strike.[13]

Governor Gifford Pinchot's special commission had completed its investigation into Pennsylvania factory conditions and issued a pre-liminary report: sweatshops existed but were not the norm in the state. "There is no reason to suppose industrial establishments of Pennsylva-nia, generally speaking, are other than wholesome and decent," asserted the commission's secretary, State Representative Eugene J. Gorman of Lehigh. But the hearings, according to *The Nation*, "produced tales of hideous working conditions, long hours and miserable wages, compa-rable only to those which obtained in the earliest years of the Industrial Revolution." As one example, the magazine offered the Adkins Shirt Company of Allentown, where only three of the dozens of girls in the shop were older than fourteen. Their average pay ranged from $1.30 to $2 a week.[14]

Several weeks of testimony at the commission's hearings gave the lie to the innocuous conclusion of the preliminary report. A Conshohocken yarn mill paid workers 6 cents an hour—and deducted the cost of ice water, a necessity in the heavy heat of the shops. At a Lebanon shirt factory, a girl received $2.73 for a sixty-hour work week. Her wage en-velope bore this message: "If you would have freedom, be thrifty. Slaves are as plentiful today as they were before Lincoln delivered his Eman-cipation Proclamation. Are you hampered in your freedom of action? Just knock the 'l' out of slave." Such sentiments were commonplace in testimony from employers and their supporters, who were especially hard on anyone who sought to improve wages or workplace conditions through collective action. "If I had my way," Charles Fox, a borough of Northampton burgess, told the commission, "I'd give no food orders to unemployed persons who urged factory workers to strike." Fox's wife, it so happened, handled relief payments for the borough. "I don't believe the strikers should be entitled to any unemployment relief, because they don't have souls," she said. The borough manager, Hale A. Guss, testi-fied that one of the owners of the notorious D&D Shirt Factory asked a state official "why he couldn't have national guardsmen to protect his mill against the 'baby strikers.'" The official wondered whether she had heard him correctly.

> Query: Aren't the police sufficient protection?
> Answer: Yes, but they won't fight.[15]

Northampton mills figured prominently in the most explosive charge to emerge from the commission's hearings: operators' demands for sexual favors from their adolescent female employees. Girl witnesses testified they were coerced into making trips to New York City "as playthings for the owners and for the purpose of enticing buyers to purchase shirts made in their mills." The accusation carried sufficient weight to prompt Pennsylvania's first lady Cornelia Pinchot to seek federal Mann Act charges against one Northampton mill owner.[16]

By and large, Pennsylvania officials responded to the hearings by claiming the abuses lay beyond their power to ameliorate. Stephen Raushenbush of the state Bureau of Industrial Relations faulted consumers first, then invoked the absence of sufficient legal authority to force mill owners to improve wages and working conditions. "Deplorable [circumstances are] responsible for $1.98 silk dresses, 3-for-10-cent cigars, 39-cent silk hosiery, $10 suits and topcoats and 25-cent shirts and neckties," Raushenbush said. And in any case, he went on, no statute, state or federal, barred women from working for a dollar a week or prevented men from working for whatever wage they agreed to accept.[17]

The Pinchots, man and wife, spoke the language of emerging New Deal liberalism, though questions about the commitment of the quondam Theodore Roosevelt protégé and suspicions about his ulterior political motives were never far from the center of the conversation. Some said Pinchot nurtured an ambition to advance to the U.S. Senate. Writer Edmund Wilson, who knew Cornelia Pinchot, speculated that she wanted even bigger things for the easygoing governor: she dreamed of taking up residence in the White House. ("He would rather fish," a friend told Wilson.) In a hostile profile, H. L. Mencken's *The American Mercury* presented Pinchot, sixty-eight years old, as a hollow politico, "America's outstanding example of a type beatified by lady civics teachers and adoring Anglophiles." The author, Isidor Feinstein, sketched in Pinchot's background: "He is a gentleman in politics. Private tutors, a childhood in Gramercy Park, Phillips Exeter, several millions inherited, are reflected in his lordly graciousness and ease of manner." The governor and Mrs. Pinchot, Feinstein went on, were masters of the empty but crowd-pleasing gesture. "His lances are still aimed, with convenient harmlessness, at Entrenched Wealth, the Plutocracy, and other decrepit hobgoblins of the Bull Moose era." In one "gesture," meant to test the commissary method of relief on trial in Pennsylvania, the Pinchots famously fed fifty paupers for $2.72, buying the groceries from the model storehouse in York. Feinstein reported that in fact only thirty-five people were present, and that the ice cream, a beverage, salt, pepper, butter, sugar, and salad dressing were paid for out of a supplementary budget and so didn't figure into the 5.5 cent cost per person.[18]

As it happened, Hickok missed an opportunity to interview Pinchot; he canceled their scheduled meeting. In strike-weary Northampton, her sources reported that workers were mistrustful of Pinchot and other politicians, skeptical of the New Deal, and increasingly susceptible to radical influences. By now Hickok felt prepared to make a couple of generalizations: people on relief deeply resented the food order system, and most wanted to work for their benefits, even if it meant mending the roads or raking leaves in the parks. While nobody lived in comfort at the expense of the county poor boards, the amount of aid struck her as adequate, if barely, and for the most part agents and social workers treated the "clients" with consideration. "The feeling seems to be that every American should have the right to earn the money he gets for relief, receive it in cash, and spend it as he sees fit," she wrote Hopkins. Then too, Hickok saw (or thought she saw) a creeping radical influence in "a sort of union of the unemployed" developing in Pennsylvania's mill towns. She sympathized with the activists nonetheless. "The people who go into these organizations it would seem to me are the people most worth saving," she asserted. "They've still got some fight in them." She believed the radical groups could "cause plenty of trouble if they are not handled properly" and that thousands of the desperate jobless were balanced on the edge. "It wouldn't take much to make Communists out of them," she went on. "The Communists are most decidedly not friends of the government. They openly say they hope the Administration program will fail. They want bloodshed. They say so themselves." People thereabouts were restive but ambivalent, Hickok thought; they "might go completely 'red' or they might go the other way and perhaps be of some help in running the show."[19]

Hickok sent Hopkins a copy of the Northampton County Unemployed League's July 28 "Program for Relief," which proposed a minimum monthly family budget for food, clothing, and shelter of $53.50, $63.50 during the winter. (The program did not include medical care.) The benefits would be generous, more than double what most people were now receiving, acknowledged John G. Ramsaye, an Unemployed League official, but he emphasized that the Northampton jobless were willing to work for them: "made work," he called it in the phrase of the day. "We could fix up the riverfronts," he told Hickok. "We could plant trees. We could repair buildings. There's plenty to do, and I'd like to know why they don't have us do some of those things, and give us a little cash for it, instead of those food orders. We'd all be better off and feel more like human beings." Curiously, when Hickok interviewed the Republican county chairman later that day, he told her more or less the same thing. "If I were broke or starving," he said, "I don't believe there's a case worker in the world who could make me accept one of those damned food orders." But the Republican wasn't broke. He hadn't been forced to make the choice.[20]

Ramsaye raised another issue with Hickok, one as galling to the clients, perhaps, as the food order system: What happened when people regained their jobs but returned to work with debts for food and shelter owed to their employers? "Should these debts be wiped off the slate?" she wondered in a letter to Mrs. Roosevelt. "If they pay them out of their wages, should relief be continued until they get back on their feet? If these bills were paid up, wouldn't it help business recovery?" When Ramsaye went back to work part time at Bethlehem Steel, Mrs. Fox struck him off the borough relief rolls. The company withheld $8 from his first paycheck to cover a debt for fuel, and he had to return, cap in hand, to the poor board. Most people wanted off the rolls at the earliest opportunity. "The percentage of those who call up and announce that they have jobs and don't want any more food orders is truly impressive," Hickok told

Hopkins. "But if their jobs don't last, or if they are expected to pay off their bills right away, what are they going to do?" Hickok actually saw a paycheck for 8 cents. The man had earned $2.08, but the company deducted $2 as pay-down on his debts.[21]

Hickok retreated into anonymous hotel rooms at the end of long days with social workers, the jobless, politicians, and newspapermen. Shuffling through her notes, she tried to make sense of what she had seen, feeling her way toward constructing a narrative for Hopkins. Forget the social worker angle, he had insisted. She dated the first field report August 6 and filed it with a cover note to Hopkins's secretary, Kathryn Godwin. "I feel faint whenever I try to imagine the expression on Mr. Hopkins's face when he gets this report," she wrote Godwin. "I can't imagine what he'll do with it. . . . Maybe he'll just never read it, and perhaps that would be just as well. But I had to get some of it off my chest. Will you please pass it on to him if you think he can stand the shock?" Hickok concluded the report itself with a disclaimer: "I've probably gone into too much detail. Only don't tell me to leave it *all* out, please, because I like this job. Believe me, it's absorbing!"[22]

Hopkins withstood the shock and absorbed the detail. The first of Hickok's more than ninety reports from the field in 1933–34 would circulate widely, ultimately reaching the president's desk. Rich in detail, breezy and colloquial in tone, the reports would allow Hopkins to see beyond the statistics for a fuller understanding of the human dimension of the crisis. In the view of historians Richard Lowitt and Maurine Beasley, only Edmund Wilson's *American Jitters*, a collection of pieces published in 1932, rivals Hickok's reports for range and descriptive power.[23] With their emphasis on the Depression's unprecedented scale and impartial reach, the relative helplessness of the states, the mood of ordinary Americans, the psychological benefits of work relief, the resentment toward food and rent order systems, and relief workers' treatment of the "clients," they would guide Hopkins as he built the first national system of welfare in the nation's history.

Hickok moved on from Northampton to Bethlehem, then to Scranton in the anthracite region. "I'm getting dizzy," she wrote Mrs. Roosevelt from the silk-manufacturing center of Easton, Pennsylvania, en route to

Scranton by rail. "You must simply be worn out, putting so much into every day," ER replied from Hyde Park, where she and the president were continuing their vacation after the annual respite at the family summer home on Campobello Island in the Gulf of Maine. "But I hope the cooler weather reaches you, for the heat adds to the strain." She went on in her affirmative way, "Gee, your reports are interesting. Your letters are grand. It's fine you get on so well with people." She had read parts of Hickok's private letters aloud to FDR, she said, and he had been attentive. Though Hickok hadn't heard back from Hopkins, nor yet the president, the first lady's response would have been encouraging, some reward, perhaps, for sleep deprivation, meals taken on the fly, the exigencies of travel, and a nagging anxiety about whether she would be up to the job.[24]

Faint signs of recovery appeared during the summer, perceptible improvements stimulated, perhaps, by the rush of the Hundred Days. *Business Week* reported July department store sales up 4 percent from July 1932, and chain store sales up 11 percent. "Retail sales, after all, are the gist of recovery," the magazine noted hopefully. The Federal Reserve Board's index of industrial production, down to a dismal 59 in March, rose to 100 in July; it had been 125 in 1929. Stock prices climbed too. But payroll increases were modest, and purchasing power had not kept pace with rising prices for food and other goods. In a paradox, the news sounded promising for farmers: widespread drought would result in the smallest wheat harvest since 1893, a boost for the Agricultural Adjustment Administration's acreage reduction program and, presumably, for farm prices too. Still, the trends toward recovery, if that was what they were, appeared fragile, with virtually no effect on unemployment, which remained at intolerable levels.[25]

Hickok found little evidence of a rebound during her second Pennsylvania trip, August 6–12. The itinerary took her northeast from Bethlehem to Scranton, then south and west to Altoona, Ebensburg, Greensburg, Uniontown, and Pittsburgh. (Mercifully, she would travel by car much of the time.) The route led through the coal regions, hard and soft, mining counties that were racked by labor troubles in the summer of 1933, with a spreading and violent strike in the bituminous districts of southwestern Pennsylvania, where a shooting war had broken out. Hickok reached hard-coal Scranton, a begrimed and hangdog town with thousands of families reliant on relief, on August 6. Mountains enclosing the narrow Lacka-wanna River Valley to the north, east, and west loomed over a drab skyline of coal breakers and factory smokestacks. The Lackawanna ran black, and the hillsides were scarred. Decades of relentless digging and blasting had created a subterranean labyrinth, undermining the city and leaving build-ings atilt on sinking foundations. So powerful were the claims of the coal barons that a district judge in August 1933 confirmed the Scranton Coal Company's right to continue mining operations under Nay Aug Park de-spite the city's assertion that they endangered "the life and limbs of people who use the park." Black diamonds had brought prosperity to Scranton, and they left it in despair. Hickok detected a general air of collapse and resignation among the city's 140,000 residents.[26]

Geological forces over millions of years had formed a type of coal of unusual purity and density, with a carbon content far higher than normal. The purest anthracite came from a 500-square-mile region of northeast-ern Pennsylvania whose mines yielded 95 percent of U.S. production. Though difficult to ignite, anthracite burned longer and more efficiently than soft coal and became the leading fuel source of nineteenth-century industrial America. By the 1930s, though, anthracite mining was a dying industry, beset by inept management, labor strife, and competition from cheaper oil and natural gas. Annual tonnages dropped off precipitously, from a record 100 million tons in the war year of 1917 to 69 million tons in 1930. By 1938 production would be down to 46 million tons.[27]

According to Hickok's main source, a laid-off newspaperman work-ing part time for the Scranton relief agency, a majority of the Lackawanna Valley's sixty-five thousand miners were idle. Miners' representatives claimed employment had fallen from 125,000 in 1925 to 20,000 in Au-gust 1933. Most of the region's big collieries and all the less profitable ones had shut down years earlier, and Hickok met men who had not worked since 1927. Many miners, the ex-reporter told her, reviled John L. Lewis, the dictatorial president of the United Mine Workers of Amer-ica and a Republican who had voted for Hoover in 1932, considering him a racketeer and a strikebreaker, and thousands of them had risen in open revolt in an effort to force the resignations of Lewis's chief lieutenants in the Scranton district.[28]

In July disaffected miners established an independent union, with as many as fifty thousand men signing up for the new organization. The insurgents regarded Lewis and his understrappers as hirelings of the coal operators who, *The Scranton Times* reported, were slashing miners' wages "under the noses of district organizers and other district officials." In the new union's view, Lewis merely used the UMW to provide soft jobs for his cronies. Iowa-born, fifty-three years old in 1933, Lewis cut a striking and carefully cultivated figure with his massive head, shaggy eyebrows, shock of dark hair, characteristic scowl, and booming voice. *Time* portrayed him as "squat, bull-necked, heavy-pawed, black-maned, bushy-browed," though it did acknowledge the "surprising resonance" of his remarkable voice. When Lewis took charge in 1920, the union had become the country's most powerful labor organization, with more than 60 percent of U.S. coal mined under UMW contract. Ruthlessly imposing one-man control, he ruled like a potentate. And he presided over a steady decline in union fortunes through the 1920s and the early years of the Great Depression.[29]

Scranton miners resented Lewis's $12,000 annual salary, his unlimited expense account, his persecution of radicals in the UMW ranks, his pitiless breaking of men who crossed him, his high-handed disregard of union local charters, and his penchant for throwing out big words unfamiliar to rank-and-file miners. For example, speaking at a miners' convention, Lewis referred to a dispute with Kansas district union leaders as an "embroglio." Wrote journalist Tom Tippett in *The American Mercury*, "No one in the hall, save some of the newspapermen, had ever heard the word before."[30]

Hickok witnessed miners' anger firsthand at an August 7 union meeting—she called it a "rump convention"—of a thousand insurgents in an indescribably filthy Regal Hall in Scranton. Lewis had sold them out, they said, with a bad contract that would run until 1935. They were determined to oust UMW District 1 president John Boylan and his entire executive board. "Surely no one believes for a moment that the workers are now properly being represented by Lewis, Boylan, etc.," insurgent leader Tom Maloney said. He and his associates parried UMW charges of radicalism by ordering Communists out of Regal Hall and swearing fealty to FDR and the New Deal. "We do not want them here," Maloney said. "We are here to meet as mine workers and to support the policies of our great president. There is no room here for Communists." The delegates sang a verse of "America," then carried an oversized American flag to the stage.[31]

Passing on an item of political intelligence, Hickok wrote Mrs. Roosevelt: "They also say that Lewis has ruined the union by pitting the soft coal miners against the hard coal miners and that he'd never have had the nerve to call that strike in the bituminous area except for the fact that he had the government behind him, that the government would force the operators to make concessions, and that he could then claim all the glory." Consumed as they were by union politics, few miners showed much interest in the relief issue, Hickok went on. Most had grown accustomed to accepting help, and anyway they reckoned the new state-issued food orders a great improvement. "Whatever they are getting now is far far ahead of what they were getting under the old poor director system," she wrote Hopkins. For one thing, people on relief could now buy soap and toilet paper.[32]

While the insurgents plotted revolt, Scranton city officials lobbied the Glen Alden Coal Company, idle for three months, to reopen three mines with jobs for four thousand men. Beyond that, prospects were bleak; the engineers reported that many long-closed mines were too damaged from misuse and neglect to ever restart. Meanwhile some miners were learning, painfully, what it meant to shift for themselves. Searching for a bright spot, Hickok seized on Scranton's backyard garden program, which provided people with useful work and fresh vegetables. "By and large," she wrote Hopkins, "the happiest and most contented people I saw were those working in the gardens." She spoke with a jobless man who swelled with pride on winning a prize for best garden. "But I'd rather have my job back in the mines than be doing this," he told her. The more enterprising of the unemployed were beginning to turn to bootleg mining—groups of men who dug their own "dog holes" where the coal lay close to the surface and with hand tools hewed out enough to earn a precarious living. Despite relentless coal and iron police persecution (company agents blew up thousands of holes and arrested scores of illicit miners), bootleggers would produce 10 percent of the anthracite in the Scranton region by the mid-1930s.[33]

A night train carried Hickok toward the turbulent southwestern counties. Reaching Altoona at daybreak on August 8, she joined forces with Clarence Pickett, the executive secretary of the American Friends Service Committee, a thin, ascetic, and earnest Quaker with millennial designs; he and his fellows were laboring to create the Kingdom of God on Earth. Hickok liked him at first sight and wished him well in his errand. Pickett and the Quakers struck her as simple and practical, despite their grand aims, and they managed their modest resources with consummate skill. "They did little talking," Hickok observed, "but they worked—right down among the people." Pickett and the AFSC promoted gardening and canning, helped women make clothes out of material supplied by the Red Cross, and taught men to knock together pieces of furniture from scraps of lumber. Touring by car, Pickett showed her around Altoona with its massive red-brick Pennsylvania Railroad locomotive and car-building and repair shops spread out along the valley. At its peak, the railroad employed 16,500 workers, but times had been hard for more than a decade. In the late nineteenth century the PRR grew to become America's largest corporation; now many of its 6,700 daily trains operated at a loss. Nationally half a million workers had been dropped from the railroads' payrolls in the 1920s. The Depression accelerated the trend of worker displacement, and employment in the Altoona shops had declined by a quarter since 1925.[34]

With Pickett at the wheel of an AFSC car, Hickok explored the hinterlands of Altoona and farm districts in Cambria and Indiana counties to the west, cruising the back country along smooth new "Pinchot roads," part of the governor's fifteen-month project to put the unemployed to work hard-surfacing thousands of miles of Pennsylvania byways. Pinchot's effort to "get the farmer out of the mud" created some fifty thousand temporary jobs, a result in which he took immense pride. Isidor Feinstein, though, presented the roads program as the governor's attempt to avoid the perilous issue of direct relief—the politically toxic dole—and anyhow he detected an ulterior motive. Pinchot "will pave his way to the Senate yet," he wrote, "even if he has to put macadam on every cowpath in the State to do it." Whatever Pinchot's motivation, Hickok would have thanked him for the ease with which Pickett's car glided over the secondary roads of central Pennsylvania.[35]

According to Pickett and others, there had been dustups lately involving the Indiana County jobless, with charges that radicals were responsible for stirring up the trouble. "The Communists came in here and tried to organize us," the chairman of the Unemployed League admitted to Hickok. "Well, we organized and then kicked them out." The league wanted official recognition, she reported, as well as a role in how county relief funds were spent. For months the group had sought a meeting with the county relief board. The board finally agreed—and then failed to show up. That was when the league members took to the streets and "simply exploded," Hickok said.[36]

She detected, too, a growing resentment of the relief boards in Indiana County and elsewhere. "They were taught to deal with 'problem' families," she wrote later, "but in the FERA we were not dealing with problem families," for in 1933 most of the people who turned up at the relief office were there through no fault of their own. Relief officials were, if not prosperous, at least comfortable. "No person on that board has ever known hunger," one man told her. And the clients resented official record keeping and intrusive questions from social workers administering means tests—"fingerprinting," they called it. But nothing Hickok had seen suggested a lightening of the relief load anytime soon. Pinchot's road scheme and other work relief projects provided only temporary jobs, and that income stream would dry up in a matter of weeks or months.[37]

Hickok parted with Pickett on August 9. As he moved off, he offered this: "If you want to see how bad things are, go down to the southwestern part of the state." So she set out for Greensburg across the westernmost of the principal Allegheny ridges in a hired car, into the center of a spreading labor insurgency in the soft-coal region. Her abrupt introduction to the embattled district came during an interview with a man named Shelley, the general manager of a group of H. C. Frick Coke Company mines near Greensburg. Shelley had lost an eye in a beating administered by an enraged out-of-work miner; he sat on the county relief board, so perhaps the miner had a double grievance. The strike that erupted in late July idled Shelley's mines, leaving him out of work too.[38]

Near Latrobe, with its big Rolling Rock brewery and, in happier days, the home of the world's original banana split (created in 1904), Hickok encountered, for the first time, the truly "forgotten men." They were cast-offs, middle-aged and older, and she found thirty or forty of them living in a sort of monastic community in abandoned coke ovens. They had no hope of work, even should good times return; stunted, bent, and mal-nourished, they couldn't pass the physical required before a man could go down the mine. The world had passed them by. "Coke ovens are obsolete, too," she wrote Mrs. Roosevelt. "They tell me there is some new process. And so—abandoned miners live . . . patiently, utterly discouraged, with no future at all, and raise pathetic little patches of tomatoes and cabbages in front of their makeshift homes." The ovens looked like brick beehives, she thought, once-thriving hives long abandoned and falling into ruin.[39]

The United Mine Workers of America had lapsed into irrelevance by the spring of 1933. From a peak of 500,000 after the Great War, member-ship fell to fewer than 75,000. The decline commenced with the postwar slump and accelerated in the late 1920s, when, with coal prices plunging, many operators simply repudiated UMW contracts. The union had all but collapsed in the southwestern Pennsylvania district under pressure from the Frick combine, which employed fifteen thousand miners, and other antiunion operators. The left-wing National Miners Union carried out such union activities as persisted there. But the National Industrial Recovery Act's protective shield for union activity, the famous Section 7(a), Title II, changed all that. Now Lewis risked all, committing the en-tire UMW treasury to a summertime soft-coal organizing drive. Frick responded with clubs, tear gas bombs, shotguns, and economic warfare in the form of pay cuts and severed credit at company stores. By June 30, though, the resurgent UMW counted 128,000 new members among Pennsylvania's miners. Lewis's organizers distributed tens of thousands of circulars. One asserted, "The President wants you to join the union," making affiliation with the UMW a matter of patriotic obligation. The UMW program called for a base pay rate of $5 a day; a six-hour day and a thirty-six-hour work week; the paycheck deduction of union dues; miners' right to select their own checkweighmen; the freedom to trade at private stores and to live in noncompany housing; payment of wages in cash rather than scrip; and arbitration of workplace grievances.[40]

Frick's holdings were "captive mines," so-called because they were controlled by bigger, stronger companies, in Frick's case the vehemently antiunion U.S. Steel Corporation. When the miners walked out under Lewis's leadership in late July, the allied mine operators joined in launching a savage attack on the strikers, mobilizing company militia and friends in the sheriff's departments of Cambria, Westmoreland, Fayette, and Washington counties. As Lewis said of Frick's chief, Tom Moses, and the others, "the law of the jungle" ruled the coal industry.[41]

The miners "walked out as if on a summer spree," *Time* reported, "full of noise and good cheer and enthusiasm." But the holiday atmosphere soon dissolved. Company guards shot four riotous strikers in front of Fayette County mine gates on July 28. Three days later, police responded to outbursts in a half-dozen Monongahela Valley coal patches with tear gas bombs and blank cartridges, injuring many strikers. As the skirmishing intensified, miners' wives fought alongside their husbands, and sons walked the lines with their fathers. A fierce battle erupted at Colonial Mine No. 3 near Uniontown on August 1, with mine guards opening fire at daybreak, when the mine shifts changed. A thousand strikers were dozing or smoking and chatting in the twilight, and a dozen American flags flew at intervals along the picket line. The guards and the sheriff's deputies fired live ammunition this time, killing one miner and wounding eighteen, three seriously. For a change, the operators' hard-fisted tactics failed them. Within a few days twenty thousand more miners walked out, shutting down all the Frick mines, twenty of them in Fayette County alone.[42]

In response, Governor Pinchot ordered three hundred National Guardsmen into Fayette County. The soldiers displaced the sheriff's men, encouraging the strikers who viewed the law in the county as a tool of the operators. Detachments of soldiers guarded the mine gates and patrolled the roads and highways, acting as a buffer between the hard men on either side of the divide. In a short article that surely caused Isidor Feinstein to grind his teeth, *The New Republic* observed that Pennsylvania's working people owed "a debt of gratitude" to the union-friendly governor and his picket-walking wife.[43]

The UMW locals focused on two immediate, intractable, and non-negotiable issues: Frick's recognition of the UMW and the miners' demand for their own checkweighmen at the tipple scales. With prodding from NRA Administrator Hugh Johnson, Lewis and the operators reached a tentative agreement in early August, a deal the UMW senior leadership expected the locals to ratify without serious debate. President Roosevelt sent NRA deputy Edward F. McGrady to Uniontown on August 8 to persuade the miners to return to work, offering to make Section 7(a) live and to give union representatives an equal voice in NRA coal code negotiations soon to open in Washington. Thousands of strikers drifted back to the mines, deciding, for the time being, to trust the president's men.[44]

But thousands stayed out. As in Scranton, many miners mistrusted Lewis and others declined to take the NRA and the New Deal on faith, both groups ignoring the return-to-the-pits edict of a leadership they viewed as remote. At Frick's Colonial No. 4 mine, workers chose an insurgent, Martin Ryan, as checkweighman. The mine superintendent refused to accept the magnetic Ryan, one of a number of younger leaders, "strong, close, cautious, bitter men," according to *The Nation*. But he had won the trust and loyalty of the rank and file, and thousands followed him back onto the picket lines.[45]

By now it had become clear that the more radical or anyhow more desperate miners meant to force a test of the union protection provisions of the NRA. "The men are giving Roosevelt a chance, but only a chance, is what I hear everywhere," wrote Daniel Allen in *The Nation*. "We come right out again if the code is no good," a miner told him. "This time when we come out we stay out." Coal code talks would begin in Washington in the Shoreham Hotel during the week of August 12 and drag on inconclusively for weeks in the stupefying heat of the Washington summer. With the deadlock, strikes continued to flare in southwestern Pennsylvania. Some ten thousand miners would stay out through mid-September in what Ryan, echoing bank regulators and the Middle Border farmers' movement, called a "mine holiday." A skirmish at one of the Frick mines on August 13 left fifteen miners and a deputy sheriff wounded by gunfire and another twenty injured by other means.[46]

Hickok reached the southwestern Pennsylvania battlefields during a lull in the fighting. Clarence Pickett drove her from Greensburg to Uniontown on August 10. The smooth pavement of U.S. 119 led through rolling country along the lower western slopes of the Alleghenies. Tranquil summer weather and the beauty of the brown, green, and blue hills masked the fury of the mine war. Perhaps thinking of the Pinchot Roads, Hickok had work relief on her mind. But she saw at once the drawbacks in launching public works schemes in coal patches where the operators owned everything. They were transient places; the average life of a mine ran to about twenty-five years, and the tumbledown company towns gave the impression of ugly impermanence, as though they would be whisked off the shabby set the day after the mine played out. She witnessed desperate people scratching a subsistence from gardens with a topsoil of coke ash. She visited places in which store shelves were utterly bare, though that hardly mattered since nobody had money to spend anyway. In the hamlet of Scottdale, a Roman Catholic priest "begged me for some aspirin for his parishioners," she would recall, saying he had exhausted the parish credit at the drugstore. When the interview ended, Hickok moved on. But the story stayed with her. "His worried eyes still haunt me," she wrote Hopkins.[47]

In chaotic Uniontown, Pickett handed Hickok off to Clare McDonough, a field representative for the Pennsylvania Emergency Relief Board, and with McDonough listening in she sat down for the last of the eighty-one interviews she conducted between August 7 and 12. Her subjects represented an extraordinary range of reporting. She spoke with town and county administrators, people on relief, Chamber of Commerce officials, priests and ministers, newspaper people. She spoke with Martin Ryan, the radical union leader (a mine boss described him to her as a "Communist agitator"), and with Clay Lynch, a senior executive with Frick. She listened, observed, and took precise notes. She heard a mine superintendent demand that McDonough deny relief to a striker. She wrote, "The coal operators . . . pay most of the taxes [and they] naturally felt they were being forced to feed their enemies." Small businessmen agreed; by keeping the strikers from starvation, they said, the poor boards were only prolonging the strike. McDonough drove her out to Gray's Landing, a hopeless patch where the mines were mostly worked out and virtually none of the "enemies" had a job or even the faint hope of one.[48]

A number of themes emerged from Hickok's interviews and observations. Cities, towns, and boroughs were tapped out; there were no local funds for relief, for public works projects, or even for basic services. In one town, the parish priest told her 97 percent of the citizens were on relief. The streets were in appalling condition—in perfect condition, actually, for made-work projects for people on the dole. When Hickok mentioned the possibility, an official replied, "Yes, but you see the town is so poor that it had to turn off its water supply a few weeks ago. If there had been a fire, the whole place would have burned up." Even if the labor cost nothing, there were no funds for paving materials. She noticed, too, the calming, almost narcotic effect of the village priests. "The Catholic priests in some of these towns represent almost the last bulwark against riot and disorder," she concluded. One priest told her he regularly gathered the parish into the church for a novena. "Sometimes it's the only way I can keep them from going crazy," he said.[49]

A fourth theme presented itself, important to Hopkins, to Eleanor Roosevelt, and to the president. Just about everywhere she went, Hickok found a simple faith in Franklin Delano Roosevelt. She wrote ER: "I seldom hear anyone say 'I'm a Democrat,' or 'I'm a Republican.' What they do say is, 'I'm for the President,' and then, 'Well, if he can't make a go of it, I guess there'll be a big change and we'll all be Reds.'" When he needed to soothe agitated, fractious people, a relief administrator told her, he shouted "Franklin D. Roosevelt" at the top of his lungs. According to Hickok, Fayette County miners showed little confidence in anyone but FDR: "Stuck up in a window [of the house] of a miner who had been out of work and nearly starving on inadequate relief for more than a year, I saw a newspaper clipping, apparently out of an advertisement, of the President's picture and a Blue Eagle." Strikers carried the president's picture on the picket line and, in Hickok's words, "in their little parades—with the American flag and queer little bands made up of saxophones and accordions—when they went back to work." This could be double-edged, though. Roosevelt had raised expectations, and ordinary folk now looked to the government for help. They would hold FDR accountable if it failed to deliver.[50]

Clare McDonough drove Hickok to Pittsburgh on August 11, and they spent the next day touring the stricken steel capital. Hickok found the city's unemployed sullen and aggressive. For one thing, sharply rising prices were eroding their food-order buying power. Since April coffee had jumped 11 cents for a five-pound tin; cornflakes were up from 17 cents to 23 cents for three boxes; rice had more than doubled to 7 cents a pound; the cost of a peck of potatoes had more than tripled, from 17 cents to 60 cents. The prices of beans, beef, and lard were all up substantially. A twenty-four-pound sack of flour, 59 cents in April, cost $1.14 in August. Hickok met with a group of relief clients for an hour; when she rose to leave, they demanded she come back later to hear elaborations on their miseries. She wrote Hopkins, "I unfortunately made a remark about being tired, whereupon one of them said, 'We're tired, too, lady—and we're living on 90 cents a week.'" She returned that evening.[51]

Hickok had trouble processing it all, though individual images remained sharp and unforgettable: the fetor of the Philadelphia bandboxes, the dispossessed gardener in Scranton, the forsaken inhabitants of the Latrobe coke ovens, the careworn priest in Scottdale. Nothing had prepared her for the breadth and depth of the misery she witnessed each day during nearly two weeks on the road in Pennsylvania. She boarded the train for Washington at 11:35 on the night of August 12 benumbed, in a state of near physical and moral collapse.[52]

In Pennsylvania, for the first time, Hickok had begun to comprehend the terrible dimensions of the crisis. "The Great Depression had never hit me personally at all," she would write, "not as it had these people." She had assumed that the job with Hopkins would be an extension more or less of her reporting career, requiring the same tools, techniques, and ability to rapidly assess a situation and explain it in accessible prose. And that had been the case, up to a point. At first she approached the FERA assignment with a hard and rather spurious objectivity; the lives and experiences she encountered were the "story." As it happened, her reports to Hopkins and the letters to Eleanor Roosevelt (letters she later bowdlerized, carefully editing out much of the emotional content specific to her relationship with the first lady) were carefully crafted little masterpieces, capturing the abject devastation of the worst years of the Depression. "There but for the grace of God," Hopkins had said. And she became part of the story.

ER caught the change in tone at once. "What a book you'll be able to write on 'how we all live.' Some day you'll really need Campo[bello Island] and quiet to do it," she wrote Hickok. And then, "What a power you have to feel and to describe. I can see what you have seen and feel as you felt, just reading your letters. How small one's worries seem in comparison to what so many human beings have been through." She reached Washington at 7:35 a.m. on the 13th. The big stories stared out from the Union Station news racks: the president was pressing the National Recovery Administration for action on the coal, steel, and oil codes; he had ordered warships to Cuba to protect Americans during a period of political unrest and transition there; two black men, charged with the murder of a twenty-one-year-old white girl, had been taken from an Alabama jail and lynched. Hickok reached ER's second-floor quarters in time for breakfast. For a hurried day or two, she and the first lady would outline the plot of the next chapter of what might be called *The Education of Lorena Hickok*.[53]

The flying visit gave Hickok her first extended look at life in the Roosevelt White House, along with an understanding, if an unwelcome one, of the frenetic pace of the first lady's days. Hickok had spent a weekend there in April, a month or so after the inauguration. She seemed ill at ease then, perhaps overawed. "You must go and say hello to Franklin," ER had said, adding after a pause, "Come on! You are a houseguest now!" Over the first months, Mrs. Roosevelt had evolved a routine that began, whenever possible, with an after-breakfast horseback ride in Rock Creek Park. From then on she rarely had a moment to relax, and she evidently preferred it that way. She confronted a heavy correspondence each morning. At Hickok's suggestion, she introduced weekly news conferences for the capital's female press corps. There would be lunch with Labor Secretary Frances Perkins and two or three other powerful women and visits to the Senate chamber to take in speeches and debates on issues of the moment and, increasingly, meetings with advocates for the poor (she had just seen "a man about the welfare of mountain children," she wrote Hickok that first spring) and for racial minorities. Every so often, she had a swim with FDR in the pool he had caused to be installed in the White House basement.[54]

Even the private family dinners usually were working affairs, with senior political and policy figures joining the Roosevelts at table. (Down the years Hickok would be an occasional guest, but she dined alone with the first couple only once. FDR offered her this advice: "Never get into an argument with the Missis. You can't win.") The president watched a movie two or three times a week, taking special pleasure, according to his wife, in the adventures of Mickey Mouse. "Though he rarely asked for a particular movie," Mrs. Roosevelt recalled, "he hated a picture to be too long, and it must not be sad." Live-in family and friends filled the private quarters of the presidential mansion: Missy LeHand, FDR's secretary; Louis Howe; Anna Dall and her two children. Before long, Hickok would give up the Mitchell Place apartment in New York and move in with the others. Some nights there were official functions, and there were semiofficial events too: concerts, speeches, charity functions.[55]

With the end of the White House interlude, overwrought still, Hickok moved on to the rendezvous with Clarence Pickett, the first stage of a journey into the desolation of the West Virginia mountain country, an experience that would take her to the limit of her power to see, experience, and record.[56]

3

COAL COUNTRY

West Virginia and Kentucky, August–September 1933

A geological curse lay upon Scotts Run. The eight-square-mile district near Morgantown, West Virginia, possessed an extraordinarily high ratio of soft-coal deposits to surface area and the yield from its four commercially valuable coal seams found a ready market in the Northeast, powering industry in western Pennsylvania, Ohio, and the Northeast. One of the seams, the Little Pittsburgh, broke the surface in places, allowing for open-pit mining; all four seams ran along a level plane, and with steep rises in elevation it became necessary to sink shafts or hollow out slope entries and send men below ground. The befouled watercourse from which the district took its name emptied into the Monongahela River after a few miles; the blight of the curse remained in the form of the human wrack in tumbledown dwellings clinging to the lower slopes and in mining camps clustered in the hills near the shafts, drifts, and open pits.[1]

A West Virginia University engineering survey in June 1933 showed that even after a decade or so of unusually intensive mining, plenty of coal remained exploitable in the Scotts Run district, at least 60 million tons. But much of it was low in quality, and the most valuable deposits had been hacked from the hillsides and exported during the district's boom era between World War I and the onset of the Great Depression; at the peak of development, thirty-three separate coal companies operated thirty-seven mines. Narrow as a ditch in places, green, red, black, and yellow with mine and human waste, Scotts Run flowed through an enclosed valley whose inhabitants were as forlorn and derelict as the landscape. "Sociological conditions throughout the area are very poor," the engineer, Dennis K. Scott, wrote. "Living conditions as they are found in the mining camps are putrid to say the least if such an expression may be used in a formal report." Malnutrition and disease were endemic. And a decade of bitter owner-miner conflict gave the district its alternate name: Bloody Run.

Scott's investigation found sharp divisions among the ten thousand inhabitants of Scotts Run. There were people of feeble capacity, who tended to make trouble when they could, and there were people who were able-bodied but demoralized and disinclined to do anything to help themselves. He also identified a third cohort: "The most pitiful of all is that group of people who try to live in a respectable manner but are victims of circumstance. In some places, soap is so scarce that sand and water are used. . . . Out of 14 families investigated recently, only two had sheets and dishes in their houses." Scott concluded with advice against investing in Scotts Run coal property. Contracting demand through the 1920s had diminished the market. As utilities became more efficient they burned less coal, and widespread use of the oil-powered railroad locomotive promised to further undermine demand. Closed mines were hardly worth reopening. Labor wars (one side or another employing machine guns, tear gas, dynamite, and evictions) racked Bloody Run during the boom seasons; by the late 1920s, technological advances had significantly reduced the need for unskilled labor. The United Mine Workers locals withered. Then came the economic collapse. Miners were grateful for any work, even one or two days a week, at any wage. As Scott wrapped up the report, he recorded the breakout of another in an interminable series of improvisational strikes, opening like an old wound, "one of those spasmodic affairs which flare up in a moment and die as quickly." Usually, he added, no damage was done—nor any good accomplished.[2]

For some years, mission-based charities—Clarence Pickett's Philadelphia Quakers, the Methodist and Presbyterian churches of Morgantown—had sought to deliver rudimentary social services to the disinherited hamlets of Scotts Run. Desperate communities straggled east to west along West Virginia Route 7: Osage, Pursglove, Jere, Cassville. Rutted dirt tracks ascended into the hills to reach the mining camps. Today the leafy valley is lightly peopled, and though some of the physical wounds of the mining era have healed the scars remain; the stream flows orange with acid discharge and mine spoil layers the barren hollows. The ghosts of want and misery haunt the flimsy wood-frame houses, rusting mobile dwellings, and corroded hulks of ancient cars. Nothing much survives along the main street of Osage; the battered brick and wood buildings are abandoned, the windows streaked with dirt. The beauty of the narrow wooded valley and the grassy hills heightens the sad contrast with the coarseness and dilapidation of the human artifacts of Scotts Run.

The Women's Home Missionary Society of the First Methodist Episcopal Church in Morgantown patterned the Scotts Run Settlement House after precursors in the big cities. For starters, the settlement workers offered English-language instruction (twenty-eight ethnic groups were represented in Scotts Run), later expanding into health education. The settlement's first permanent quarters, a sturdy red-brick building that still stands, opened in Osage in 1927. In November 1928 a young woman named Mary Behner started a Sunday School under Presbyterian auspices in an abandoned schoolhouse in one of the coal patches. The energetic Miss Behner soon diversified into social services, offering Bible classes for miners, a charm school, singing groups, a sewing club, and a nursery school for women and children. In 1932 the Pursglove Mining Company gave Behner an abandoned company store, which she dubbed "The Shack." (Like the settlement house, it remains in business today.) Beginning in 1931, American Friends Service Committee social workers ran their relief programs out of The Shack.

Behner continued to expand services, and over time she developed a nutrition program that fed two hundred miners' children a daily lunch of vegetable soup, crackers, raisins, and milk. She seemed to possess a gift for making religious uplift palatable for a debased population. As many as thirty miners used to attend her Sunday afternoon Bible classes. "The men stayed till 9.00 playing checkers, cards, jigsaw puzzles and reading Sunday papers and the like!" she wrote in the detailed diary she kept in 1933–34.

She cut and pasted into the diary newspaper clippings that marked her out as an enthusiast for the New Deal. "If ever a president had an opportunity to lead a people it is Roosevelt of the U.S.," she wrote shortly after the inauguration. "There is reason for 'hope.' Why should Roosevelt not turn the tide?" For all her inexperience, Behner had seen enough of conditions in Scotts Run to know that it would take more than any conceivable combination of church volunteers and private charities, however well-intentioned, to make life worth living for the people of the West Virginia hills.[3]

The Presbyterian Church paid Behner a salary of $125 a month, and she commuted to Scotts Run from an apartment in Morgantown. The salary just sufficed to sustain a precarious middle-class existence, allowing her to enjoy the common sort of genteel relaxations: church activities, movies, restaurants, and other amenities of a university town. There was, for instance, Harry Pullins, a Red Cross agent with responsibility for distributing flour to the Morgantown poor. "I have a date (?) with a Harry Pullins," she recorded in the diary. "We are going to see 'The White Sister' at the Metropolitan Theatre. Fancy that! I have felt it coming. . . . Well, we'll see." As it happened, no date with Pullins could prepare her for a close-up look at relations between the sexes in Scotts Run.[4]

Marie was twenty-one years old, her husband thirty-six. She was small-boned and frail, her husband large and powerful. Marie married at thirteen and delivered her first child within a year. Three more children followed at intervals. They were "almost naked for lack of clothes," wrote Behner. "To think that a fifth one is on the way! Marie said she'd rather die than have another child." She had tried quinine, iodine, "and everything she could get her hands on and nothing seemed to cause a miscarriage, so she had decided to go to the doctor and have her womb opened." Behner either didn't know the term *abortion* or chose not to use it. As her friendship with Marie developed she would learn a great deal, some of it confirmation of things she had studied at the College of Wooster in the late 1920s, much of it new—and terrifying—to her.[5]

"When I first talked to her about it I thought to myself—I hardly blame her," Behner went on, "and I didn't say much!" The more she considered the matter, though, the more certain she became that it was her duty to persuade Marie to carry the child to term. "I tried to show her that a human soul had been formed in her body and explained the biology of it which was all new to her. I also said that perhaps that unborn child might be some genius someday, or might do something wonderful in this old world. A new light came into her face, and she changed in an instant as if struck by something. We dedicated the child then and there to God, and I know that the nurturing of that child will be different from all the others she has had!"[6]

Still, as Behner recognized, nothing likely would change between husband and wife, however much the notion of motherhood now exalted Marie. "He is still a brute," she wrote, "and demands of her every night in the world that he is home. Each night's experience is nothing but agony to her because she is so small and he is so large. And if she doesn't give in to him, he beats her, and sometimes doesn't speak to her for weeks. . . . I had always known this to be a general condition in Scotts Run, but never before had I experienced so intimately the facts of a specific situation . . . and now I *know*."[7]

From time to time, on the rare occasions when her husband let her off "the hill," Marie made her way down to The Shack to find refuge with Mary Behner. Strange as the comparison sounds, Lorena Hickok, buffeted in different ways, found her own (often unquiet) refuge in the White House with Eleanor Roosevelt. After the brief mid-August respite there, another overnight train trip and a punishing two-hour bus ride delivered Hickok to Morgantown on August 16 for a rendezvous with Clarence Pickett. Headlines in the Morgantown newspapers would have caught her eye. The morning *Dominion News* reported that Harry Hopkins, meeting in Washington with Governor H. G. Kump, had issued an ultimatum: West Virginia must substantially increase its contribution to relief, now at 5 percent of the total, or face a cutoff of Federal Emergency Relief Administration grants. The governor entered a plea of poverty, certainly a reasonable one in the circumstances. West Virginia would flourish or decay with coal and steel. With coal, it seemed prudent to anticipate further decay. Where were the tax revenues to come from? A few days later Hopkins relented, saying FERA would continue to fund relief programs while the state cast about for ways to increase its share. And he authorized another $1 million in funding for federal relief assistance.[8]

Pickett showed Hickok the shabbier neighborhoods of Morgantown and then led her out to Scotts Run. It was, she would write simply, "the worst place I had ever seen." The inhabitants had only the stagnant, filthy creek for drinking, cooking, and washing. Children splashed about in it. The houses (hovels really, places "most Americans would not have considered fit for pigs") were black with coal dust; it permeated everything and mocked even minimum standards of cleanliness. The coal tipples loomed over the ravaged valley, thrown into weird relief at night by single bright lights like low-hanging stars. "Everywhere, grimy, undernourished, desperate people—so hungry that they could not wait for the vegetables to mature in their pathetic little gardens," Hickok wrote. Incessant, gnawing hunger led the miners to dig up tiny, bitter potatoes long before harvest time and to pick tomatoes while they were still green.[9]

In an uncharacteristic fit of activism, impelled now to do more than take notes and file reports to Hopkins, Hickok rang long distance to summon Mrs. Roosevelt from Washington to see for herself—and for the president—this travesty of the American Dream. ER reached Morgantown on August 17, driving (alone and, much of the time, with the convertible top down) from Washington. She and Hickok spent the night at the Crown mining camp in Arnettsville, in the home of Glenn Work, a former mine superintendent who now made a living as a caretaker for a group of closed mines. In the morning Mrs. Roosevelt toured a craftsmen's cooperative at the Crown camp, a joint venture of Pickett's AFSC and Work. A miner's wife made her a present of a hand-woven scarf.[10]

Hickok, Mrs. Roosevelt, and Pickett motored to Scotts Run on Friday in Mrs. Roosevelt's car. Hickok would have been startled, and probably unnerved, to see a photo of herself alongside the first lady's in *The Morgantown Post*. The coverage, though, would have struck her as familiar enough, some of it "women's pages stuff." Mrs. Roosevelt, *The Post* reported, wore a blue skirt, a white blouse, a soft hat, and "shoes of the kind commonly known as sensible." Indulging her interest in what *The Post* called the "back to the land movement," Pickett showed her a community garden in Cassville. Later they toured a mining camp above Jere and The Shack in Pursglove. (Mary Behner was away on vacation and missed the visit.) Mrs. Roosevelt traveled without an entourage; there were no Secret Service agents, nor were any West Virginia politicians along for a photo opportunity. "I did not come here on a handshaking visit," she told reporters, "but only to observe for myself, without interference, exactly the things I wanted to see." The newsmen were charmed, and perhaps disarmed, by the absence of any sign of political hoopla in connection with the visit. According to *The Dominion News*, the first lady blended so easily into the Monongalia County landscape that nobody recognized her for twenty-four hours.[11]

Still, she could hardly have failed to stand out. Mrs. Roosevelt may have been less innocent of the calamitous effects of hard times than Hickok, but she would not have preserved her incognito in Scotts Run, if for no other reason than the sensible shoes. Most of the children, and many of the adults, went about barefoot in all seasons. She spoke with miners who had forgotten what it felt like to have a job. She met children who had never known the experience of sitting down at a table for a proper meal. The houses leaning precariously on the hillsides were scarcely fit for human habitation. In one, a miner showed her his weekly paycheck; deductions for a bill at the company store, rent, and oil for his miner's lamp left him with less than $1 to support his wife and six children. "I noticed a bowl on the table filled with scraps, the kind you or I might give to a dog, and I saw children, evidently looking for their noonday meal, take a handful out of that bowl and go out munching," she wrote later. "That was all they had to eat." Two of the children hovered near the door, fascinated by the crisply dressed stranger but too timid to come closer. One, a boy, held a white rabbit, obviously a pet, in his pencil-thin arms. His sister, clothed in rags, approached the first lady and said, "He thinks we are not going to eat it, but we are." The boy turned and fled down the road, clutching the rabbit to his heaving chest. A former schoolteacher, Mrs. Roosevelt observed the children of Scotts Run intently; some clearly were "sub-normal," in her phrase, and in later years she often wondered how, or even whether, they grew up.[12]

The first lady returned to Washington on August 19. Hickok continued her investigations with Pickett as guide, touring Wheeling on the Ohio River and returning briefly to the warring coal districts of southwestern Pennsylvania. A few weeks after her visit, Mrs. Roosevelt sent Mrs. Work an electric mixer as a thank-you gift. The gesture charmed the superintendent's wife. "It is something I have wanted for a long time," she wrote ER. "Sometimes I think it is a dream, and I'm afraid I might awaken. I think I am the happiest person in the state of West Virginia." As for Hickok, she moved about as though in another sort of dream, a profoundly disturbing one. "I just couldn't believe that in this great, still potentially rich country in which I had grown up, such conditions existed," she would write. Afterward she wondered what the miners and their women and children had thought of the tall, slender patrician lady "who walked among them, asking questions and listening attentively to their hopeless replies." Hickok found it impossible to put the accursed inhabitants of Bloody Run, listless and slowly starving, out of her mind. As it happened, fresh unbearable experiences awaited her in Coal Country, only they had to be borne. Toward the end of the West Virginia assignment, she would write ER, "I don't believe I'll ever feel complacent again in all my life."[13]

The road south led through a romantic landscape: deep wooded valleys with a sudden upthrust of hills, lowland hamlets twilit till midmorning, mine camps in the hollows where the days drew in early when the sun dropped down behind the western ridges. Below Charleston, the state capital, loomed the craggy citadels of the Open Shop, with their grim backdrop of lawlessness, violence, reprisal, and vigilante justice. "The hills are still beautiful," Hickok wrote ER, "but I'm beginning to hate them for all the misery that the stuff inside them makes for people." Men and women in this wild country went about the business of living in a desolation of everyday scarcity and brutality the equal of which Hickok had never seen. These mountains had been hostile to the chattel slavery that had flourished in neighboring Virginia, Kentucky, and Tennessee until the 1860s. So far as Hickok could tell, though, no antebellum American of African descent had been any more thoroughly enslaved than the coal miners of southern West Virginia.[14]

She reached Charleston on August 21 and made her accustomed reportorial rounds, meeting with state officials, the Associated Press bureau chief, relief investigators, and union organizers at the frowsy United Mine Workers office at 142½ Summers Street. Headlines in *The Charleston Daily Mail* served up shorthand accounts of Governor Kump's negotiations with Harry Hopkins, the NRA coal code talks, a grisly and spectacular local murder, and a powerful hurricane that raked the Virginia Capes. Traveling from coal patch to coal patch in sound trucks and ladling out free beer, the union men had been in a frenzy of activity since the signing of the National Industrial Recovery Act in June, and their assaults on the fortified positions of the operators in coal-rich Logan and Mingo counties were showing gratifying results. As the journalist and literary critic Edmund Wilson put it, "The miners hail the organizers as wrecked men hail a ship." Operators in the southern counties claimed an imperative to shortchange the miners because greater distances from northern markets meant higher transportation costs. Something had to give; the owners weren't making money, and miners' wages were that something. The operators called it the "wage differential," and even they conceded their pay rates were disgracefully low.[15]

The UMW locals weren't buying the owners' argument, and miners were streaming into the union by the hundreds. For the time being, Hickok reserved judgment about whether the union's ascendancy would be a good thing. Her senses were overwhelmed and her nerves raddled from a visit to a community of miners, most of them on the companies' blacklist, near Ward in the Kanawha coal district south of the capital. The men and their families had been living in tents along a hillside a mile down the road from the Ward mine since the fall of 1931. For two harsh winters they had subsisted under thin, patched canvas. Hickok wrote Mrs. Roosevelt, "Gosh, I wish I could make you see that place as I saw it! The tents, all black with coal dust and dampness, are huddled together along the highway near a river. In the background, those beautiful—and rather terrible—hills. A little group of men sitting silent and thoughtful on a big rock. Ragged, discouraged, bitter. Women messing around, trying to do a little washing and clean the places up. A few pathetic little gardens. And those terrible looking children." A social worker told her there were five-year-olds in West Virginia who had never tasted milk. She saw a baby, fifteen months old and born in one of the tents, all covered with sores. A lot of the children were afflicted with open, running sores; they had contracted some sort of skin disease, probably from playing in the mine-poisoned river.[16]

The women, slatternly beyond description, wandered about barely covered, showing thin white arms and legs. Hickok spoke with one prematurely aged miner's wife who stood before her in a ragged slip and an almost transparent dress. "Not another stitch," Hickok noted. "No shoes or stockings. And she told me those were all the clothes she had in the world." The Ward mine superintendent had worked in Soviet Russia, and he swore he'd never witnessed anything there more distressing than the tent colony he passed every day. She heard from miners who hadn't drawn a coal company paycheck for eight years. "Thirty-four of the men are perfectly able-bodied and could work, but they can't get jobs," the superintendent said, because of the blacklist. The undercurrents of rage and violence in Coal Country were shocking to Hickok. "Even the children talk in the most matter-of-fact way about shooting mine bosses," she wrote ER. If someone supplied the guns, she thought, the children certainly would use them.[17]

Violence. This was, after all, the country of the Hatfields and McCoys. The West Virginia Hatfields and the Kentucky McCoys were warring families separated by the Tug Fork River, which formed a stretch of border between the two states. Two or three generations back, Hickok learned, a son of Devil Anse Hatfield, the head of the West Virginia clan, eloped with a McCoy girl, reigniting a feud that had smoldered since before the Civil War. When the McCoys raised the alarm, a Hatfield crossed to the west bank of the Tug Fork, raided the McCoy farm, cut off the tail of a McCoy cow, and beat a McCoy woman half to death with it. A decade of bushwhacking and arson claimed the lives of more than a dozen members of the clans. Hickok actually met a Hatfield, "a handsome old rascal if I ever saw one" and a minor celebrity. "He was trying to 'chisel' some relief for himself," she found, "even though he has a railroad pension of $20 a month, a neat little farm, several cows, some pigs." The Hatfield-McCoy feud had ended around the turn of the century, but it lived on in 1933 as a symbol of the mountain anarchy that fueled the operator-miner wars.[18]

The stakes were high in Coal Country. In 1932 Logan County ranked seventh among ninety-two U.S. coal regions in tonnage mined (12,471,000). Hickok judged the NRA coal code negotiations crucial, predicting unprecedented violence should the code fail to protect the union, with Logan and Mingo counties the chief zone of battle. "They've got two gods, those miners, the President and John Lewis," she noted. Then too, they were courting trouble. "They're in the union now," she reported to Hopkins, "and they want to strike—if for no other reason than to 'get back at' the operators." The idea of an FDR dictatorship seemed more appealing to her now: "Both gangs need someone to stand right over them with a whip and make them behave. If we're going to get anywhere at all, those operators and miners have got to be made to pull together. And only a good strong Big Boss, with plenty of authority behind him, can make them do it." She implored the first lady to tell the president he should claim, and assert, the broad powers of a strongman.[19]

Hickok traveled south from Charleston early in the afternoon of August 22, a long, slow bus trip along State Routes 12 and 17, a back-bone-jarring ride through some of the most beautiful mountain scenery she had ever seen. The highway worked its way down a narrow valley through which the Spruce River ran swift and dark with mine waste. Clearing Madison, the self-proclaimed gateway to Coal Country, the bus continued south toward Logan along a route that passed the site of the battle of Blair Mountain. This affray in late August 1921, the largest armed uprising in the United States since the Civil War, had seen battalions of striking miners in blue overalls with red handkerchiefs knotted at the neck clash with police, private detectives, American Legion vigilantes, and strikebreakers. Upwards of fifteen thousand men exchanged more than a million rounds of small-arms fire in a week-long series of skirmishes. Don Chafin, the despotic sheriff of Logan County, commanded the forces of the Open Shop. He deployed machine guns and other up-to-date weaponry and hired private aircraft to bomb the strikers' lines. U.S. Army warplanes carried out reconnaissance missions for the operators. The fighting ended with as many as a hundred dead and hundreds wounded, a decisive victory for the mine owners; in the aftermath, nearly six hundred miners faced charges of murder, conspiracy, and treason.[20]

The bus pulled into Logan in a cloud of exhaust fumes a few minutes before 5 o'clock. Hickok's first impressions weren't favorable: the little valley town ringed by high hills wore a dreary, godforsaken aspect. "The streets are so narrow that there is barely room for two cars to pass, and the whole town looks crowded and mean and miserable," she wrote Mrs. Roosevelt. With two begrimed hotels to choose from, she checked into the outwardly less dingy one, resolving to inspect the mattress carefully before turning in. She managed only one interview that evening, with

Mabel Sutherland, the tired and discouraged-looking head of relief distribution for Logan County. Sutherland at least might have tried to put up a cheerful front, she thought, for after all a lot of miners were working at the moment. That was owing in part to the strikes in western Pennsylvania, and also because the operators were trying to stockpile as much coal as possible before the impending NRA code changed the capital-labor equation. Sutherland's relief load had been cut almost in half.[21]

Working or idle, the men and their families were forlorn and debilitated, afflicted with dysentery, tuberculosis, diphtheria, asthma, heart trouble, and arthritis. An unvarying diet of sowbelly and pinto beans left them vulnerable to disease, and Sutherland anticipated widespread illness with the onset of winter. So many had died during the winter of 1932–33, Hickok heard, that county agents "established as one of their relief projects the making of coffins!" Many smaller coffins doubtless would be filled soon with the wasted bodies of child victims of diphtheria; an early outbreak of the highly contagious bacterial disease in Logan and Mingo counties deeply worried Sutherland. The best Logan County could do for the most desperately ill children was to try to pour nutrients into them in the detention home that served as a makeshift hospital. The day Hickok visited, someone brought in a little girl from one of the mining camps. "In the afternoon they operated on her," she wrote Hopkins, "putting the tube in her throat (so she could breathe). They had her isolated in a building back of the home, and later it occurred to me that it must have been the garage!" Private hospitals were uncooperative, and there appeared to be no hospital beds for indigents anywhere in the state.[22]

There were, too, the immemorial hazards of the mines. A crippled miner—he had lost a leg on the job—wrote UMW organizer William Blizzard to beg for work, an all too typical case: "Now brother. The department of mines will not allow the operator to hire me in the only trade I know." Unfit for below-ground work, he wanted a place as a checkweighman, and he wanted it desperately. "I have no means of support at all," he went on, for none of the Hoover-era Reconstruction Finance Corporation works projects would take him on. A day or two after Hickok reached Logan, an explosion at the Hutchinson Coal Company's Dabney mine killed two men outright and left a third so badly burned he died a short time later.[23]

Hickok had come to credit the miners' claims that the operators cheated them out of wages by short-weighting. ("Believe me," one swore, "they take a ton off every carload.") She did not, however, warm to the two UMW organizers in Logan, Lee Hall and H. E. Smith, both of whom were staying at her hotel. "They showed up after I finished writing you last night, and ever since then I've had them on my hands—whenever they could find me," she wrote Mrs. Roosevelt. Hall and Smith believed they were on the verge of a great triumph. The mines soon would be unionized and paying out a uniform $5-a-day wage; the operators would be tamed and the miners prosperous and happy. "They have no idea of what this coal situation is," she went on. "I didn't argue with them, my dear, I just sat and listened—with my mouth open. What a jolt these boys are going to get! It all came out when I asked them if they had any ideas about what to do with the miners who are not going to be able to get back in the mines." They were the stranded ones, and they numbered into the thousands here—men older than forty-five, the ailing, men a step slow or with their wits astray. Neither the operators nor the union would have any use for them.[24]

She didn't much care for the UMW, she concluded; she found Hall and Smith puerile, and she suspected they were out to settle scores. Extolling the rival company union, the biweekly *Logan Banner* called the UMW "a great industrial leech" and carried full-page ads from the operators warning miners not to be deceived. But she didn't like the operators any better, at least in the person of their Logan County representative, Jesse Sullivan. "We just didn't speak the same language; and, since I have neither the qualifications nor the authority to argue with him, we didn't get very far," she wrote. She summarized Sullivan's attitude: "The miners don't want to go back to work. They'd rather stay on relief." That might well have been the case, and she thought she could see why. Compared to the Logan and Mingo operators, the Pennsylvania mine barons were Coal Country humanitarians. As for relief, almost anything would be preferable to working below ground in circumstances such as the men described them.[25]

A miner might labor in a vein as shallow as thirty inches, Hickok learned. He might work on his knees the entire shift, "almost in the position in which he lay in his mother's womb." On her tour of the Logan County districts, an investigator called her attention to a man slouching along the verge of the road. He had gauze patches on his back, between his shoulders. "That's from rubbing his back against the top of the vein," he told her. "They get callouses there too." A Logan man named Woodrow Mosley first went down the mine in 1929 at age sixteen, starting at a wage of $2.10 a day and working with picks and shovels on his hands and knees. "You'd go in at 6 o'clock in the morning, and you wouldn't get out no more till next evenin' after dark," he recalled. "It was all hand-loadin' coal. You stayed till ever' man got his coal cleaned up so he could get his coal cut back for the next day." The mine boss didn't bother to keep track of hours; a man stayed till the job was done, and he stayed for the daily wage, more often than not paid in scrip or thin, crude aluminum coins. Out of that wage came various deductions for rent and provisions; powder and explosives required to "shoot the coal" could claim 20 to 25 percent of a miner's pay.[26]

A working man had next to nothing; a man on relief had about the same, perhaps a little less. Some of the better Logan County operators showed interest in relief programs and (so long as it didn't cost too much) in their miners' welfare. The Island Creek Coal Company drew commendation, even though the bosses had insisted upon yellow dog contracts until 1932 and continued to discharge men who traded elsewhere than in the company store. An Island Creek foreman named Parsons used to require miners to work a certain number of hours to be eligible for Red Cross flour handouts. When UMW organizers reported Parsons for this, Island Creek fired him in spite of his seventeen years with the company. Visiting the Island Creek camp, Hickok found decent housing and other amenities. On balance, though, the visit left her glum and discouraged. "They simply own the men, body and soul," she observed. Still, the company president, T. B. Davis, seemed to show genuine sympathy with the miners' plight and expended some effort on their behalf.[27]

Davis and his company were the exception. "The operators have not taken very much interest in [relief] work, even though the work done has not only relieved them financially, but has also put off hunger marches, unemployment demonstrations, etc.," wrote J. W. Colley, secretary of the Logan County Coal Operators Association and a member of the State Relief Board. In a survey of Logan relief efforts, Colley determined that the most effective assistance in 1932–33 had come from private groups, including Pickett's

AFSC, the Salvation Army, and the Red Cross. The Quakers sustained 42 percent of the Logan County school population in January 1933. "They are doing splendid work, and they do it without a great deal of publicity," Colley reported. Red Cross agents distributed flour, clothing, and shoes. The Salvation Army looked after transients, supplying nearly a thousand meals and several hundred beds in 1932–33 to people drifting through Logan.[28]

Private agencies could not meet the demand, though, and government work relief programs were ineptly managed. The federal government offered funds for road mending, for example, but required the counties to provide tools. Logan County refused. "Consequently, we have a great many men on the roads but no tools," Colley wrote. "The reaction of the public when they see men standing around loafing on various jobs is not good." In February 1933, 3,325 families—between 40 and 50 percent of the population—were subsisting on work relief in Logan County. Colley claimed miners chose made-work on the roads over low wages and dangerous, back-breaking toil in the mines. He wanted the public works wage of 30 cents an hour reduced so that jobs in the mines would be more appealing.[29]

Hickok wrapped up her tour of the southern districts on August 24. Bernice Chambers, a Logan County relief investigator, drove her over the mountains into Mingo County—"Bloody Mingo," Hatfield and McCoy country. In Williamson, a major coal-shipping center on the Tug Fork River, the Norfolk & Western Railroad shops were mostly shuttered and the marshaling yard ghostly. She returned to Charleston that evening with Chambers and Mabel Sutherland, leaving them with a promise to lobby for a free medical clinic in Logan County and to press the secretary of labor to conciliate the warring factions once the coal code went through.[30]

With the state relief director, Major Francis Turner, driving, Hickok traveled north to Wheeling on August 25. Turner's forecasts were gloomy. West Virginia tax receipts were falling off, he said, and prospects for raising new revenue were bleak. The Associated Press man in Charleston had told Hickok that a proposal to increase the cigarette tax would go nowhere; the state's powerful tobacco lobby held the veto. Patronage and political interference were hampering the relief effort. Said Turner, "Here we are with our entire civilization built on rotten foundations and tottering, and you've got a lot of damn fool capitalists and petty politicians fiddling away while the thing collapses." Everywhere he looked, the indications were ominous.[31]

Yet Hickok thought she could detect signs of hope. Turner used his military connections to open National Guard camps to children; more than four thousand destitute boys and girls from families on relief had fattened up on three decent meals a day for a two-week period that summer. Turner showed her around a camp for a thousand boys ages eight to fourteen. People on work relief did the cooking and cleaning. The camp's doctor, on salary at $200 a month, looked after the boys' most obvious health problems. It cost 30 cents a day to feed them. "It was good food, too, and all they wanted," she wrote Hopkins. "Supper, a good, filling meal, was served cafeteria style, and I saw some of the youngsters go back for three servings." The average weight gain per child was five pounds over the two weeks. Hickok met some of the boys' families in their homes a few days later. "The faces of their parents simply glowed when I described the camps to them," a contrast with home life that nearly broke her heart.[32]

Other items of good news: idled nurses were being put on work relief and assigned to public health agencies; clinics were opening in abandoned stores and empty miners' cabins. (Still, the need for free hospital beds remained acute.) The state's subsistence gardening program appeared to be a success, at least in locales—the university town of Morgantown came to mind—where expert advice, tools, and seed were readily available. And on their first quick trip to Wheeling the weekend before, "Major Turner almost jumped out of the car for joy—because there was nice, rich, black smoke pouring out of almost all the steel mill stacks!" Steel's labor wars were yet to come. For now, smoke from the millstacks signaled a step back from the edge. And it meant money in workers' pockets and receipts for landlords and grocers.[33]

In working up her second report to Harry Hopkins, Hickok confirmed a number of tentative conclusions: however flawed, work relief programs were superior to the dole; relief agents deserved protection from the politicians; health issues were paramount and improvements to public health essential; there were frightening prospects for unprecedented levels of labor-capital conflict; and a peaceful settlement between the coal operators and the United Mine Workers, however desirable, would do little to alleviate the distress of the thousands of West Virginia discards—men and women for whom there seemed to be no place and no solution. Turner drove her to the Allegheny County Airport near Pittsburgh on August 26, where she indulged in a contemporary travel novelty and bought an airline ticket for Washington, paying a $3.04 surcharge for excess baggage. (Hickok probably did not know this, but in 1933 travelers were seventy-two times more likely to perish in a plane crash than in a railroad accident.) The aircraft fluttered to a safe landing at the newly christened Washington-Hoover Airport in Arlington, Virginia, at 7:30 in the evening. Hickok settled into her quarters in the White House, a small chamber adjacent to the first lady's bedroom, in time for a late dinner.[34]

Woodrow Mosley, the Logan County miner, gestured toward a wooded hillside. "You ought to go up there," he told an interviewer in 1988. "It looks good from our way, where you see. It looks good. But you get on the other side. See what you see. There ain't nothin' there. They ain't even pushed no dirt over where they got the coal." The method is called mountaintop removal, and it lets the mining companies inexpensively and efficiently exploit the rich coal seams lying near the surface. The miners put explosives to what they call the overburden, layers of soil and rock that cover the seams. Giant earthmoving machines lop off the summits and dump the spoil in the upper reaches of the valleys. This type of strip mining is concentrated in southern West Virginia and southeastern Kentucky, and it alters the mountain landscape in a drastic—and shocking—way.[35]

The ridge and valley system known as Pine Mountain stretches northeast to southwest for nearly a hundred miles, angling through Harlan and Bell counties, Kentucky, the scene of bitter mine wars in the early 1930s. U.S. 119 ascends the ridge via long S curves to summits with a 360-degree view to the rim of the world. In the middle distance to the west and north the bare yellow-brown earth of the scarred peaks stands out starkly against the vivid green of the lower slopes. The highway drops down into the valley near Cumberland, passes just to the west of the city of Harlan, and terminates, abruptly, at Pineville, the Bell County seat.

Judging by the signs in the shop windows, mercantile Pineville today is a loyal ally of the mining industry. "We Support Coal," the signs read, and a banner proclaims, "Coal Keeps the Lights on in Bell County." The center of Pineville hasn't changed much since the 1930s, and it is easy to imagine posters bearing the Blue Eagle, with the legend "We Do Our Part," taped to the windows of the same buildings that fronted the four sides of the Bell County courthouse square back then.

After another overnight trip from Washington, this one twenty hours in duration, Hickok stepped onto the platform at the Pineville railroad station a few minutes after 2 o'clock in the afternoon of August 31 and moved off in the late summer heat to the Continental Hotel. Later she met her escort, Caroline Boone, a Kentucky Relief Board field supervisor responsible for ten counties with 28,000 families—roughly 150,000 people—on the rolls. "For the present there will be no more help," read a typewritten notice affixed to the relief office door. Boone explained that the state had been unable to distribute any assistance for nearly three weeks. Kentucky's relief funds were exhausted, the state couldn't find a way to meet FERA's matching grant requirements, and the last food orders had gone out on August 12. Boone told Hickok, "Every morning little groups of people—those who still have enough strength to walk anywhere from one to ten miles—come straggling in and stand staring helplessly at those notices. Many of them cannot read." One of the staffers read aloud from the morning paper every day to people waiting outside the courthouse, delivering the latest news of the special legislative session in Frankfort. There was not much to report. "They listen dumbly, and then they go away," the staffer said. Caroline Boone had an aversion to watching human beings starve. One morning she sent all the cash she had in her purse over to the bank to be changed into 50-cent pieces, which she handed out to the forlorn, bedraggled women queuing up outside the relief office.[36]

The citizens of Harlan and Bell counties had all but lost hope in the late summer of 1933. The intermittent coal wars there entered a more violent phase in the spring of 1931, when the United Mine Workers disavowed an especially hard-fought strike, abandoning southeastern Kentucky miners to the Communist-led National Miners Union. This added the element of red-baiting to the capital-labor equation. An uneasy truce held for a year or so, but when miners were working at all it was only one or two days a week. Capital in Bell and Harlan counties played to win, and justice, if that is the right word, invariably served the operators. "If the court doesn't get you, the gunmen will," the saying went; a few men plotting a strike were criminal syndicalists, easy targets for the deputies. Journalists with left-wing sympathies turned up to compile a documentary record of Coal Country's wars. The novelists Theodore Dreiser, John Dos Passos, Sherwood Anderson, and others toured Harlan County in November 1931 and a few months later published *Harlan Miners Speak*, a book-length report on conditions there. Bringing four truckloads of food, the literary critics Edmund Wilson and Malcolm Cowley, the novelist Waldo Frank, and several associates came to Pineville in February 1932 on a fact-finding mission for the Communist-inspired Independent Miners' Relief Committee of New York City (outside agitators, to the Kentucky overlords). J. C. Byars followed a bit later, visiting Harlan County with a view to collecting material for articles in *The Nation*.[37]

The writers experienced intimidation and the overt threat of violence. Wilson called Bell County a "war zone." Frank, the head of the New York delegation,* believed the power of exposure would assure protection, and he boasted to the authorities in Pineville that he and his friends would use the platform of *The New Republic* to raise the alarm from New York to California. Byars presented himself as a plain newspaperman in search of information. "Inevitably, the coal operators and officials warned me—some with hostility, others kindly, that I should leave," he wrote. Mayor J. M. Brooks of Pineville instructed Frank not to arrange meetings with miners. Wilson's lecture on freedom of speech left the mayor unmoved. Cleon Calvert, an attorney for the Straight Creek Coal Company and other operators, let it be known that in Bell County Communists had no constitutional rights. There were Communists in the New York delegation, and Wilson, though not himself a party member, aligned himself with the comrades. Plainclothes detectives loitered day and night near their hotel entrance, and everyone went about armed.

---

*According to Malcolm Cowley, Frank won the appointment because he had published more books than the others.

The authorities deployed machine guns outside the courthouse, in case the miners came too close.[38]

The New Yorkers' dealings with the satraps of Bell County were icily polite, darkly humorous, and, ultimately, violent. Walter B. Smith, the county attorney, wore a Phi Beta Kappa key to their meetings, perhaps to show off his highbrow credentials to the city men. Wilson thought Smith's ornate manner masked nervousness. Lawyer Calvert was there, along with Herndon Evans, editor of the *Pineville Sun*, county chairman of the Red Cross and a share-owner in a coal mine. "These Bell and Harlan county miners can live on less than any other people in the world," Evans once claimed, as if that were a matter of local pride. Frank sought "permission" for the delegation to meet with miners. Smith asked Frank and the others who had paid their fares to Kentucky. Then the two had the following exchange.

Frank: I assume you believe in Jeffersonian democracy.

Smith: As a matter of fact, I've always been a Republican. I've heard about it, though.[39]

Smith warned Frank, Wilson, and the others against stirring up the miners. "You can distribute food as much as you want to, but as soon as you buck the law, it will be my pleasure as well as my duty to prosecute you," he said. That afternoon, the New Yorkers distributed milk and groceries to miners under the baleful eyes of armed deputies, who confiscated newsreel footage of the event, then overturned one of the trucks and helped themselves to the food. The writers were under virtual house arrest, according to Frank. Evans advised against their leaving the hotel that night, but they wandered out anyway, walking around the square and stopping at a drugstore to buy cigarettes. The sheriff awaited them when they returned. He escorted the New Yorkers to the courthouse for a sort of arraignment charade while deputies searched their rooms. Frank kept asking to see a warrant, as though forms of law had any currency in Bell County. Around midnight, the authorities ordered Frank and his associates to collect their baggage and pay their bills. Bundled into cars, they were driven to the Virginia line at Cumberland Gap. The headlights were doused. "Get out of the car and don't ever come back to Kentucky," the commander of the escort told them. Somebody whacked Frank in the head with a blackjack or a pistol butt; he could feel his blood warming the back of his neck. The nightriders roughed up Allan Taub, the delegation's Communist lawyer, leaving him badly enough wounded to require medical treatment at the Virginia hotel where they found shelter in the early hours. Afterward Mayor Brooks said the outsiders left Pineville of their own free will, and he suggested Frank and Taub had quarreled and assaulted one another in the darkness and confusion.[40]

Working as a journalist rather than an organizer and working alone, *The Nation's* Byars had less difficulty with the authorities. Bell County social workers were candid, telling him pellagra and flux were endemic among miners' children, with malnutrition and medical ignorance the chief causes. Ruth Etheridge, a "home demonstration" agent, and Beulah Dittoe, a nurse, tended to blame the miners (they were "aggressively contemptuous" of the clients, according to Byars), for they usually failed to follow the weekly menu the county health office recommended. For $8.83 a week, a family of five could enjoy a two-pound roast on Sunday and two pounds of bacon; the other twenty meals were meatless. Byars noted that few miners were working more than a couple of days a week at $2.50 to $3 a day (before deductions for rent, light, heat, and doctor's fees), so $8.83 menus were beyond the reach of just about everyone. In reality, people were living on forage from the meadows and woods: violet tops, wild onions and lettuce, forget-me-nots, and such weeds as cattle consumed. Besides, the county menu lacked many of the items the U.S. Department of Agriculture deemed essential: milk, chicken, fish, cheese, cereals, tomatoes, and greenstuff.[41]

The coal operators Byars spoke with were candid about their views. J. T. Bradley ran three mines in Bell and Harlan counties, leasing the coalfields from absentee owners and paying land rent and royalties. "The operators have got to make their carrying charges or go broke," he said. "They are under duress to do things to their workers and they do them." Bradley, as it happened, paid wages in scrip usable only in company stores. Were the men compelled to shop there? "Well," he said, "I just told my miners, 'Now boys, if you don't want to trade with me you can move along.'" Of course, he admitted to Byars in his open-handed way, his prices *were* a little higher than everyone else's.[42]

By consensus, the best mine in Harlan County belonged to R. W. Creech, president and general manager of the Creech Coal Company and "a genial old gentleman of the Kentucky colonel type," a man with fierce white moustaches who slept with loaded guns at his bedside. The local operators' association regarded Creech as a model employer; Byars saw him, arsenal and all, as a "feudal humanitarian." His $18,000 annual rent payment to a New York landowner obliged him to act in certain ways in the cause of self-preservation. Byars wrote, "He is compelled to practice in his mine the same policies which have resulted in sinking the living standards of a whole population of old-stock American miners into the depths of destitution, starvation and disease." Creech told him, "They'll bring a union in here over my dead body. I would rather close this mine forever than work with a union. I can do it. I have got mine [enough, that is, to live on] and I will never submit to a union."[43]

Byars wrote, too, of a National Miners Union soup kitchen that shared a hollow with the Creech mine. The day Byars visited, the union fed 157 children a stew of boiled potatoes and beans and a piece of cornbread. Union organizers had been subject to blacklists, beatings, kidnappings, and arrests for distributing leaflets. But it wasn't only the operators, Creech and his colleagues, who stood against the union. The entire power structure of Coal Country mobilized to defend the immemorial foundations of authority. Even the charities fell into line. The American Red Cross chapter had its Pineville office in a coal company headquarters, and the chapter refused assistance to strikers. "We made a policy," said Herndon Evans, "a local policy, whether it's in conformity with the national organization or not—when men on strike come to us for aid, we turn them down because of limited funds."[44]

Hickok saw a lot of this for herself during four days of intensive investigation in "notorious" Bell and neighboring counties. The suspension of relief had converted a general widespread destitution into a full-scale humanitarian crisis. Like Byars, she detected a lack of sympathy and even contempt in the authorities' response; the men, women, and children who were suffering were "poor white trash" and expendable. As it happened, the denizens of southeastern Kentucky appealed to Hickok. Most were descendants of colonials who had poured through the Virginia gaps and settled the eastern valleys before the Revolution. They were intensely patriotic. She reported that there had been no need for a draft in Bell County during the World War; man and boy, everyone volunteered. They were deeply religious, and they often opened their feeble protests with a hymn, their favorite being "Where Were You When They Crucified Our Lord?" "They all carry guns and shoot each other," Hickok wrote Hopkins. "And yet they desperately never think of robbing people. I can't for the life of me understand why they don't go down and raid the Blue Grass country." Many, she saw, were so weakened by hunger they could barely stand up for themselves. In Middlesborough, a group of unemployed men tried to organize a raid on the stores. "Since they all carry guns, it looked as though it might be serious," Hickok wrote. But it fizzled. "They came all right, but only about a hundred of them. They stood around a little while and listened to some speeches. By the time the speaking was over most of the crowd had drifted away—slowly, listlessly." They were so vitiated, it seemed to her, they couldn't even pull off a riot.[45]

Outside the towns, in the country districts of Bell and Knox and Harlan counties, in company with Earl Mayhew, a University of Kentucky agricultural extension agent, Hickok found people living in abandoned mining camps and in scattered communities, "rather like Indian villages," at the headwaters of creeks far up the barren, eroded hillsides. The summer had been dry, and the subsistence patches of corn and the kitchen gardens were burned yellow. And the settlements were crowded now. The young people had drifted away during the prosperous 1920s to find work in Cincinnati, Indianapolis, Detroit, Chicago. The Depression had driven them back to live with the old folks, who would share out such meager stocks of flour, cornmeal, lard, and coffee as they could spare.[46]

Rattling up to the head of one of the creeks in Mayhew's old Ford, they encountered a gnarled, ancient woman carrying a handful of string beans she'd begged off someone. Mayhew called her "Aunt Cora." Hickok spoke to her briefly, and before Aunt Cora moved off up the creek she laid a withered hand on Hickok's arm and said in a whisper, "Don't forget me, honey. Don't forget me."[47]

Perhaps thinking of Aunt Cora, she emphasized in her September 3 report what happened to people when FERA cut off assistance as a tactic to pressure the states to pick up a greater share of the relief burden. "This stuff may sound a bit sobby," she wrote Hopkins. "I can only say that it's all true and not a bit exaggerated. I hesitated a little at turning in this sort of report. I don't want anyone to think I'm trying to argue about policy. It certainly is NOT my job. But I don't know—perhaps this kind of report IS my job." As she reminded herself, Caroline Boone had told her 62 percent of the people in the ten counties she looked after were on relief—six men, women, and children out of every ten.[48]

But Hickok could see, too, that the New Deal and the man far away in the White House were beginning to make a difference. And in Harlan County, at least, a bloodless revolution soon would take place. By midautumn miners of the Black Mountain Coal Company would be fully organized. In Evarts, where a dozen men had been killed in a pitched battle with the forces of order a couple of years before, five thousand miners would turn out for an open-air meeting. No Harlan County official would try to break it up, for Harlan County officials would be friendly for a change. The coal operators' men, Sheriff John Henry Blair, County Judge D. C. "Baby Face" Jones, and Commonwealth Attorney W. H. Brock, all had been turned out of office.[49]

The blustery Hugh Johnson's threats, blandishments, and tantrums, coupled with the president's lectures to soft-coal operators in two late-summer meetings at the White House, yielded results at last. After weeks of onagain, off-again negotiations, the operators and the United Mine Workers agreed to the NRA code on September 18. Covering 340,000 miners, it gave the UMW close to what it sought, though not the closed shop: an eight-hour day and a five-day workweek, a $3.36 daily minimum wage, a check-off of union dues, and arbitration of disputes. President Roosevelt signed the coal code on the 18th and the pact dealing with pay and hours of work five days later, sealing perhaps "the most important wage agreement made in American labor history," according to The New York Times.[50]

With word of the deal, "Scotts Run literally went wild," The Dominion News of Morgantown reported. The code set the local wage at $4.36 a day for skilled labor, $3.36 for unskilled. News broke that the Samuel

Pursglove family would reopen the Connellsville mine on the Little Pittsburgh seam, idle since January 1, adding five hundred jobs. The Connellsville camp's hundred houses would fill soon, with electric lights and "city" water among the amenities. In bloody Logan County, the mines were to be UMW-organized, with a $4.20 daily minimum wage for a forty-hour week. The miners got their checkweighman too, along with assurances the operators no longer would be able to force them to live in company houses or trade in company stores.[51]

The coal code did nothing, though, to create jobs or boost the market for coal or address miner redundancy. "We have to face the prospect that hundreds of thousands of persons must find jobs elsewhere if those miners who are needed are to have enough work to earn a decent living," *The New Republic* reminded readers. Share-work programs were not a long-term answer.[52]

Meanwhile strikes continued to spread, especially in southwestern Pennsylvania. The mid-September walkout in the Uniontown area pressured reluctant operators to reach a deal with Johnson's NRA, but Tom Moses of the Frick combine remained adamant in his refusal to sign the code. *The Morgantown Post* reported the Scotts Run miners, euphoric just a few days earlier, now were inclined to follow the Pennsylvanians out of the coalfields. With the Frick mines idle, Pittsburgh steel mills were importing West Virginia soft coal, and the Pennsylvanians wanted the miners there to stand with them. "If we have to eat grass, we will fight on until [Moses] comes around," their leaders vowed. Frick managers cut down credit at company stores to 10 cents per person a day and, playing the race card, imported black strikebreakers.[53]

"FDR is having real trouble with the steel crowd over the coal code," Mrs. Roosevelt wrote Hickok at the end of September, and there were rumors of a general strike that would shut down steel as well as coal and deal a setback to such recovery as had occurred. The coal strike had already cost the economy an estimated $20 million. But ER sounded more concerned, for now, about what would happen to the "redundant" miners of Scotts Run. During her August visit to West Virginia, she had inspected a run-down 1,200-acre estate near Reedsville east of Morgantown, property of the once-prominent, now faded Arthur family. Returning to Washington, she arranged with Louis Howe for government purchase of the estate with a view to settling surplus miners there. This was the genesis of her famous Arthurdale project.[54] Her vision was to give families subsistence plots of two to five acres, with each of the initial fifty families supplied with a cow, a pig, chickens, and garden seed. The Quakers who ran the program chose the first settlers based on need and the likelihood of their making a success of it. Just before Thanksgiving, the first lady returned to West Virginia on an inspection visit. When Mary Behner learned she would be coming, she invited her to a fifth-anniversary celebration of the missionary project in Scotts Run. Mrs. Roosevelt declined, so Behner made the trip to Reedsville on November 22, hoping for a view of "the pet hobby of the First Lady." People lined the main street several deep to watch the motorcade pass; Mrs. Roosevelt drove her own car, with a motorcycle escort. "It was a thrill to see the First Lady," Behner wrote, "and to realize that she was here to help the people who have inspired my work of the past five years—and to know within myself that I had a small part in helping create a background for her interest."[55]

Behner may have unknowingly inspired Mrs. Roosevelt, but Hickok, with her letters and reports, exerted a direct influence on the first lady and her husband. ER assured Hickok that the president had read the Pennsylvania, West Virginia, and Kentucky reports carefully. "How funny you are about your reports, of course they are good, absorbingly interesting," she wrote. "FDR told me he wished your letters could be published! He is hard to please and always asks if I've anything to read from you." Soon there was additional evidence. *The Literary Digest* reported that FDR had summoned a "hard-boiled" mine operator to the White House for a discussion of conditions in Coal Country. The magnate told the president the only miners who were suffering were those who were shy of work. FDR responded with details of desperate conditions in the operator's own mining town. People in Washington were curious about the president's informant, according to *The Digest*, and discovered that the chief source was Lorena Hickok. "Relief Administrator Hopkins is accumulating an encyclopedic knowledge of conditions," the magazine reported. "It is no longer a secret that her reports are seen, exactly as written, not only by Mr. Hopkins but in the White House."[56]

4

STRANDEES

New York and Maine, September 1933

Here, finally, Lorena Hickok encountered a healthy community, at least on the face of it: Corning, New York, a small Southern Tier industrial and trading center, population 15,700, curiously resistant to the contagion of economic collapse. Glass had been manufactured in Corning since 1868, tableware, thermometers, incandescent red and green lightbulbs used for railroad signals, Edison lightbulbs, and, since 1915, heat-resistant Pyrex. A gateway to the Finger Lakes tourist district, the city had hardly felt the effects of the Great Depression before 1931 and now, in September 1933, the Corning Glass Works, a complex of forty brick buildings grouped along the Chemung River, were running at full capacity; the company had just rehired five hundred workers and regained 1928 production levels. For some reason, specialty glass had not suffered as severely as other industries.[1]

Hickok reached Corning on the bright, mild afternoon of September 12, driven from New York City in her own newly acquired automobile, a secondhand Chevrolet convertible, christened "Bluette," which Eleanor Roosevelt had helped her buy. She rode in the passenger seat for most of the 225-mile journey, her chauffeur a young man, jobless until now, who would travel with her during the fourth in a series of reporting expeditions for Harry Hopkins, this one through upstate New York and Maine. She was learning, if painfully, to drive, and though a novice herself she could be cuttingly critical of the youth at the wheel, a New Yorker she referred to, rather heartlessly, as "the unemployed boy." Once, when his foot slipped off the clutch and Bluette's gears shrieked, "I wanted to murder him," she wrote ER. One wonders what she and the young man had to say to each other as the miles unwound. Perhaps the clatter of Bluette's engine, the metronomic click of the tires as they ran over the creases in the pavement, and the roar of the wind made conversation impossible. At any rate, the boy must have had the forbearance of Job. Hickok would not be a quick study as a driving student, and her white-knuckle turns at the wheel would test his nerves and the little Chevy's stamina over hundreds of miles of New York and New England roads.[2]

Hickok had won a five-day respite in Washington after the grueling, emotionally wrenching West Virginia–Kentucky trip. She moved into the anteroom off the first lady's study and the White House became her legal address. The night train had delivered her to New York City from Washington before dawn on September 9, and she spent the weekend tidying up her affairs there, subletting the Mitchell Place apartment, making long-term arrangements for Prinz, her German shepherd, negotiating to buy the car, and working out an agreement with her driver-instructor. The responsibility of car ownership seemed to daunt her at first, but she understood that Bluette would give her unexampled freedom of movement. The terms were favorable too: a government travel allowance of $5 a day and 5 cents a mile for oil, gasoline, and wear and tear.[3]

Conditions in Corning were so strikingly different from those Hickok had observed in Pennsylvania, West Virginia, and Kentucky that she wondered whether "things were running almost too smoothly" there. "I got the impression that the relief people . . . had begun to look about for new worlds to conquer and were, perhaps, 'case-working' their people too much," she wrote. She cited a so-called escrow system in which the county board withheld a percentage of a client's weekly work relief earnings so he could be laid off after a few weeks. Living on the escrow money, he would pass his job along to someone else in need. That struck her as paternalistic. "I honestly believe it is the right of every American citizen, even though he *is* working on a relief project that pays only minimum subsistence wages, to collect his money and do what he wants with it," she wrote Mrs. Roosevelt. That said, she admired the creativity and ingenuity of Corning's work relief projects. One entailed curbing and guttering the city's streets with stone. In another, crews took down thousands of poplars whose roots were compromising the sewer system, replacing them with donated maples and elms.[4]

New York State's relief program had been in place since the autumn of 1931, when then-Governor Roosevelt persuaded the Republican-dominated Assembly to establish the Temporary Emergency Relief Administration. At least a million New Yorkers were out of work in the summer of 1931; the jobless rate approached 25 percent in Buffalo and other upstate industrial cities. Roosevelt went to the legislature in late September with a proposal for an independent state relief agency to operate for seven months with an appropriation of $20 million, to be covered by a 50 percent increase in the state's graduated income tax. "It is clear to me," Roosevelt told the Assembly, "that it is the duty of those who have benefited by our industrial and economic system to come to the front in such a grave emergency and assist in relieving those who under the same industrial and economic order are the losers and sufferers." The creation of TERA marked the beginning of his association with Harry Hopkins, the New York City social worker who became the agency's first executive director. By February 1932, with unemployment at 1.5 million and climbing and most of the initial $20 million used up, FDR fell back on a flexible definition of the word *temporary*, moving to extend TERA's life to January 1934, obtain an additional $5 million for immediate needs, and place on the ballot in November a $30 million bond issue to fund relief. (It passed.)[5]

Hopkins ascended to the chairmanship of TERA in the summer of 1932, overseeing a relief operation that eventually would provide assistance to 10 percent of New Yorkers—a precisely tabulated 386,884 families, a total of 1.6 million persons. Hopkins and his cadres of professional social workers identified significant weaknesses in a slapdash emergency system that had not yet attempted to address fundamental questions such as technological displacement. Strandees were "a new and permanent insecure group," wrote David Adie, New York State's commissioner of public welfare: "musicians thrown out of work by sound pictures; factory workers displaced by the belt system and automatic machinery; clerks [supplanted by] calculators; laborers sent home by the scores by the steam shovel, the mast hoist, and the conveyor." The "temporary" designation of the state's relief operation suggested, according to Adie, that too little attention was being paid to the larger issues.[6]

At first glance, Hickok judged the TERA system remarkable, a model of fairness and efficiency. Benefits were generous, "dazzling," she put it, especially "to one just out of Kentucky." Payments ranged up to $16 a week, depending on family size. TERA provided rent subsidies up to a maximum of $16 a month, and the agency helped with clothing, mortgage payments, home insurance bills, medical assistance, and even hospital coverage. The state classified medical care and medicines as "necessities of life." A December 1932 survey of 1,600 families, chosen randomly from eleven communities, showed that illnesses weren't much more common among the unemployed but were far more prolonged. Forty percent of those who were ill on the day of the survey had been that way for more than a year. Death rates among the long-term jobless were higher too, TERA concluded.[7]

On average, heads of households in the TERA survey had been out of work for nearly two years but on relief for only nine months. These physically and emotionally distressed families had survived on savings and help from relatives, and more often than not medical care was the first expense to go. Only two of the eleven communities in the survey provided nursing services for the jobless. Here TERA clearly found a match: nurses in those communities worked an average of ninety-four days in 1932, earning $478 for the year. Most said they would be happy to accept work relief at wages of $3 or $4 a day. In February 1933 TERA launched a work relief program for nurses, and by April two hundred nurses were on the payroll in fifty-three communities, with an average $17.50 salary for a five-day week.[8]

Albany delivered the goods, and Hickok detected surprisingly little political interference from the state capital, far less than she had seen from elected officials and bureaucrats in Harrisburg, Charleston, and Frankfort. In New York State both major political parties were in basic agreement on the relief effort, and Herbert Lehman's Democratic administration made a good-faith effort to work with Republicans. "I am a Republican, and I come from a Republican city," Dr. Christopher Parnall, Rochester's welfare director, told Hickok, "but when I ask the state board for anything, I feel that I am getting the same consideration I'd get if I were a Democrat." From the start, Hopkins had refused to play the game of welfare politics, knowing the hardships such antics could cause; his lingering influence at TERA had much to do with the atmosphere of social worker professionalism that so favorably impressed Hickok.[9]

Parnall and others suspected, though, that New York's beneficent, smooth-running, and responsive relief operation, with its means tests, home visits, checks and balances, and nannyish experiments in coercing people to live the right way, could yield unintended consequences. Hickok suspected that too. "Gosh," she wrote ER, "I wonder what would happen to all these pretty theories if the unemployed organizations moved in." In Rochester, Parnall told her, it *had* happened; in midsummer, 5,500 men on work relief organized and went on strike. They were being paid 30 cents an hour, and they demanded, and won, a raise to 40 cents. Now they wanted 60 cents. "The thing that bothers me," Parnall said, "is that they are forming a political minority—a grand field for a small-time politician to work in." Implicit in his comments lay the notion that challenges to the authorities were ill-mannered and even impious and that the plain people could throw up few defenses against demagoguery. The politicians and the professionals knew best, and they expected a measure of grateful deference from New Yorkers who were surviving on the state's largesse.[10]

"Let the title of this opus be 'The Forgotten Woman to the wife of her President,'" Hickok headed her September 13 letter to Mrs. Roosevelt. She wrote it late that night in her room at the Hotel Seneca on Clinton Street in downtown Rochester, a 500-room brick and stone confection after, some way after, the French Renaissance style. She and her instructor-chauffeur reached the Flower City at 7 in the evening after a tiring drive via Dansville, where the forgotten men, women, and children of that Livingston County market town were being instructed in the elements of a proper diet. In Dansville, Hickok learned, relief officials actually were rationing some commodities. With the price of flour on the rise, social workers directed clients to find a cheaper substitute, and they were permitted to purchase only so much flour with their relief payments. "Of course, there's no doubt the average family buys unscientifically, eats according to personal taste rather than the best dietary rules, and wastes food," she wrote ER. "And boy, how any of us would resent being told what to buy and what to eat!" Running to fat, diabetic, unable or unwilling to keep off rich or heavy foods, sweets, tobacco, and liquor, Hickok wrote from the heart. "Somehow," she went on, "this paternalistic attitude, well-intentioned though it doubtless is, goes against the grain with me." New York's system literally kept the forgotten ones alive, but Hickok recognized the perils of trying "to do too much social work on these people." Like the restive work relief men in Rochester, they might rise up someday.[11]

The state's third-largest city, population around 320,000 in 1933, Rochester had weathered the Depression pretty well. The city produced cameras and optical equipment, dental apparatus, shoes and textiles, canned foods, and mail chutes. Rochester's modern history commenced with the arrival of the Erie Canal in 1823. Farmers in the hinterland grew wheat that Rochester milled and exported along the canal. When western wheat began to flood the market, the city turned to the nursery industry, and the Flour City became the Flower City. The citizens showed a lot of social, political, and religious earnestness during the second half of the nineteenth century. Frederick Douglass published his abolitionist sheet *North Star* in Rochester beginning in 1847, and the three mystical Fox Sisters held their communions with the spirit world around the same time. There was innovation too. In 1888 George Eastman launched the revolutionary Kodak camera, introducing the urban middle classes to the snapshot.[12]

Labor peace reigned in Rochester. The city's needle industries had learned to accommodate the Amalgamated Clothing Workers of America, and capital and labor had been collectively bargaining for years. The news Hickok picked up from Rochester's evening daily, *The Times-Union*, reflected a sense of comparative well-being amid chaos. Most of the front-page headlines that September 13 topped out-of-town stories: 250,000 people marched in New York City's NRA parade, "the greatest parade in American history," according to the Associated Press dispatch; in southwestern Pennsylvania, union leaders blamed the mine owners for continuing strikes and an impasse in the coal code talks; three more states, Colorado, Minnesota, and Maryland, voted to repeal Prohibition. For tragicomic relief, the paper carried a short item about the arrest of a Sacramento, California, mother on a charge of inhuman treatment for clamping her four-year-old's tongue with clothespins to "break him of babyish habits." Locally, *The Times-Union* reported that Rochester already had experienced job and wage growth under the NRA. The city's NRA Committee credited the agency with creating more than nine thousand jobs and adding $6.7 million to workers' annual income. For example, the Beech-Nut foods concern hired a hundred operatives for the September canning rush, bringing the company's total employment in Rochester to 637. The short news item provided a vivid illustration, too, of the NRA's byzantine complexity; three NRA codes governed Beech-Nut operations: the canning code, the coffee-roasting code, and the biscuit and cracker code. The NRA called for a forty-hour work week and a minimum wage of 50 cents an hour for men, 40 cents for women. The codes did permit longer work hours in the canning department, because operations there dealt with perishables.[13]

Hickok's eye doubtless alighted on this story: M. L. Wilson, the head of the Agricultural Adjustment Administration's subsistence homesteading program (the agency that would sponsor Eleanor Roosevelt's Arthurdale in West Virginia), hinted that the city would receive federal funding to help place twenty-five jobless families in a planned rural community on the outskirts. She would have taken note of the advertisements as well. The "Help Wanted—Male" classified columns were anemic, two items only, one clerical and the other sales. In the next day's paper, Flickinson's food shops offered flour at 89 cents for a 24½-pound sack, Red & White Coffee for 29 cents a pound, California oranges for 27 cents a dozen. Rival Loblaw's advertised eggs at 25 cents a dozen, four packages of spaghetti for 29 cents, two tins of corned beef for 33 cents, and pork and beans at 8 cents a can. As for jobs, there were classified ads seeking a dry goods salesman, three men for the production department of an unnamed firm, and "two neat-appearing young men for a special advertising campaign."[14]

Hickok traveled east from Rochester to Syracuse on a showery September 14, the temperature in the 60s, cool for late summer. State Route 104 ran through green and gold fields south of Lake Ontario, with sudden glimpses of gray-blue water on the left hand. Once a salt-mining cap-

ital responsible for most of the U.S. supply, Syracuse had spread beyond
the swampy southeast shore of Lake Onondaga and grown to maturity
as a general manufacturing center. It had developed in other ways too.
Charles Dickens, visiting the city for a reading in 1869, complained bitterly of the food and drink: only two wines on the list, both the same but
one priced at 6 shillings and the other at 15, and "an old buffalo for supper
and an old pig for breakfast." The tone and quality of the place improved
materially as the century advanced. The railroads, notably Commodore
Vanderbilt's New York Central, and then the highways succeeded the
Erie Canal as the main avenue for Syracuse's exports, now chemicals,
auto parts, typewriters, air-conditioning equipment, and door knobs.[15]

By late summer Syracuse appeared to be sharing in what some state
officials characterized as a modest industrial recovery, or anyhow the beginning of one. A survey of nearly 1,600 representative manufacturing
firms showed factory employment in New York State up 6.2 percent between July 15 and August 15, along with a 6.7 percent increase in factory
payrolls. Still, on an index of 100 for the prosperous years of 1925–27,
factory employment lagged at 56 and factory payrolls at 51. As in Corning
and Rochester, Hickok found a clean-run relief program, the sort, in her
view, "the Federal Emergency Management Administration is aiming at
for the rest of the country." But she wondered whether at least some of
the city's ten thousand relief-dependent families had become a bit too
comfortable. Ralph Drowne, a TERA field representative, suggested that
liberal benefits sometimes put the state's relief offices in competition
with private employers, far-fetched as this might sound. "Wouldn't it be
better, perhaps," Drowne wondered, "to make relief a little less adequate
and therefore less attractive?" He told her of a case, admittedly atypical,
of a man who turned down a job paying $25 a week, more than twice his
relief dispensation, because he had earned $35 a week before the Depres-
sion and refused to return to work for less.[16]

Hickok accompanied a Syracuse case worker on his rounds on the afternoon of September 14, "an average case worker with an average load—
neither the best nor the worst." She had turned up unexpectedly, so he
hadn't been able to hand-pick the clients. Two families were living in a
double, "as comfortable and as well furnished as any home I ever lived in

as a child," she noted. Another, a couple with a baby, lived in a small but clean and sturdy house. A big Italian family inhabited a large, down-at-heel dwelling, and an old man and his son doubled up in a shack they had built themselves in an abandoned stone quarry. "Even these last two places were well above the average I saw in Pennsylvania," Hickok noted. For the Italians, the issues were hardly dire: should they burn coal or wood for heat, and should the boy have two pairs of trousers or only one.[17]

While relief might be working well, there were rough patches in Syracuse. The Hearst-owned *Syracuse Journal* concluded that business had slowed since the July upswing, outdating those sunny midsummer employment figures. (One index of production, at 101 in July, would sink to 71 in November.) *The Journal* placed the blame on the NRA, its "impulsive and sometimes intimidating" head, Hugh Johnson, and Johnson's "Socialistic assistants." In a front-page editorial, the newspaper accused Johnson of headline-grabbing and reminded readers that "prosperity cannot be recreated through a slogan." The government-business partnership should be voluntary; the president ought to make it clear that it would be up to business to decide how far it would go in bartering better labor relations for greater freedom to fix prices and manage competition. In the news columns, *The Journal* reported that business and government officials were complaining about delays in setting up a Syracuse office of the Home Loan Corporation, a New Deal agency established to relieve homeowners harassed by mortgage obligations. Thousands in the city were facing foreclosure, the Chamber of Commerce claimed, and sought to shift their mortgages from cruel banks and insurance companies to a benevolent government. Finally, *The Journal* covered the bitter dispute between Syracuse's welfare commissioner, Elwood P. Boyle, and TERA. Boyle had refused to replace a departed case worker with a state-approved successor. "Highly educated social workers with little practical experience are very dangerous people to have spending the public's money," said Boyle. They were "visionaries," he charged, people who were committed to shaking up the established order of things, and he wanted nothing to do with them.[18]

There were signs, too, of the Syracuse jobless rising above their station and mobilizing to fight for their interests. At first, Leon Abbott, a senior welfare administrator, judged their demands reasonable, and he had little trouble with them. Now they wanted more. Abbott, and Hickok with him, regarded one of their leaders, a Syracuse University junior named Charles Rinaldo, as particularly troublesome, a bumptious boy who had read too much Tolstoy—and Trotsky—at too early an age. "He apparently is just a young egoist out for glory," Hickok decided. "My personal feeling about him is that he ought to be spanked and sent to bed without his supper." The mayor, to his credit, believed the citizens of Syracuse ought to be allowed to have their say, and he let Rinaldo use the Central High School auditorium for a meeting of men on work relief. Rinaldo cannily asked for police protection, saying he feared disruption from "Communists and other radical influences." During the week a group of radicals had circulated a handbill that demanded trade union wages on all relief jobs and a thirty-five-hour work week. It went on to denounce the NRA and stigmatize Rinaldo as "the bosses' man." Police arrested two men for handing out the broadside and sent a dozen plainclothes policemen to Rinaldo's meeting.[19]

Hickok and Drowne went to hear him on September 15. Rinaldo harangued the audience of five hundred or so, in English first and then in Italian. ("He offered to make the address in several other languages if necessary," according to the *Journal*.) In what struck Hickok as "a somewhat florid speech," Rinaldo demanded a work week of at least thirty-five hours at a minimum wage of 40 cents an hour and circulated petitions calling on Governor Lehman to speed approval of two big work relief projects planned for Syracuse. "What we are asking for is reasonable," Rinaldo said. "If we get no satisfaction, we'll get the cooperation of every relief worker in the state. Then the state will have a job on its hands." There were no outbursts at the meeting, and the radicals responsible for circulating the handbill spent the night in the city lockup, confined there without bail.[20]

The next day, a rain-swept Saturday, the third day in a row of intermittent downpours, Hickok and Drowne executed a quick round-trip to Watertown, the gateway to the Northern Tier counties. The route led through country districts that had been caught up that spring and summer in a long-running, violent, and near-revolutionary dairy farmers' strike. In a day or two Hickok would have an opportunity for a more considered examination of the issues of the dairy belt and the North

Country. Conditions clearly had become more tolerable in the mid-state cities, and it might be said that many broken lives in those places were on the mend. As it happened, Hickok was about to encounter—rather, to encounter again—the corrosive effects of rage and woe, of grievance and lack of redress among the desperate and the dispossessed—or anyway, among those who still had some fight left in them.

Dairy farmers in upstate New York were producing too much milk, or perhaps milk had become a luxury too few city dwellers could afford. Whatever the cause, the region's dairymen were operating at a loss, forced to accept less than the cost of production from the distributors, using up their savings, falling deeper in debt, and facing the loss of their farms. In Syracuse for the New York State Fair a few weeks after a brief civil war over milk ended inconclusively, Henry Wallace, President Roosevelt's secretary of agriculture, cautioned farmers about relying on the government to guarantee an adequate return. "Agreements and licenses are ultimately unenforceable if they are out of line with economic facts," he said, and the facts were incontrovertible: the supply of milk outran demand. A twenty-one-year-old cow on the Frank Robideau place near Massena, St. Lawrence County, illustrated the point; a living symbol of the farmers' dilemma, she continued to deliver a steady twelve to fourteen quarts a day years after she ought to have been turned out of the milking barn. Owing to a loss of teeth, the average cow began to go dry at age twelve or thirteen. Robideau's amazing bovine kept a full set through her eighteenth year, and even now she retained all her teeth but two. She could graze almost as efficiently as ever, and she continued to produce at the rate of animals half her age.[21]

Milk and milk products generated a quarter of all U.S. farm income in 1933. Dairy cows stocked five of every six American farms, and they were mostly small farms: two-thirds of the fluid milk sent to market came from dairymen with herds of twenty or fewer animals. If oversupply was the problem, the University of Wisconsin agricultural economist Benjamin H. Hibbard wrote in The American Mercury, it was a problem without an obvious solution. "The farmer cannot close up his plant or cut the output to 20 percent, as does the United States Steel Corporation," he wrote. "He cannot stop cultivating his fields, for they would only be taken by taxes and weeds, not to mention the mortgage. He cannot discharge his labor, since it consists of his wife and children, and they would still be on his hands." To produce at current milk prices was disastrous, Hibbard asserted; to reduce the yield might make things worse.[22]

Big distributors such as Borden and National Dairy Products were making money, or at any rate they were paying dividends to shareholders while farmers went underpaid and city consumers were overcharged. *The New Republic* acknowledged an excess supply of milk, "not, God knows, in terms of what people ought to consume but in terms of what they can afford to buy." As it happened, Hickok interviewed a state dietician with a possible short-term solution, and a creative one at that. Mary Bittner wanted TERA to buy up the milk surplus and provide a quart a day to children and undernourished adults. "We've got in this state between 400,000 and 600,000 children on the relief rolls," she told Hickok. "We don't want them to grow up invalids." Such a program would address a major issue that Hibbard had raised: farmers could not expect a surge in demand given the "flattened pocket books" of the unemployed.[23]

Hickok headed north for Ogdensburg and the St. Lawrence Valley on September 17, following U.S. 11 along the western flank of the Oneida and Lewis county farm districts the milk strike had singed a few weeks earlier. The country, pasture, woods, and plowlands, thick with black and white cattle, looked forlorn in the mist and rain. Dairymen were willing, even eager to discuss their plight, though somewhat reticent about the two-week August upheaval. Hickok got a slant on the story from one hard-used farmer, she wrote Mrs. Roosevelt: unclearable and growing debt, grinding poverty—and these on top of the usual country vicissitudes of weather, blight, and accident. "One thing he told me rather horrified me," she went on. A prolonged early summer drought had seared the meadows and ruined the hay crop. "Some farmers, unable to feed their cows, are shooting them. . . . It hasn't been done as much yet, but he predicted there would be a good deal of it this coming winter."[24]

The milk war had broken out on August 1 with a call to thousands of dairy farmers to withhold their product from the market. On behalf of the distributors, the Dairymen's League vowed to keep the milk supply flowing and assured consumers that there would be no shortage. As it turned out, there wasn't much of a holiday spirit among the farmers, and a passive strike escalated into active rebellion almost at once. Strikers felled trees and laid spiked planks across the highways. They flung stones at the police. They poured kerosene into milk cans or dumped the milk of dairymen who tried to run the blockade, and they fired at the big metal containers on the cars of the long, slow, city-bound milk trains. The stream of milk contracted to a trickle in Oneida, Lewis, Chenango, and Herkimer counties. By the second day, central New York dairy plants reported deliveries down by 50 to 75 percent.[25]

The authorities responded with disproportionate force, with the focal point the northern Oneida County town of Boonville, the distribution center for a large dairy region. Roving bands of farmers four hundred to eight hundred strong stopped delivery trucks and spilled thousands of quarts of milk. When a party of some four hundred farmers armed with stones, axe-helves, and pick handles tried to bar the passage of two Dairymen's League trucks and their State Police escort, steel-helmeted troopers hurled tear gas bombs and charged the strikers' ranks, swinging nightsticks. Some forty farmers were injured. The State Police commander, Major John A. Warner, claimed the farmers had assaulted the troopers; a delegation of Boonville politicians and merchants filed a protest with Governor Lehman, accusing the police of misconduct and brutality—of "medieval atrocities," in their phrase.[26]

According to Edmund Wilson, the New York City newspapers dismissed the strikers as Communist-inspired "ruffianly bands of marauders—some not natives or even farmers," spilling milk, poisoning wells, and shooting out the tires of delivery trucks. Wilson tended to travel the same roads as the comrades and often in company with them, and he sometimes referred to himself as a Socialist and a cultural critic (with *Axel's Castle*, a 1931 study of Yeats, Joyce, Proust, and other moderns, he had already gained an impressive foothold as a literary critic); all the same, the charge surprised him. From his early childhood Wilson had spent summers at the family place in Talcottville, a Lewis County hamlet a dozen miles up Route 120 from Boonville, and he'd known the country people thereabouts all his life. When he came up from the city to investigate, they told him right off that they were indignant at being called Communists. And they were thoroughly aroused. Wilson had visited the turbulent eastern Kentucky coal districts, he had written about a bitter textile strike in Lawrence, Massachusetts, and he had investigated labor conditions in Henry Ford's Detroit. "I have never seen such furious feeling in any industrial strike," he wrote. "The industrial workers of the towns are accustomed to having their standards of living cut away, and then, when they try to rebel, having the police called to suppress them. They are not surprised by bullets or clubs." Upstate New York farmers had not been clubbed before; their innocence had been injured, and they did not intend to get used to rough treatment.[27]

Reporting for *The New Republic*, Wilson presented the August 1 clash outside Boonville as a police riot. The farmers gathered at midmorning to block the road leading to Sheffield's dairy plant. The state troopers left their cars and moved among the pickets. As Wilson narrated the story, "the crowd did not hesitate to make fun of the troopers," who marched back to their cars for gas masks and steel helmets. The unearthly masks seemed to increase the farmers' mirth. A moment later, though, the laughter died in their throats. "The troopers set upon the crowd, shooting gas bombs at them and clubbing them, old and young, men and women alike," Wilson wrote. "They pursued people into fields and woodsheds, beat them over the heads when they got stuck in the barbed wire." The troopers fired a tear gas bomb into the back of a fleeing striker, setting his clothes alight. They called the insurgents sons of bitches and Reds and rats. Later, the strikers concluded the troopers must have been drunk. No other explanation could account for their behavior.[28]

Within a few days fifteen thousand farmers in a dozen milk-producing counties were in arms. With violent confrontations by day and by night, casualty totals mounted. In some places farmers upgraded from stones and clubs to shotguns and high-powered rifles. Along with tear gas and billies, the troopers went into battle with revolvers and Thompson submachine guns. The politicians turned up the volume. Republican Congressman Hamilton S. Fish Jr., already a strident critic of the New Deal, called the strike a Red "reign of terror." The Associated Press reported plots to dynamite bridges and culverts. Responding to the reports,

Democratic Assemblyman Louis A. Cuvillier said, "Russia in its worst days couldn't be any worse than the situation we have right now, when milk cannot be safely moved over the highways for babies or anyone else." For the time being, though, Governor Lehman resisted Cuvillier's demand to call out the militia to suppress the farmers.[29]

Renewed violence on August 5 rocked Oriskany, Vernon, and the outskirts of Rochester. In what farmers called the second battle of Oriskany (in the first, on August 6, 1777, Revolutionary forces and American loyalists and their Indian allies fought a bloody drawn battle), 150 strikers dropped spiked planks across the Rome–Oriskany highway and swarmed over an idling delivery truck and its police escorts. Eight state troopers and twenty strikers were injured. In McDougall, Seneca County, strikers stormed a dairy, drained away ten thousand quarts of milk, and threatened to break up the machinery if the plant opened the next morning. In a skirmish in the woods near East Creek on the Herkimer–Montgomery County line, farmers and police exchanged three hundred rounds of gunfire. (Evidently the marksmanship left something to be desired, for no injuries were reported on either side.) Scattered outbreaks occurred over the next few days before a climactic spasm of disorder on August 10, when police swept up some 250 insurgents on charges of unlawful assembly, attempting to incite a riot, and rioting.[30]

Wilson and others accused Governor Lehman of favoring the big distributors. Perhaps so, though in spite of a lot of tough talk the governor resisted pressure from conservatives to send in the heavy battalions, an action Wilson believed might have touched off actual civil war. "This is no ordinary strike," Lehman told New Yorkers in a statewide radio broadcast on Saturday evening, August 12, "it is not the usual conflict between worker and employer. It is a strike to nullify and defy the authority of the state itself." Still, even though supplies of milk had been choked off in Syracuse, Amsterdam, and other places, the authorities sensed that the crisis had passed. "It's just about over," State Police commanders concluded. Farmer leaders asked for a truce; Lehman insisted on unconditional surrender, a demand he softened with a promise that the Milk Board would listen to the farmers' troubles once the strike ended. He made it clear too, after a quick trip to Hyde Park, that the president had taken notice. (Many farmers would have seen the photos of Roosevelt and Lehman in the rotogravure section of the Sunday papers, "Roosevelt looking up at the camera with his usual alert affability," according to Wilson.) One of the strike leaders, Albert Woodhead, a Rochester lawyer, moved to call off the Milk War, declaring victory on the grounds the politicians had pledged to give the farmers a hearing. Another strike leader, Boonville dairyman Stanley Piscek, ready to give in but unwilling to say so, simply announced he would observe a truce.[31]

The August 13 stand-down quelled the violence but provided no real solution. In Wilson's view, the strikers settled for vague assurances from Albany and Washington that their grievances would be investigated. The farmers were gloomy, pessimistic. "They do not trust their own representatives," Wilson wrote. "There is only the chimerical smile of Roosevelt, and that is so far away, hovering on the horizon; while what they have in front of them is . . . that peculiar phenomenon of American life which has come to figure so prominently since the war—the military policeman." The uneasy truce held. But some dairymen began shooting their cows, and Boonville farmers would call for a renewal of the strike in early October in protest of milk price-cutting in New York City.[32]

In the North Country, summer shaded into autumn. Hickok's route led through a weather-beaten landscape, less well-tended than the dairy region of central New York. "All in all, things look pretty tough," she wrote Hopkins. "Farmers who used to employ two or three men are doing all the work themselves now and letting their buildings and land go to pieces. There are public auctions all the time." She discovered that the Northern Tier had struck an attitude of watchful neutrality during the Milk War. Most dairymen in Jefferson and St. Lawrence counties declined to join the strike, or even to observe a brief "holiday." Although they greeted the settlement with relief, Hickok wrote, "the farmers don't feel any too happy about it."[33]

Approaching Ogdensburg, the road led past clusters of summer cottages hidden among the pines along the south bank of the mile-wide St. Lawrence River; the valley's attractions gave a significant seasonal boost to the local economy. A port of entry and a small manufacturing center (paper, brass, and casein, the protein of milk, used in cheese, as a food additive, and as a binder for matches), Ogdensburg had been founded as a French fur trading post, and more than half the population of around fifteen thousand had French Canadian antecedents. Quebecois or Yankee, they were having a mean time of it. Hickok learned that some of the paper mills were running, though paper's future looked bleak given competition from Canada. The quays that lined the Oswegatchie River for three hundred feet upstream from its junction with the St. Lawrence were somnolent. Thousand Islands tourism had fallen off, damaging small businesses dependent on the summer trade. Captain Peter Fleming, a St. Lawrence River pilot, reported fewer pleasure craft on the great river than in any summer in forty-five years. He had piloted only three yachts, down from the seasonal average of twenty or so. The river towns looked to the visionary Seaway, a projected deepwater route from the Atlantic to the western shore of Lake Superior, as an economic lifeline. The president favored the scheme, or so he said, but the initial $160 million for hydroelectric development awaited the outcome of treaty negotiations with the reluctant Canadians.[34]

Front-page headlines in the *Ogdensburg Journal* for September 18 announced that five men would face trial for a fire that heavily damaged the Reichstag in Berlin; Americans in Cuba were uneasy over continuing political disturbances on the island; and FERA granted another $3 million to New York State for relief, bringing the total since May to $21.5 million. A story on an inside page noted the success of TERA's relief garden program; an Ogdensburg family subsisted for two full weeks in late summer solely on food grown in their own backyard plot. The little city's merchants and tradesmen, anyway "those who were conscientiously trying to live up to the rules," told Hickok they were feeling the exactions of the NRA regulations. Official Ogdensburg put the best face on things, though. A big parade planned for September 27, with a half-holiday already declared, would "demonstrate Ogdensburg's patriotism and her loyalty to President Roosevelt's NRA program," according to *The Journal*. Loyal or otherwise, an editorial faulted the administration in Washington for "permitting hopes to outstrip practical facts," citing Hugh Johnson's brash prediction that the NRA would put 5 million men back to work by Labor Day "as an example of ill considered optimism." The help-wanted ads in the classified section bore out the editor's view, with only one job on offer: an experienced cook—female.[35]

Taking turns at the wheel with her driver, Hickok pushed on to Malone on the afternoon of September 18, spending the night in another dreary small-town hotel and doing interviews on the fly before striking southeast along Route 374 through lovely lake and mountain scenery to Plattsburgh for a brief stop on the 19th. (She meant to reach Montpelier, Vermont, by evening, and she was moving fast now.) While relief operations were competently managed in the Southern Tier and FERA's 40 percent welfare reimbursements kept local programs afloat, Hickok reported delays in other projects meant to assist the jobless, particularly public works. Whether the holdups were in Albany or Washington she couldn't tell, though Harold Ickes of the Public Works Administration had been in no rush to spend the $3.3 billion the National Industrial Recovery Act had authorized for the agency. For whatever reason, federal highway money wouldn't reach Clinton County in time to help the strandees there this autumn. She wrote Hopkins, "The man at the head of the Federal Reemployment Bureau had 834 men all ready to go to work on a highway job when the contractor announced that, [with] the approach of cold weather, the laying of the concrete top would have to be postponed until next spring." Road workers, he told her, couldn't pour unheated concrete when the temperature dropped below 40 degrees. So 834 weekly paychecks were postponed, in a county where 85 percent of the farms were mortgaged and where the Plattsburgh pulp and paper industries were shedding jobs.[36]

The editors of *The Plattsburgh Daily Republican* selected stories for the morning's front page on FDR's signing of the coal code, suspected Nazi responsibility for the Reichstag fire (the allegation would turn out to be true), and the third marriage of actress Jean Harlow, this one to a studio cameraman. As it happened, *Hold Your Man*, a film with Harlow and Clark Gable, was playing that night at The Strand. A story in the afternoon *Daily Press* evoked Hickok's sobbie days: a ninety-seven-year-old woman, Henrietta Young, had finally judged an apple her mother had given her in 1858 to be ripe, if rather shrunken. "It was a little green then, but I've given it plenty of time," she said, explaining that she had preserved the apple for three-quarters of a century with a stuffing of cloves.[37]

The rush through the Northern Tier meant a delay in Hickok's report to Hopkins. From Plattsburgh she drove north to U.S. Route 2, crossing the narrows of upper Lake Champlain at Rouses Point via ferry (a bridge would open in 1937) to Alburgh in Vermont. The weather had finally cleared. Route 2 led south through the Champlain islands, battening down for the autumn with the inns and motor courts and small boat harbors quiet now that the summer visitors had gone, to Burlington and then east to Montpelier, Vermont's diminutive (population seven thousand) and charming capital. Hickok worked on the report at night, collating notes, searching for details that would catch Hopkins's attention, compressing, struggling to render her impressions tangible: Corning had been only a week ago, but time passed at a different and unsettling pace on the road. She would post the report from Ellsworth, Maine, on September 23.

"Sorry the report is so late," she wrote Kathryn Godwin, Hopkins's secretary, "but learning to drive that darned automobile has left me pretty much frazzled every night. I'm getting the hang of it, however, and now about my only dreads are having to stop about halfway up a very steep hill and New York and Washington traffic.

"If I don't break my neck, I'll be back in New York a week from tomorrow night."[38]

Long days in the car, lonely nights in second-class hotels: Montpelier to South Paris, Maine, via St. Johnsbury and New Hampshire's Mount Washington Valley; overnights in South Paris and Augusta, Maine's capital; the weather changeable, the meals indifferent. Eleanor Roosevelt wrote to lift Hickok's drooping spirits: "I hope you get accustomed to 'Bluette' and have a grand time." Times fell some little way short of grand. "You sounded low," she added a few days later, "and I know just how cheerless those horrible hotels are." Hickok encountered little to chase away the blue devils in Depression-stunted upstate New York and Maine, though she found temporary relief, sometimes comic, in the newspapers, astonishing in the range and variety of their coverage. *The Plattsburgh Daily Press*, for instance, had run a brief on a Lowville farmer's three-legged pullet; *The Bangor Daily News* carried a wire service dispatch about a Texas woman who had drawn up an NRA code for housewives.[39]

But grim news predominated in late September. In midcoast Rockland, she found quarrying and shipbuilding moribund, the fishing and canning industries quiescent, and at least thirty storefronts along the mile-long Main Street vacant. With construction slumping everywhere, Rockland's biggest employer, a limestone quarry, lapsed into receivership and owed the cash-strapped city $76,000 in back taxes. To the southeast, in the town of St. George on the narrow peninsula that forms the western shore of Penobscot Bay, the granite quarries were on short time, demand slack for their chief product, paving blocks. The deep pits of the quarries were visible from the road as it approached the picturesque weather-stained village of Tenants Harbor, the wind-lashed setting for Sarah Orne Jewett's novel *The Country of the Pointed Firs*. At the tip of the peninsula lay Port Clyde (fishing boats, a packing house, the pungent aroma of fish), along with Tenants Harbor a long-time attraction for summer visitors, "rusticators," in the local idiom. Fewer rusticators had come this summer, increasing the town's distress. "When New York City is doing lots of paving," Hickok wrote, "St. George is prosperous. When New York City isn't doing any paving—and it hasn't in recent years—St. George is in the dumps." Then too the quarries would be exhausted someday, just as so many coal mines in Pennsylvania and West Virginia were playing out, an adumbration of another stranded population.* The townsfolk, docile for the most part, tended to fault themselves when things went wrong; Mainers struck Hickok as "almost tragically patient." The Finns and Swedes working the St. George quarries were an exception. Communists had gotten among the Scandinavians, she reported, and a couple of weeks earlier fifteen of them had organized a march on the town relief office—an act not far short of stark, staring rebellion by Maine standards.[40]

Rockland, with literary associations of its own as the birthplace of the poet Edna St. Vincent Millay, appeared to be even worse off than St. George; the city had been steadfast (or perhaps stubborn) in its refusal to solicit aid from Augusta. "A Maine-ite would almost rather starve than

---

*The last granite quarry in St. George shut down in the early 1960s.

ask for help," Hickok observed. "In fact, his fellow citizens would expect it of him. It is considered a disgrace in Maine to be 'on the town.'" Rockland had received no state or federal relief since June. "They think in Augusta that they ought to have some help, and I think so, too," she wrote Mrs. Roosevelt. "They can have it whenever they want it, but they won't ask for it!" The mayor and the city employees already had taken a 20 percent reduction in pay, and as a last desperate measure they were prepared to volunteer for another 20 percent cut.[41]

Hickok found the Rockland waterfront derelict and eerily quiet. The shipyards, rigged out for wooden vessels, had built nothing since the Great War. The fish canneries, some closed for years, were in ruins. She interviewed two fishermen who had been out in Penobscot Bay all day and set down their grim accounting: eight gallons of fuel at 19 cents a gallon, a hundred pounds of bait at 2 cents a pound, and a 200-pound catch that sold for 1 cent a pound. "After they got all through," Hickok reported, "they had 20 cents apiece for their day's work!" Yet she seldom detected bitterness among the people; wistfulness, perhaps, but no more.[42]

U.S. Route 1 ran east by a little north from Rockland: Camden, Belfast, and Stockton Springs, where the federal highway bore north to Bangor. Hickok followed State Route 3 for Ellsworth, crossing the Waldo-Hancock Bridge at Bucksport, built in 1931, the first permanent structure to span the Penobscot River below Bangor. At Ellsworth Route 3 rejoined U.S. 1, traversing lonely country to Machias and beyond to Eastport; on either hand, coves and dark tidal streams, blueberry barrens, wind-tortured second-growth pine, gaunt farmhouses that hadn't known paint in decades. Like just about everything else along the Maine coast, blueberries were slumping. The Machias harvest, the smallest in twenty years, plunged 40 percent in volume from 1932.[43]

The tarred surface of State Route 190 ran along Passamaquoddy Bay toward Eastport on Moose Island. Hickok reached the easternmost city in the United States on September 24, the end of daylight savings time; the sun set at 5:30 that afternoon. Not that she enjoyed a long northern twilight; the weather continued dreary, damp, and cool. *The Eastport Sentinel*, the local weekly, would report September 1933 as the wettest and cloudiest September since 1909. The little city, famous for its July 4 cel-

ebration, with annual visits from U.S. warships, impressed her as "one of
the bright spots." The coal yard, the ship's chandleries, the ice and provisions dealers were active, and the Water Street business district, with its
cluster of a half-dozen tall, narrow red-brick buildings all dating from
an 1880s economic boom, seemed prosperous, anyway by contrast with
Rockland. It had been a good tourist season, owing partly to President
Roosevelt's annual summer visit to Campobello Island, visible from the
waterfront on clear days. The busy Eastport summer art school, whose
students sought to capture in paint the elusive effects of the vaporous atmosphere of Quoddy's land- and seascapes, provided a seasonal boon to
the city's boardinghouses, restaurants, and shops. Eastport showed creativity in housing some of its many unemployed, buying fishing shacks
and fixing them up. "They could hardly be called luxurious," Hickok
observed, but at least they were warm and dry.[44]

It had been a hard year for fishing. An Eastport firm had been the first
to can sardines, in 1876, and the little herring helped define the place. A
popular 1930s guidebook noted, "The women of the town, young and
old, seize their aprons and knives, and run to the factories where the siren
gives warning of a new catch." But the siren calls were infrequent this
September. Canneries in Eastport, Lubec, and West Pembroke, though
ready to open, were holding off until the fishing picked up. The runs
were late this year, for mysterious reasons. "The weather here has been
fine," *The Sentinel* reported in late August, "there are plenty of pollock in
the harbor and apparently all the conditions are right for good catches,
but for some reason, there is very little doing right now." The indifferent fishing continued through most of September. The newspaper said
inspectors were condemning some catches on account of "red feed" (the
small crustaceans, copepods, perhaps contaminated, that sardine herring consumed). A mid-September storm wrecked some of the outer
weirs, further reducing the catch. The mayor told Hickok a pod of five
whales out in the Bay of Fundy had been worrying the schools. "What
they haven't eaten they've scared away," he said. Toward the end of the
month sardines became more plentiful, but by then Norwegian imports
were crowding the market and driving down prices. *The Sentinel* called
for tariff protection for the Maine fishery.[45]

Eastport may have been an island of comparative prosperity, but the Washington County school nurse's report for 1932–33 suggested that four years of economic hardship were taking a cumulative toll on Down East children. The nurse's office examined 3,500 school-age children during the year and identified 2,000 with "defects." Ten to 15 percent were underweight. Around 250 suffered from poor eyesight. Worse yet, there was a lot of tuberculosis. Diagnostic testing prompted closer examinations of thirty-four children in Lubec; twenty-one were tubercular. There were similar results for Eastport, where ten of sixteen tested positive for TB, and Calais, where thirteen of twenty-four were found to carry the bacillus.[46]

The big news in Eastport in September 1933, the great hope, was the Passamaquoddy Tidal Power Development Project, a scheme to exploit the extraordinary rise and fall (more than eighteen feet at Eastport) of Bay of Fundy tides. The project would raise all boats in the region, providing a powerful inflow of resources that would keep the Down East economy afloat for decades. *The Sentinel*'s editor, Roscoe Emery, a former Eastport mayor with business interests in real estate and insurance, championed the project, using the news and editorial columns of the newspaper to boost it.

Emery's vision encompassed not only the export of cheap electricity—once it went on line, Quoddy would exceed the capacity of all the existing power stations in Maine—but also a vast economic exploitation of the entire region, Lubec to Calais, Eastport to Machias: a deepwater anchorage off Eastport with an international seaport's infrastructure (land transport connections, warehouses, docks, ship repair facilities) and industrial concerns such as an aluminum smelter and fertilizer and chemical plants. "Should it prove practical," *The Sentinel* observed, "there will be opened a magnificent new storehouse of power, not only in Quoddy, but in the entire Fundy area, which if exploited may become a region of great industrial activity, the more so because of its accessibility to the sea through an abundance of spacious ice-free harbors." Visionary too, or maybe chimerical, was Federal Power Commission member George Otis Smith, who saw greater potential in Quoddy than in the hydro projects of Niagara Falls and the Tennessee River Valley. "It is said that Ralph Waldo Emerson was inspired to make his famous remark 'hitch your wagon to a star' by watching the operation of a tide-mill at Lubec," Smith told a gathering of Eastport businessmen in early September. "Perhaps the time has come for Eastport to 'hitch its wagon to a star.'" More prosaically, the Eastport City Council urged President Roosevelt to approve the project to provide jobs. The engineers estimated the Quoddy project would employ eight thousand men at living wages for two and a half years.[47]

Emery and his friends were so enthralled by the material potential of God's own tides that they were prepared to accept a dominant federal government role in developing, building, and managing the project. After all, government ownership of public utilities was Socialism, wasn't it? Wrote Hickok, "One man asked me if it was true that Socialists don't believe in God. 'Anyhow,' he added, 'I don't see what God has to do with a dam out here in the bay.'" With such rationalizations and an assist from Power Commissioner Smith, Quoddy enthusiasts filed an application with the Public Works Administration on September 11 for a dam connecting Eastport and the mainland, following the line of an old wooden railroad trestle. The project would be restricted to American waters at first, because (as with the St. Lawrence scheme) the Canadians were reluctant to enter into the partnership.[48]

Moving on to Calais and Houlton on September 25, Hickok again met with what she now recognized as a characteristic reluctance on the part of the Yankee element in Maine to concede that many respectable people simply had exhausted their resources. An old friend of Eleanor Roosevelt's, Calais lawyer Helen Hanson (Hickok had met her in July when she and ER passed through on the homeward leg of their Quebec jaunt), spoke in bitter tones about the city's refusal to solicit aid from the state. A short interview with the mayor confirmed Hanson's account. He actually boasted of the city's self-sufficiency, oblivious to the misery it caused. "I could see he thought it would be a disgrace to ask for state or federal help," Hickok observed. But it wasn't only mean-spiritedness; there was indifferent ignorance too, and not just among the town and county gentry. She wrote Hopkins, "The Red Cross official who sent up a lot of cotton goods up into Northern Maine last winter was a bright boy!" As a result, Washington and Aroostook counties would need plenty of clothing for the winter—warm wool clothing.[49]

Attitudes in northern Maine ranged from ruggedly individualistic to robustly anti–French Canadian. One man told Hickok that accepting relief, taking something for nothing, would be "pauperizing." She wrote, "You hear so much in Maine about 'deserving cases.' And to be a 'deserving case' in Maine, a family has got to measure up to the most rigid Nineteenth Century standards of cleanliness, physical and moral. They just haven't any patience with people who don't. As a result, a woman who isn't a good housekeeper is apt to have a pretty rough time of it. And Heaven help the family in which there is any 'moral problem'!" People on relief, Hickok remarked, were "subjected to treatment that is almost medieval in its stinginess and stupidity." A man would have to be hollow with hunger to run the gauntlet of Yankee contempt and seek out help. Often the most desperate were the French Canadians, a despised class; the old-line Mainers, she observed, regarded the Quebecois much as southerners regarded the downtrodden class they referred to as "poor white trash."[50]

From Calais she ventured north along U.S. 1 to Houlton, the Aroostook County seat, with dozens of bent figures in the flat brown potato fields and distant views of Mount Katahdin to the southwest. According to the Maine guidebook, Houlton combined "the qualities of the old-fashioned country town with those of the modern city." Hickok walked elm-lined residential streets and the handsome business district; in the center of town, Market Square had been rebuilt to ample dimensions after a devastating fire in 1902. Houlton had boomed with the arrival of the Bangor & Aroostook Railroad in 1893 and the expansion of potato farming. Factors graded and sorted hundreds of thousands of bushels a year in the potato warehouses in the Bangor & Aroostook freight yards, and Houlton remained a major shipping center in spite of the Depression.[51]

In late August 125 Aroostook County potato shippers, accounting for 95 percent of the region's tonnage, approved and sent to the NRA in Washington a code establishing a forty-eight-hour work week during the shipping season (October 21–August 31), a sixty-hour week during digging and harvesting season (September 1–October 30), and a $14 minimum wage scale for the shorter week. Northern Maine potatoes were selling for $1.75 to $2 a barrel that autumn, up from a calamitous 35 to

40 cents in 1932, when angry farmers had dumped tons of potatoes into the rivers, damming the flow and causing serious flooding, rather than accept prices below the cost of production. Nationally the forecast called for a lighter potato harvest in 1933, at 293 million bushels the smallest crop since 1919.[52]

The shippers estimated that Maine would export 39 million bushels of seed and consumption potatoes in 1933, most of them from Aroostook County. A good year, so it seemed, with prices on the climb, but they added that liens tied up three-quarters of the crop, that many farmers were seriously in arrears with mortgages and taxes, and that many would be unable to wait for an anticipated price increase in the spring because they couldn't afford to store the harvest. That was the landowners' plight. The farmhands, mostly casual and seasonal labor, were far worse off. "Right now everyone is picking potatoes," Hickok wrote Mrs. Roosevelt. "It will all be over in about two weeks, however. By that time the people will have earned enough to pay up a few bills, buy a few clothes, and keep themselves during the period while they've been working. Then they'll be back on the relief rolls." The casuals used to migrate to the woods for winter work; they did so no longer, for the paper pulp and long-timber business in Maine had all but expired. Canadian and Russian pulp were cheaper, and the building trades remained in a Depression-long slump.[53]

In Aroostook County, then, Hickok encountered another stranded population. Economic calamity and technological change accelerated the loss of farm jobs; the introduction of labor-saving machinery meant those jobs were gone for good. In an interview with Hickok, three substantial growers were alternately buoyant and glum about their advance into what they called the "machine age" and the displacement of farm laborers. "I've got on my farm a potato-digging machine that will do the work of 15 men," one of the farmers said. "I'm certainly not going to throw that machine away to give work to 15 men. I can't afford to. I suppose, if all industry and all agriculture went back to the methods we used 40 years ago, there would be plenty of work for everybody." But there were few alternatives to farm labor. The Houlton weekly, *The Pioneer-Times*, published only a handful of help-wanted classifieds in August and September 1933: ads for a maid and a housekeeper, for a "distributor" for a New Jersey firm who could "write quick," for a nursemaid, and for a State Farm Insurance agent in the Houlton office.[54]

Desperate times bred daring thieves. With prices on the rise, potatoes caught the attention of the region's minor criminals. In late August, farmer George Rugan reported the theft of eight barrels of Irish cobblers from one of his fields. The thieves needed two car trips to carry off the contraband; they sold the potatoes to a shipper for $18 and split the proceeds.* But they underestimated the investigative skills of the county detectives. "The police said they traced tire tracks in the road beside the potato field to the door yard where [Wilbur] King lives," *The Pioneer-Times* reported. King, twenty-six, led police to the second suspect.[55]

Mornings were chilly now and frosts a nightly possibility. The fierce northern winter would arrive in early November, and with the end of the harvest and the clamping down of the cold Houlton officials predicted a steep increase in the relief load. Hickok met on September 26 with the Board of Selectmen and an official of the Maine Emergency Relief Board, Charles S. Brown, to discuss conditions in the town. (*The Pioneer-Times* account of the session appeared on page 1, with star billing for Hickok.) Houlton, they told her, carried 136 families on relief with an expenditure of $1,000 a month for groceries, $500 for rent, $250 for medical care, and $150 for fuel. The taxpayers also supported thirty-two children at $100 a month for board and other costs, twenty-two paupers at $150 a month, and thirteen inmates of the Town Farm at $400 a month. Altogether Houlton's welfare budget approached $30,000 a year, an insupportable figure given tax delinquencies ($58,000 and rising) and the impossibility of raising the tax levy. Hickok made no promises, according to the newspaper, though she would limn Houlton's circumstances and prospects in her field report to Hopkins.[56]

Hickok's sympathies were aroused, and a close examination of the relief operation in Maine appalled her. She graded the administration of relief "awful" in many places, mostly owing to ignorance and lack of sympathy among local officials. "Last winter, we used to give 'em dried fish

---

*Agricultural larceny happens in our own hard times. "Farm Thieves Target Grapes, and Even Bees," ran a front-page headline in the *New York Times* on July 22, 2011.

which would knock the plaster off if you threw it at a wall," one relief official confided to her. Weekly food orders were written out by men with a less than rudimentary knowledge of the basic principles of nutrition. She saw one order, totaling $1.83 and meant to feed a large family for a week, for potatoes, cornmeal, rolled oats, dried beans, dried peas, rice, and condensed milk. There was hardly any meat, no fish this time, no fruit of any kind, no fresh milk, no sugar, "in fact, practically nothing except starch and a little fat and a little molasses." Here was plain stupidity, and perhaps negligence too; the Houlton A&P advertised five tins of sardines, a food full of essential nutrients, for 25 cents, but sardines appeared nowhere in the food orders.[57]

Beyond Houlton, U.S. 1 led north to Presque Isle, Caribou, and Van Buren before curving west to Fort Kent, its northern terminus 2,300 miles distant from the starting point in Miami. Potato and oat fields stretched away on either hand. Hickok made a brief excursion to the remote settlement of Allagash, "away up at the end of the road in timber country." She discovered that all but three of the village's ninety mostly French Canadian families were on relief. "I was told in Augusta," she reported to Harry Hopkins, "that when Allagash . . . wrote down to the capital for help last winter it had to borrow a postage stamp to send the letter."[58]

5

THE GHOSTS OF WALL STREET

New York City and Washington, October 1933

How, Lorena Hickok would have wondered, had she missed no much? She had lived and worked in New York City since the mid-1920s, through the years of the spurious Coolidge prosperity, the Wall Street collapse, the onset of the Great Depression, the advent of the apple sellers, the lengthening breadlines, the packed soup kitchens, the noisy demonstrations in Union Square, the empty storefronts, the Hooverville in Central Park, the filled-to-capacity municipal shelters. She saw it now, in early October 1933. "The City of New York," she would write Harry Hopkins in a lively approximation of a lede from her time with the Associated Press, "is struggling today with the biggest community relief job on earth—the biggest job of its kind undertaken by any city since the world began." A million and a quarter New Yorkers were wholly dependent on public assistance. Another million, desperate for relief, went without help owing to a lack of resources. "These [people] are skating along on thin ice," Hickok went on, "barely existing, undernourished, in rags, constantly threatened with eviction from their homes, utterly wretched and hopeless, their nerves taut, their morale breaking down." The city spent $6,330,981 on relief in August; Hickok told Hopkins $15 million a month barely would meet the need.[1]

The crisis had taken the city unawares, boiling up, in Hickok's words, "with the dizzy, terrifying force and speed of a tornado." In 1931 New York City's public and private charities supported a client load of fewer than 500,000, with a total annual expenditure of around $30 million. During the first six months of 1933, 1,417,675 men and women received official or private agency assistance, at a cost of $50.5 million. Plainly the numbers didn't add up; the relief load had tripled, while spending increased only 40 percent. The 1.25 million New Yorkers on public relief represented a cross-section of the population, "the most intelligent, the most highly educated and the most helpless and most ignorant," according to Hickok. At one end of the range were thousands of needy immigrants (some thirty nationalities), many of whom spoke hardly a word of English. At the other were business and professional people whose annual pre-Crash incomes ran deep into five figures. "There they are, all thrown together into a vast pit of human misery, from which a city, dazed, still only half awake to the situation, is trying to extricate them." How, she surely asked herself, had she overlooked all this?[2]

Sprinting to catch up, Hickok worked long shifts during these first golden days of October. New York skies were fair, with temperatures in the pleasant 60s and 70s, and she pounded the beat in taxis, buses, and the IRT subway, Battery Park to the Bronx, with her characteristic swift efficiency. Still, she admitted in a letter to Kathryn Godwin, Hopkins's secretary, she labored to make sense of things. "One reason why it's so difficult is that it's so damned big," she wrote. "Getting appointments to see people is hopeless. . . . Incidentally, they take the five-day week seriously here. Saturday might as well be Sunday." Nevertheless, over a period of ten days, from October 2 to 12, she would interview dozens of relief officials, New Yorkers on the dole or on work relief, homeless men, unattached women, striking workers, superfluous stockbrokers, and the lead reporter for a New York World-Telegram investigation that had alleged, in a series of stories in late July, Tammany Hall meddling and graft in the city's relief operation. As she would report, the relief agencies, public and private, were overwhelmed, underfunded, and failing.[3]

Then too, Hickok could attend to personal matters. An evening with her sister Ruby and her husband, Julian Claff, brought the crisis home, into what remained of her fractured family. "Julian, who had had a few cocktails and was feeling very bitter anyway, having been out of work for more than two years, pounded the Hell out of everything, especially NRA, which he termed 'boy-scoutism,'" she wrote Eleanor Roosevelt. Claff concluded the outburst with a harrowing flourish: "We're damned discouraged and disgusted with life." He spoke for his wife as well. Ruby Claff saw no hope of her nurse's salary lifting to pre-Depression levels, and in the meantime higher prices had driven up her expenses by 25 percent.[4]

In an unpleasant break from the round of interviews, Hickok spent a couple of hours in the dentist's chair. Rotting teeth had become an emblem of the Great Depression, for dental care turned up near the bottom of the priority list for the jobless, below such discretionary items as coffee and tobacco; with her FERA salary Hickok could afford a visit. It was the heroic age of dentistry; he pulled several teeth, and she left the office a picture of misery. Solicitous as always, ER wrote, "Hope the x-rays show all well, and you are safe for the next year on teeth. I do feel a beast to hound you about the doctor, but you should watch your blood sugar, and I will feel happier when all that is done." (She needed, too, to check her chain consumption of Pall Mall cigarettes.) After two months of virtually uninterrupted travel, Hickok had begun to fray. She could look forward to a brief break in Washington in mid-October; for now, though, she returned to the task of negotiating the New York City relief maze and of thinking through what ought to be done for her sister and brother-in-law and the tens of thousands of middle-class New Yorkers who shared their predicament.[5]

The *World-Telegram* exposé showed scant mercy toward New York City's public relief program. While hundreds of thousands of New Yorkers were falling into the abyss, the newspaper charged, "politicians in Tammany Hall and allied with it are using the machinery of the Department of Public Welfare for their advantage and are exploiting human misery in anticipation of the coming Mayoralty elections." And it wasn't only waste. Political interference jeopardized the state Temporary Emergency Relief Administration's contribution, now 55 percent of all public relief funds distributed in the city, the newspaper claimed.[6]

Established in 1931 with the merger of Joseph Pulitzer's venerable *World* (which dated from 1860) and Scripps-Howard's *Evening Telegram*, the *World-Telegram* seemed to be searching for an identity. Longtime

readers were curious to see whether it would remain progressive in outlook; the Scripps holdings generally were conservative. For a few years
the hybrid would uphold the Pulitzer tradition. The relief "survey," as
the paper called its investigation, was one example; the retention of star
columnist Heywood Broun, a larger-than-life troubadour of lost causes,
was another. The *World-Telegram* published a lively front page every afternoon, with vivid accounts of Giants and Yankees baseball games a sta-
ple of the upper left-hand corner. Sports aside, the editors assigned one
of the paper's top reporters, Joseph Lilly, to the relief story and gave him
ten—*ten*—staffers to track down and interview top relief officials, relief
investigators, social workers, people on relief, and the police. Lilly relied
heavily on blind sources, not the best practice, the *World-Telegram* conceded, but hardly anyone, high or low, critical or laudatory, would speak
for the record, evidently out of fear of Tammany reprisal.[7]

Among the *World-Telegram*'s findings: relief benefits barely supported a subsistence living, and appropriations frequently were delayed.
Tammany had applied pressure from the start; administrative jobs went
to the politically favored, and officials with political influence received
higher salaries than more qualified functionaries who lacked Tammany
connections. Many persons were allowed to jump the queue for assistance through the intervention of machine hacks.[8]

Lilly's survey also found fraud, graft, inadequate record keeping, and
slipshod accounting, especially in the ticket system of food distribution
and rent assistance. Grocers discounted the tickets, so people's grocery
baskets were lighter because they couldn't pay in cash. Relief employees were working rackets with dishonest landlords. Clients endured long
waits, sometimes as long as two months, for visits from relief investigators; they were imprisoned for days in their own homes because, under
the rules, everyone in the family had to be present when a case worker
called. The practice of assigning people on work relief to home investigations meant "hundreds of persons quite unqualified by education and
by temperament have been retained," Lilly wrote. In the final analysis,
the *World-Telegram* survey found New York City relief to be "tragically
inadequate," the system for delivering it inefficient, wasteful, slow, and,
it appeared, riddled with corruption.[9]

At first Hickok sounded skeptical of the *World-Telegram*'s survey, especially the allegations of heavy Tammany influence. She tried to independently confirm some of the newspaper's findings but found people evasive, "except for the protest crowd," she wrote Godwin. Relief officials simply wouldn't talk about Tammany. "They'll tell you plenty about how much money is needed," she went on, "but you don't hear much about politics. That's all under the surface." A long talk with Joseph Lilly convinced Hickok that he meant well and had done his reporting conscientiously, though she thought he might "have gone wrong in the matter to some extent through ignorance and lack of understanding of the problems of administering relief." For instance, one of the top officials with Tammany connections, the administrator in charge of personnel (and thus jobs) for both the home and work relief bureaus, turned out to be a fully qualified Catholic Charities veteran. A city relief bureau investigator did concede, though, that a fair number in a group of 235 families he examined were on the rolls through influence, if not always Tammany's. Still, she tended to discount Lilly's sharpest criticisms of Welfare Commissioner Frank Taylor and of Mary Gibbons, who headed the Home Relief Bureau.[10]

Certainly the vast relief machine offered plenty of opportunity for plunder and lots of jobs to dispense to the politically loyal. Writing in May in *The New Republic*, Matthew Josephson predicted that relief, public and private, would be a $100 million business in New York City in 1933. Along with city and state bureaus, there were more than seventy-five private charities; the bewildered and confused could dial the Information Service at GRamercy 5-7000 for advice on where to turn for help. The agencies' leadership, "social workers of yesterday, drawn from the ranks of the YMCA, the Salvation Army, the Jewish and Catholic charities and the various non-sectarian and university groups," directed a swollen bureaucracy staffed by men and women drawn from the ranks of the jobless. Collectively the social workers' views may have been old-fashioned, but they were on the front lines now. "Slum workers along the seamy edges of town, they now find almost a third of the city's area given over to slums," Josephson wrote. It was a wonder, he thought, that such a vast, antiquated, and cumbersome system worked as well as it did.[11]

The men and women who directed the relief operation believed they were saving New York City from social disintegration. "We social workers regard this as *preventative* work," a senior official told Josephson. Then, gesturing toward an office crowded with clerks busy with their files and index cards and telephones, he added, "If it were not for all that there would be riots and bloodshed all over this town." Social work stood out as one of the few growth industries in the early 1930s, but the relief agencies were overmatched. At the end of 1932, according to Josephson, 391,000 New York City families were afflicted with unemployment, and joblessness continued to rise through the late spring of 1933. By September the agencies carried more than 230,000 families on the books, with applications pending from another 38,000. The City Work Bureau employed 36,000 men and women during the first nine months of 1932 at a cost of $9 million; by September 1933, 72,000 New Yorkers were earning a paycheck from work relief, and the bureau chief estimated that with $3 million more a month he could provide jobs for another 50,000. Still, that would cover only the most urgent cases, heads of households who had been without work for a year or more. As matters stood, Josephson estimated that a beggared New Yorker had roughly two chances in five of getting on the dole or obtaining made-work.[12]

As it happened, social workers asserted that matters actually were growing worse, owing to the exhaustion of personal savings, the collapse of the middle class, and the depletion of relief budgets. For example, the President's Emergency Unemployment Relief Committee,* a private agency that since 1930 had raised $11 million from private charities to fund jobs for forty-four thousand heads of families, was running out of money and about to disband. In February the top monthly relief rate for a New York City family reached $39. By August it had dropped to $23. The professional standard for New York City stipulated $25 a month for food and $20 for rent, rates that would require a monthly expenditure of $12 million just to accommodate the existing client load. Besides that, the relief agencies no longer had enough money to operate for a full thirty-one days, a circumstance that gave rise to the phenomenon known to the darkly humorous

---

*Also known as the Gibson Committee, named for its banker chairman, Harvey D. Gibson. The committee specialized in relief for white-collar workers.

as "foodless holidays." When the money gave out, the agencies dropped people temporarily from the rolls, leaving clients to shift for themselves for a week or more. The shortfall affected those on work relief too; they could never be certain when—or whether—they would be fully paid for their labor. Wrote Hickok, "The practice of appropriating relief funds late in the month, this uncertainty as to whether there will be enough money to carry through the month, and the failure to plan ahead and prevent 'foodless holidays' have done more to break down the morale of everybody—the people on relief and those administering it—than any other factor." And to make matters worse, consumer prices continued their steady increase; a grocery tab of 96 cents in March rose to $1.10 in August.[13]

The effects of unemployment on families were excruciating; they were hardly less painful, if not quite so visible, for the unattached. Matthew Josephson caught something of the special condition of the long-term jobless: "undernourishment, indignity, vacuity, leisure, chronic fatigue." Far more people, mostly men but some women too, were living rough on the streets than there were beds in the East Twenty-fifth Street municipal shelter or its annexes, such as the notorious rat-infested city shelter in an abandoned ferry house on South Street. The "freer and hardier spirits," Josephson observed, encamped in Hoovervilles, slept in doorways, or, in winter, subsisted below the frost line in subway stations. He toured a makeshift Hoover settlement at the foot of Tenth Street near the East River, a hundred or so dwellings, "each the size of a doghouse or chicken coop," constructed with surprising skill and imagination out of wooden boxes, metal cans, strips of cardboard, and old tarpaper. "Here human beings lived on the margin of civilization," Josephson wrote, "foraging for garbage, junk and waste lumber." Most of the inhabitants survived by begging, though lately this had become an even more precarious vocation; the Brooklyn-Manhattan Transit Company now prohibited "solicitations for alms" on subway cars and in stations. The announcement of the BMT ban led with a quote from City Magistrate Mark Rudich: "It is a mistaken kindness to give money to street beggars." When street charity failed, the homeless shuffled off to soup kitchens or public canteens for their meager meals.[14]

Josephson found the East Twenty-fifth Street munie and the South

Ferry annex filled to capacity. The shelters served two meals a day: watery oatmeal and thin black coffee for breakfast, twenty ounces of coarse reddish-brown vegetable stew, sometimes, though not often, with a gobbet of beef in the broth, three pieces of stale bread, and black coffee for supper. "The place was warm enough, almost too warm," he wrote, "and filled with a nightly human stench." The men slept in shelter-issued rough cotton nightshirts on army cots, packed like immigrants in the steerage compartments of old passenger steamers. ("Truly," Josephson noted sardonically, "a man no longer need feel himself alone or 'forgotten.'") The ailing and the tubercular coughed all night; others snored like hogs. After a 6 o'clock breakfast the wardens turned the men out into the streets. Some passed the hours in the comfort of the public library and its branches. ("The libraries are a godsend," one man said.) Others shuffled from park to square to park, and still others enlisted in New York City's 6,000-strong army of panhandlers. Men foraged for cigar and cigarette ends and read discarded newspapers with close attention.[15]

As the population of the munies increased, its character altered. "We are getting a very good class of people in here nowadays," one of the shelter officials told Josephson. "Half of them are not bums at all." Ruined professionals, too fastidious, perhaps, for the flophouse, the "derelict bourgeoisie," in Josephson's phrase, could seek a bed in the up-market Gold Dust Lodge, an abandoned flour mill at the foot of Grand Street at a bend in the East River. The mill housed two thousand men, who maintained it themselves, doing all the work of the place, from sweeping up to keeping the books, in rotating shifts. Accommodations were spartan but clean except for the flour dust (white rather than golden), and the meals were an improvement on those at the munie: beef stew, spaghetti or beans, and codfish on Fridays. The inmates were subjected to less regimentation than the unfortunates on East Twenty-fifth Street; they could stay home during the day and read or smoke in the public rooms. The more docile among them remained for as long as five or six months. "They have no fight in them," Josephson observed; they were reluctant to complain or make trouble for fear of being cast into the streets.[16]

★   ★   ★

In her report to Hopkins, Hickok detailed the elaborate routine required of an applicant for relief. The New York City welfare operations were decentralized, intentionally so. Once you worked up the nerve, you approached one of the city's seventy-nine neighborhood Home Relief offices, usually in a school (you would be apprehensive about encountering your children; they came and went by a different door, but you wouldn't know that) and nearly always within hail of a police station. Welfare Commissioner Taylor told Hickok that placing relief offices near precinct houses discouraged crowds from gathering, reducing the likelihood of serious trouble. But he added, "Sometimes I think maybe we've done this job too well—that it might be better if we had a few disturbances." A policeman stood guard at the entrance to the office. Once inside, you squeezed into a place on a bench in the back of a dismal room reeking of disinfectant and packed with fellow supplicants. Wrote Hickok, "If you are the kind of person the government really should be interested in helping, you go there only as the last resort. You have used up all your resources and have strained the generosity of your relatives and your friends to the breaking point. Your credit is gone. You couldn't charge a nickel's worth at the grocery store. You owe several months' rent. The landlord has lost patience and is threatening to throw you out." From the bench you would see a line of wobbly desks up front, where interviewers were taking down people's stories and making judgments about whether (or not) they were deserving.[17]

You're hungry. There's no food in the house, not even a crust of bread. Anxieties gnaw at you too. You try not to fidget: Do your features, your posture betray your fears? "And there you wait," Hickok wrote, "wondering if they're going to make you sell the radio, which wouldn't bring in enough to feed the family two days." Eventually, three or four hours later, your turn comes. "Maybe the questions aren't so bad, but you hate answering them, just the same," she went on. "If the person asking the questions were sympathetic and tactful, qualified by experience and temperament for the job, it might not be so bad. But the person asking those questions is just another victim of the depression like yourself. He's apt to be without experience or training. Possibly he hates the job—and hates you because you're part of it." The interview ends, the worst is over for now, and all you can do is go home and wait for an investigator, probably someone on work relief, to come to the apartment with more questions—and then you steel yourself for the Home Relief Bureau's verdict.[18]

TERA auditors indicted the city's system as inefficient and inhumane. "Crowded precinct offices, occasional hostile police guards, long waits for interviews, long delays in investigations tend to sap the courage and self-respect of clients," they observed. *The Christian Century* magazine stigmatized relief officials as "stupid and heartless . . . so that the plight of thousands is such as to move even the callous." True, inadequate resources limited social workers' freedom of action. Hickok wrote Hopkins, "They simply have not had enough money to provide the proper housing and equipment for the Home and Work Relief Bureaus and to pay a decent salary to that most important person in the whole relief machinery—the interviewer or the investigator who actually contacts the people on relief." For a change, though, she endorsed the harsher critics, including Lilly and the *World-Telegram*. Hickok tended to be careful, reserved in her judgment of relief workers, ordinarily giving them the benefit of the doubt. But not this time. "There is no question in my mind that we have done and are doing some terrible things to people on relief in New York City," she wrote. "For instance, we have let families be evicted three times in six months! We have starved them, failed to provide them with clothing or medical care, and have brow-beaten them on top of that.

"Just how much more of it they can take nobody knows."[19]

Given budget constraints, there could be no margin for clothing, medical or dental care, or for mundane household necessities such as soap and tooth powder. Gas and electric bills might be paid—or they might not. Hickok met a woman who had been reduced to trying to heat milk for her two children by burning newspapers under a pan. Experimenting with an electric grill, she had blown all the fuses in the building. Evictions were on the rise, and bureaucratic obstruction and delay made matters worse. As *The Nation* pointed out, "Destitute families no longer received money for rent until they were actually evicted and their household effects on the sidewalk." City marshals turned 1,257 families out of their apartments in August, Hickok reported, compared to 420 evictions in August 1932. Increasingly New York landlords were refusing to let apartments to people on relief. The attitude of the rentier class hinted at a deeper problem, or so argued *The Nation*: "Probably there is hardly an American who would allow another man to starve on his doorstep if there was a loaf of bread in the house, but we are reaching a point where we are willing to let thousands die of starvation provided only they crawl out of sight to do it. . . . Callouses grow on compassion in time."[20]

Michael Scheler, reporting for *The Nation*, witnessed up close the torments the relief system inflicted upon the family of "Mr. S." For the most part the newspapers, Scheler wrote, emphasized the impressive sums paid out to New Yorkers on the dole and on work relief, the implication being that the authorities had matters well in hand. Only rarely, with the *World-Telegram* an honorable exception, did the press cover the system's inefficiency, negligence, and unpardonable delays. Out of regular work for two years, Mr. S supported his wife and four children (the oldest was twelve) by doing odd jobs such as canvassing for a printing house and selling door-to-door. Inevitably an inadequate diet began to take a toll on his health. He grew thin and pale, and in early 1933 a bout of influenza kept him bedfast for three weeks and under doctor's orders to go slow for another two months after he regained his feet. Even so, he hesitated to ask for help. Finally Mrs. S swallowed her pride and paid a morning visit to the neighborhood relief office.

Her turn came after a four-hour wait. A clerk handed her the application forms. She went home, answered the questions carefully, and returned with the completed application that afternoon. Pleading desperation, for S had not paid the rent for two months, Mrs. S begged the clerk to rush the case through. He seemed sympathetic and assured her an investigator would call within a day or two. Meanwhile the landlord became importunate, threatening S with eviction and making good on the threat a couple of days later with a notice of dispossession. S delivered it to the relief bureau that same day, together with another urgent plea for help, but a week passed with no sign of a case worker from the relief office.

An eviction notice from the city marshal reduced S to a state of physical and moral collapse. He asked his wife to solicit the local Democratic Club for a politician who could intervene with the relief board on their behalf. Mrs. S had "socialistic leanings," according to Scheler, and appealed to the neighborhood Socialist Committee instead. The committee head approached a relief supervisor, a woman with left-wing inclinations, and an investigator appeared at S's apartment a day or two later. By then, though, it was too late. Rather than cash, the agencies issued relief tickets to landlords, redeemable, if all went smoothly, in two or three weeks. S's landlord refused the ticket and advised him to find someone who would accept it in place of cash for the first month's rent. S trudged from building to building, super to super, searching for days without success. When his wife returned empty-handed to the relief office, a supervisor told her:

"You must find a landlord. We cannot find one for you. If you find yourself in the street you cannot blame us for it."

Relief officials refused Mrs. S's request for cash to cover the rent, saying they couldn't change the rules for her. The marshal handed the eviction order to S at 10 o'clock on a Thursday morning. A policeman escorted the marshal and a corps of expressmen. "Within 30 minutes," Scheler wrote, "all the family's earthly possessions were on the sidewalk." They were homeless for five days. Three members of the Socialist Club volunteered to take in a child each. A fourth comrade, a teacher in a workingmen's education program, allowed S, his wife, and their two-year-old daughter to sleep in his classroom. Within a few days, the Socialists had raised enough for a month's rent.

By now S had all but given up. But not his wife, even when the conundrum of gas and electricity confronted her. She took the previous tenant's overdue bills to the bureau, explaining that without gas she couldn't warm the baby's milk. A week passed; investigators visited, and Mrs. S filled out more forms. Finally the bureau handed her tickets to cover the previous month's bills. But the gas company refused to act unless she cleared a second month of arrears. A relief official told her he couldn't issue a ticket for a two-month overdue bill. With yet another appeal to the comrades and a two-week round of Socialist hat-passing, a penny here, a nickel there, the gas ring burst into flame. But it was anybody's guess how long the lights and the gas would burn, or indeed how long the S family would be able to keep the apartment. Scheler, or anyhow his editors, drew a simple moral from the story of Mr. S and the spectacular indifference of the bureaucrats, condensing it into a headline in *The Nation* of November 8, 1933: "Relief That Does Not Relieve."[21]

The best of the relief officials deplored situations such as the one that tormented Mr. S. Hickok's sources acknowledged housing as "the most aggravating problem" the authorities faced. What people had told her in Philadelphia and Pittsburgh in August—that the time would come when landlords would refuse to rent to people on relief—had become a reality in New York City: "one month's rent for a cheaper apartment, AFTER a family has been evicted." Not much would change, her sources said, until the federal government assumed full responsibility for relief and provided national standards, national oversight—and plenty of money. Josephson's contacts said much the same. He added this twist, what he called a "cosmic joke" on the old laissez-faire system: "If the relief expenditures [in New York City] were by some device made five times greater, say $500 million a year, the old order might be saved, through correcting the fatal want of buying power in the proletariat. However, intelligent social workers believe that if any effective relief is to come out of the present blundering system, it must be national in scope and command." Harry Hopkins doubtless agreed, though he also had a hard-headed grasp of political and fiscal realities. Nevertheless he and his associates—with an assist from Mrs. Roosevelt—had come up with a new idea, one that could be characterized as "national in scope and command," and he had gone up to Hyde Park in late September to present it to the president.[22]

They met in FDR's comfortable, pleasantly dowdy study for three hours. Hopkins emerged to tell the White House press corps that a new federal relief program, with funding of up to $700 million, would distribute surplus food, clothing, and coal to the needy during the winter of 1933–34. "We'll be going in a week," Hopkins told the reporters. FDR would create a new agency, the Federal Surplus Commodities Corporation, by executive order, with Hopkins as its chairman. "We are going to get enough coal to see that these people are warm this Winter and that goes all along the line," Hopkins said. The food would be drawn from the agricultural surplus (one commodity would be salt pork from the Agricultural Adjustment Administration's late summer pig-slaughtering program*), and it would be healthful. The finer points would be decided later, but the reporters had a hint about the menus, at least: Hopkins car-

---

* The pig killing outraged Eleanor Roosevelt for what she saw as its sinful waste, and her protests to senior AAA officials helped spur the federal surplus program.

ried under his arm a large volume between red covers, the U.S. Navy's commissary list.[23]

A few days later, Hopkins dropped down to New York City to address the National Conference of Catholic Charities' annual meeting at the Metropolitan Opera House. The 15 million Americans on relief "face a desperate winter unless heroic action is taken," he said. He called the existing level of benefits a "pittance" and urged social workers to resist demands for cuts— indeed to insist on more money to meet the crisis. "There are some people who still think that these people are naturally or entirely made up of the unemployables, the ne'er-do-wells, the drunkards, the bums—people that never could get on," he said. "You know perfectly well that that's absurd. You've got a cross-section of the American people on this relief roll—the finest people in America, mainly working people, because in the main it's been the workers who have taken the beating in this depression." City relief administrators responded to Hopkins's call for action, meeting October 3 with Mayor John O'Brien to plan the distribution of 2 million pounds of AAA pork and other surplus commodities.[24]

The president addressed the Catholic Charities convention-goers at their final session at the Waldorf-Astoria on October 4, his first speech in New York City since the inauguration. He told the 3,000-strong gathering that the hardest part of the recovery had yet to come, and he called for a redoubling of the relief effort. Cardinal Patrick Hayes, the archbishop of New York, closed out the four-day conference by invoking a Catholic tradition of social justice dating from the late nineteenth century:

"The depression which marked a major breakdown in the prevailing economic and social order has cleared our vision. Now we can see that the old order was built upon a foundation of selfishness, unrestricted competition and a craving for economic power. Our social order needs to be reconstructed upon a different basis. . . . Our able-bodied citizens should be assured of a family wage, decent hours, safe working conditions and steady work."[25]

How much more could New Yorkers take? The leftists who rallied downtown in Union Square—colloquially, New York City's Red Square— looked to the miserable masses expectantly, "possessed," in the words of the writer Malcolm Cowley, "by a daydream of universal brotherhood." Radicals of every denomination gathered there: implacable Communists, millennial Trotskyists, unruly Anarchists, disputatious Socialists, quizzical fellow travelers. Their doctrinal disputes were venomous, but they all accepted as an article of faith that the old system had rotted and soon would fall apart, or be dismantled, despite the patchwork repairs of the emergent New Deal. But the timidity of the dispossessed vexed the comrades. Large groups turned out for demonstrations and marches on City Hall during the winter and spring of 1933, but the protests invariably were peaceful. As Cowley remarked, "There were no riots unless the police started them." Now, in autumn, there were signs of more robust activity, perhaps because FDR's renovations had raised expectations. In mid-October, for example, mounted police, edging their horses into the packed crowds, broke up a gathering of four thousand needle trades unionists besieging the NRA headquarters on Seventh Avenue, arresting fifty-five men and women for disorderly conduct.[26]

The Communist-led Unemployed Councils were astir, demanding reforms in the city's relief operation. In her report, Lorena Hickok mentioned an account of a march from Union Square to City Hall from one of the participants, a woman she regarded highly, the veteran social worker Mary Simkhovitch, who had founded the Greenwich House settlement during Theodore Roosevelt's presidency. As Hickok reported to Hopkins, dissidents from the soft left to the Communists all demanded "cash instead of food orders, clothing, medical care, more consideration at the hands of interviewers and case workers." Above all, she went on, they sought benefits more nearly approximating a level that would sustain a decent living.[27]

Hickok and Simkhovitch shared an interest in a mostly invisible group of Depression victims, young single women—not only the middle-class, often college-educated girls with artistic and political leanings one could meet at the John Reed Club headquarters in a Sixth Avenue loft in Greenwich Village, but women adrift, anonymous, without work or family: "white collar girls, self-respecting, independent," in journalist Marlise Johnston's words, though not very sophisticated. "I was unable to get much dope on what was happening to these people," Hickok conceded; Simkhovitch "seemed to know more about them—and be more inter-

ested in them—than anyone else." Like their young male counterparts in
the munies, they had largely escaped the relief agencies' attentions.[28]

"Single women? Why, they're just discards," Simkhovitch told
Hickok. "I'll tell you how they live! Huddled together in small apartments, three or four of them living on the earnings of one, who may have
a job. Half a dozen of them, sometimes in one room. Sharing with one
another. Just managing to keep alive. They've left the YWCAs and the
settlement houses. They can't afford to live in those places any more."[29]

In the monthly *Review of Reviews*, Marlise Johnston offered a glimpse
of how these strandees survived, proposing a tentative theory about why
they were so easily overlooked. "Women hate the idea of charity," she
wrote. They went for help only as a last resort, after they had pawned
or sold the last of their possessions. "According to the reports of social
workers," Johnston went on, "food is the first thing that goes when a
woman gets up against it, and appearance and clothes are the last. This
is not vanity as much as self-preservation. They know that 60 percent of
their chance of getting a job depends on their appearance." No one knew
how many thousands of New York City's 1,150,000 unemployed persons
were single women. The relief agencies were set up for families, leaving
the unattached to fend for themselves.[30]

They were half-starved. It was rare to see women on the breadlines,
according to Johnston; they found the lines degrading. Sometimes they
patronized the penny kitchens around the flower markets in the neighborhood of Sixth Avenue and Twenty-sixth Street, agreeable sights and
smells thereabouts, presumably. Bean soup cost a penny, beef stew a
nickel, coffee with cream and sugar 3 cents. "You stand up to eat," Johnston wrote, "and if the atmosphere is not cheering the food is nourish-
ing. It is cheap. It is not charity." At night a few hundred free beds were
available, two hundred at the munie (though these were "more for the
drifting type of woman"), some at various private lodgings and shelters,
and, for the fortunate ("white-collar girls only, and white girls"), seventy-
five beds at the Salvation Army Canteen on Twenty-ninth Street, where
during the Christmas season the girls worked as bell-ringers for $3 a day
and could look forward to a holiday gift packet of lipsticks, a compact, and
silk underwear. All too many, though, spent their nights in the subways,

a precarious form of lodging but dry and, usually, safe. One could ride the cars all night for a 5-cent fare, "up and down and back and forth, if you know the right places to change." The subway could be cold, though, especially toward dawn, and one managed little sleep. But a girl could rest up during the day in one of the department store lounges.[31]

Hickok thought she detected a tone of bitterness in Simkhovitch's voice. Born Mary Kingsbury in comfortable circumstances in Chestnut Hill, Massachusetts, she had been an ally of the left at least since 1919, when she stared down the red-baiters who had complained to a congressional investigating committee about Bolshevik influence at Greenwich House and other New York City settlements. Then as now, she made no apology for her radical views. So far as she was concerned, the younger social workers and the Greenwich Village intellectuals, writers, critics, artists, and musicians were only just now catching up to her, and about time too.

Fellow travelers Malcolm Cowley, Edmund Wilson, Matthew Josephson, John Dos Passos, and their colleagues at *The New Republic* gave a powerful voice to the left, and to the millions who were overwhelmed by the tragedy of the Great Depression. Wilson, thirty-eight years old, stout and balding, a two-finger typist, had been the first to arrive, joining the magazine in 1925 as a reviewer-critic. Cowley, thirty-five, the Pittsburgh-raised son of a homeopathic physician, a veteran of the American Field Service during the Great War and a 1920 graduate of Harvard, signed on as a copy editor in 1929 and took over as literary editor in 1931, when Wilson decided to cut loose from the desk and experience the Depression firsthand.* The offices, the general effect "shabby-genteel," according to Cowley, were in an old brownstone in Chelsea between the Ninth Avenue elevated line and the Hudson River docks. Founded in 1914 with a subsidy from J. P. Morgan partner Willard Straight, *The New Republic* under its influential longtime editor Herbert Croly promoted Progressive ideas of the era of the first Roosevelt and Woodrow Wilson: interventionist government, the regulation of business for the

---

*Wilson's travels took him from one end of the country to the other and yielded *The American Jitters: A Year of the Slump* (1932), in which he reported on Henry Ford's Detroit, race in Chattanooga, coal miners in West Virginia, evangelists in Los Angeles, suicide in San Diego, and a textile strike in Lawrence, Massachusetts.

public good, and social welfare policies designed to soften the roughest edges of industrial America.[32]

The magazine drifted leftward after Croly's death in 1930 and, as the Depression deepened, its mission became more urgent. The mainstream press played up small signs of recovery, Cowley charged, such as a temporary rise in stock prices or a modest increase in hiring, while underplaying or ignoring bank failures and factory closings. Even a cursory review of news coverage in the years 1933–34 would suggest he passed an unduly harsh judgment. Yet Cowley had a point about *The New Republic*, for all its modest subscription list of about twelve thousand. "This musty house on a side street, where the stairs creaked and the radiators pounded, was for a time curiously close to the center of what was happening in America," he wrote. Cowley, Wilson, Dos Passos, and, to a lesser degree, Josephson were writers of unusual understanding, imagination, and depth. Cowley would work through much of 1933 on *Exile's Return*, a memoir-study of the "lost generation" of writers in Paris during the 1920s. Wilson had begun to think about a survey of the development of revolutionary thought from the utopian Socialists through Marx and Engels to Lenin's arrival in St. Petersburg in 1917, the genesis of *To the Finland Station.**** Dos Passos, thirty-seven years old, had emerged in the 1920s as an important younger novelist. Though born on the wrong side of the blanket, he had enjoyed a privileged upbringing: the Choate School, private tutors, the Grand Tour, and Harvard. Dos Passos saw *The 42nd Parallel* into print in 1930 and brought out *1919* two years later, the first two novels in his *USA* trilogy. In 1933, between bouts of rheumatic fever and agitation for the movement, he worked away on the third, *The Big Money*.[33]

When the writers and editors of *The New Republic* turned their considerable talents to on-the-scene reporting on coal and textile strikes, milk holidays, and Hoovervilles, when they invited eyewitnesses into the brownstone for exhaustive interviews and combed the printed record to inform their weekly political commentary, they enormously enhanced their

---

*Viking Press published *Exile's Return* in May 1934. The book, now regarded as a classic study of the literature of the 1920s, appeared to generally hostile reviews, and fewer than a thousand copies were sold in the first year. Parts of Wilson's *To the Finland Station* were serialized in 1937; the book, which remains a compelling read, came out in 1940.

readers' understanding of events—and they greatly enriched the historical record. Wrote Cowley, "People now came to see us on their return from Pennsylvania mining towns or the Imperial Valley or the textile mills of the South. The stories they told were of incredible poverty leading to strikes and demonstrations that were suppressed by clubbing, flogging, kidnapping, sometimes lynching—in other words, by the criminal violence of the 'better people' and the lawlessness of the law." Cowley, Wilson, and the others listened and took notes and wished they could do more.[34]

A Roosevelt loyalist, Hickok had little use for the radicals. Nor did she move in their circles. Indifferently educated, a middlebrow, she preferred the rough-and-tumble of covering crime, scandal, and big-time politics to the theorizing of the intellectuals. Still, she must have wondered why the radical left attracted so many imaginative people. In Josephson's view, the conviction had grown among writers, artists, actors, and composers that capitalism had fallen into desuetude and that dictatorships of the left or right were bound to replace the old freewheeling individualism. Less charitably, a sarcastic piece in the *Forum* magazine suggested the "old fashioned phenomenon of bourgeois disillusion" as an explanation. The Sacco and Vanzetti case of 1927 evidently induced Wilson's leftward swing.* For Wilson too, daily vignettes of calamity stirred latent doubts about the American system. "I saw somebody after food or old shoes or whatever in our garbage cans in East 53rd Street almost every time I went out on the street or looked out the window," he recorded in his 1933 notebook. For others, the infatuation began with admiration for the achievements of the Soviet Union. Viewed from the vantage of drab and dormant Depression America, Stalin's Five-Year Plan seemed almost miraculous, Cowley remembered: Russians now had more of everything, wheat, steel, electricity, and "nobody walked the streets looking for a job." He went on, "Under communism, it seemed that the epic of American pioneering was being repeated, not for the profit of a few robber barons, but for the people as a whole." Even then, though, reports were filtering in about a terrible and spreading famine, a consequence of

---

*Nicola Sacco and Bartolomeo Vanzetti were Italian American anarchists accused of robbery and murder. After a controversial trial and a series of appeals, they were executed, many believed at the time, for being Italian American anarchists.

Stalin's collectivization policy that would kill millions, and about more millions held in slave conditions in Stalin's labor camps. Americans on the left, dreamy and willing to suspend disbelief, suspected press exaggeration if not fabrication, and for a long time they remained untroubled in their reverence for the Soviet experiment.[35]

Cowley and other writers and artists longed for cooperation, community, and comradeship, values hardly anyone would associate with traditional American business culture. He and his literary friends, looking back on the individualism of the 1920s, in some ways as destructive to writers as to the victims of unrestrained capitalism, sought "a faith that would supply certain elements heretofore lacking in their private and professional lives as middle class Americans." The movement promised to supply that faith. "The party performed for its members the social and institutional functions of a church," he observed, "and communism was, in effect and at that moment, the only crusading religion." Cowley made his public confession of faith in 1932 by marching in the 1932 May Day parade, a holy day of obligation for radicals.[36]

That said, few of Cowley's friends actually joined the party, however powerful its allure. Authentic Communists found Dos Passos, if touchy, to be made of fairly stern stuff, although he once identified himself as "a 'camp follower' of radical parties." Sincere and a bit naïve, an early admirer of Stalin, Cowley could be useful to the party. The comrades dismissed Wilson as vacillating, unreliable. A writer needed to surrender his autonomy when he accepted the party card; no one could evade the discipline of the Communist line. "I don't see how a novelist or historian could be a party member under present conditions," Dos Passos said. "The Communist party ought to produce some good pamphleteers or poets. By the way, where are they?" Communist doctrines were rigid and the jargon was barbaric, a painful thing for someone with a passion for language. Then too, most writers are intensely self-conscious. Wrote Cowley, "At best one suspected a masquerade, for the Communists one met were mostly intellectuals and politicians disguised in workingmen's clothes." Most real Communists, when they were fortunate enough to be employed at all, were to be found on the shop floors in the city's garment district.[37]

So Cowley, Wilson, Dos Passos, and other accomplished literary leftists were fellow travelers, people who would "sign petitions and join delegations and write about the struggles of the working class—while always retaining [their] independence and [their] right to criticize." True, the movement offered certain social advantages. Cowley recalled that when he turned up for a party in April 1931 at Theodore Dreiser's studio on West Fifty-seventh Street, the author of *Sister Carrie* and *An American Tragedy* employed a butler and served Scotch, a marked improvement on the Jersey lightning Cowley and his friends were accustomed to. The younger writers liked and admired Dreiser, in spite of his affectations and inconsistencies. "His mind, it often seemed to us, was like an attic in an earthquake," Cowley wrote, "full of big trunks that slithered about and popped open one after another, so that he spoke sometimes as a Social Darwinist, sometimes as a Marxist, sometimes as almost a fascist and sometimes as a sentimental reformer." Dreiser may have been a political muddlehead, but the party at his place led to the establishment of the writers' delegation, operating under Communist sponsorship, that would venture into the enflamed and deadly eastern Kentucky mountains in the autumn and publish *Harlan Miners Speak* early in the following year.[38]

Not surprisingly, *The New Republic* expressed editorial skepticism about the strength and constancy of American writers' political convictions: "It isn't true that all of them have simultaneously boarded the Red Express; the train in which they are traveling might be better described as a leftbound local." Still, Cowley, Wilson, Dos Passos, and Josephson were among the fifty-three writers and artists who signed a manifesto endorsing the Communist Party leader William Z. Foster for president in September 1932. They claimed to see little difference between Hoover and Roosevelt, though they conceded that FDR was personally more engaging.

The radicals' views of FDR and the New Deal were complex. At first, anyway, Dos Passos regarded Roosevelt as "a sleek wire artist," shallow and manipulative. "The upshot of it is, you and me and The Forgotten Man are going to get fucked plenty, but it is almost a pleasure to be liquidated by such a bonny gentleman," he wrote Wilson. At times Wilson cast FDR in the role of jester, a befuddled lightweight. His ideas about currency manipulation, for instance, "evidently derived from the *American Boy's Handy Book*: all the things you can do with a dollar." Said the

Communist labor journalist Benjamin Stolberg, "There's nothing [the New Deal] has done so far that could not have been done better by an earthquake." Leo Wolman, a labor economist and NRA staffer, dismissed the president as a dizzy experimenter, according to Wilson: "Roosevelt kept smiling and didn't really know what it was all about—didn't understand the bills he signed." Meanwhile, according to Wolman, the long-established capitalist masters of American economic life remained firmly in command.[39]

In the end, though, it may have been more about plain Americans than plutocrats for writers on the left. Certainly they believed the stakes involved the shaping of what seemed an indeterminate and faintly sinister future. In a *Modern Quarterly* survey of fifteen writers in the summer of 1932, a dozen responded that they believed "American capitalism is doomed to inevitable failure and collapse"—not today, perhaps not even in ten years, but eventually.[40]

In a passage in a 1933 notebook, Wilson described an image seen from the train to Red Bank, the seaside New Jersey town where he grew up: "a pretty looking girl in blue, well dressed middle-class, wheeling a baby carriage—that was the next generation, what would they do, what would they be? in the future that someone was bringing them into—that future that looming seemed so strange, and they were just an ordinary baby (though mysterious with the future as babies are) and an ordinary American mother."[41]

Hickok left New York on the evening of October 13, driving solo now through the New Jersey swamps and south along U.S. Route 1 for Washington. She had earned a ten-day break, a holiday in the private quarters of the White House with the companionship of her particular friend Eleanor Roosevelt. By any measure Hickok had gotten off to a fast start with FERA. Taken together, her reports from Pennsylvania, West Virginia, Kentucky, New York, Maine, and New York City had confirmed most of Harry Hopkins's conceptions about the federal relief program and amended others, presented hard-won evidence to suggest where practices should be altered and execution improved, and provided a checklist of the states' progress in carrying out FERA's basic policies. The reports were of immeasurable value to Hopkins as he moved to replace poor boards and private charities with a national system of public welfare that eventually would expand to include the temporary Works Progress Administration and the greatest of all permanent entitlement programs, Social Security.

By statute and by administrative writ, FERA obliged the states to establish their own emergency relief agencies and staff them with professionals in return for federal aid; where this had been done, in Pennsylvania for instance, programs were effective, Hickok's reports showed. Hopkins sought to establish and maintain uniform national standards and benefits, but as Hickok had discovered, this was proving to be all but impossible. Aid packages varied widely from place to place, and while some relief workers were trained professionals, others were holdover hacks from poor board days, and still others were people on work relief, most of them ill-suited to the task. Hopkins stipulated that all the needy—the unemployed and their dependents, the underemployed, and strikers too—were eligible for relief. But as Hickok had found, millions who qualified were receiving nothing as yet. Payments were supposed to be sufficient to maintain a civilized standard of living. Her reports showed Hopkins how far FERA and the states needed to go to approach that goal; relief assistance averaged 50 cents a day per family in the autumn of 1933. Hickok's investigations made it clear that cash disbursements were superior in every way to food and rent tickets; cash maintained clients' morale and reduced occasions for sin in the form of graft. More than anything, she again emphasized, Americans wanted work—any sort of work—rather than the dole.[42]

Returning to 1600 Pennsylvania Avenue as a permanent resident, Hickok continued to have difficulty fitting herself comfortably into the first lady's day. She felt out of place at ER's official functions—and perhaps with reason, for White House press agents regularly cropped her out of official photos. Her expectations were a flight of fancy: she wanted America's most famous (and perhaps overscheduled) woman to herself. By one estimate, Mrs. Roosevelt's workday stretched sixteen to twenty hours; she received 301,000 pieces of mail between March and December 1933, and she answered a lot of it herself. Then too, she kept up with myriad connections: family, intimate friends of many years, secretaries and other staffers, and compelling new social and political acquaintances in Washington. "Remember one thing always," she had written Hickok, "no one is just what you are to me. I'd rather be with you this minute than anyone else and yet I love many other people and some of them can do things for me probably better than you could, but I've never enjoyed being with anyone the way I enjoy being with you." It's impossible to say whether Hickok found the words reassuring, or whether it seemed to her that ER intended them to delineate the limits of their relationship. She kept a calendar on which she circled the days they were together and drew an X through the days they were apart. Sometimes she made brief notations that indicated whether the White House days had been satisfactory. Not many were, given the claims on the first lady's time.[43]

The midsummer economic boomlet had fizzled by Labor Day, and with recovery stalled Hickok found a White House preoccupied by growing labor conflict, insubordinate industry's challenges to NRA authority, rising demands for currency inflation, and continued misery—and potential for violence—in the countryside. With winter coming on, the sense of urgency in the Oval Office mounted. In Ambridge, Pennsylvania, the authorities shot and killed one striking steelworker and wounded another fifteen. Textile workers shut down mills in South Carolina and Georgia. Arkansas sharecroppers trying to organize touched off a violent response from planters and the police. Senator Robert F. Wagner's National Labor Board struggled to mediate a bloody ten-week-old strike involving thousands of silk workers in Paterson, New Jersey. New York City window cleaners and bushelmen* had struck, and now corset makers and underwear workers were threatening to walk out. The American Federation of Musicians filed a lawsuit challenging the New York police band's free concerts on the radio and at ballparks, parades, and social events, tax-supported performances that were keeping at least some of the city's seventeen thousand union musicians from gainful work. Heywood Broun, the *World-Telegram*'s celebrity columnist, shook his considerable bulk into

---

*Laborers who alter or repair garments, in this case for New York City's big department stores.

motion to launch an organizing drive for notoriously independent, competitive, and crotchety newspapermen, with a call for a minimum wage, a forty-hour work week, notice of dismissal, and collective bargaining. In late October, Broun would charter the Newspaper Guild of New York, with signed commitments from five hundred journalists.[44]

The frequency and severity of strikes—there would be twice as many stoppages in 1933 as in 1932—threatened the entire enterprise of recovery, at least according to NRA director Hugh Johnson. In a speech carried over the NBC network, the splenetic Johnson told an American Federation of Labor convention gathered in Washington during the second week in October that workers now had ample protection under the law and must lay aside the strike weapon—"economic sabotage," he called it. "The plain stark truth is that you cannot tolerate the strike," Johnson said. "Public opinion is the essential power in this country. In the end it will break down and destroy every subversive influence."[45]

From the start, Communists had attacked the NRA, as they attacked all New Deal programs, dubbing the ubiquitous thunderbird emblem the "blue buzzard." Now *The New Republic* wondered whether Johnson's speech foreshadowed a calculated program of coerced government-labor partnership, threatening "a rapid drift toward fascism." The magazine feared that Johnson was moving toward "a labor movement fettered by the state, forbidden to strike." Government was doing all it could, Johnson seemed to be saying, and workers could expect no more from the economic system than they now were getting.

"The judgment of the government on these matters is final and must be accepted" was *The New Republic*'s interpretation of Johnson's speech. "If organized labor disagrees, it will be suppressed."[46]

Yet Hugh Johnson faced issues more pressing than the doubts of *The New Republic*'s editors about his goodwill toward organized labor. The NRA's economics of scarcity meant prices were climbing, a good thing for profits but an added burden for millions whose wages or relief benefits were stagnant or falling. Farmers and small businessmen regarded the NRA as a vast "price-fixing conspiracy" of big industrialists and industrial-scale farmers, and consumer advocates complained that Johnson ignored their concerns. Some New Dealers warned that corporate greed could wreck recovery. According to George Soule, *The New Republic's* economics writer, business used the NRA to pile up profits by the time-honored methods of monopoly and curbs on output. Meanwhile Johnson fretted about the possibility of a constitutional challenge to the NRA. He wanted to keep the program out of the courts for as long as possible, and that mandated a cautious, conciliatory approach to business. Prosecutions of code violators were rare, and Johnson understood that persuasion and aggressive huckstering were his most potent weapons. Hence his ceaseless flow of flamboyant commentary and the inspired NRA ballyhoo campaigns: parades in September in a thousand cities big and small and, in October, a widely publicized "Buy Now" drive.[47]

Critics—and they were legion, left and right—charged that Johnson, and the administration generally, delivered more ballyhoo than substance. The "Buy Now" campaign opened on October 10 in New York City with 130,000 merchants pledged to sell at "fair and square" prices, according to *The New York Times*. Johnson issued a call to arms to the massed legions of female shoppers: "The housewives of the country, the purchasing agents who spend 85 percent of the family income, will realize that now is the time to buy, not only to save money but because every dollar spent now is helping to keep the wage earner in her family on the payroll." Eleanor Roosevelt lent a first lady's prestige to the campaign, saying it offered women opportunities for patriotic service such as had not been seen since the Great War. *The New Republic* countered, with some justice, that most Americans "spend nearly all their income on a hand-to-mouth basis, and cannot buy to anticipate future wants."[48]

With the NRA's loss of momentum, the experimenter in chief looked toward other expedients as the autumn advanced. FDR's haphazard flitting from policy to seemingly contradictory policy appalled the tidy-minded George Soule. There appeared to be hardly any central direction at all, only FDR's whim, or so it seemed to him. "Little is heard anymore about the 'Brain Trust'—always a picturesque fiction," he wrote. "What there ever was of trustification in brains has now succumbed to the free competition in ideas. . . . Ideas and projects of all kinds—good, bad and indifferent—go up to the president; he asks advice and takes what action seems right to him at the moment." Where, Soule wondered, was the guiding hand, operating with reliable data pouring out of a command center with charts on the walls showing payrolls and production, farm and factory prices, money in circulation, indexes of purchasing power—all collated in a master "control chart extended into the future, which would show what goal was expected by, say, July 1934."[49]

Rising profits notwithstanding, prices continued to hover below healthy levels. Mindful of the rural revolt, Roosevelt strove to restore the balance between what farmers received for their commodities and what they paid for essentials. He understood, too, that recovery would gain strength only when workers had more dollars to spend. Demands grew for increasing the money supply to make money and credit cheaper, in an effort to ease Americans' debt load. Rummaging among the monetary policies available to him, Roosevelt resolved to try tinkering with the dollar's gold value. The United States would not return to the gold standard, as some were calling for, but it would buy and sell gold on the world market to try to increase its value. The Cornell economist George F. Warren argued that gold purchases would spur inflation, raising commodity prices. To encourage this outcome, FDR held daily breakfast-in-bed sessions with Henry Morgenthau, the acting treasury secretary, at which they fixed the price for that day's government transactions in gold.[50]

Any salutary effects of the gold program were imperceptible. The influential British economist John Maynard Keynes would sharply criticize FDR's monetary policies in a year-end "open letter" published in *The New York Times*, labeling as crude the notion that "income can be raised by increasing the amount of money." Keynes, with his remarkable gift for striking imagery, added that Roosevelt's program seemed "like trying to get fat by buying a larger belt." He implored the president to launch a massive public works program, more wide-ranging than anything yet contemplated, to be paid for by government borrowing rather than by raising taxes. Conservatives shrank in horror from deficit spending, prophesying dire consequences in the long run. But as Keynes once famously quipped, "In the long run we're all dead."[51]

While he waited (in vain) for the gold program to show results, Roosevelt moved decisively on two other fronts to inject more cash into the system and to deal with agricultural surpluses accumulating in storehouses in the South and Midwest. In mid-October he authorized the creation of the federal Commodity Credit Corporation to grant interest-bearing loans to farmers who agreed to keep their crops off the market until prices rose. Cotton planters would receive 10 cents a pound at 4 percent interest. Agriculture Secretary Henry Wallace announced a similar program for corn on October 25; the government would lend farmers 30 to 35 cents a bushel for grain stored on their places. The new agency would issue the first corn loan check on November 25 to a farmer in Pocahontas County, Iowa, a center of rural unrest.[52]

Finally, too, the president moved on public works. The National Industrial Recovery Act had allocated $3.3 billion to the Public Works Administration for long-term projects such as the Lincoln Tunnel connecting New York and New Jersey, the Grand Coulee Dam on the Columbia River, and aircraft carriers for the U.S. Navy. But these projects required months and years for planning, design, and construction.* Up to now, the Civilian Conservation Corps, a pet Roosevelt project an editorialist in *The Nation* magazine derided as "a militarized body of boy scouts," had been the only substantial provider of federal public works jobs. In response to complaints from the American Federation of Labor about the plodding pace of PWA spending, the agency's administrator, Harold Ickes, announced that $500 million in construction projects, mostly road work, would be under way by mid-October. An independent survey projected that the PWA would put a million men to work by winter.[53]

That failed to satisfy the relentless Hopkins. Malcolm Cowley remarked that the success or failure of a New Deal program usually turned on the strength, determination, and political savoir-faire of its leading advocates. Hugh Johnson, for one, was unsteady; Assistant Secretary of Agriculture Rexford Tugwell, for another, terrified conservatives. "Harry Hopkins, the spender, was a more effective administrator for all his raffish manner, and therefore his undertakings had a chance of success," Cowley wrote. In early November FDR accepted Hopkins's Keynesian plan for an immediate public works program, hundreds of thousands of comparatively simple "pick and shovel" jobs that would see the needy through the

---

*The Lincoln Tunnel would not open for traffic until December 1937.

winter in thousands of American communities. Hopkins told the president he could create 4 million jobs by mid-December at a cost, ultimately, of about $4 billion; the initial funds would be drawn from Ickes's unspent PWA budget. The president issued an executive order creating the Civil Works Administration, with Hopkins at its head, on November 9.[54]

By then Hickok had been on the road for the first two weeks of a nearly two-month investigative trip that would take her to Minnesota, the Dakotas, Nebraska, and Iowa, the heart of the farm insurgency. The traveling would be arduous; she would encounter dust storms, blizzards, biting cold, and the incessant enervating winds of the Northern Plains, and the scenes of human suffering would tear at her emotions. She would ache with loneliness, too, as a passionate correspondence with Eleanor Roosevelt would show. But she would observe the results of New Deal relief and recovery policies up close and witness the initial impact of the corn loan and civil works programs. She would record a half-starved Dakota woman's recipe for Russian thistle (tumbleweed) soup: "It don't taste so bad, only it ain't very filling." So concerned was Hopkins about the revolutionary potential of the Middle Border in the late autumn of 1933 that he instructed Hickok to send off her first reports by telegraph. Matters were too urgent for the mails.[55]

6

AMERICA'S SIBERIA

The Dakotas, October–November 1933

Good boys, now go home and feed the hogs."[1]

For a decade, farmers of the Middle Border had taken away this message from their encounters with government, the banks, insurance companies, railroads, and processors. It had become tired (and irritating) with repetition, and as the economic crisis deepened groups of farmers began improvising forms of rough justice: embargoes and blockades, milk dumping, violent resistance to the wave of foreclosures crashing over the countryside. Farmers in a broad arc from Wisconsin and Iowa through Minnesota and the Dakotas down to Nebraska had discovered how to gain the attention of the men who exercised political power. President Roosevelt told key aides that he judged an agrarian revolution likely if the New Deal failed to deliver higher prices and debt relief to farmers. As it happened, FDR misconstrued the rural insurrection, often spontaneous, as a systematic challenge to the established order. "The word 'revolution' often occurs among them," labor journalist Mary Heaton Vorse wrote, "but what they mean is a farmers' revolt. They do not understand revolution in the communist sense." Perhaps, but Roosevelt nonetheless transmitted his anxieties to Harry Hopkins, and when Hopkins sent Lorena Hickok to the Middle Border for the next in her series of field investigations, he insisted on frequent reports by wire.[2]

She left the capital on an 8:20 train the evening of October 24. En route to Chicago, she wrote Hopkins to say that Roosevelt confidants Louis Howe and Henry Morgenthau had asked her to freelance for them, reporting on how officials in federal agencies were treating people. "I am perfectly willing to give Colonel Howe anything I may hear on this subject—provided my doing so meets with your approval and provided I am NOT placed in the position of spying on other federal employees," she wrote. In reply, the bureaucratically sure-footed Hopkins wired her to send everything to him; he would sort through her findings and forward the key points to Howe and others. From Union Station Hickok took a taxi and then a bus to the Chicago Municipal Airport (today's Midway, in 1933 said to be the world's busiest landing ground) for the three-hour flight to Minneapolis. She spent the next day working at her customary tearing pace, darting out of the Leamington Hotel for a flurry of interviews: the director of the Minnesota Farm Bureau (flour mills dominated the Minneapolis skyline; Pillsbury's A mill, six stories high, ranked as the world's largest flour producer in the 1930s), the city editors of the region's two largest newspapers, and a senior Farm Credit Administration official. Hickok compressed what she had learned into a telegram to Hopkins on October 27, a staccato report with an emphasis on politics, unusual for her. "Told little likelihood of violent disturbance, now chiefly work of professional agitators with opposition party certainly looking on if not secretly participating," she wired. "Undoubtedly growing bitterness and restlessness among farmers. Personal prestige of big boss at stake. Still feel generally he [FDR] is sincere and acting in good faith but listening too much to the theorists. Administration has lost a good deal of ground."[3]

Hickok met too with Thomas Dillon, the editor of *The Minneapolis Tribune*, her mentor when she worked as a reporter there in the 1920s. "Had five-hour confab with former boss one smartest newspaperman in the country," the telegram went on. "His comment on present Middle West situation is two bullfrogs in a puddle can make a lot of noise. Keep your shirts on and don't worry." Even so, as Dillon and others informed her, the problems were acute and the insurgency rattled people because it drew on such unlikely sources. Wrote journalist Lillian Symes, "It was not among the long-peonized sharecroppers and tenant farmers of the South and Southwest that these amazing events were occurring but among the formerly comfortable owning farmers of Iowa, Nebraska and Wisconsin, facing the loss of their middle class status after a ten-year battle to maintain it." Even still-solvent farmers complained about old-line bankers making decisions on farm loans, excessive interest rates on government loans, and too much red tape. They demanded government-mandated minimum prices for their products, claiming that the big food corporations were passing along to farmers the taxes they paid to fund the Agricultural Adjustment Administration's crop reduction program, leaving them no better off than before. They complained that the hog-killing campaign hadn't helped much,* and they were skeptical about the just-announced Commodity Credit Corporation—informally, the corn loan program. The NRA also continued to arouse strong resentment, especially among small operators.[4]

The "theorists," objects of derision and scorn to many farmers, included Iowan Henry Wallace, the agriculture secretary, the assistant secretary, Rexford Tugwell, and any member of the New Deal cadre generically described as "young men with their hair on fire," in the critics' vivid phrase. "Wallace would make a second-rate county agent if he knew a little more," Milo Reno, the Farmers' Holiday Association leader, said tartly. In mid-October, with spring wheat dropping to 75 cents a bushel, 60 cents below Reno's (exaggerated) estimate of the cost of production, Governor William Langer of North Dakota ordered an embargo on his state's wheat; when the railroads signaled they would refuse to honor it, Langer threatened to order National Guard troops to keep Dakota wheat off the market. But Langer's words rang hollow. "The only way to obtain effective enforcement would be to put a national guardsman in every [grain] elevator in the state," *The Bismarck Tribune* observed. That was not only impractical, it was impossible: there were 1,800 elevators in North Dakota and 1,300 militiamen. Like Langer, Governor Charles W. Bryan of Nebraska (a brother of the plain people's hero, three-time presidential candidate William Jennings Bryan) sounded more like a Red agitator than a chief executive: "The people are now being plundered. The prices of the farmer's products are decreasing so his throat is being cut from both

---

*The federal government eventually bought 6.2 million piglets and 200,000 hogs and supervised the slaughter.

ears at once." In late October Reno, that "bad weather bird," in *Time*'s phrase, issued a new call for a national farm strike, urging farmers to withhold their products from the markets until scarcity forced prices to rise. They were asked to buy nothing unnecessary, to refuse to pay debts or taxes, and to fight evictions.[5]

Hickok moved from interview to interview on October 27 and 28: Governor Floyd Olson of Minnesota, representatives of dairymen and stock farmers, relief administrators. She complained to Hopkins tongue-in-cheek that the press of work would keep her from attending the Iowa–Minnesota football game, homecoming for the Golden Gophers. (Minnesota won, 19–7.) "If I tried to tell you all the complaints and theories and 'isms' I've heard in my talks with people these last two days . . . it would take all night," she wrote. "The feeling seems to be that the Public Works crowd, NRA, the Department of Agriculture, AAA, and so on—are trying to do a lot of funny things, but aren't getting anywhere." When she met with Olson, a Farmer-Labor Party leader with pronounced New Deal sympathies, she reported "nothing but gloom" from him. "Governor Olson gave the President 30 days more," she wrote. If things hadn't changed for the better by then, he suggested, FDR's prestige would begin to dissolve.[6]

Hickok: And where do we go from there?
Olson: Darned if I know.[7]

The Farmers' Holiday Association's Reno raised the rhetorical stakes, placing the blame for the rolling catastrophe in the Corn Belt on Secretary Wallace and predicting doom if the administration ignored Reno's demands. "So far my confidence in President Roosevelt has not been destroyed but it has been cracked mightily," he said. "He'll either make good his promise or he'll be the last President of this American Republic." To the editors of *The Bismarck Tribune* embargoes and strikes were futile, though "no one who knows the real plight of the farmers can blame them for grasping at straws in their present dilemma." Iowa Governor Clyde Herring responded to Reno's strike proclamation by ordering out the National Guard. Farmers in western Iowa renewed the blockade of Sioux City, a center of the 1932 uprising; picketers thrashed a trucker delivering a load of cattle to the Sioux City stockyards. In Wisconsin strikers drained ten thousand pounds of milk out of the vats of a Milan cheese factory and clubbed a farmer trying to sell a load of wood. A blockade runner shot and killed a picketer near Madison.[8]

As it happened, the end of October brought slight signs of improvement. Nationally the price of wheat advanced to 85 cents a bushel, and with a poor 1933 harvest, the smallest in thirty-seven years, prices might be expected to climb a bit higher before long. News of the corn loan program also lifted farmers' spirits. In fourteen states, farmers' groups declined to vote for a strike. Judges for the eleventh annual North Dakota Corn Show in Bismarck reported good-quality field corn, alfalfa, and sweet corn despite a poor crop season over all. (McLean County won the state's corn championship.) In Washington, the New Deal hurried the Commodity Credit Corporation into being with a promise of payments of 30 cents a bushel for corn not grown in 1934 and $5 a hundredweight for notional hogs so long as farmers agreed to a 25 percent cut in production. Sober-minded newspaper editors counseled patience, even in Iowa. "The Government's proposition is part cash and part gamble," *The Cedar Rapids Gazette* observed. "Reno's proposition is all gamble." Despite outbreaks in some places (dynamiters blew up two cheese factories in Wisconsin), rank-and-file farmers were turning cautious, or anyhow were inclined to wait and see.[9]

Five Middle Border governors—Langer, Olson, Herring, Tom Berry of South Dakota, and Wisconsin's Albert Schmedeman—nevertheless decided it would be foolhardy to assume the strike would fizzle. They gathered at the rococo State Capitol in Des Moines on October 30 to hear out Reno and prepare for a lobbying trip to the White House. The Farmers' Holiday Association wanted a farmers' NRA code with government price-fixing, compulsory controls on production, and marketing and licensing of producers and processors, what Reno called currency "reflation," and a national moratorium on mortgage foreclosures. Reno even proposed an NRA-style banner for the FHA: a green eagle clutching a pitchfork. The governors endorsed key elements of Reno's program, potentially the most far-reaching restraint on private enterprise in the nation's history, in return for a pledge to suspend the farm strike.[10]

But the strike was wilting even as the governors made their way to

Washington. They met with the president for four hours on November 2, with Wallace voicing skepticism about the code proposal and a smiling and solicitous Roosevelt leaving the governors with the impression that he favored their nostrums. "A tentative plan was worked out," the White House announced after the meeting. "Further conferences will be held tomorrow morning." But Wallace prevailed in a private session with the president, and the conferences were stillborn. Roosevelt deflected the governors' request—demand—to reconvene and instead sent them into meetings with Wallace and his aides.[11]

The president recalled the governors a couple of days later. Candid this time, he categorically rejected their demands for a system of compulsory marketing controls, "what amounts substantially to the licensing of every plowed field and marketing by a ticket punch system of all grain and livestock," according to a statement he read to them and later released to the press. The Corn Belt might accept regimentation, but states with large urban populations and the prickly and independent farmers of New England and the South likely would resist. "The Governors can most promptly increase the money in the hands of their farmers . . . by cooperating to the limit with plans which have already been set in motion," the handout asserted. Publicly the governors graded their mission a failure. "I am very disappointed and disgusted," North Dakota's combustible Langer said. "The farmer is the forgotten man. Everybody else has been here before him. The banker, the insurance man, the railroad man have got all the money. There is nothing left for the farmer." Reno ordered an end to the truce, and the strike resumed with new episodes of exhibitionist violence. Insurgents burned a railroad bridge near Sioux City and plundered some boxcars. Still, the incidents were isolated. The vitality had seeped out of the movement, and the strike would sputter to an end within a few days.[12]

Privately, South Dakota's Berry told Hickok that the governors agreed they had received a fair hearing in Washington. They had met too with Harry Hopkins, who may have told them about the just-approved and soon-to-be-announced federal civil works program, unquestionably an item of good news. (In a November 9 letter, the first lady would pass word of the new program to Hickok: "Mr. Hopkins' new idea is to be put into effect, and he hopes to put 2,000,000 men back to work and then 2,000,000 more.")[13]

FDR ordered Hopkins and other senior New Dealers to Des Moines to provide political cover for the governors. South Dakota's Tom Berry, a rancher—"Did you ever notice his walk?" Hickok wondered. "He walks as though he still had on chaps and high-heeled boots!"—saw humor in the Washington interlude in spite of himself. According to Berry, Governor Schmedeman of Wisconsin was afraid to go home. "I told him he'd better come on out here with me, and I'd protect him," Berry told Hickok. "When he got off the train in Madison I told him he'd better walk in the center of the street because they just might accidentally blow up a cheese factory as he was going by. He just gave me a dirty look."[14]

West of Bismarck a dirt road, rutted and barely passable, led over smooth rounded hills to a worn church where Hickok found a dozen men bent against a lacerating wind, waiting for a word with the Morton County relief agents. Paintless and frail-looking, encouched in dry grass, the church stood alone in the vast wind-scoured prairie. The men grouped near the entrance had been "hailed out" during the summer, their crops destroyed by ferocious storms in June and July. With winter coming on, they were desperate for help. On the way to this bleak rendezvous Hickok passed withered and stunted cornfields, desiccated stalks the hail had beaten into the ground. Only one or two of the men wore overcoats. The others shivered in faded, thin, shabby denim. "Cotton denim doesn't keep out the wind very well," she observed. When she returned to the car, it was full of men. Seeking warmth, they had crawled in and rolled up the windows.[15]

Hickok had left Minneapolis on October 29 in a Farm Credit Administration car with a young man from the Land Bank, Richard Freeman, as her codriver, pushing west along U.S. 10 in a long, imperceptible climb to the Red River and across the drift prairie toward the Missouri uplands: Fargo, Jamestown, Bismarck for the night. Next day, she endured her first taste of celebrity. She had spoken with Mrs. Roosevelt in Chicago the night before. In the morning a reporter for *The Bismarck Tribune* turned up at the Prince Hotel to scout her identity, her North Dakota errand, and her business with the first lady, saying he'd heard she had put in a long-distance phone call to the White House. A heavy cold exacerbated her irritation, and she brusquely declined comment. Judge Adolph Christianson, the state emergency relief director, a bit more forthcoming, told *The Tribune* that Hickok—a grand-niece of the notorious Black Hills gunman, he said—worked for Hopkins and the Federal Emergency Relief Administration and had close White House connections. The paper called her a "woman sleuth for Harry Hopkins."[16]

Over the summer, a meteorological calamity of biblical proportions had deepened the Dakotas' long agricultural depression. Hail and three-inch-long grasshoppers devastated the standing grain, assuring yet another in a succession of poor harvests.* (Hickok would interview a Dakota farmer who claimed he hadn't made a profitable crop since 1916.) The scattered clouds that flew across the cruel blue sky were cottony and dry. Scorching winds and a full-scale drought that set in during the summer of 1933 would shrivel and crack the plains and hollow out the Dust Bowl.

The gaunt, weather-beaten men outside the Morton County church once were prosperous farmers. Most owned substantial holdings, at least 640 acres. "A 640-acre farm at $10 an acre—which is about what land is worth hereabouts these days—means only $6,400 worth of land," Hickok calculated. If immediate conditions were desperate, long-term prospects struck her as hopeless, for the region appeared to be in the process of drying up and becoming what the geologist and explorer John Wesley Powell had called it a half-century ago: a desert unsuitable for intensive cultivation. The farmers kept lots of stock, thirty to forty head of cattle, a dozen horses, some sheep, hogs, and chickens, but the animals were in pitiable condition, thin and rangy for lack of feed; the cows had gone dry and the hens weren't laying. Some farmers had tried feeding the grazing animals Russian thistle (colloquially, tumbleweed); this made their mouths sore and, given its digestive effects, they might as well have eaten barbed wire. Many animals would die of hunger or exposure over the winter. The men's families weren't much better off. They needed everything, espe-

---

*With 1932 an exception: a bumper wheat harvest that year, but ruinous prices for Dakota farmers.

cially warm clothing. "Everything I own I have on my back," one farmer told a relief investigator. He wore two pairs of overalls and two ragged denim jackets. His shoes were so battered Hickok wondered how they stayed on his feet. Clothes? The men had mortgaged their animals and land up to the limit. All were in arrears with taxes, some by as many as five years. There was no money left for clothes.[17]

The relief agents at the church had scant aid to offer. In conversations with Hickok they blamed the state government in Bismarck. The Morton County relief operation carried a thousand families, mostly farmers, on the rolls, a third of the population. The state, suspecting local officials of playing politics with relief, pressed for a reduction in the caseload and refused to send the county commissioners more than $6,000 a month—$6 per family. "And most of the families are huge—eight or ten children," according to Hickok. The state declined, too, to support a county plan to put men to work on the roads at $15 a month for three months in the fall and early winter. She wrote Hopkins, "The commissioners say that, if they could have $15,000 a month these next three months—until the people get clothed and stocked with fuel—they might be able to get along, by half-starving them, on $6,000 a month for the rest of the winter." On the face of it, Hickok went on, "it looks as though somebody was responsible for a pretty rotten job," though she promised to report the other side of the story when she returned to Bismarck at the end of the week.[18]

Officials in the capital had warned her that she would find significant unrest—the "farm holiday" spirit—in the countryside. "I can't say that I did," she told Hopkins. "They seemed almost too patient to me." True, farmers complained about the AAA crop and livestock reduction programs. Twenty-five years ago, the old-timers told her, they routinely recorded crop yields of twenty bushels of wheat an acre. Today ten bushels made a bumper crop. Dakotans didn't need to farm fewer acres or raise fewer cattle and hogs; they needed better prices for what they produced. In order to make a living, their wheat had to sell for $1 a bushel. On October 30, 1933, North Dakota farmers were getting 70 cents. They complained, too, that federal agencies granted loans only so they could meet their obligations to the Twin Cities bankers who held their mortgages. Hickok suggested that even if the money did go to the banks, it probably saved their farms for them.

"Well, the farms aren't worth saving now," one of the farmers replied.[19]

Hickok's itinerary took her west from Bismarck to Dickinson and, on October 31, north to Williston via U.S. 85, skirting the western slopes of the Killdeer Mountains. Actually two long, flat-topped buttes, the Kill-deers rose seven hundred feet above the plain, their grassy flanks scored by deep ravines. Scattered stands of aspen, oak, and ash bestowed on the district an air of mystery, as though those lonely hillsides and dark copses were enchanted. Williston, population five thousand, the Williams County seat and the market town for northwestern North Dakota, spread out along the banks of the Missouri River, but the river had rerouted itself and now flowed a mile south of town. When the railroad came in 1887 Williston "was said to have a saloon at either end of its one busi-ness block, with seven or eight in between," according to a contemporary guidebook. Now the city claimed the biggest cooperative creamery in the state.[20]

Hickok found plenty of shortcomings in relief arrangements in Wil-liams County. "I wish I could find words adequately to express to you the immediate need for clothing in this area," she wrote Hopkins. "All I can say is that these people have GOT to have clothing—RIGHT AWAY. It may be Indian summer in Washington, but it's Winter up here. They've had their first snow. Snow is in the forecast for tomorrow. It's COLD." She met a farmer in the Williston relief office, a small man with leathery skin, dressed stylishly if incongruously "in a worn light flannel suit of collegiate cut, a flashy blue sweater, also worn, belted tan topcoat and cap to match." The outfit belonged to one of his seven children, the oldest son, and they took turns wearing it. They were the only clothes the two of them owned.[21]

Williams County was wheat and livestock country, and the farmers and ranchers and their crops and stock were in a bad way. Williston re-lief workers told Hickok that 95 percent of the farmers thereabouts were bankrupt. Some 450 families were on relief and the county added forty families a week to the rolls. Even so, Bismarck refused to increase the state's $6,000 a month allotment. She sat in on a Farmers' Loan Associa-tion interview with an applicant, a quiet Scandinavian who said he had been "hailed out again" last summer.

Hickok: Why do you stick it?
Farmer: No place to go.

The farmer tallied his assets: thirty head of cattle, sixteen horses, some hogs, miscellaneous farm equipment, a tractor (though he hadn't used it for years because he couldn't afford the fuel), and 320 acres. His liabilities: an $800 Bank of North Dakota mortgage, $400 owed to a farm implement dealer, $300 to a blacksmith, $1,000 to a hardware merchant, $600 in back taxes, and $500 in federal feed and seed loans, for a total of $3,600. He asked for the new loan to pay off his old ones or at least keep his creditors at bay for a few more months. The association secretary asked him whether he had sufficient food and clothing to see his family through the winter. Silent for a long moment, he answered finally by wiping away tears with the back of his hand.

"And for the second time since I've been on this job I found myself blinking to keep tears out of my own eyes," Hickok confessed.[22]

She sent Hopkins a canceled check and a bill of sale from a cattle transaction in Ray, a quiescent village on U.S. Route 2 a hundred miles east of Williston. Frank Herbaugh sent four cows, total weight four thousand pounds, to market in Chicago. They cost $20 apiece to raise. Herbaugh's check from the Stockyards National Bank came to $3.61. In an hour's conversation with two cattlemen in the shuttered bank in Ray, Hickok learned that one man had sold the other thirty head of cattle for $310. The buyer sent twenty-seven head to market and, after deductions for freight and commissions, cleared $178. "They weren't prime," the rancher told her, "but good stuff. Better than canning grade. And at that I did fairly well. Some cattlemen around here have netted as low as 35 cents an animal. . . . We figure everybody'd be better off if the government bought them up at a low price and slaughtered them here and delivered them to the starving farmers."[23]

Hickok pushed east along Route 2 to Minot, arriving in the afternoon of November 1. "Came on here over a grand road," she wrote Mrs. Roosevelt, "eating an apple and some pecans in the car for lunch." For the most part, though, she found North Dakota traveling hard. "The hotels are Godawful," she complained to Kathryn Godwin. "And I'm turning into a flaming 'Red.' Also, I haven't got my voice back yet. Otherwise, all is lovely." For once, the quotidian details pleased her: a better class of hotel in Minot, and in the smoke shop she bought a pack of Pall Mall Specials, the first she'd seen in North Dakota. (Still, she complained that the out-of-town newspapers came a day late.) "I'm warm and comfortable," she went on, "and pretty soon I shall enjoy probably a fairly good dinner. But I don't feel very happy about it—not after what I've seen and heard today. Damn it, what right have we, any of us, to any comfort and security when there is so much misery in the world?"

She wrote Hopkins that night too, another in a series of letters, posted every couple of days, meant to meet the boss's demand for timeliness while preserving a measure of discretion and confidentiality. She sensed that circumstances would compel her to say some hard things about the administration of relief in North Dakota. "Telegraph wires don't lend themselves very well to the sort of things I hear," she wrote him. "These are pretty small communities, you know, and what goes out on the telegraph wire is apt to be all over town within a few hours." But she promptly violated her new rule, wiring to Hopkins that night, "TO REPEAT URGENT NEED FOR CLOTHING." And she posted the letter by airmail.[24]

Next day, November 2, Hickok drove north along U.S. 83 from Minot before turning east a dozen miles south of the Canadian border to follow State Route 5, unpaved for half its nearly 400-mile course through the state. The car sped over a flat, featureless plain, the *spang* of gravel steady on the undercarriage, toward Bottineau in the shadow of the Turtle Mountains. Writing in *The American Mercury*, Alfred Klausler saw North Dakota's treeless landscape as "a living symbol of a T. S. Eliot poem," that is to say, a wasteland bleak and beyond hope. But the muted beauty and the subtle color palette of the prairie country retained the power to stir Hickok emotionally. The Dakota skies shone a metallic copper and blue. "Sunlight brings out all the gold and blues and reds and orchid shades in the prairie landscape," she wrote ER. "These plains are beautiful. But, oh, the terrible hushing drabness of life here. And the suffering, both for people and animals." She responded, too, to the absence of things: austere expanses of plowland, isolated farmhouses, gray-white grain elevators sharp against the horizon, long, arrow-straight roads leading off into an ever-receding distance. Hereabouts one could see the weather coming from a long way off.[25]

A wide, windswept street bisected Bottineau, population 1,700. Points of interest: the grain elevator, a cooperative creamery, a three-story brick Masonic Hall, and a state college offering a two-year program in forestry. North Dakota had legalized 3.2 beer, but in listless Bottineau nobody had applied for a permit to sell it, perhaps because no café owner could afford the $100 license fee. The town claimed its share of the eight hundred Bottineau County families on relief, with fifteen to twenty new applicants every week and many turned away for lack of resources. Hickok settled in on a frigid afternoon after an aborted excursion into the Turtle Mountains; she and Freeman had had to turn back or risk being benighted on roads blocked with ice and snow. There wasn't any snow down on the plain, only a savage northwest wind and the mercury at zero. She took a room in perhaps the worst hotel she'd experienced in all her travels. "There isn't— there can't be—any reason for a hotel to be so hopelessly uninviting as this one is," she wrote ER. "The odor alone is enough to knock you down. Stale soapsuds, old wet rags, some sort of disinfectant. Oh, gosh." And the room was hot, so hot she would find it impossible to sleep.[26]

Bottineau County might have been the most distressed district in North Dakota in the fall of 1933. The inhabitants moved about in a daze. "A sort of nameless dread hangs over the place," Hickok wrote. And it wasn't just the past summer's hail. Harvests had been poor for four years running. Grasshoppers had infested the region during the previous two summers, depositing their eggs in the soil, the farmers said, assuring a return of the scourge in 1934. Hickok had grown up in Wisconsin and South Dakota, but perhaps the ferocity of the plains winters had faded from her memory. In early 1933 the temperature had dropped to 40 below in Bottineau and hovered there for ten days, with fifty-mile-per-hour winds blowing ceaselessly. "And entering that kind of winter we have between 4,000 and 5,000 human beings—men and women and children—without clothing or bedding, getting just enough food to keep them from starving," she lamented. Dreadful, but Hickok knew she'd be away, and for good, at 7 the next morning. Otherwise, she confided to ER, she'd simply call it a day and commit suicide.[27]

Leaving town, Hickok and a county agent visited a relief client's farm, one of the "better" places, or so the agent said. Still, no repairs had been done for years. They crossed the threshold into a bitterly cold interior, falling plaster, newspapers stuffed into cracks in the windows, daylight showing through the walls, the kitchen floor patched with thin metal: old license plates, a wash boiler cover, tin can lids. The two children, boys ages two and four, wore frayed overalls and were barefoot, their toes purple with cold. Their mother, bare-legged, shuffled about in a pair of battered sneakers. She was pregnant and expected to deliver "IN THAT HOUSE" in January. In a tentative voice Hickok asked the investigator whether a doctor would be available to attend her. How to say "Probably not," gently? "I could hardly bear it," Hickok wrote. They inspected the only bed in the house. "One iron bedstead. A filthy, ragged mattress, some dirty pillows—her bed linen, she said, all gave out more than a year ago—and a few old rags of blankets." The family had to pile into it together, to keep from freezing.[28]

"We just hardly know where to begin," the chairman of the county relief board told Hickok. She sent Hopkins a request from teachers at the school in Newburg, a village in the southern part of the county, for overshoes, shoes, mittens, caps, stockings, underwear, dresses, coats, shirts, and overalls to outfit the students. The Newburg Mercantile quoted $55.21 for the full order; the Newburg Cash Store came in at $67.26. Not an extravagant sum, but where would the funds come from? O. T. Strom, a school official, had a notion. "I am taking this up with the Home-makers Club," he wrote the county Emergency Committee. "Will you kindly advise me if you are in position to do anything about this, so as to protect the children's health." Meanwhile the relief chairman told Hickok he needed—now, this minute, urgently—1,200 quilts and 2,000 blankets for families on relief. He needed 3,000 overalls for children, 5,000 suits of underwear, 5,000 pairs of socks, 20,000 yards of dress material, 40,000 yards of flannelette for nightgowns, slips, and bloomers. At retail, the cost would approach $35,000. Perhaps the Home-makers Club would rally round. Up to now, so far as Hickok could tell, the Red Cross hadn't been of much use. The head of the local Red Cross committee had shown her a padlocked storeroom stocked with flannel, cartons of quilts, stockings, sweaters, and underwear. It wasn't enough, Hickok saw at once, but it would help.[29]

She wrote ER, "What really burns me up is a statement made to me today that the Red Cross is holding here, under lock and key, a quantity of sweaters, underwear and blankets—for an 'emergency.' Good God, I wonder what constitutes an emergency in the eyes of the old ladies who run the Red Cross?"[30]

Hickok had reached adulthood in the Dakotas and, hard as life could be at times, or even most of the time, she had never known such distress as she witnessed among the Dakotans of 1933. "At the moment, I'm angry, through and through," she wrote Mrs. Roosevelt. "Almost as angry as I was when I came back from Ky. last Fall." Even so, a brief conversation with Minnie D. Craig of the State Emergency Relief Commission caused her to question whether she had begun to lose perspective. Still more disconcerting, she had a suspicion that her sources were misleading her. "[Craig] told me I'd received an exaggerated impression—that I'd seen the worst places and none of the good places," she informed Hopkins in a handwritten addendum to her November 3 letter. "Well, maybe so." But where were the good places? And in any case, local agents in every part of the state overwhelmed Craig with pleas for help. She passed clothing and bedding requests along to the Red Cross and received a paltry response, only some boys' shirts and ladies' unions and vests and bloomers.[31]

Besides, Minnie Craig surely knew better. She supervised relief in the state's hardest-hit counties. There were few trained social workers in North Dakota, and local men, volunteer experts, sat on the county relief boards. Some were sympathetic and some were not; none had any background for the work. Craig hadn't wanted the post, but the state relief chairman pressed it on her. "You have proven that you can get along with men," Judge Christianson told her. A native of Maine, fifty years old, and an experienced political operative,* Craig left a brief memoir of her months in what, in 1933-34, might have been the most difficult and emotionally draining job in the state. Part of the task involved meeting with—and lecturing—relief clients in county courthouses. Here is a

---

*Minnie Craig served in the North Dakota House of Representatives from 1923 to 1933 and was the first female speaker of the House.

sample question, not necessarily representative, from a client: "Do you think they would send us a hatchet to cut off the county worker's head?"[32]

In her lectures, Craig insisted that clients use their relief benefits solely for the "necessities of life." She recalled an encounter in a grocery with a woman who carried canned pineapple and marshmallows in her market basket:

Craig: Are those necessities of life?

Client: I've wanted to try them my whole life and now's my chance.[33]

Dakotans resisted in other ways too. Craig recorded the story of a wheat farmer near Crosby in the northwest corner of the state who went on the offensive against the grasshoppers. He improvised a hopper killer out of a twelve-foot-long plank attached to a backboard sheathed in galvanized iron, then carefully placed three pans of motor oil on the plank. "With three horses attached to the rig he drove across his field—walking behind the backboard," Craig wrote. "The hoppers rising as the team advanced, flew up—hit the backboard & fell into his oil. He had to dump his load at each end of the field. Huge piles of dead hoppers caused a terrible stench." Later the farmer's wife showed Craig the ruins of her garden. The beans were sticks, "like small pencils stuck in the ground." Everything green had been devoured. Shallow depressions yawned in the arid soil where onions, carrots, and radishes had grown. For this family, disaster came in threes. The farmwife had carefully guarded her turkey poults until she judged it safe to let them range in the barnyard. Before she could intervene, every one had gorged itself on grasshoppers. The poults' craws were so full they suffocated or choked to death.

"This was only one case," Craig wrote. "Multiply it by hundreds and measure the catastrophe!"[34]

Hickok returned to Bismarck on November 3, arriving just ahead of a snowstorm. ("Think of you in snow," ER wrote from temperate Washington. "And I rode this morning without a coat!") In a room at the Hotel Prince that night, wind howling, icy flakes flying slantwise, Hickok attempted a survey of the scene for Hopkins. Federal loan programs weren't working in North Dakota, mostly owing to delays, red tape, an absence of sympathy. She blamed a lot of the trouble on the Minnesota bankers. "Having worked on the [Minneapolis] Tribune for 10 years, I think I know the attitude of the 'money crowd' in the Twin Cities toward the ND farmers. Or any other farmers. They regard them as peasants," she wrote. As it turned out, her initial esteem for Judge Christianson, the state relief director, failed to survive the week's experiences and observations. Hickok left Bismarck on November 4 and wrote Hopkins a summary letter from Ortonville, Minnesota, a couple of days later. She had covered two thousand miles of North Dakota roads. Politically, attacks on the administration were coming from every point of the compass: Republicans complaining about too much New Deal, Democrats complaining about too little, graybeard radicals from the Nonpartisan League ascendancy in 1915 renewing the call for state-owned grain elevators and hail insurance and complaining about the arrogance and power of the Minneapolis bankers.* She sensed trouble on the boil just beneath the state's cracked, frozen surface. Klausler, *The American Mercury* writer, had sensed that too. "The underground grapevine quivers with stories of clubs that resemble the clubs of the days before the French Revolution," he wrote. People were in dire need of food, clothing, fuel. Christianson and other senior relief administrators seemed out of touch, indifferent, or incompetent—and sometimes all three.[35]

Hickok's letters from North Dakota reached Mrs. Roosevelt toward the end of the first week in November, quickening the first lady's sympathies. She wrote, "Poor dear, what sad things you are living through! But you will be able to help, things will be done, and it will be because you have the power to see, feel and write." Not for the first time evidence reached Hickok that things *were* getting done. "The letter from Bottineau came, and I read parts of it to FDR, and he said he hoped clothes and blankets could be got out in a few days," ER wrote on November 5. "That [pregnant] woman haunts me. How do they live through it?" And a few days later: "You are doing a grand job, my dear, and I'm helping where I can. I used your stories yesterday, and shall again today."[36]

---

*A. C. Townley himself, the founder of the Nonpartisan League, came out of retirement to excoriate FDR. "They say he manages to put quite an effective bit of sarcasm into his voice when he says 'the *Pres*–dent,'" Hickok reported.

Mrs. Roosevelt's replies caught up to Hickok in South Dakota, her home country. There she would revisit scenes from adolescence, a time when circumstances forced her, abruptly and prematurely, to come of age and enter the harsh, lonely, and ruthless world of the grown people.

The South Dakota Hickok remembered was "a vast treeless prairie, round and flat, like an empty plate, white in winter, soft, grayish-green in spring, golden in summer." She would claim, as her first memory, light: bright, yellow, probably the sun shining through a window. She recalled too the steady, cleansing Dakota winds, the morning sun rising out of the snow, and the long views to the west at day's end: "the most glorious sunsets I have ever seen." Driving west on U.S. 12, she passed through her girlhood hometowns, Milbank, Summit, and Bowdle, during the week of November 6. The towns and the countryside struck her as gloomier and more desolate than she remembered. Possibly it was the time of year: bleak, chill November. Possibly it was the memories of growing up in the three moribund towns.[37]

"Miles and miles of flat brown country," she wrote Hopkins. "Snowdrifts here and there. Russian thistles rolling across the roads. Unpainted buildings, all going to seed. Hardly a straw stack or a hay stack for miles. Now and then a shabby little town spread out around two or three gaunt, ugly grain elevators. What a country—to keep out of!"[38]

Nothing much had changed in Milbank, Summit, and Bowdle. "They were all the same size as they were when I left Dakota 25 years ago!" she went on. "Hardly a new house. On the main street of Bowdle there was a big gap where there were no buildings at all. Someone said they'd had a fire there 15 or 20 years ago." *The Bowdle Pioneer* reported that twenty-nine families were on relief in early November and that the relief board had taken delivery of 320 pounds of AAA salt pork. A brief article summarized the benefits of the corn-hog loan program. The high school football team was about to play its first home game of the season. Wheat prices were disastrous: No. 1 at 64 cents a bushel, durum at 63 cents.[39]

The New Deal can't have made much of a difference in such places. Even in 1933 their time had passed. Today Bowdle's streets are dusty still, the concrete sidewalks cracked; the inevitable grain elevator rises "gaunt, ugly" above the railroad tracks on the northern edge of town. In summer the place is quiet and shady under an umbrella of trees. The burnt-out block, rebuilt some decades ago, houses Lassle's Café, the Bird's Nest Inn, and the Black Hat Tavern. Few people are about; the place has a forlorn feel. The wind blows ceaselessly, stirring the dust and hurrying along bits of paper and plastic, the twenty-first-century equivalent of Russian thistle. There are two substantial stone churches, St. Augustine's Roman Catholic and St. John's Lutheran. Fields of sunflowers lap the skirts of town, the only cheerful sight thereabouts aside from the metal cap of Bowdle's water tower, painted turquoise.

In parts of South Dakota the farm strike still flared. Writing to Hopkins on November 7, Hickok reported most of the creameries were shut down along the Yellowstone Trail (U.S. 12) from the Minnesota line to Aberdeen, the state's third-largest city and, in the 1930s, the biggest place along an airline distance of a thousand miles from Minneapolis to Butte, Montana. Ralph Hansmeier farmed three thousand acres and owned a grain elevator near Webster, fifty miles east of Aberdeen. In better times he employed twenty men on the place; drought, grasshoppers, and falling prices forced him to lay off a dozen hands and reduce the others' wages. Now Hansmeier headed the Day County Farmers' Holiday Association. His aims were modest. "All we ask is that we get what it costs to produce our crops," he said. "We don't even ask for a profit. Don't you see, we have only one weapon left. We've exhausted our voices. All there is left for us is resistance." He didn't believe the strike would accomplish much, but he could imagine no other option.[40]

"Cheer up," Hickok wrote Hopkins from Aberdeen. "I'll be brief. It's been a long day, and I'm tired." The letter contained scarcely a cheerful word, though. In Webster Hickok interviewed the Day County attorney, a man named Lewis Bicknell, who blamed Communists for the farm agitation. Hickok had seen enough by now to dismiss the charge. Even so, she noted about the Communists, "There's no doubt that they are very, very busy. Getting right down among the farmers and working like beavers." Just as she finished up in North Dakota, farmers had broken up a foreclosure sale in Oaks and chased a state relief investigator out of the town of

Ellendale. There were outbursts, too, at foreclosure sales in South Dakota, most recently in Milbank and Watertown. "All that sort of thing, Bicknell believes, may lead to a good deal of bloodshed and disorder before the winter is over," Hickok reported. Then too, the FHA's Hansmeier asserted that conditions in his state actually were worse than those in North Dakota.[41]

The farm strike led the *Aberdeen Evening News* for several days running. NRA director Hugh Johnson shared front-page billing with the FHA on November 6, the story appearing under the headline "Johnson Midwest Tour Aims to Pacify Strikers." A champion scold, the director would have seemed more likely to inflame than soothe the rustics. "Somebody ought to come out here," Hickok advised Hopkins. "NOT General Johnson or Mr. Wallace . . . making speeches in Chicago, the Twin Cities or Des Moines. Someone who could travel about quietly, without a lot of puff and blow and newspapers." The envoy should *talk* to the farmers and *listen* to what they had to say. This sounded curiously like her own job description, but Hickok doubted she could handle the larger task. She thought she had mastered the relief setup but lacked confidence in her ability to explain the intricacies of the array of New Deal grant, loan, livestock, acreage reduction, and other expedients intended to improve the farmers' lot.[42]

In a joint meeting with the Brown County FHA chapter, Aberdeen merchants and businessmen expressed support for the farmers, the *Evening News* reported. In Pierre, the capital, Governor Berry said he doubted the strike would be effective and declined to intervene. The FHA vowed on November 8 to try to block all sales of farm products except in cases of actual distress. To keep people from falling even deeper into debt, the strikers agreed to allow sales of poultry, cream, butter, and eggs. With FHA approval, an occasional sale of livestock might be permitted. Berry refused the strikers' request to embargo the state's grain, cattle, and hogs. "We didn't raise enough farm products in South Dakota this year to supply New York City with one good breakfast," the governor said. Nobody knew that better than the Brown County strikers. The parched and pestilential summer left them with hardly any wheat to withhold, and so far the autumn had been dry too. In Webster the weekly *Reporter and Farmer* noted that only trace amounts of rain had fallen during the month of October.[43]

Ordinary life went on in Aberdeen as elsewhere. The season's first snow drifted down the night of November 4, whitening the ground and clinging to the bare branches of the trees. The comic melodrama *Tillie & Gus*, with W. C. Fields, had feature billing at the Capitol Theatre. At the Astor, Ginger Rogers starred in *Professional Sweetheart*, playing a singing and dancing pitch girl for Ippsie-Wippsie washcloths. In a banner headline, *The Evening News* announced the demise of Prohibition, anodyne to drinkers everywhere. The Aberdeen Public Library lent 18,838 books in October. In distant Washington, President Roosevelt announced the Civil Works Administration jobs program and the allocation of $150 million for corn loans.[44]

West of Aberdeen, the once-thriving town of Mobridge wore a forsaken look, its railroad lifeline all but severed. Established on the site of Arikara and Sioux villages in 1906, when Milwaukee Railroad engineers threw a bridge across the Missouri River there, the place gained its name from a telegrapher's abbreviation, "Mo. Bridge." The railroad built maintenance and repair shops that once employed hundreds in the town. As Hickok explained to Hopkins, the development of longer-haul locomotives all but put Mobridge out of business. The shops were moved west into Montana, and Milwaukee Railroad employment in Mobridge declined to fewer than twenty men. She wrote, "Most of the men who used to work in the shops have been out of work for two or three years! They haven't even enough money to get out of Mobridge! And so there it sits—with the west wind howling down its wide, empty streets. Everybody just stays home and mopes." Even the ranchers, confident, sun- and wind-burned men in their ten-gallon hats and cowboy boots, still a common sight on the streets and in the shops and speakeasies, seemed diminished now.[45]

Living out of a suitcase, Hickok observed, gave one a measure of the desolation of the country. Even the newer hotels were abysmal. She had stayed in fairly modern places in Aberdeen and Mobridge. "They are simply going to seed," she wrote Hopkins. "Practically empty most of the time—I don't believe there were half a dozen guests in the Mobridge hotel last night—they don't bring in even enough money so their furniture, plumbing and so on can be properly kept up." These days, the bromide "safe as houses" had been drained of meaning. Real estate was only a tax liability now; one couldn't "raise five cents at a bank on any of it," even newish hotel buildings.[46]

Hickok dropped down to Pierre on November 9, stopping at the state capitol to listen, "incog," as she put it, to a powerful current of complaint from farmers, merchants, Rotarians, and a delegation of "malcontents" from west of the Missouri. Much of the anguish expressed to the state relief administrator involved the so-called "4-4-2" limit on federal livestock aid: four horses, four cows, two brood sows (and twenty chickens). Hickok took down the comments more or less word for word, collated them that night in her room at the St. Charles Hotel, and mailed them off to Hopkins.

Cattle are so cheap now that the man who has to sell down to four will lose so much—well, he can't do it, that's all.

If you make our farmers reduce to that limit, they'll be on relief for years to come. You'll be making paupers of them. You'll be forcing them into bankruptcy.

If prosperity should return next summer, the city man gets a job and becomes self-supporting. But a farmer on that 4-4-2 basis can't be self-supporting. When the government confiscates the factory where the city man earns his living, we'll be satisfied to let the government sacrifice our stock.[47]

Later, meeting privately with Hickok, Governor Berry conceded the farmers had a strong case; the 4-4-2 limit was too low. She liked and respected the bantam cowboy and believed his views were worth a hearing: "I don't know a Hell of a lot about being Governor," he told her, "but there ain't a damned thing I don't know about a cow!" A strong supporter of the administration, Berry declined to challenge the 4-4-2 policy publicly, and he shied from asking Harry Hopkins to increase the limit. "He is afraid you will think him ungrateful," she wrote Hopkins. "He asked me several times to be sure not to give you the impression that he was kicking. Well, he certainly is NOT."[48]

"Dammit," Hickok's November 10 report to Hopkins began, "I don't WANT to write you again tonight. It's been a long, long day, and I'm tired." She halted for the night in the town of Winner in grassland and hill country south of Pierre, one of the youngest settlements in the state and "one of the most typically western in color," according to a South Dakota guidebook. Still, things were looking up a bit for Hickok, despite her weariness. Arriving just before dark after a spectacular Dakota sunset, she found "a nice little town with a fairly decent hotel," she wrote Mrs. Roosevelt. The afterglow "covered the whole sky," she went on, "and the colors on the buttes were beautiful beyond description." In better times the town had prospered as a shipping point for poultry raised in the hinterland and as a busy trading center for a long stretch of U.S. 18, an east–west trunk road. Good pheasant shooting thereabouts drew crowds of hunters in the autumn, a boon to Winner's lodging places and restaurants. As additional evidence of the aptness of the name, the future legendary Notre Dame football coach Frank Leahy went to high school in Winner.[49]

On balance, though, the day had been discouraging, like so many others since Hickok first took to the roads in Pennsylvania in August. She spent it in Rosebud country (wild roses bloomed in profusion there), a lovely name for a desolate region. A treaty of 1868 set aside a vast expanse of what is now western South Dakota for the Sioux; by 1910 most of the area had been opened to white homesteaders. In 1933 only Todd County, perhaps the poorest county in a beggared state, remained in reserve. Berry had told Hickok the lands west of the Missouri probably never should have been opened to settlement. The prairie grasses long since had been overgrazed or plowed under, leaving the Rosebud region's sandy soil vulnerable to wind erosion, especially now that drought had taken hold. Half the population consisted of Indians living abjectly in tents and shacks.[50]

Hickok stopped to inspect a country school near Mission, "a horrid little town" at the crossroads of U.S. 12 and 83. She wrote ER, "I found to my astonishment a ladylike youth with all the mannerisms of a 'fairy,' teaching a crowd of the dirtiest and toughest looking children you ever saw—mostly Indians." The building was crowded and dirty, the air vile. There were picturesque elements too: "Wandering about the schoolyard were six or eight shaggy cow ponies, and beside the door a pile of saddles. They ride to school." The teacher remarked that the students were fairly warmly dressed and brought decent lunches to school. But their teeth were terrible. As elsewhere, relief payments in South Dakota failed to

cover dental care. Indian or white, Hickok observed, families in the Rosebud country produced bumper crops of children. She met one woman
near White River with ten offspring and an eleventh on the way. The
mother couldn't remember all their names, referring to them in Hickok's
presence as "this little girl" and "that little boy."[51]

Turning northeast on November 11, Hickok shaped a course for
Huron, Beadle County, set in a once fertile region of level, unvarying
prairie, home of the South Dakota State Fair. The route led through what
Hickok called "the grasshopper area," thousands of acres that looked as
if they'd just been plowed. "They haven't been," she informed Mrs.
Roosevelt. "What happened was the grasshoppers simply cleaned them
off—right down to the earth, even eating the roots. And there they lie,
great black patches on the landscape, completely bare." Grasshoppers devoured the standing grain and every spear of grass. They stripped the
bark off trees. "People were afraid to hang their washing out," she went
on. "They even ate the clothes off the line." The hoppers left nothing
for people or animals. The horses were dull-eyed, gaunt, with protrud-
ing ribs. "Sometimes they would come toward us with a sort of hopeful
look, as if they thought we might be bringing them something to eat,"
she wrote. "The owners . . . have simply turned them loose to get along
as best they can, hoping that a few of them would survive. It would be
more merciful to shoot them." Horses dropped dead from starvation in
the barnyards. And they dropped dead in harness, on work relief road
jobs that were far beyond their feeble strength.[52]

The wind picked up during the night, rising to a sixty-mile-an-hour
gale by daybreak. When Hickok arose at 7:30 and looked out the window
of her hotel room in Huron she noticed "a queer brown haze—only right
above was the sky clear." The wind shrieked and the brown haze climbed
higher and higher into the sky. She and her guide, a polished and attractive half-Indian social worker, a woman of forty or so, finished breakfast
and were ready to start for a tour of the countryside by 9 o'clock. By then,
she wrote ER, "the sun was only a lighter spot that filled the dust in the
sky like a brown fog." They set out anyway, driving ten miles or so out
of town before the black blizzard forced them to turn back. The wind
roared. The Weather Bureau would report visibility at zero during the

fiercest hours of the storm, from about ten in the morning until noon, when the sky was dark as moonless midnight.[53]

The gale rocked the social worker's Ford so violently Hickok wondered whether it actually might be blown off the road. When they stopped—able to see only a foot or so ahead, they just crept along—they engaged the emergency brake to keep the car from rolling forward, driven by the wind at their back. Hickok had experienced dust storms as a child, though none like this one. "It was a truly terrifying experience," she wrote ER, "as though we had left the earth. We were being whirled off into space in a vast, impenetrable cloud of dust." They crept back to Huron. The street lights, those still standing anyway, were burning, and by noon the thick brown blanket of airborne earth blotted out the sun. Hickok sought the safety of the hotel, no longer a flea trap but a refuge. "I was lying on the bed reading the paper and glanced up—the window looked black, just as it does at night," she went on. "I was terrified, for a moment. It seemed like the end of the world." The wind began to abate by sundown, and later, as the dust settled, one could look straight up into the sky and see the stars.[54]

With pardonable exaggeration, the local newspaper, *The Evening Huronite*, called it "the most severe dust storm in history." Huron and its hinterland were a moonscape of disaster. Brown sand lay in broad drifts. Phone, power, and telegraph lines were down. The storm blew out windows and shrouded homes, shops, and offices in layers of dust, while the ditches filled with silt. Communications went awry; static disrupted transmissions over the few lines that remained in service. Dust worked its way into the mechanism of the paper's linotype machines. "For about the first hour this morning," according to *The Huronite*, "they turned out type that might have been used for a Chinese newspaper." Still, the presses rolled heroically, and the paper, packed with storm coverage, appeared on schedule on November 12. The staffers thought they detected a silver lining: "The wind took off so much dirt that plants will have about a foot-and-a-half less to go before reaching subsurface moisture next spring." Were the editors being heavily humorous? Perhaps they were providing a form of public service, the newspaper's contribution to maintaining readers' morale as they coughed and wheezed their way back to normality.[55]

As Hickok made ready to exit the state, she offered Kathryn Godwin advice on how she might make use of her experiences there. "If your son misbehaves and you want to make him mind, just say to him: 'You do as I say, or I'll send you to Dakota!'" She would forward Hopkins a wrap-up of her South Dakota investigations from Lincoln, Nebraska, a week or so later. The strongest theme was fear: Dakotans were afraid of grasshoppers, afraid of drought, afraid of dust storms, afraid of their debt load, afraid their livestock would die, afraid of losing their farms, afraid for their children. "Those people are afraid of the future," she saw. "Some of them are almost hysterical." For dinner, Russian thistle soup: people cut the thistles green, dried the marrow of the plant, and stewed it up with flour and water.[56]

"If the President ever becomes dictator," Hickok suggested to Hopkins, "I've got a grand idea for him. He can label this country out here 'Siberia' and send all his exiles here. A more hopeless place I never saw."[57]

7

"THE RICHEST VILLAGE IN THE WORLD"

Nebraska, Iowa, and Minnesota, November–December 1933

The splendors of Omaha's Castle Hotel had faded. Faded, too, were the prospects of the farmers who crowded into the Castle's smoky, flyblown lobby during the third week in November 1933. Looking in on a National Farmers Union convention for Harry Hopkins, Lorena Hickok found the venue of the Castle lowering to the spirit, "with worn, sagging leather sofas and chairs, paintings of naked ladies on the walls, cigar ashes all over the floor, untidy bellhops in worn, soiled uniforms." The place had a hangdog air, only too familiar to Hickok after nearly a month of travel in the region of the Middle Border. The farmers, up to five hundred of them, gathered for their meetings in the hotel ballroom, "probably the last word in elegance west of the Missouri forty or fifty years ago." Not any longer; to Hickok the city and the visitors seemed of a piece. According to a New Deal–era guide-book, "Omaha has not yet lost a sense of surprise over becoming a big town: at least it is still a city in the making, with Saturday night brawls, 'drug-store cowboys' and packing house workers on parade." The place and the crowd struck her as funny and pathetic, in more or less equal parts.[1]

A woman on the margins, Hickok nearly always wrote with sympathy of the people she encountered, shell-shocked victims of a calamity nobody had foreseen. Not this time. The convention—the speeches, the resolutions, the ballroom—unsettled her, perhaps because the atmosphere so powerfully evoked her own Dakota years. "It had elements of a country church social, an old-fashioned camp meeting, and a 'red rally' in Union Square, New York," she wrote Eleanor Roosevelt. Possibly the farmer-politicians' strong antiadministration tone put her on the defensive. The cowboys in their high-heeled boots looked nervous, the dirt farmers ill at ease in their "store clothes." The men turned up with cruel haircuts that left strips of unhealthy-looking white above their leathery necks. Their wives, timid and frumpy, wore styles four or five years out of date. An off-key trio from western Nebraska warbled freshly made-up words to the tune of "Happy Days Are Here Again." The homespun entertainment also included a "home talent" orchestra from South Dakota and the Williams Sisters of Endicott, Nebraska, a three-child ensemble that reminded Hickok of her own youthful public singing ordeal. After the performance their father, a little man with curly hair and spectacles, marched the children to the ballroom entrance to position them for the anticipated shower of compliments from the hayseeds.

"God, it was depressing," she wrote ER.[2]

The politicians worked the lobby crowd confidently, pumping hands and thumping backs. "Town men," Hickok observed. "Perfectly at ease. Accustomed to being in cities and hotels." They flattered the rustics, pushing their panaceas—cooperatives, cost of production plus profit, cheap money, direct action—in confidential murmurs while a dance band caterwauled from a radio loudspeaker. John Simpson, the Farmers Union president, reminded Hickok of the more furtive sort of evangelist. "Calls everybody brother," she complained to ER. "God how his type irritates me." The thirty-one-year-old farmers' union, a mild-mannered offspring of the 1890s Populist movement, lobbied for producer co-ops and other sales and marketing initiatives. Simpson called, too, for the immemorial Populist nostrums: curbs on bankers' power, the remonetization of silver, and a cascade of greenbacks: $27 billion worth. H. G. Keeney, the head of the politically conservative Nebraska chapter of the union, promoted grain, dairy, and livestock cooperatives and machinery, clothing, and food exchanges.[3]

Quoting *The Omaha World-Herald*'s farm beat reporter, Hickok reserved her harshest words for the frontman for the Farmers' Holiday Association. "Nine of ten farmers have no use for Milo Reno," Kenneth McCandless told her. "He's just a racketeer. He got control of the Farmers' Union over in Iowa, took all its money, and wrecked it." Agricultural Adjustment Administration benefit programs were beginning to undercut the FHA, and expectations were that Reno and his executive committee would soon call off the farm strike. "Checks from the AAA were descending in a gentle rain on the land, damping the prairie fires of farmers' anger," *Time* magazine waxed poetically. More people turned out for the National Cornhusking Championship on Ben Stalp's farm in West Point, Nebraska, than were turning up to walk Reno's picket lines. (A Nebraska man won the title, with a precisely tabulated 27.62 bushels in the allotted eighty minutes, out-husking finalists from Indiana, Illinois, and Minnesota.) Said McCandless of the FHA leaders, "Right now, they're licked, and they know it. Reno may think up some new ideas—if he stays sober." Hickok presented Reno as a "cheap little organizer" and to add insult to injury likened him to a fat Judd Gray, the corset salesman who had been electrocuted at Sing Sing Prison in 1928 for collaborating with his mistress in the murder of her husband.[4]

Hickok passed up an opportunity to interview Reno, writing ER, "I took one look at the guy, heard him talk for a few minutes, whispered to myself, 'Oh, hell.' Then I left. I couldn't bear it." Writing in *The New Republic*, Bruce Bliven permitted Reno to speak for himself. With 25 million hungry Americans there could be no overproduction, he said. *"For the government to destroy food and reduce crops at such a time is wicked. The scheme won't work, and it would be wrong if it did."* Wheat allotments and corn loans were simply a dole, according to Reno. Instead, the government should fix prices to guarantee farmers an adequate return on their capital and labor. *"That seems to us a reasonable demand. We intend to keep on agitating until we get justice."* Still, Bliven's reporting tended to confirm Hickok's impressionistic view: nobody could say how many farmers backed Reno (Bliven guessed only one in ten supported the farm strike), the uprising had little discernible economic effect, and most farmers were perfectly willing to accept the government's checks.[5]

The Des Moines Register and Leader had compiled the most detailed survey yet of the trend of corn and hog farmers' thinking. The newspaper deployed a brigade of reporters armed with carefully crafted questions into selected Iowa counties, talking to scores of farmers in each locale. The result: 14 percent of those polled approved of the farm strike; 77 percent were opposed. Most said a strike would never attract enough support to make a difference, and more than a third favored the AAA's corn and hog reduction program. Most farmers wondered what the government planned to do with all the corn it bought, but 56 percent approved the loan scheme. FDR drew nearly a 75 percent approval rating. As H. G. Keeney told Hickok, "The average of us believes in giving the President and the crowd down there in Washington a chance. We don't like Mr. Wallace much, but—we're willing to wait awhile and see what happens." Even Simpson endorsed Roosevelt's efforts as far as they went.[6]

As always, Hickok read the local press with close attention. The critical tide flowed strongest against Agriculture Secretary Henry Wallace, the architect of the AAA's reduction schemes, in Minnesota and the Dakotas, where nearly all the influential newspapers were Republican. "Up until recently," she explained to Hopkins, "they haven't dared to attack the President. They are now, and getting a little bolder all the time." The Omaha convention worked overtime in abusing Wallace, but Nebraska's governor Charles Bryan, an anti-administration Democrat and one of the keynoters, assailed FDR without restraint. The president had not done nearly enough. "Old man depression needs more than a shot in the arm," Bryan said. "He needs a load of slugs in the face." Hickok listened to the radio broadcast of the speech, Bryan's first after a long, debilitating illness. He had a balky heart, had only just gotten back on his feet, and spoke haltingly, in a weak, high voice. (She wondered, "Can this be the brother of the man who made the 'Cross of Gold' speech?") The substance centered on a call for cheap money. When she interviewed Bryan at the capitol in Lincoln, he spent an hour or so "yowling" about inflation, then ended up boasting "with the naivete of a child" about the sumptuousness of his office furnishings.[7]

As it happened, the leading Nebraska newspapers were friendly to Roosevelt and the New Deal. By Hickok's count, page 1 of The World-Herald on November 20 carried five stories favorable to the administration, including an advance on Eleanor Roosevelt's White House conference on women, the Depression, and the Civil Works Administration. In Lincoln, The Star came on strong for Roosevelt. James E. Lawrence, The Star's managing editor, told her as many as 80,000 of the state's 117,000 farm families subscribed to one paper or the other. "It isn't only their editorials that count," she wrote Hopkins. "They play up in a favorable way the things Wallace and [Assistant Treasury Secretary Henry] Morgenthau and [AAA Administrator George] Peek are doing. They do a lot of that 'missionary work' that, it seems to me, is so badly needed in the Dakotas and Minnesota." Then too, Lawrence impressed her as more knowledgeable about the relief situation in Nebraska than were many top officials. From what he suggested, Hickok calculated that the state's relief effort lagged eighteen months or so behind others she had investigated.[8]

Problems were most acute in the sprawling, sparsely settled western counties; one covered 9,500 square miles. In some districts out there, Hickok told Hopkins, the relief rolls contained only two or three families, and not because most western Nebraskans were holding their own. Grasshoppers and drought had hit the western regions hard. Keeney, the state farmers' union head, predicted that relief applications would spike in the west as Hopkins's Civil Works Administration gained momentum. "Those fellows don't like to go on the county," Keeney said. "They'll almost starve first. What they want is jobs." The jobs would be coming, and soon. In contrast with the relief bureau, Nebraska's Public Works Board had moved aggressively to plan jobs projects, including an ambitious $42 million irrigation scheme. In Lincoln, men were already at work digging a sewer system. So when the first installment of Hopkins's CWA money arrived, perhaps as soon as the end of the month, the Nebraska board would be prepared to spend it.[9]

The farmers' convention closed with a flourish. The FHA executive board called a face-saving "temporary truce" in the farm strike. The delegates voted one of the few leaders who had spoken in support of Roosevelt off the union's national board and reelected Simpson to another term as president. He celebrated by throwing a punch at one of his fiercest critics, a farm paper editor from Minnesota named A. W. Ricker. It landed on the side of Ricker's head.

"I'm only sorry I didn't knock him down," Simpson said.[10]

"Three loud cheers for CWA!"

Hickok moved in and out of Sioux City over the course of a week, operating from the Warrior Hotel as she observed the start-up of the Civil Works Administration program in Iowa. Tough and gritty, climbing from the river bottoms onto the wooded bluffs between the points where two tributaries empty into the Missouri, the town had become the chief livestock market for a five-state region. As the saying went, Sioux City's seventy-nine thousand residents relied on "crops and litters" for their prosperity;* by 1929 the city's stockyards and packing plants employed fully a third of the workforce. An average of nearly five hundred truckloads of livestock rolled into Sioux City every day, making it the largest trucked-in stock market in the United States, with a capacity of 45,000 pigs and 25,000 cattle. But by the early 1930s the packers were shedding jobs, cutting wages, and assaulting unions. For more than a month in 1932 the FHA farm strike had convulsed Sioux City, virtually shutting down the yards, feedlots, slaughterhouses, and packing plants. More than a thousand Woodbury County farmers blocked the main routes leading into town, U.S. 20 from the east, U.S. 75 from the north and south.[11] On April 17, 1933, Sioux City became the first municipality in Iowa to make the sale of 3.2 beer legal, boosting workers' morale, if only temporarily.

A center of International Workers of the World agitation as early as 1914, Sioux City glanced back on a proud history of radicalism. The Social Gospeller Wallace Short's pro-labor views led to his ejection in 1914 from the pastorate of the First Congregational Church; with workers' backing, he won election as mayor in 1918 despite the intense opposition of Sioux City business leaders and the two principal newspapers, *The Tribune* and *The Journal*. Short's tolerance of the IWW during his six years in office earned the city the nickname "Wobbly Capital of the United States." In 1932 Woodbury County recorded three times more pending farm foreclosures than any other county in the state. The farmer uprising thus unfolded with unusual ferocity in western Iowa, with Wallace Short a major force in the Holiday movement.[12]

> *Let's call a farmers' holiday*
> *A holiday let's hold*
> *We'll eat our wheat and ham and eggs*
> *And let them eat their gold.*[13]

---

*Sioux City's first Corn Palace, a wooden skeleton with a skin of sheaves of grain and red, yellow, and white corn, went up in 1887.

Farmer discontent boiled over again in the autumn of 1933, "the Sioux City farm war," *The Tribune* called the renewed outbreak. Once again, strikers and truck drivers skirmished along the main roads leading into town. In a series of incidents in early November, pickets stopped trucks and turned loose two hundred hogs and cattle, spoiled a butter delivery valued at $200, and fired on blockade runners. Three truckers were stabbed or beaten. By November 3, *The Tribune* reported, the city's milk supply had been cut in half. A vigilante group, the Law and Order League, mobilized flying squads to reinforce the police and carry out offensive operations. The insurgents were less steadfast now, partly because they resented the intrusions of professional radicals, and also because New Deal cash benefits were beginning to flow to farmers. By November 7 the Law and Order League claimed to have put the strikers to the rout. By the 9th, *The Tribune* reported, all roads into Sioux City were open.[14]

On first impression, Hickok concluded that Sioux City native Harry Hopkins's CWA would quell the radical threat, or anyhow undermine it. She inspected a road project on the damp, gray morning of November 23, twenty-man crews building up shoulders along a narrow paved thoroughfare. "It was a nasty morning. Cold. And sleet," she wrote Hopkins. "But they looked cheerful. Thirty-hour week, 40 cents an hour—CASH, instead of grocery orders." Sioux City, she reminded Hopkins, "is a hotbed of reds," with strikes and demonstrations endemic. A few days earlier, a mob had threatened to kidnap one relief director and lynch another. Police arrested some "known Reds" and an uneasy calm prevailed for now. "Of course there are only a few of them who are communists," Hickok went on. "The rest are dissatisfied unemployed who follow along." Those CWA paychecks, she thought, were bound to reduce the ranks of the disaffected, at least temporarily.[15]

"Here's ONE spot in the United States where things are 'looking up.' Today was the first CWA pay day in the state of Iowa," Hickok reported from Des Moines on November 25. "Something over 5,000 men, who went to work with picks and shovels and wheelbarrows last Monday morning, lined up and got paid—MONEY." Hundreds if not thousands of men were handling greenbacks and silver for the first time in months. "They took it with wide grins and made for the grocery stores, NOT to shove a grocery order across the counter, but to go where they pleased and buy what they pleased, with cash," she wrote. "And along about a week from today these and many thousands more will be dropping into the dry goods stores, too, and the clothing stores." The effects on people's morale were immediate and, Sioux City mayor W. D. Hayes told her, almost beyond calculating.[16]

The launch of the CWA was an astonishing demonstration of bureaucratic agility and dash. "If we are talking about putting four million men to work by December 15, somebody has got to step on it," Hopkins had said in mid-November. The CWA program in Iowa was up and running within twenty-four hours of the state relief director's return from a November 17 conference in Washington with Hopkins and his staff. F. W. Mullock stepped off the train at Union Station in Des Moines at 7:30 Sunday morning the 19th, and on Monday men in Iowa's sixteen most populous counties were on the job. "And did they want to work?" Hickok's question was rhetorical. "In Sioux City they actually had fist fights over shovels." Officials there launched seven separate public works projects at 7 o'clock in the morning of November 20, including grading and landscaping at Bridges Park, where two hundred workers filled seventeen trucks with soil to be recycled from hilltops to low places. The city ran two shifts totaling 1,100 men, 7 to noon and noon to 5, paying 50 cents an hour or $2.50 a day. Jobs initially went only to married men with dependents, and hundreds of applicants were turned away. "There will be work for all," they were told. "Just be patient." By November 23, 1,300 men had been taken off relief and added to the CWA payroll; 1,700 were working altogether. The first paychecks were handed out in Sioux City on November 27, $13,442 to 1,567 men for four days of the first CWA work week.[17]

By late November, fifteen thousand Iowans were employed on $13 million worth of projects, the first installment of a projected fifty-three thousand CWA jobs in the state. Nationally the CWA transferred 2 million men from relief rolls to payrolls almost from one day to the next.[18]

Hickok went out again on November 24, a cold, raw, breezy Friday, to observe the CWA in action; Sioux City crews were building a swimming pool in a public park, mending roads, and expanding a waterworks system. "You never saw shovels fly faster in your life," she wrote Hopkins. At Stone Park, with its hilltop view of three states, men using spades and wheelbarrows leveled a site for a water tower. From the first, officials and workers overflowed with enthusiasm for the program, a powerful political boost for the Roosevelt administration. "They tell me they are feeling better than they have in years," Hickok reported, "and that anyone who was through here a month ago wouldn't even recognize the state now! Why, they're not even panning Mr. Wallace around here!" In addition, she cited a major advantage (other than speed) of the CWA over Harold Ickes's Public Works Administration projects. Ickes's contractors preferred using heavy machinery to men with hand tools. Machines were easier to manage and more efficient. CWA workers were unskilled; in many cases, they were professional people or artisans, inexperienced and awkward in handling their tools. But the point of the CWA was to employ people, to put *earned* money into people's pockets.[19]

The CWA checks arrived two days after the first two corn loan payments reached Woodbury County farmers, one for $1,350 for three thousand bushels and another for $800 for two thousand bushels. For the most part, people used the newfound cash to cover daily living expenses and pay overdue rent and bills. There were occasional indulgences, pleasures more or less guilty. Hickok happened to be visiting a relief office in South Sioux City, Nebraska, when a tall, gray-haired man of sixty or so approached an investigator. "Well, I bought that ring," he confessed. He'd allowed his daughter to order a high school class ring, price $4.95, the previous spring. "When, because of the newspaper ballyhoo, people got an erroneous impression of how fast the New Deal was going to move, this man felt sure he would have a job by now," Hickok explained. In the event, he could find only a couple of weeks of temporary work toward the end of the summer. That job had ended, and in a week or so he figured to be back on relief. "Most of the time, while she's been growing up, I've been out of work," he said. "It's always been, 'You can't have this' and 'You can't do that,' because we couldn't afford it." The relief director had taken a procedural risk and told him to go ahead and buy the ring. The tale ended happily. The girl would get the bauble, the director escaped a reprimand, and the paterfamilias had been told to turn up at a CWA job site on Monday morning.[20]

Though Hickok's reports generally trumpeted the CWA, she included a couple of caveats. Sources told her the unions were trying to "coerce" workers into joining, saying they wouldn't be eligible for CWA jobs unless they could produce a union card. American Federation of Labor leaders wanted to reserve available jobs for union members. "I don't think they're playing fair with us," Hickok wrote. She suspected, too, that American Legion organizers were working a similar racket. "I've heard repeatedly that the American Legion, under the soldier preference law, is trying to use CWA to build up its membership—i.e., telling the boys they have to belong to the American Legion to get CWA jobs." And the loan sharks were moving in, preying on workers clutching their first paychecks in a long, long time. "They're getting busy—right on the job," she reported. "I don't see how anything could be done about this, however. But, gosh—if the average American only had more brains!" The CWA conjured up all manner of good feelings, but everybody knew the program would cease to exist after four months. In an allusion to Ickes's notorious caution, she added that the Public Works Administration should be prepared to take up the slack when the CWA passed from the scene: "They simply MUST be ready."[21]

Hickok continued to pass along strong reactions to Hugh Johnson's National Recovery Administration. "You see," she wrote Mrs. Roosevelt, "a Blue Eagle doesn't mean much when it's unpopular both with the retailers *and* the consumer. Why, half the stores here don't even display them, and most of those you do see are all faded and curled up and covered with dust." NRA codes? Lots of Iowa businesses, especially smaller ones, simply ignored them. "Hotels, for instance," she went on. "You see the same crew on all day and far into the night. Some hotels have only one waitress." She cited the example of the Warrior, a new hotel with three hundred rooms. Built for $1.25 million, it had opened in 1930. She had taken daily board at the hotel coffee shop; the waitress who served her dinner in the early evening turned up the next morning at 6:30 to serve breakfast. Hickok doubted the hotel could take on any more help and remain solvent. "Walk up to the desk in any of these hotels and look over the mail boxes," she suggested. "Certainly 80 percent of them will be empty, with the keys lying in them." Consumers complained too. "NRA is not at all popular," she told ER. "Well, how *could* it be? Their prices *did* go up faster than their incomes." Still, she guessed that most small businesses would comply with the codes—so long as they could afford to. As matters stood, though, she thought the NRA should simply leave the small merchants and businessmen alone.[22]

With the Land Bank man Richard Freeman driving, Hickok headed east from Sioux City to Des Moines late on November 24. The leaves had fallen, the crops were gathered in, and the stubble fields, the sodden dark earth, and the country towns along U.S. 20—Moville, Holstein, Rockwell City, Webster City—showed the drab tones of early winter. She spent Saturday in the capital in meetings with Governor Clyde Herring, the state relief director, the federal reemployment director, and her newspaper connections. For the moment, her mood turned uncharacteristically buoyant, despite the rigors of the carpetbagging life. "Another letter for the boss," she wrote Kathryn Godwin from Des Moines. "As for me, I haven't felt so optimistic for months. This thing is going to WORK!" She and Freeman shoved off Sunday morning, following the valley of the Des Moines River southeast to Ottumwa. Hickok slept through most of the three-hour drive. "I've been living in hotels so long I'm beginning to get grouchy," she told Godwin. "But, even so, I wouldn't give up the job. Maybe you think this trip hasn't been interesting! And when I get through working for the Government, I think I'll run a hotel. Believe me, I've got plenty of ideas!" They reached Ottumwa around 2 o'clock and she descended into a heavy sleep not long after the bellhop let her into the room.[23]

Hickok awoke at 5, just as the day was drawing in. Her room looked to the west across undulating country into the afterglow of a glorious sunset. "The day has been simply beautiful," she wrote ER that night. Ottumwa was the girlhood home of one of her heroes, the novelist Edna Ferber. But her irritation mounted as she turned the pages of the Sunday papers. "I think I shall have to quit reading *The Chicago Tribune*. Their latest was to run—today—two weeks after it was all over—pages of farm strike pictures. Battles! They looked to me as though they'd been posed, by the scrub football teams of Northwestern and Chicago! They do make me so damned mad!" At least the Des Moines papers, irredeemably Republican though they were, gave prominent play to the arrival of the first corn loan payments. Even as she went on with the letter to ER, an unaccountable weariness settled over her, and she could feel her mood retracing the arc. She meant to tot up two weeks' worth of accounts that night, dine early, and maybe take in a movie. "*Should* work—see people," she wrote, sounding groggy. "But the week has been strenuous, and I seem to be about at the end of my rope. . . . Think probably 'the curse' is imminent, and that's perhaps what's the matter with me." She felt gloomy, uncertain, strung out emotionally—and alone; another night in another anonymous hotel.[24]

Such moods burst upon her with adamantine force. By now Eleanor Roosevelt had learned to anticipate the exactions of her friend's turbulent spirit. She could read between the lines of Hickok's letters and hear trouble in the timbre of Hickok's voice over the long-distance wire. As before, she fussed over Hickok's health and habits—her liquor intake, tobacco, diet. "Well, if I have stopped your drinking of too much corn liquor I probably have increased your chances for health for the next two years," she wrote, "& as hangovers can't have added much to the job of life perhaps this last year's changes aren't all bad." ER wrote frequently during this most intense phase of their relationship, brief letters packed with the mundane details of a protean first lady's daily routine. But they usually closed with words of warm affection.[25]

"Dear one, I would give a good deal to put my arms around you and to feel yours around me. I love you deeply & tenderly," ER wrote in a typical passage of this period. They had started the countdown to Hickok's return to Washington: "*Darling*—only eighteen more days," Hickok reminded her. ER already had sketched out a series of holiday excursions for the two: a trip to Charlottesville, Virginia, and Monticello or, if Hickok had wearied of traveling by car, picnic lunches and country walks on the outskirts of Washington. And they might steal a day or so in New York City. "Dear one, I always want you here in this room with me," she wrote from the East Sixty-fifth Street town house. "Somehow you visualize easily here because we've been here to-gether so much. Well perhaps you'll come up and spend the night of Dec. 21st here with me." The countdown continued, both women with expectations for a White House reunion that would be impossible, perhaps, to meet.[26]

Meanwhile, hour after monotonous hour in the Land Bank car: due east to Burlington on the Mississippi River on Monday, November 27;

Iowa City by midday Tuesday; then north on U.S. 218 Wednesday to Charles City in north-central Iowa, by repute one of the least amenable towns in the state. The tractor had been invented at the Hart-Parr works there thirty years earlier.* The first machine, delivered in 1902, saw seventeen years' service on a farm near Clear Lake. In flush times at peak production, the company shipped out trainloads of tractors daily, and by 1930 some 920,000 machines were in use on U.S. farms. Now one shipment of ten tractors for export to Italy made news. Hickok felt too jaded that night to stroll the little city's business district, two-story brick and stone buildings stretching for three or four blocks up from the Cedar River. The place has been much knocked about by tornadoes and floods in recent years, though today the center remains much as Hickok knew it. The Hotel Hildreth on North Main Street is no more, though, and perhaps that is just as well. Writing to ER on hotel stationery, she drew an arrow to a window at one corner of the building. "My room—for Two Dollars! And I suspect bed bugs!"[27]

The CWA's first projects in Charles City, the graveling of streets, rock crushing, water main and storm sewer work, and grooming the park, were under way by November 23. The projects employed 153 men at the start, with another 150 ready to go. "Working at feverish speed the past week, the civil work agencies have seen the local phases of the gigantic program successfully set in motion," *The Charles City Press* reported. There were high hopes for employment with a plan to resurface a hundred miles of Floyd County roads with crushed rock. *The Press* sent reporter Helen Payne out to interview workers at a big quarry near the town of Floyd. "It is a cheerful scene of systematic routine, with an atmosphere of good cheer among the workers," she wrote. The first CWA paycheck went to a strandee named Joe Siplon. "It will be mighty fine to get a check again after being off the payroll for three years," Siplon told the paper. The foreman told *The Press* that output had increased considerably since the men learned they now would be paid in cash rather than in grocery orders.[28]

Hickok sloughed off her lethargy the day before Thanksgiving

---

* Hart-Parr manufactured gasoline-powered traction engines, and when they adapted one to power a farm machine the advertising manager dubbed the vehicle a "tractor."

and walked the streets of Charles City. One day during the summer, she learned, a mob had kidnapped the Floyd County relief director and chased her out of the county. Someone introduced Hickok to the leader of the vigilantes and they went to his home, chatting as his wife bustled around the kitchen making preparations for the holiday. He had just drawn his first CWA paycheck. His wife said, "The first thing I did was go out and buy a dozen oranges. I hadn't tasted any for so long that I had forgotten what they were like." Earlier, the butcher in one of the Charles City groceries told Hickok he knew people who hadn't tasted meat for six months. Now former customers were trickling in with their first CWA earnings, some offering to pay at least part of what they owed before they had gone on relief.[29]

Hickok went back to Sioux City in early December for a last round of interviews. When she called on Mayor Hayes, he all but flung himself into her arms, booming, "Why, our people here in Sioux City are now saying that in another 20 days we'll be out of the depression!" A number of sources told her the corn loans and CWA checks had released so much pent-up demand that the city's department stores were more crowded than they had been at any time since 1921.[30]

After more than a month on the road, Hickok returned to Minneapolis for a four-day break at Thanksgiving, spending the holiday with Thomas and Clarissa Dillon. Dillon had been more than an editor when she worked on *The Minneapolis Tribune* in the 1920s; he had initiated her into the higher mysteries of the journalist's trade. Dillon saw promise in Hickok; she could write a bit, and she flourished at *The Tribune*. As the years went by, her memories of those days would become tinged with a warm glow of nostalgia and longing. "We were a wild, boisterous, cynical, unmannerly crew," she wrote long afterward. "Only the bootleggers loved us."[31] She owed a lot to Dillon. All the same, she tested their friendship over the long Thanksgiving weekend. In the course of a year or so Hickok had become wholly committed to Eleanor Roosevelt and, by extension, to her husband's presidency. *The Tribune* had carried wire service stories with allegations that Mrs. Roosevelt sold reproduction furniture from her workshop at Val-Kill near Hyde Park to the government for the Arthurdale subsistence housing project—and made a handsome profit from the deal. Hickok regarded the charges as Republican-inspired and resented Dillon for publishing them. Mrs. Roosevelt denied the accusations, which turned out to be without foundation, and advised Hickok to let the matter drop. "I hope you & Tom Dillon don't let that feeling [of] estrangement grow," she wrote, "there are so many other things besides politics you can talk about!" Anyway, she added, Dillon and the others had published her denials along with the charges and the controversy would soon be forgotten. Even now, the first fifty houses in Arthurdale, thin prefabricated dwellings manufactured in Massachusetts,* were being assembled on the grassy plateau below the western slopes of the Alleghenies.[32]

ER promised to phone early on the afternoon of Thanksgiving Day, and doubtless they talked over the Arthurdale matter down the long-distance wire from the Roosevelt cottage at Warm Springs, where she and the president were spending the holiday. Hickok found it difficult to suppress her resentment over the first lady's brief vacation—and about her richly textured public and private life. Hickok often railed against the notion that she was only one of many in ER's ambit. "Well, I'd probably not be happy there," she wrote of Warm Springs. "Oh, I guess I'm probably a little jealous. Forgive me. I know I shouldn't be—and it's only because it's been so long since I've seen you." ER replied a few days later, "I had a little longing (secretly) that FDR might think I'd like you to be here & insist on your coming to report to him! You know how one dreams? I knew it wouldn't be true but it was nice to think about." In the event, the two would enjoy their own holiday at the Georgia retreat in January, when Hickok would break for a few days from the first of her investigative trips through the South.[33]

Though Mrs. Roosevelt most often sustained the role of protector as their relationship developed, Hickok's anxieties about what she regarded as ER's lack of discretion—motor trips to Charlottesville, for example—were growing. "I know they [reporters] pester you to death because you

---

*Unsuitable for West Virginia's cold, damp winters, the cottages soon would have to be rebuilt—and at considerable expense.

are my friend," ER wrote, "but we'll forget it & think only that someday I'll be back in obscurity again & no one will care except ourselves." Perhaps the second-most recognized American by now, the first lady saw her every move, gesture, and utterance anatomized. Hickok too had gained a small measure of notoriety as Hopkins's confidential agent and particular friend of Mrs. Roosevelt, with East Wing access to the president. "Dear one, so you think they gossip about us," ER wrote. "Well, they must at least think we stand separation rather well!" Both women had seen the short piece, with a rather severe photograph of Hickok, in *The Literary Digest*, and the first lady had posed for the cover portrait of *Time* magazine's November 20 issue. Seated, with admirable posture, dressed in flowing garments in complementary shades of green, she held what appeared to be an appointments book in her lap, certainly an appropriate prop. The accompanying article detailed Mrs. Roosevelt's relentless routine: a swim with the president in the White House pool, a press conference, a small luncheon party, an afternoon reception for the Persian minister and his wife, tea for women executives of the state and treasury departments, dinner with Rochester, New York, publisher Frank H. Gannett and his wife—and that was only Monday's schedule.[34]

The first lady recoiled at her first glimpse of the *Time* front. "*Time* has a dreadful cover picture of me & pages *on* me, not too scathing I'm told," she wrote Hickok. In fact the account was altogether admiring. The author emphasized Mrs. Roosevelt's "unrouged freshness, amazing vitality," and patrician frugality; baked beans, meatloaf, prune pudding, and oatmeal appeared regularly on the menu for long-suffering White House inhabitants and guests. *The Literary Digest* presented Hickok as an intrepid veteran newswoman turned FERA legman. Neither woman relished press coverage of any kind, however flattering, though Mrs. Roosevelt accepted it as inevitable; she knew years would pass before she could disappear into the character of her alter ego, the anonymous, unremarkable Mrs. Doaks. She mused in a letter to Hickok, "Does it ever occur to you that it would be pleasant if no one ever wrote about me? Mrs. Doaks would like a little privacy now & then!" As for Hickok, she detested being on the other side of the reporter's notebook.[35]

According to *Time*, the first lady's mid-November Tuesday opened with a morning horseback ride and proceeded with a consultation with FERA representatives about setting up urban clubs for single unemployed women that would be a near-equivalent to the Civilian Conservation Corps's winter camps. From the start, Hickok had sought to call attention to the largely invisible problem of women in the Great Depression; nationally 10.5 million women, 22 percent of the labor force, were employed in 1930, and the calamity had devastated this group. Hickok had no difficulty enlisting the first lady's sympathies. "We are going to get something done for the single women, I think," ER had written her in September. She found Hopkins attentive; as a result, the two arranged a November 20 White House conference (the day the farmers' convention opened in Omaha) with a buffet luncheon for forty women—the legendary settlement house reformer Jane Addams among them—that promised "just and fair provision for women" in the new civil works program.[36]

Mrs. Roosevelt opened the conference with a bold statement: "As a group, women have been neglected in comparison with others, and throughout this depression have had the hardest time of all." Hopkins admitted that the early New Deal programs had largely ignored women, and he offered a rough estimate of as many as 400,000 in desperate need of FERA relief or CWA work. "The immediate problem," he told the conference, "is to find jobs for these women where they now are, and get them to work with as little delay as possible." He pledged an initial focus on New York City, where relief sources put the number of unemployed and distressed women as high as 250,000, and said he would consider setting aside a percentage of all CWA jobs for women. The first lady's powerful patronage drew wide attention to the problem; *The New York Times* gave the conference front-page coverage the next morning. From Minnesota, Hickok reported that relief officials had found eight hundred jobs for women in Minneapolis alone. "Out in the smaller cities and towns it's harder to get them interested, though," she wrote Hopkins. "Your average businessman just won't believe there are any women who are self-supporting!" But in the end, of the 4 million Americans CWA put to temporary work in late 1933 and early 1934, only 300,000 were women.[37]

★　　★　　★

The country was vast, the drives long, the roads icy, the wind bitter off the snows: Minneapolis to Fairmont near the Iowa line, another fast run to Sioux City, then a long northward pull up U.S. Routes 75 and 59 to Fergus Falls. In spite of the previous summer's drought, western Minnesotans seemed to be making do, at least by contrast with the downtrodden Dakotas. Hickok and Dick Freeman stopped for lunch in Luverne, a town of 2,600 set in fertile grain and dairy country in Minnesota's southwestern corner. The woman who owned the restaurant and the man at the post office told Hickok the pace of economic life had begun to accelerate, especially in the past two or three weeks. "Business around here is a lot better," the postmaster said, adverting to the CWA, "with all these men going to work on those projects." Hickok noticed too that in all the little towns along the route the Christmas decorations were up, with festoons of evergreens atop the light poles along Main Street in downtown Fairmont.[38]

Fergus Falls, prosperous before the Depression with more than a dozen factories, two big flour mills, the largest cooperative creamery in the state, and a 2,000-patient mental hospital, lay along the southern edge of the drought area. The town had more or less recovered from a devastating tornado that ripped through Otter Tail County in 1919, killing sixty people and destroying much of the town center. "Freaks of the storm included a shingle driven through a fence post, a flock of chickens picked clean, and the walls of a house carried away bodily, leaving a cupboard full of unbroken china," according to a Minnesota guidebook. Reaching Fergus Falls on December 5, Hickok found a rebuilt business district, neat, tidy, and regular, and a kind of knock-on-wood feeling that the worst of the hard times, disasters natural and man-made, had passed.[39]

To her surprise, Hickok discovered that relief operations in Otter Tail County had barely gotten under way. Her inquiries revealed that county officials had not sought federal relief and that until recently only about a quarter of Minnesota's eighty counties were receiving any assistance. Lack of organization and management experience meant that the CWA was off to a slow start there too. In some municipalities not a single man (or woman, for that matter) had gone to work under CWA auspices. Hickok tended to fault Governor Floyd Olson. "I gravely suspect [Olson] of playing politics with relief," she wrote Mrs. Roosevelt; he wanted to run the show, Hickok believed, but didn't have time to manage it efficiently.[40]

Hickok's views about Olson were ambivalent. In April he had threatened to declare martial law in Minnesota unless the state legislature and the federal government "made provision for the sufferers" of the state. "There is not going to be misery in the state if I can help it," he promised. Charismatic and ambitious, he was "about the smartest red in the country," Hickok thought. Should the New Deal fail, Olson's Jacobinism would carry him a long way.[41]

Still, she sensed needs weren't as pressing in Minnesota as elsewhere. "So far as destitution is concerned, I can't see that there is any comparison between what I've seen in Western Minnesota and what I saw in the Dakotas," she wrote Hopkins. "If Floyd Olson ever gave you the idea that the need in the drought area could even touch that in the Dakotas, he was either crazy or a liar." The effects of drought were sporadic, even capricious: "In some cases, I was told, one farmer would have a good crop, and his neighbor would have nothing." Then too, the dry spell lasted only one growing season rather than for several years running, as had been the case west of the Red River.[42]

That is not to say there weren't isolated cases of acute misery. The county people told Hickok about a family that had been reduced to living in a tent; already two of the children had gone to the hospital with frozen feet. As it turned out, the head of the family, a drunkard, went "on the county" every winter. In Perham, in the heart of the drought region, she asked a member of the relief committee whether people were adequately clothed. "They're a bit shabby, but they're warmly dressed," he said. Drought-seared meadows were the problem, the official added. "What our people need mostly is a little money to carry their livestock through the winter. This is dairy country. There's been no feed." As a result, farmers were sending their milk cows to the slaughterhouse at $5 to $6 a head. Unless help came, he warned, there would be nothing left of the drought-area dairy herds by springtime.[43]

Another long drive on December 6: Hickok and Freeman struck north from Fergus Falls and Perham to Bemidji in cut-over timber country, the wheels of the Land Bank car churning up the snow. "We drove for miles and miles, it seemed to me, through second-growth pines," she wrote ER. "When it got dark . . . the road—where the sun hadn't had a chance to melt the ice—was terrible. This is beautiful country, though. I'd forgotten how beautiful it is." The journey, if hair-raising, revealed something Hickok hadn't encountered before. A horse trader she met along the route boasted that his business had never been better. He bought colts in Montana, trucked them east, and found a ready market among North Dakota and Minnesota farmers. In the past year he had sold three thousand head. Long-term trends were bleak: the horse and mule population on U.S. farms had decreased by 9 million between 1918 and 1932. For now, though, it was a seller's market, for it cost less to feed livestock at market grain prices than to buy fuel for a tractor. She had seen machines abandoned in the fields, "apparently right where they ran out of gas!" That, she told Hopkins, explained why the tractor plant in Charles City had all but shut down.[44]

Hickok checked into a third-floor room at the New Markham, "not a bad hotel," she wrote Mrs. Roosevelt, before noting that in only eight more days she would be back in Washington. Then she descended to the half-full lobby to eavesdrop on the political conversation there. Men in denim shirts and sweaters and ill-matching coats and trousers had gathered to listen to the radio broadcast of the president's speech to the Federal Council of Churches of Christ. Some of the men were talking about their expectations for recovery. They impressed her with their patience and resignation.

"I think things will hold just about as they are for a while," one of the men said. "They're just getting organized."

"Yeah—we can't expect things to get going in a big way for a few months," one of the others agreed.[45]

The first lady sat with the audience for FDR's speech, wondering whether Hickok would be listening in ice-shackled Minnesota. Roosevelt's plummy patrician voice came crackling into the New Markham's lobby. The early churches were united in a social ideal, and government today "is seeking through social and economic means the same goal which the churches are seeking through social and spiritual means," in the president's phrase, "a more abundant life" for everyone. Church and state should work together, he went on, with the churches teaching the ideals of social justice and the government guaranteeing the churches' right to worship God in their own way. Characteristically, Roosevelt ended on an optimistic note, adumbrating an era of steady progress, with growing material prosperity shared out equitably among all the nation's 120 million citizens. Hickok tried to gauge the lobby crowd's reaction. "One of them listened so hard that he didn't realize he was leaning on the cigar lighter, which burned a hole in his coat!" she wrote Hopkins.[46]

The CWA may have started slowly in Otter Tail County, but officials got off the mark right away up in timber country. Bemidji had outgrown its origins in the 1890s as a wild and lawless lumber settlement to become the trading center of a rich north-central Minnesota forest, lake, and farming region. But the Depression released long-suppressed tensions, and Hickok reported that the little city "has been the scene of a good deal of Communist agitation and resultant disorder," with a near-riot at the relief office only a few days before her arrival. Relief money had been flowing into Beltrami County for more than a year, but it had been badly handled, with slapdash record keeping, inadequate investigations, and a bloated caseload. From what she could tell, the county board chose to "buy off the agitators by giving them plenty of relief." She heard of one malcontent who collected $65 worth of grocery orders, clothing, and medicine during the month of July alone.[47]

Everyone wanted work, and Bemidji's merchants strongly backed the federal jobs program, a stance the local newspapers amplified. "Prosperity can only be achieved when workers are getting a living wage," the Beltrami County weekly *Northland Times* asserted, noting that the CWA's prospective 55-cent hourly scale ran well above prevailing local rates. The county's initial CWA allocation of $58,900 would support around three hundred jobs at thirty hours a week, with heads of families given first priority. Scanning the papers, Hickok contrasted what she called their ballyhoo with the realities she encountered. The county carried nine hundred heads of families on the relief rolls, so only a third would be employed at first. Altogether, three thousand men had registered for jobs—ten times as many as the CWA initially made available. *The Bemidji Daily Pioneer* reported in late November that so many men were being hired for the initial projects that the clerical force had fallen behind with the paperwork; the first week's paychecks were late because the bureaucracy couldn't cut the checks fast enough. There were hopes for many more openings, and a *Northland Times* story claimed 1,500 men would soon be hired for tree planting in Chippewa National Forest, the first installment on a promise (almost certainly exaggerated, according to Hickok) of as many as 3,500 jobs.[48]

Still, it would be difficult to overstate the impact of the CWA on this Minnesota community. The benefits were psychological as well as practical, and the leading citizens of Bemidji were appreciative, as the local press suggested. "The President has done everything in his power to bring back the return of prosperity," a *Northland Times* editorial argued. "Perhaps miracles haven't been performed, but Mr. Roosevelt . . . didn't maintain that he would perform miracles. He is working for the salvation of the country and if we give him time and the necessary patience we will be rewarded by the much sought after prosperity." Doubtless men who cashed their first weekly paychecks (a substantial $16.50) in months—or in some cases years—beheld the CWA as miraculous. Probably the merchants did too. By December 8 the weekly CWA payroll in Beltrami County totaled $9,600. On Saturday the 9th, market day, the *Northland Times* reported that Bemidji's streets were packed as though it were circus day. The receipts showed merchants had their best sales day since the Christmas season of 1929.[49]

With the arrival of a weather front from Manitoba, a dome of arctic air settled over northern Minnesota, the temperature plunging to 12 degrees below zero during the night of December 6. But the chill failed to match the low for the season so far, 15 below on November 15, a harbinger of what would go down as one of the coldest winters on record. Hickok and Freeman pushed south for Brainerd in the morning, following State Route 371 through frozen, snow-covered lake and pine country, spent the afternoon and evening there, and regained the road on December 8 in the nostril-pinching cold of early dawn, bound for Hibbing in the Mesabi district of northeastern Minnesota's Iron Range. In peak times the mines were a $100-million-a-year enterprise, supporting more than two dozen communities along the range and employing fifteen thousand men. With a population of about that many, Hibbing was the largest community in iron-rich St. Louis County, a vast region of more than six thousand square miles, larger than the states of Connecticut, Massachusetts, and Rhode Island combined.

Before the Depression, flush with tax revenues from U.S. Steel Corporation holdings, Hibbing had won the title of "the richest village in the world."[50]

First with lumber, then with iron ore, Hibbing had prospered for a long time, a storybook town. When mining engineers found rich veins under the streets, U.S. Steel bought up the village in 1919 and moved it a mile to the south. "Towed by log-haulers, churches were slowly moved down the street—spires, pews and decorations all intact," according to the Minnesota guidebook. Some buildings were cut into sections and moved. Steam shovels dug up graves, "reverently" scooping up the dead for reburial in the new cemetery. Iron money built Hibbing High School, completed in 1921 at a cost of $4 million, with a swimming pool, an indoor track, two gymnasiums, an 1,800-seat auditorium with a $25,000 pipe organ, and, so Hickok reported, a medical clinic "that would do credit to the most perfectly equipped metropolitan hospital." A doctor, a dentist, and a staff of nurses all drew full-time salaries. The school board, she added, had a difficult time finding ways to spend the $1 million annual budget. The fire chief drove around in a Cord luxury automobile "half a block long," and the town recorder made more money than the governor.[51]

All the same, Hibbing had begun to experience severe social and economic stresses. Wrote Hickok, "The other day the town went 'red' and elected a linotype operator in the local newspaper office mayor!" Some of the mines were slack, and displaced workers and transients, several hundred of them, had collected in Hoovervilles on the outskirts of Hibbing and Virginia. "Mostly Finns," she informed Hopkins. "Mostly aliens. And mostly, I gather, communists." There were calls to deport them and fears that crowded and unsanitary conditions in the camps could touch off an epidemic; some years earlier, Hickok remembered, an outbreak of black smallpox spread from the Iron Range to Duluth and eventually south to the Twin Cities.[52]

There were stark contrasts in miners' prospects along the Iron Range. In the Vermilion district the ore lay deep underground, reachable by vertical shafts. The subterranean mines around Ely and Tower were hiring—fully three hundred men over the past ten days at $20 a week. But in the open-pit region of the Mesabi (the largest strip mine in the world lay near Hibbing), giant earthmoving machines were displacing men. "Electric shovels that can be operated by one man, instead of six or eight needed on a steam shovel," Hickok explained. "Electric cranes that, in moving track about, can do the work that used to require 40 or 50." She regarded this as a new industrial revolution, creating an unemployment problem that might never be solved. And the temporary expedient, the CWA, had been laggard so far in St. Louis County, with only 3,000 or so men working out of 5,500 who were supposed to have been hired on local projects.[53]

Only six more days to go, Hickok wrote ER from the Androy Hotel in Hibbing. The letter contained a sort of warning: "You are going to be shocked when you see me. I *should* be returning to you wan and thin from having lived on a diabetic diet, but I'm afraid I've gained, instead of losing, weight. Just you or Doctor McIntire★ try to live on green vegetables and fruit, without starch or sugar, in country hotels, where they have nothing but meat, potatoes, pie and cake." Besides, she felt well; she tramped over the CWA sites without difficulty in spite of her bulk, and the cold northern air— 10 below in Hibbing Friday morning—gave her a Bunyanesque appetite.[54]

Then there was the elevator boy at the Androy. Hickok was wearing an old dark gray skirt and a gray sweater with a red scarf knotted at the throat, a black felt slouch hat and low-heeled golf shoes.

Boy: Are you a Girl Scout leader?
Hickok: God God, no. Whatever put that idea in your head?
Boy: Your uniform.

She wrote ER, "I wonder how many people in the farm belt these last few weeks have thought I was a Girl Scout leader! My very soul writhes in anguish."[55]

As the day of their reunion drew nearer, the letters grew more ardent. "Good night, dear one," Hickok wrote ER from Hibbing. "I want to put my arms around you and kiss you at the corner of your mouth." The reply: "Never are you out of my heart & just one week from to-morrow I'll be holding you." Hickok boarded a train in Minneapolis on Decem-

---

★Ross McIntire was President Roosevelt's White House physician.

ber 14, arriving before daybreak the next morning in Chicago, where she took a taxi to Midway Airport for a 9:30 a.m. United Airlines flight to Cleveland, paying $4.86 for fifty-four pounds of excess baggage. For the onward journey, she boarded a Pennsylvania Airlines flight to Washington. Bad weather forced a landing in Pittsburgh, canceling the onward stage. After a six-hour layover and another overnight train trip, Hickok stepped onto the platform at Union Station at 6 a.m. on December 16.[56]

Far from an idyll, the interlude in the White House graded little short of a disaster. The first lady was consumed with juggling the public events of the holiday season, the normal White House social activities and visits from children, grandchildren, and old friends. Despite her good intentions, she saw little of Hickok. She had tried to hint at how it might be. "We had all the world to tea," she had written a week before. "Now I must get ready for dinner & I feel rather weary not a good way to begin the evening is it?" And a few lines later: "I am half afraid of being too happy. It's the way I felt as a child when I dreaded disappointment." She promised they would have tea in her suite as soon as Hickok arrived, but travel delays forced a change in those plans and she could not find time for them to be alone. After Hickok's remonstrances, she reserved the night of December 22 for her, but she ended up spending it instead with her daughter Anna Dall, then ensnared in a contentious divorce. Hickok flew into a tantrum, packed, and fled to New York City to spend a cheerless holiday there. In phone calls on Christmas Eve and Christmas Day, ER apologized ("I went to sleep saying a little prayer," she would write, "'God give me depth enough not to hurt Hick again'") and persuaded Hickok to return to Washington for New Year's weekend.[57]

Hickok buried herself in work, investigating New York City relief and the CWA program for Harry Hopkins. She found that the management of relief had improved somewhat since October, that with the arrival of winter the numbers on the rolls were rising, and that more than 100,000 New Yorkers were now earning CWA paychecks. Not that many checks had been distributed yet; the $7 million CWA payroll hadn't made much of an impact owing to delays in getting the money into workers' hands. "The whole thing had to be done with a force of stenographers some of whom had not worked for two years or longer," she explained. "They had forgotten how to use the typewriter." There were complaints, too, among private employers that wage rates were so high—15 cents an hour above prevailing scales—that they couldn't compete with the CWA for labor.[58]

The city's CWA administrator, Travis Whitney, took a creative approach in finding employment for professionals and white-collar people, hiring newspaper reporters, for instance, to work as troubleshooters. "When I hear that something is going wrong on a project," he told Hickok, "I'll send one of those boys out there to find out—and he'll find out." Among the boys now working for Whitney were former *World Telegram* reporters involved in the graft and influence-peddling investigation of New York City relief the previous summer, probing charges of political meddling in the distribution of CWA jobs and administrative positions.[59]

CWA jobs also would be available for physicians. The head of the Kings County Medical Society told Hickok that the telephones of 30 percent of Brooklyn doctors had been disconnected, suggesting they had gone out of business; he suspected an even higher percentage for Manhattan doctors. CWA physicians, she proposed, could identify people who weren't healthy enough for manual labor and also carry out a comprehensive survey of the health of the jobless. Most people, it seemed, would accept work of any kind. Strong and nimble or otherwise, thousands of men registered as "common laborers" in the belief they would land work sooner that way. Hickok met a former chauffeur assigned to a pick-and-shovel job at Hunter College in Manhattan. He spent several hours at the job site the day before he was to report for work, "watching the men to see how they handled shovels so that he wouldn't look so awkward when he started!"[60]

8

THE STRICKEN SOUTH
Georgia, Florida, and the Carolinas, January–February 1934

The New Year saw a sharp spike in the numbers of Atlantans on relief. The capital of Henry Grady's New South,* the Georgia metropolis had risen from the ashes of Sherman's visitation to become a powerful regional commercial, industrial, and financial center. A leading sociologist went so far as to call Atlanta, with its go-ahead values, "the most 'yankee' of the southern cities." By early 1934, though, the executive and clerical forces of the national firms with regional headquarters in Atlanta, the traveling salesmen based there, and the managers of Georgia financial institutions and commercial and industrial enterprises were in deep trouble. The Great Depression had overtaken, overwhelmed, and undone so many. "The plight of some of them is pitiable," Hickok wrote Harry Hopkins. Many once comfortable Atlantans, she found, had been compelled to draw down to the last of their resources.[1]

Characteristically, though, the newspapers were buoyant. *The Atlanta Constitution*'s January 1 edition saw "a future bright with omens of good fortune." According to its afternoon rival, *The Atlanta Journal*, "Nineteen Thirty-three, a guy who couldn't take it, retired at midnight Sunday in

---

*Grady's "inspired imagination and equable, progressive attitude" as managing editor of *The Atlanta Constitution* promoted reconciliation between the North and the South during the post–Civil War era. He died in 1889.

favor of a younger and fresher champion, Nineteen Thirty-four, who promised to put up a better fight than his predecessor." The city's New Year's Eve celebrants were noisy, cheerful, and law-abiding, evidently hoping that 1934 would bring "a little more prosperity, a little less depression," *The Journal* noted. Encouraging augurs revealed themselves here and there, Hickok would find, but it remained to be seen whether the new contender could deliver a knockout blow to the catastrophe.[2]

After a New Year's holiday with Eleanor Roosevelt in the White House, Hickok set out in Bluette on January 5, Friday, for a six-week tour of the Old Confederacy that would take her as far south as Miami. She reached Atlanta Monday morning, the start of the first full work week of 1934, arriving to find the city's larger hotels had put up their prices 15 percent to cover National Recovery Administration wage increases and restrictions on working hours. The minimum for a room had climbed to $2.50 a day, straining her $5-a-day expense account right from the start.[3]

She spent the cold, breezy midweek with a relief investigator, calling on sixteen new cases, "all white collar people, living in a very good residential section of the city." One, a salesman in his late fifties, had paid for his home and put two sons through college. When hard times got harder in 1932 he lost his job, but calculated that his savings would see him through. Market fluctuations all but wiped out his investments. One of the sons was studying for the priesthood in Washington; he had taken the vow of poverty and couldn't help. The other, a Georgia Tech graduate, had been jobless for a long time. The ex-salesman mortgaged his house and supported his wife and son, the son's wife, and two grandchildren until the money ran out. During his first visit to the relief office, he said he expected to be able to make do with a delivery or two of coal. Then the grocer cut off his credit. All this came out as the investigator went down the checklist of questions. After a while the salesman's wife burst into tears and fled from the room.[4]

The social worker, a native Atlantan, had endured mortifications of her own. "A couple of times lately I've found myself in a most embarrassing predicament," she told Hickok. "I discovered I was being sent to investigate people I'd known all my life—one man whose son I had once been engaged to!" For such people, Hopkins's Civil Works Administration offered an opportunity to claw back some self-respect, and they clamored for a share of the CWA payroll. By now, though, the CWA was approaching the midpoint of what would be a brief life; the initial $400 million allocation would be spent by mid-February. Private interests were challenging the program, claiming that the government put them at a competitive disadvantage for available labor. Still, Hickok had the impression that hard-pressed Atlantans wanted to believe that the CWA would go on generating payrolls forever.[5]

Reconciled with Hickok, ER put through a series of late-night phone calls to her during the second week in January, apologizing for the hour because she knew Hickok slept uneasily even when in tranquil spirits. "It was a crime to wake you last night, but I was glad to hear your voice," she wrote on January 9. "Oh! dear one it means so much to me to talk to you for a few minutes even at 2 a.m.!" She went on to recommend that Hickok read poet Stephen Vincent Benét's *John Brown's Body* as she toured the South. Notwithstanding the provocative title, there would have been little in Benét's 1928 Civil War epic to offend those with southern sensibilities. "The book came as a revelation of what the Civil War meant," Douglas Southall Freeman, the historian of the Confederate Army of Northern Virginia, would write in the introduction to the 1948 edition. It meant, he suggested, nobility, sacrifice, suffering, and woe. Freeman said little about the chief cause of the war, though, and Benét dealt with the matter of freedom for American slaves in tones acceptable to most whites:

> *They stray from lost plantations like children strayed,*
> *Grinning and singing, following the blue soldiers,*
> *They steal from the lonesome cabins like runaways*
> *Laden with sticks and bundles and conjur-charms.*

Should a hoped-for rendezvous at Warm Springs materialize later in the month, ER proposed she and Hickok read Benét's poem aloud together.[6]

During the Atlanta investigations, Hickok's contacts emphasized three key issues, along with the impoverishment of the middle class: race, the status of women, and the impact of the CWA. Malcolm J. Miller, the FERA administrator in South Carolina, had told her that he expected the jobs program to work a hardship on that state's planters. The standard rate for farm labor ran to about $3 a week for a six-month year; CWA projects paid three times that figure. Planters complained they couldn't compete with the government; besides, CWA wages would spoil the hands, white and black. Some of Hickok's Georgia sources questioned the critics' claims. Few planters paid cash wages; instead they let land to tenants and croppers on a share basis. CWA workers were responsible for their own housing, food, fuel, and implements; landowners supplied their tenants with mules, seed, tools, and advances to cover rations during the growing season through laying-by time in late summer. And so far as Hickok could tell, Georgia's "surplus" population could supply more than enough workers to fill the available jobs.[7]

Even so, Georgia governor Eugene Talmadge protested—insistently—that CWA paychecks were luring laborers away from the state's farms, shops, and factories. In its saucy way, *Time* suggested the "dictatorish" Talmadge's concerns were more about politics and patronage than unfair competition. Hopkins was scathing. "All that guy is after is headlines," he said. "He doesn't contribute a dime, but he's always yapping. Some people just can't stand to see others make a living wage." He followed through with a major administrative shake-up on January 5, promoting Gay Shepperson, a former Red Cross associate, to take charge of Georgia direct relief and civil works programs, bypassing the Talmadge-appointed management boards. Like Hopkins, Malcolm Miller saw a positive in the CWA's higher pay. "I'm strong for the federal wage scale," he told Hickok. "For sixty-five years the South has been the sweatshop of the nation. That's because we were afraid of the Negro. We wanted to keep him down." The South kept him down. And much of the white South stayed down with him.[8]

Cotton was an embattled king in Augusta. The dealers along Cotton Row and in the ornate Queen Anne and Second Empire–style Cotton Exchange* at Eighth and Reynolds were satisfied for now with a 10-cents-a-pound return, and Augusta in 1934 remained one of the ten largest inland

---

*The building, all turrets and gables, dates from 1886. The last of the cotton brokers closed up in 1964; the Exchange (2011) now houses a bank.

cotton markets in the world. But they were gloomy about the region's economic future, particularly about the prospects for agriculture. Farmers in Georgia and neighboring South Carolina might be better off than they'd been for a long time, with cotton prices double their 1932 values and a share of $100 million in Agricultural Adjustment Administration payments for plowing under a quarter of the 1933 crop, the most bountiful in years. For 1934, the AAA called for a 40 percent reduction in cotton acreage, with $3 to $11 per acre to Georgia cotton planters who let their land lie fallow. Yet even with acreage reduction, enough cotton remained in the South's warehouses—13 million bales, equal to a year's crop—to meet the world demand without the harvest of another boll.[9]

Then too, the locus of cotton production had shifted west. "Generally speaking the feeling seems to be that [the southeastern] states are just about through as cotton producing states—that they can't compete with states like Texas, where more cotton can be produced per acre at lower cost," Hickok wrote Hopkins. A number of factors conspired to offset the Augusta region's advantages in variety of soil types, 236-day growing season, ample rainfall, and sunshine 68 percent of the time. Decline set in during the early 1920s as the boll weevil worked its inexorable way north and east from Mexico. Depleted soil, the need for quantities of high-cost fertilizer, the expense of weevil antidotes, the wastefulness and inefficiency of the tenant farming system, the development of new techniques for cultivating and picking, the advent of synthetics such as rayon: all foretold trouble for the Lower South's traditional cash crop. In the words of sociologist Howard W. Odum, cotton was "a drainer of land and men." That said, it was as much a cultural as an economic feature of Georgia life. After all, in 1793 Eli Whitney had experimented with his cotton gin on a plantation near Augusta, and no crop had a closer association with slavery.[10]

Hickok now confronted race, the South's all-pervasive social, political, and economic reality, for the first time. She drove out of the university town of Athens on the evening of January 12, weaving along U.S. 78 through low red-clay Piedmont hills toward Augusta. The weather turned treacherous, with wind and downpours of rain; the roads were bad, the cotton and corn fields impenetrably dark. The wipers clacked metronomically; the headlights fitfully illuminated the rain-blackened pavement. Lexington, Washington, Thomson, Harlem: few cars were traveling in either direction. Hickok reached the hotel exhausted, her nerves raddled, half an hour before midnight. Next day the Richmond County relief director scolded her for driving alone after dark without a gun on the seat beside her. "I laughed and remarked that I would be more afraid of the gun than of anyone who might molest me," she told Hopkins. "Whereupon she assured me that it wasn't any joking matter." Hickok dismissed the warning as a "hangover" from carpetbag days, but revised her thinking after talking to a northerner who had lived in Georgia for twenty years.

"I came down here thinking all men were equal, Niggers and whites," he said. "I've been forced to change my mind. There are good Niggers and bad Niggers, and I'm sorry to say that almost any Nigger is apt to turn bad Nigger if he catches a white woman alone on a country road at night."[11]

Nothing in Hickok's experience had prepared her for an intimate encounter with the southern burden. In the beginning, she tended uncritically to accept her white contacts' views and prejudices. "Some of the Negroes down here are rather terrifying, at that, in appearance," she wrote Hopkins. "They seem so much bigger and blacker than the Negroes up North, and many of them look more like apes than men." She could not get used to masses of black faces. She had interviewed, with sympathy, African Americans in Philadelphia and New York and in the Pennsylvania coalfields. But fully half of Augusta's population was black.[12]

White folks told Hickok that blacks weren't good for much more than tending cotton. They said blacks with CWA jobs squandered their paychecks on white-mule whiskey and secondhand cars. A black preacher told her white officials systematically denied black laborers the opportunity to work on federal Public Works Administration projects, even one that built a new school for Augusta's black children. NRA codes mandated minimum wages, which in Augusta meant higher wages. "Whenever the higher wage scale is adhered to, they say, the tendency is to throw out Negroes and hire whites," she noted. "Negro workmen are uniformly lazy and shiftless, they say—and judging by the color of some of the bathtubs in some of these Southern hotels I'll say they are—but heretofore have been tolerated because they were cheap." Hard times accelerated trends that saw white workers displacing blacks in the lower pay and skill ranges. Whites were working as bellhops and waiters, jobs Hickok had expected blacks to fill. As long as black labor remained plentiful, she figured, white wages would hover near the level for blacks—a theory that seemed to make little impression on the whites she interviewed.[13]

She also met that familiar southern figure, the paternalistic white community leader who believed he loved and understood blacks "as one loves horses and dogs," said Hickok, who in this case at least retained a vestige of her journalist's breezy skepticism. Though she didn't name him, circumstances suggest her informant was Dr. Frederick Smith, the pastor of the upscale First Baptist Church on Greene Street and, by virtue of his pulpit, one of Augusta's leading citizens. "He also indicated, though he didn't come right out and say so, that he still believed in slavery!" Smith assured her that blacks had been better off socially and economically under the Peculiar Institution. As it happened, the pastor expressed a denominationally orthodox point of view: southern Baptists in 1845 moved to secede and form their own religious convention, breaking with northern churches over the issue of slavery.[14]

Built on sand hills rising from the flood plain of the Savannah River and established as a fortified trading post in 1745, Augusta had been much knocked about in modern times. Sherman had bypassed the city in late 1864, his army veering from Milledgeville southeast for Savannah. But a destructive flood in 1908 led to the construction of a $1 million levee protecting Cotton Row, the industrial quarter in the flats, and the business district. In March 1916 fire broke out in Kelly's dry goods store on Eighth and Broad downtown. Fanned by high winds, the conflagration consumed thirty-two city blocks—118 acres and 764 buildings—and left three thousand Augustans homeless. At least the rebuilt city felt secure behind its fourteen-mile-long levee. Then a 1929 freshet tested the protective wall. The Savannah crested at forty-five feet and breached the levee in several places, temporarily isolating the city except for airmail deliveries to Bush Field on high ground to the west. Repairs to the levee were continuing; in late 1933 the CWA fielded a thousand casual laborers to raise and shore it up.[15]

By early 1934, Augusta appeared to be on the cusp of recovery. The city billed itself as the "Winter Golf Capital of America," with the Augusta National Golf Course designed by Bobby Jones, which had opened in 1933, as well as links of less exalted pedigree. The big resort hotels were doing a brisk trade during Hickok's brief stopover in the city. "Merchants, particularly the little fellows, are most enthusiastic about improved business," she reported. "Every merchant I've seen has told me that his business is a whole lot better than it was a year ago." Another indicator: bankruptcies declined 50 percent over the first nine months of 1933, a total of 59 cases, down from 116 during the comparable period of 1932. The city had barely regained its footing, though, after a brief, costly, and intermittently violent textile strike in the autumn of 1933. Even so, Augusta bank deposits increased by $2 million in 1933, "cash evidence that business is better," according to a report early in the new year in *The Augusta Chronicle*.[16]

Hickok heard plenty about the textile strike. Then and now, labor leaders told her, the mill operators were violating the spirit of the NRA wage codes. "They have raised the hourly wage, or lowered it, in the case of skilled labor, to the minimum," she explained to Hopkins, "but they have seen to it that no man earned any more per week than he was earning before by cutting down the number of hours the mill operates." In consequence, there had been no increase in mill payrolls and no increase in the number of hands employed.[17]

Textiles were an ailing industry in the South as elsewhere. Two big Augusta mills had shut down permanently in the early 1930s, throwing hundreds of people out of work. On a Friday morning in late October 1933, some three thousand operatives in four mills in Augusta and across the river in South Carolina walked off the job in protest of the bosses' abuse of the "stretch-out" system, the practice, as Hickok understood it, of making one man do the work of two for marginally higher wages. Augusta prepared for a siege, and city officials authorized the police to carry tear gas bombs for the duration of the strike. In Atlanta, Governor Talmadge requested National Labor Relations Board mediation. The newspapers reported groups of mill hands idling in the streets but no violence at first; the strikers were in tearing spirits. Textile union representatives sounded anything but cheerful, however. Union members had been fired, they claimed, and nonunion hands hired in their place. The union expected, demanded NRA protection. A big crowd gathered at the gates of the still-running John L. King Manufacturing Company in Augusta on October 23, and a police squad car "heavily loaded with tear gas" raced to the scene. The King works shut down that evening, reopened the next day, and fell silent again on October 25, the operators citing fear of violence.[18]

Across the Savannah, National Guard troops set up machine-gun posts outside mills at Grantville and Bath. Pickets from Augusta joined the South Carolina strikers in late October; when workers threw rocks at their tormentors, the police and soldiers responded with tear gas and twenty-four arrests. In Augusta three thousand workers and their families surged into Municipal Stadium to hear national labor leaders denounce the arming of police and the deployment of troops with automatic weapons. They assured the crowd, too, that strikers were eligible for relief payments. One of the union leaders, George L. Googe, said Harry Hopkins himself had told him that strikers would qualify unless the U.S. Labor Department declared the walkout unjustified, an unlikely outcome here. In the event, the strike ended with a whimper on November 4. *The Chronicle* reported that workers could return without fear of retaliation, a win for the union, and that an NRA board would mediate wage and stretch-out issues, a draw at best.[19]

Hickok left for Savannah on the afternoon of January 14, shaping a course south and east along U.S. Routes 25 and 80 via Millen, the site of a notorious Civil War prison camp,* and Statesboro, where Sherman's troops had paused briefly on the march to Savannah. That Sunday *The Augusta Chronicle* reported cotton at 11.16 cents a pound at Saturday's close; it had sold at 5.79 cents on the same day a year ago. The route led through cultivated country, with cotton predominating south of Millen. Spring plowing already had begun, men in denim shirts, osnaburgs, and battered cloth hats negotiating with slow-stepping mules, for what would be a much-reduced cotton crop in 1934.[20]

---

*The camp, built by slave labor, housed roughly ten thousand Union prisoners from the notoriously overcrowded Andersonville Prison. More than seven hundred prisoners died in the three months of the camp's existence.

1

Breadlines lengthened as the Great Depression deepened. Here New Yorkers form a long queue for sustenance in 1932.

Eleanor Roosevelt as a debutante, 1902. She married her second cousin, Franklin Delano Roosevelt, in March 1905. It would be, in her biographer's phrase, a partnership of "labyrinthine complexity."

2

3

Candidate Roosevelt delivers a major speech on farm policy in the burning sun in Topeka, Kansas, September 1932. Critics judged it short on substance.

Eleanor Roosevelt campaigns for Lieutenant Governor Herbert Lehman in Binghamton, New York, October 1932. Lorena Hickok, shadowing Mrs. Roosevelt for the Associated Press, follows a couple of steps behind.

Franklin Delano Roosevelt delivers the inaugural address on the steps of the Capitol on March 4, 1933. Associated Press reporter Lorena Hickok had seen a final draft of the speech with Mrs. Roosevelt the night before, but let the opportunity for the scoop pass.

6

Depositors line up to withdraw their assets. Runs on banks accelerated in early 1933, prompting President Roosevelt to declare a bank holiday shortly after he took office.

7

A creditor forecloses on an Iowa farm in 1933. Burdened by debt and falling prices, thousands of farmers lost their property and their middle-class status in the early years of the Depression.

A relaxed President Roosevelt takes the sun in the cockpit of *Amberjack II* in May 1933, before sailing from Marion, Massachusetts, to the Roosevelt cottage on Campobello Island, New Brunswick, where the first lady joined him for their annual vacation.

Franklin and Eleanor Roosevelt take tea on the lawn of the Roosevelt place, Springwood, in Hyde Park, New York, August 1933. Mrs. Roosevelt wrote solicitous letters from Hyde Park to Lorena Hickok as she made the rounds in Pennsylvania in sweltering heat, carrying out her first investigative trip for the Federal Emergency Relief Administration.

10

Eleanor Roosevelt and Lorena Hickok (*right*), with two of Mrs. Roosevelt's large circle of women friends.

11

Labor boss John L. Lewis in 1922. With protection from the National Industrial Recovery Act, Lewis built the United Mine Workers union into the largest labor organization in the United States in the summer of 1933.

A coal washer and the coal tipple (*background*) dominate the Scotts Run, West Virginia, mining community of Pursglove. The desperate conditions of miners there appalled Lorena Hickok.

12

13

A miner's children in Pursglove, West Virginia. Social workers reported most children in the district undernourished and underweight. Eleanor Roosevelt wondered what would become of them, and even whether they would live to reach adulthood.

A mining "patch" in Scotts Run, West Virginia. The streamlet in the foreground is the settlement's sewer system. Inhabitants bathed in and drew drinking water from the polluted Scotts Run watercourse.

14

Harry Hopkins established the first Federal Surplus Commodities program in the autumn of 1933. The program eventually would supply millions of schoolchildren with lunch.

A quiet street in Rockland, Maine. Lorena Hickok found the town's mile-long Main Street moribund when she stopped there as part of an investigation of conditions in Depression-stunted upstate New York and Maine in September 1933.

A farmyard in Morton County, North Dakota. Northern Plains farmers endured falling prices, grasshopper infestations, and weather calamities such as hail and drought. Lorena Hickok called the Dakotas "America's Siberia."

A street scene in Ray, North Dakota. Ranchers discussed their woes matter-of-factly with Lorena Hickok at a meeting in the town's shuttered bank in late October 1933.

A dust storm begins to blow in South Dakota in 1934. Lorena Hickok's experience of a "black blizzard" near Aberdeen in November 1933 frightened her witless.

19

20

A woman affixes the National Recovery Administration's Blue Eagle to a shop window in 1934. The NRA's efforts to set prices and wages and to curb competition came under sharp criticism, particularly from small businesses and consumers.

21

A one-mule Georgia sharecropper plows for cotton. Agricultural Adjustment Administration curbs on cotton production threatened to turn thousands of croppers loose on the countryside.

Harvesting tomatoes in Florida. Traveling through the state's farm regions, Lorena Hickok learned that tomato picking was an art handed down from father to son.

22

23

Lorena Hickok joined a group of reporters for Eleanor Roosevelt's official tour of the U.S. dependency of Puerto Rico in March 1934. Here the group inspects a poverty-stricken village on the island.

24

Some French Quarter restaurants continued to operate in the grand old style when Lorena Hickok visited New Orleans for Harry Hopkins in April 1934, but the unemployed still haunted the city's Federal Emergency Relief Administration's offices in search of work.

A Colorado farmer displays a sugar beet. Growers were hard-pressed and migrant workers lived on the edge of destitution; only the big sugar companies prospered.

A woman with her youngest child, one of seven, on U.S. 99 near Brawley, California. The family was en route from Phoenix to San Diego, where the man of the family once had lived. He hoped to get on relief there.

A California migrant worker trudges toward his next temporary job.

28

California pea pickers encamp along a roadside in Imperial County, California. The growers and their allies savagely suppressed union activity among the migrants in 1933 and '34. Dorothea Lange took this photograph in 1935.

29

An accomplished equestrienne, Eleanor Roosevelt is pictured here with rangers in Yosemite National Park in August 1934. A hoped-for idyll there with Lorena Hickok dissolved into discomfort and recrimination.

30

President Roosevelt delivers his sixth Fireside Chat in September 1934. FDR made brilliant use of the radio. His calm, conversational approach left many Americans feeling he was addressing them directly. The president's charming elusiveness could exasperate aides, advisers, and neutral observers alike, though. The writer Edmund Wilson saw his "alert affability" and "chimerical smile" as deceptive. But many ordinary Americans remained under FDR's powerful spell.

★ ★ ★

White Savannah seemed fractious, on edge, "an argufyin' bunch of people," Hickok wrote Harry Hopkins. The city itself impressed her as the loveliest she had ever seen, excepting San Francisco. Bay Street fronted Factors Row, two-story weathered brick buildings reached by iron fretwork bridges over cobblestone ramps winding down to the Savannah River wharves. The offices and warehouses were the entrepôts for two longtime Georgia mainstays now slumping: cotton and naval stores. Along Bull Street, five Georgian squares, actually small parks, formal in their arrangement, mossy and inviting, marched south from the waterfront to the magnificent Forsyth Park. Live oaks and English yews shaded clumps of camellias and oleanders, with drifts of azaleas and gardenias aflame with color in season. Skies were fair on January 15, the temperature reaching the low 60s; the *Savannah Evening Press* predicted a light frost overnight.[21]

The elegant city, languid and louche, concealed its secrets under a canopy of luxuriant semitropical vegetation, courtly manners, and easy tolerance. But Savannah whites were fretful, as Hickok noticed right away. They seemed obsessed with race, and in early 1934 they projected their anxieties onto the CWA. While white retail merchants and the city's majority-black population celebrated the jobs program, most others denounced it. Hickok found it difficult to take the complaints seriously. Savannah had been given a disproportionate share of CWA jobs, more than 10 percent of the state's allocation. City officials asked the CWA to build a new hangar out at Travis Field, and the CWA promised to oblige. In Atlanta, CWA headquarters gratified Savannah business interests by adjusting wage rates downward, though city-employed white clerk-typists who saw their pay reduced to $12 a week complained that black women working as aides earned more than that. Will Artley, Savannah's CWA administrator, told reporters that "the federal government takes no notice of race, color or creed when making its regulations for base pay and there was nothing he could do about it." That was the problem, so far as Hickok could see. Whites in Savannah certainly took notice of color. It determined everything.[22]

Front-page headlines in *The Savannah Morning News* reported administration plans to revalue the dollar, the details of a Soviet spy case,

Herbert Hoover Jr.'s denial of corruption allegations involving airmail contracts, and the death of Francis J. Chapman, the last surviving Confederate veteran in neighboring Long County. (Twenty-six years old in April 1865, Chapman had walked all the way home to Jones Creek from Appomattox Court House after Lee surrendered the Army of Northern Virginia there.) An editorial celebrated 11-cent middling cotton in the Savannah market, then reminded readers it had closed at 17.77 cents on October 15, 1929, nine days before Wall Street's Black Thursday touched off the Crash.[23]

Notwithstanding higher prices, times were hard for Savannah cotton. The shipping houses along Factors Row were quieter than they had been at any time since Union warships blocked up the port in 1862.* The volume of cotton shipped from the wharves of Savannah, the busiest U.S. port between Baltimore and New Orleans, dropped off dramatically in the early 1930s. The great days of the Georgia yellow pine lumber industry had passed too. Naval stores—spirits of turpentine and rosin chiefly, once essential in wooden ship construction and maintenance and now used as components in soap, paint, shoe polish, and lubricants—were in what seemed like a fatal decline, partly owing to the development of synthetic substitutes. Leasing agreements for new stands of pine were down; wages were slashed, with labor largely paid in rations; the 1934 outlook indicated the smallest output in half a century, according to *Gamble's International Naval Stores Yearbook for 1932–1933.*[24]

The yearbook's publisher, Thomas Gamble, a former reporter for *The Evening Press*, had taken office as Savannah's mayor in June 1933. He could point to some compensation for the slump in naval stores: a modest increase in shipments from Georgia and South Carolina textile mills, a big sugar refinery that employed 650 workers, and a new paper mill where several hundred operatives produced bags, wrapping paper, fiberboard, and dried pulp. Still, the city's long-term economic prospects remained uncertain. "Here in Savannah," a merchant told Hickok, "we eat Land o' Lakes butter. Do you know where that comes from?

---

*Cotton piled up in Savannah. When Sherman reached the city on December 21, 1864, he wired President Lincoln word of a Christmas gift of thirty-one thousand bales stored in warehouses there.

[*She knew.*] But do we ship Georgia peaches to Minnesota? [*They did not.*] But we might if we had better distribution and storage facilities." Georgia lagged in making infrastructure improvements that would facilitate moving Georgia peaches, pecans, peanuts, textiles, truck crops—and naval stores too.[25]

Reflecting his constituents' views, Gamble emerged as a leading critic of the CWA. Hickok detected five sources of discontent: racial prejudice led the list, followed by a belief that masses of blacks were flowing into Savannah from the countryside, lured by direct relief and by CWA jobs; charges that CWA rolls were padded with people who had no need of work; fear of a labor shortage; and politics. Racism was virulent: "If you compare it with the feeling down in Savannah, racial prejudice simply doesn't exist in Northern Georgia at all." Savannah whites actually were afraid of blacks; Hickok's own newly aroused racism led her to believe that she understood why. She could not forbear quoting blacks in the exaggerated dialect of the Old Plantations: "De Messiah hab come," she reported grateful blacks speaking of FDR and the CWA. "SUCH Negroes! Even their lips are black, and the whites of their eyes! They're almost as inarticulate as animals. Many of them look and talk like creatures barely removed from the Ape. Some of them I talked with yesterday seemed hardly more intelligent than my police dog." One wonders about the broad-minded Hopkins's reaction to such drivel. And surely it's suggestive that Hickok steered clear of the most blatant caricatures and stereotypes in her correspondence with Eleanor Roosevelt, an exemplar of tolerance.[26]

While she clearly shared whites' fears and prejudices, the reporter in Hickok quickly discovered Mayor Gamble's story about country blacks' streaming into Savannah to be mostly myth. A city police investigation of one hundred black relief applicants found that only six were from out of town. Nor did claims of a labor shortage stand up to scrutiny. Artley found no evidence that blacks were leaving domestic service for CWA jobs. However, he and others did credit widespread complaints about wage scales. "Any nigger who gets over $8 a week is a spoiled nigger, that's all," one official told Hickok. The arguments for paying blacks less ranged widely: their diets were different and their requirements were simpler, the costs of living were lower for blacks, and anyway they spent a lot of their earnings on drink. She dutifully passed these assertions along to Hopkins.[27]

As it happened, Mayor Gamble offered strong support for the NRA. When he reported a city vendor, the Wall Coal Company, for failure to comply with NRA codes on wages and hours of work, the local NRA board revoked the company's Blue Eagle. Exposed too were the operators of a burlap bag factory who had been accused of a sort of "bait and switch" with young white female workers. They had been hired at learners' wages, $8.93 a week. After a six-week training period, they would move up to the skilled category, at $12 a week. The catch: an increase in the daily quota of bags from a few hundred to 1,800, and then to 2,500. "Mister, I've tried it," one of the workers told Hickok. "I've worked just as fast as I could all day, never taking my eyes off the machine, and the best I could do was 2,050." The company perfected the art of hiring novices at low wages, sweating as much work as possible out of them for six weeks, raising the quotas, then replacing them with new learners.[28]

Jesup, Baxley, Macon: the route led south through pinewoods and cultivated country, then bent northwest toward Atlanta. Hickok returned to the Georgia capital in the late afternoon of January 18. Eleanor Roosevelt's flight touched down at Candler Field the next morning in time for breakfast with Hickok at the Henry Grady Hotel on Peachtree Street. Did the two remark upon the juxtaposition of ER's thoroughly up-to-date equipage with a front-page report in *The Constitution* that Atlanta had supplanted St. Louis as the leading mule-trading center in the United States? Some forty thousand mules had changed hands at Atlanta auction barns in 1933, and the mule business was brisker than at any time since the Great War, though prices hadn't risen much since 1918. ER intended to return to Washington by air, weather permitting, after a weekend with Hickok. In the meantime, the first lady toured the federal penitentiary, then motored south to Warm Springs with Hickok. She told the afternoon *Journal* that she had come to Georgia for rest and quiet and would make no public appearances or offer any commentary on public affairs.[29]

With the caretakers occupying the Little White House, ER and Hickok stayed in the "old cottage," FDR's retreat when he first came to Warm Springs in 1924 for the curative effects of the waters.* The accommodations were Spartan and the weather indifferent, with showers of rain and temperatures in the 50s. Neither woman left a detailed account of the interlude on the lower slopes of Pine Mountain. Mrs. Roosevelt paid informal calls in the village of Warm Springs, though she was unloved there, mostly owing to her views on race. ("She ruined every maid we ever had," a local woman told her biographer decades later.) They passed a damp Sunday morning with the newspapers in the old cottage. The editors gave front-page play to stories on House approval of a bill to devalue the dollar, a railroad expert's call for nationalization of the rails, a request for planters to comment on the licensing of cotton gins, and the escape of a dozen black convicts from the state prison at Powersville.[30]

The first lady set out for the return to Washington early Monday, the Eastern Air Transport plane heaving skyward through racing clouds and light rain. Headwinds delayed the first leg, to Greensboro, North Carolina, where stormy weather prompted Eastern to cancel the onward flight. The airline carried the U.S. Mail, so the pilot received orders to shift to another aircraft to take the cargo through. The passengers were left to fend for themselves. Though marooned, Mrs. Roosevelt was charmed by the intimacy and romance of this exotic new technology. She wrote, "We all lunched together & saw the little mail plane come in . . . & I got a feeling of what a lonely epic this flying the mail all alone is!" She rested for a few hours in a Greensboro hotel, boarded the evening train to Washington, and reached the White House in the early hours of Tuesday morning.[31]

Hickok's spirits wilted with the separation, though she tried to mute her sense of loss in a letter to ER. "Dearest, it was a lovely weekend," she wrote. "I shall have to think about it for a long, long time." In reply, ER sounded relieved: "It was good . . . to find you had gotten over the first wrench well. I always have a lost feeling & then the infinite succession of things takes hold." Hickok had plenty of time to think. Not so the first

---

*The springs averaged a tepid 88 degrees, the warmth thought to be ameliorative for people with polio.

lady. The daily exactions of White House routine left her benumbed, an anodyne effect, she seemed to suggest.[32]

Returning to Atlanta, a glum Hickok arranged for lunch with Wright Bryan, a young *Journal* reporter she had befriended. She picked up the tab out of a sense of guilt for hanging up on Bryan when he'd phoned the previous Friday to confirm a tip about the first lady's visit. Hickok followed up with a long interview with Gay Shepperson, the new state CWA director, whom she warmed to at once. "She's simply swell," Hickok wrote ER. "She's a most unusual woman, truly. Attractive and feminine, and yet she has the breadth of viewpoint and impersonal attitude of a man." Shepperson told her that a lot of the $7 million a month for federal relief flowing into Georgia was going to waste, that outside the cities "this isn't an emergency down here but chronic." She sought a permanent solution, possibly a subsistence farming program on the grand scale. On Hopkins's instructions, Shepperson already had moved to curtail the CWA. With funds draining away, she ordered a reduction in working hours, to twenty-four a week in cities and larger towns and fifteen a week in country districts—and this despite her acknowledgment that tens of thousands of Georgians remained without work.[33]

On the road again, alone with her thoughts, she headed south from Atlanta along U.S. 41 and Georgia 36 to Thomaston, a mill town (sheets, pillowcases, and fine-combed shirtings) set in farm country (peaches, pecans, and Spanish peanuts). With year-round grazing, dairy and beef cattle enterprises were expanding. Hickok experienced another violent oscillation of mood, this time from sadness and longing to near euphoria. "I was terribly low and felt lost this morning after I left you," she wrote ER from the Hotel Upson in Thomaston. "I always feel that way." But the sessions with Wright Bryan and Gay Shepperson restored her equanimity; they reminded her, too, of how much working for Harry Hopkins, seeing the country and its people in all their ragged, down-and-out glory, doing reporting that really mattered, actually meant to her. She went on, "Oh, Lord, dear—this *is* a fascinating job of mine! . . . Now I'm sitting on top of the world again—even though I had a little ache when I unpacked my briefcase and realized that I was in the cottage at Warm Springs *with you*, when I packed it early this morning."[34]

The long, emotionally trying day left Hickok exhausted, and she dropped into bed early, leaving a wakeup call for 5 o'clock. But with fog and drizzle visible in the dim light of the streetlamps, she fell back to sleep until 6:45. The clouds were just breaking up as she drove south out of Thomaston on U.S. 19 around 9 o'clock. "Hoofed along the road," she would write that night. "It was warm, sunny, lazy weather, and, anyway, I was afraid to drive very fast on account of the damned stock in the roads. Had to come to a dead stop twice—once for a calf and once for two very small piglets. Lunched on doughnuts while driving." She reached Moultrie in the late afternoon, shadows drifting across the quiet streets and the declining sun lighting up the dome atop the imposing white pile of the Colquitt County Courthouse.[35]

The local newspaper, *The Moultrie Observer*, carried mostly national and foreign news on Tuesday's front page. Hickok would have scanned an Associated Press dispatch from Washington reporting an investigation into allegations of graft in the CWA and PWA programs. Japan insisted it wanted friendship with the United States. Intense cold tormented Nova Scotia. French royalists were rioting in the streets of Paris. The cotton tally showed that the 1933 U.S. harvest exceeded the 1932 figure, even with last summer's AAA plow-ups. Because of the CWA, Moultrie merchants told Hickok, business had picked up to levels not seen since the Crash. "They sold shoes that they'd had in stock, covered with dust, for years," she wrote Hopkins. She managed to pay a call, too, on the county CWA administrator, who now had to comply with Shepperson's order to reduce the weekly payroll.[36]

Hickok detected tenuous signs of recovery in Colquitt County, the stagnant local economy stirred out of its torpor by New Deal spending. The Moultrie Cotton Mills were running day and night shifts, 325 workers turning out sheetings, drills, and osnaburgs. *The Moultrie Observer* sounded optimistic. "We think we are close to a general business revival throughout the country and throughout the world," read an early January editorial. In a meeting with Moultrie's "leading citizens" (a banker, the managers of the textile mill and packing plant, a turpentine operator, a couple of big planters), Hickok heard strong support for the CWA and other programs that aimed "to pour money in at the bottom." Except

for tobacco, it had been a good crop year in southwestern Georgia. Expectations were that 95 percent of the county's tobacco planters would
sign up for the AAA's cash-infusing crop reduction program. Stockholders of the Moultrie National Bank awaited an 8 percent dividend, up 2
percent from the year before. CWA crews worked on drainage projects
and painted county schools. More laborers, perhaps as many as a hundred, were to be employed soon in a CWA war on rats, baiting the entire
county with poison. The first CWA payrolls had been distributed in early
December; in five weeks some four hundred Colquitt County workers
earned $36,000. Already the merchants were fretting about what would
happen when the CWA met its foreordained end, which would come
in mid-February unless Congress moved to replenish Hopkins's budget.
The textile and packing house executives made it clear they had no plans
to add payroll anytime soon.[37]

Hickok reported fewer complaints than she expected about the CWA
cutbacks. According to the county CWA administrator, the workers took
it this way: "It's a whole lot better than being laid off. I'd rather work for
$3 a week than be laid off." Such grumblings as Hickok heard tended to
involve overindulgence of the destitute. CWA wages put pressure on Swift
and other employers. And anyway, why were people taking relief or CWA
paychecks also getting flour, lard, pork, and other surplus commodities?[38]

A drive into the country brought Hickok face-to-face with Georgia's
tenant farmers, Colquitt County's portion of a statewide tenant population of 175,000 households. Relief officials related the story of a country
girl who delivered a baby at 9 o'clock on an early winter morning. By late
afternoon, when county agents and a doctor went to the cropper's cabin
in response to a call for help, "*the cord had not been severed yet*," Hickok
wrote ER. "Did you ever hear anything much more awful than that?"
(The baby died; the mother survived.) Lincoln McConnell, a state employment agent, had tried to prepare Hickok for conditions in the country districts, where people subsisted in a twilight world of deprivation and
perpetual debt. "Why, there are thousands and thousands of Niggers living in this state in slavery just as real as it ever was before the Civil War,"
he told her. A typical planter considered everyone living on his place to
be in his employ. He might furnish his croppers the equivalent of $50 to

$60 a year in rations and other goods—for a family of five, about 3 cents per person per day. "For a few weeks each year, perhaps, he actually will pay the head of the family 30 or 40 cents a day," McConnell went on. "BUT—he works the whole family all year." In passing McConnell's assessment along to Hopkins, Hickok emphasized that she had promised him confidentiality. After all, she explained, things were tough enough already for any Georgian bearing the name of Lincoln.[39]

The tour guide, a county relief agent, introduced Hickok to "a situation where half-starved Whites and Blacks struggle in competition for less to eat than my dog gets at home, for the privilege of living in huts that are infinitely less comfortable than his kennel." The unpainted and unchinked board shacks, usually one room and a kitchen, stood amid fifteen-acre patches of cotton or tobacco or, sometimes, watermelons. They enclosed large families outfitted in patchwork clothes, sometimes mere swatches haphazardly stitched together. (The price of overalls had doubled since the spring of 1933 to a dollar a pair.) Cropper families survived on the traditional slave diet of fatback, cornmeal, and molasses. They had no concept of proper nutrition; they were, a social worker told Hickok, "eating their way into pellagra," with all its gruesome effects: grotesque skin lesions, physical weakness, mental confusion, and, eventually, dementia and death.[40]

Yet Hickok concluded, perhaps surprisingly, that she had witnessed worse conditions during her travels in West Virginia and Kentucky, North Dakota, and northern Maine, even though she understood that Colquitt County croppers might be better off than country Georgians elsewhere—in the neighborhood of Warm Springs, for example, where black folks lived in appalling circumstances. Possibly it was the spring-like weather in semitropical southwestern Georgia. She supposed the mild climate would take some of the edge off hardship, soften the effects of ignorance and want.

She wrote Hopkins, "It's true of course that these people WILL buy shotgun shells and snuff instead of shoes for their children—but somehow it doesn't seem so terrible for children to run about with bare feet on days like today. Camellias were blooming in Moultrie dooryards."[41]

When they met in Atlanta, Shepperson had suggested a comprehensive subsistence farming program as an answer to Georgia's labor surplus, which Moultrie sources placed at two thousand persons in Colquitt County, half of them farmworkers. Hickok could think of no better nostrum. In the North, objections to subsistence farming turned on the notion that it offered a man virtually no chance of redeeming the American Promise. Settling for a mere competence would destroy all initiative. "That wouldn't enter in with the present generation of poor whites and Negroes down here, I gather," she remarked. "They're so messed up with pellagra, and tuberculosis, and one thing and another that they simply haven't any morale to ruin at all." They lived, she saw, much as their fathers and grandfathers had lived, expecting nothing, demanding nothing.[42]

Something needed to be done, though. Journalists Webster Powell and Addison Cutler, writing in *Harper's Monthly Magazine*, predicted that the New Deal's crop reduction program—"human boll weevils," farmers called the AAA agents—would create a class of wandering rural refugees across the South. "Smaller crops and fewer farmers is the government's program in all its ramifications," they wrote. "They will certainly relieve the small farmer—of his livelihood." Powell and Cutler estimated that 800,000 southern families, as many as 5 million men, women, and children, were in danger of displacement. Other sources prophesied that technological changes—a mechanical cotton-picker, for example—would lead to massive job losses, potentially touching off the largest mass migration in U.S. history.[43]

As Hickok surveyed southern Georgia's human wreckage, letters from Mrs. Roosevelt heightened the contrasts in their daily lives. While Hickok observed the ravages of pellagra, ER entertained celebrities in the nation's first mansion. "I could cry that you won't be here tomorrow to hear [Fritz] Kreisler," she wrote on January 15, a day on which Hickok had felt a powerful undertow of emotion about race and caste in graceful Savannah. The first lady noted that she would receive seventy-six guests at an "intimate little dinner" in the White House for the half-Jewish violin virtuoso from Vienna. A week later, the Roosevelts would host Albert Einstein and his wife overnight. Mrs. Roosevelt found the couple "priceless, so German & so simple with many wise gentle German qualities." Still, she would have sensed the sinister loom of Nazism in Germany, where Hitler had been in power for ten months now, though nobody, however farsighted, could have envisioned the unimaginable outcome of a dozen years of Nazi rule.[44]

A day or so after leaving Savannah, Hickok caught a glimpse of a peculiarly homegrown form of totalitarian horror in the turpentine camps of south-central Georgia. It began innocently enough, with a stop in the hamlet of Odum, nine miles west of Jesup. The railroad and U.S. 341 ran in tandem through swamplands and thick stands of yellow pine, the village straggling along on either side of the rails. The inhabitants were small farmers and turpentine operators, mostly white and mostly poor. "Except for a paved road and a couple of filling stations, it probably looks much as it did before 1861," Hickok remarked. "Unpainted buildings. Not a spear of grass in the place. Just dust—gray dust—and tall pines." A conversation with half a dozen men on the village square developed into a sort of "pep meeting" for the CWA. The postmaster told her that sales of stamps had increased 30 percent since mid-December. One of Odum's two merchants reported that his business had spiked 200 percent. "If it hadn't been for CWA, I reckon both us fellows wouda gone clean under," he said. Leaving Odum, Hickok saw a man go into a dooryard with a blacksnake whip in his hand, an image, ambiguous and disturbing, that would remain with her long after the CWA passed into history.[45]

In the turpentine camps, the laborers were mostly black and entirely abused. Thirty years earlier the operators had routinely leased Georgia convict labor, and now and then intimations of unspeakable cruelty would waft out of the camps deep in the piney woods. Nothing much came of the occasional legislative investigation. Hickok and her escort followed a sandy track into a southern Heart of Darkness. A week later, still shaken by the experience, she wrote Hopkins, "I wish I could make you see the place—away off in the woods, miles from everywhere, years away from civilization itself. A few unpainted, tumbledown shacks. A turpentine still. All hidden away in the pines, cut off from all the world by trees and swamps." Her guide, a turpentine operator, explained that the black laborers were restive because they'd heard people were getting $9 to $12 a week working for the CWA. Some of the men had been giving him trouble, he said, and he clenched a fist. It was badly bruised and painted with mercurochrome. Then he gestured in the direction of the camp boss.

"You have seen Simon Legree," he said. "That fellow has killed a couple of niggers in his camps."

"What do you mean?"

He refused to say more. Hickok had difficulty putting the scenes out of her mind: the aromatic woods, dampness and the fetor of decay, profound silence, the notched pines leaking gum, a smoking still, the reek of turpentine, sullen black workers, the primitive pine barracks, the man with the damaged hand, and a murderous camp boss.

"I just can't describe to you some of the things I've seen and heard down here these last few days," she admitted to Hopkins. "I shall never forget them—never as long as I live."[46]

"Something has bitten me, six times and savagely on my left ankle," Hickok wrote Eleanor Roosevelt from Orlando, Florida. Mosquito or flea? Bedbug or spider? Perhaps it was her mood, which had turned dark again, or maybe it was the heat, but she disliked Florida. She found the tourists off-putting. "Too many Middlewestern voices," she went on. "Too God damned many old people from 'Ioway'—sitting in the sun." The ankle had swollen and pus oozed through the dressing she improvised. And it hurt.[47]

She reached Orlando on the afternoon of January 26 after a dreary couple of days in Tallahassee and Lake City. Rain fell, a novelty in what had been a dry winter so far in northern Florida; some districts were experiencing drought conditions. Cattle crowded into the road, and she noticed they were lapping up rainwater that collected in shallow depressions in the pavement. "All the water holes are dried up," someone told her. There were short crops this year, she would learn, owing to the usual culprit, weather: it was either too dry or too wet. In Dade County, for instance, excessive rainfall had drowned the fields. Markets for beans, tomatoes, and other truck crops were depressed, and though people were able to find work in the fields, wages were even lower than usual.[48]

Hickok compiled a "State of Florida" survey for Hopkins, a grim accounting. In citrus, a leading industry, prices for oranges had dropped to 50 cents a box, compared to a New York City retail price of $6 a box, and wage and employment prospects were uncertain. She could hardly find a good word to say about the growers she interviewed; collectively they were a "mean-spirited, selfish and irresponsible" group. "They'll undersell each other every chance they get," she told Hopkins. "They won't voluntarily abide by any rules." She saw little chance they would "play ball" with the AAA, and they detested the CWA. The growers complained about CWA projects poaching their labor, but when pressed they could offer no evidence to support the charge. They were cruel too: "If the labor department were to send investigators down here, they'd find plenty of evidence of peonage." The growers provided barracks and extended credit at their commissaries, charging extortionate prices for inferior products. They could, and did, turn people out of the groves at whim.[49]

Prospects were more promising for Florida tourism, another mainstay industry, though the verdict wouldn't arrive until after the peak months of February and March. "Winter vacationing, almost a lost art in recent years, is bounding back almost to boomtime proportions," *Business Week* magazine reported. In New York City, Pennsylvania Railroad officials predicted that travel to Florida would approach the peak years of 1926–28. The streets of Miami were choked with cars with out-of-state license tags, and the local newspapers waxed enthusiastic about prospects for the season. The merchants and hoteliers and real estate brokers offered a more sober assessment. Rates and rents were up, though not by much. Restaurant prices were low. Hickok found one could dine decently on 50 cents a night. At her Miami hotel, the Alcazar along Biscayne Boulevard, Miami's promenade, she discovered that no singles with baths were available. The elevator boy told her all the cheaper rooms were occupied most nights, but that the $14-a-night suites were always vacant.[50]

Newish and brash, Miami had risen out of mangrove swamp, jungle, and sand dune. The Florida land bubble of the 1920s fueled Miami's growth, and the population more than doubled over a five-year period. The white and buff skyscrapers along Biscayne Bay, the tropical vegetation, the intense blue of the waters, the glaring sunlight made the city "appear as ephemeral as a motion-picture set," in a contemporary guide-book's description. Journalist Bruce Bliven found the place uninviting, possibly because one bayfront hotel after another, ten altogether, had turned him away in his search for a room. Writing in *The New Republic*, Bliven reported hotel reservations up 20 to 30 percent in the state, with Miami recording its busiest winter since 1925. In part, he suggested, the upsurge represented a vote of confidence in the president and his poli-cies. Cuban exiles (supporters of the ousted strongman Gerardo Machado who feared going home), Americans who could no longer afford Europe, and the bitter cold of the northern winter of 1933–34 also contributed to the influx. Bliven accented the contrast between the sun-scorched tourist crowds and a backdrop of grinding poverty. Aside from the tourist trade, Florida was "completely down and out," dependent on federal money. *Time* reported that 27 percent of the state's families were on relief, com-pared to a U.S. average of 11 percent. Bliven saw, too, an element of make-believe in the skies, where a sleek silver monoplane cruised over Miami every day with a streamer advertising a club that featured "female impersonators."[51]

North along U.S. 1 to Daytona Beach, St. Augustine, Jacksonville: Hickok endured a snowbird's Florida holiday, eleven days altogether. She discovered that real skills, of the kind passed down from father to son, were necessary for tomato picking, and that fruit theft had become a significant cost of doing business; she met a woman who claimed that her five-acre grove had been stripped in a single night. She learned that health officials estimated there were as many as 90,000 cases of malaria in the state and 250,000 cases of hookworm. She heard complaints that women's workrooms in Daytona and Jacksonville were producing un-needed clothing, but a glance told her that these opportunities were transformational for the women involved. "They came in sullen, de-jected, half-starved," Hickok wrote. "Working in pleasant surroundings, having some money and food have done wonders to restore their health and their morale." Besides, why not send the surplus to Aroostook County, Maine, or Bottineau County, North Dakota, where thousands perished with cold for lack of adequate clothing? She found that outside Miami the tourist boomlet had been exaggerated. Mailboxes yawned empty behind the desk at her Daytona hotel, and she had the dining room to herself at breakfast on February 1. The Flagler Hotel in St. Augustine offered a room with breakfast and dinner for $5, about half the pre-Crash rate.[52]

Hickok motored north and west from Jacksonville on February 4, reaching Columbia that evening, a month after her first visit to the South Carolina capital. The Florida trip had been anything but restorative; she was jaded and road-worn, and she had acquired a heavy and persistent cold. She relayed her woes to ER over the long-distance wire. "I wish I'd been there when you felt rotten & wanted me," she replied the next day. The women started the countdown to Hickok's projected February 20 arrival in Washington, and they spoke about an official visit to Puerto Rico planned for March. Hickok already had begun to think about her next—and, as it turned out, last—investigative trips for Harry Hopkins, epic journeys that would describe a long southwesterly arc from the national capital to San Francisco.[53]

In South Carolina the talk focused on the CWA, cotton textile manufacturing, and farm labor. As in Florida, Hickok detected anxiety about the approaching end of Hopkins's civil works initiative. (In mid-February Congress approved another $450 million to "wind down" the CWA, a slow withdrawal.) By now she had more or less made up her own mind about the program. "Well—CWA came, fulfilled its purposes, and, I believe, should go," she advised Hopkins. South Carolina planters and truck farmers thought so too, as did W. W. Long, a professor of agriculture at Clemson College, and B. E. Geer, the president of Furman University, a former mill executive who headed the state's textile code authority. They struck Hickok as giddy in their optimism. "So far as [Long] is concerned, the South is immediately embarking on a golden age of prosperity," she noted acerbically. Howard Odum, the University of North Carolina sociologist, would make a forceful case to Hickok for an extension of the CWA, though mainly for white-collar workers. As for Geer, he asserted that the mills were running above normal in the Piedmont, and that if cotton prices continued to rise, the employers would be "begging for labor" and would resent having to compete with CWA wages.[54]

Mill villages crowded the skirts of Carolina cities such as Greenville, a characteristic semipaternalistic social arrangement reminiscent of the old grouping of slave quarters behind the plantation house. Few mill hands would have made the connection with the old plantation system; most retained an unbroken link to their native places in the mountains, visible from Greenville on the western horizon. In "The Mind of the South,"* an influential essay published in *The American Mercury* in 1929, South Carolinian W. J. Cash argued that four decades of southern industrial development had wrought only superficial changes. The South remained local, poor, and benighted. Laborers were still of the farm rather than of the factory, had failed to adapt to industrial patterns of life, and were in more or less "constant flow back and forth between the soil and the mills." Greenville's output helped vault South Carolina into the lead among cotton goods producers by 1925, with more than 5 million spindles turning in the state. Whether or not they recognized it, Carolina mill workers had emerged as a distinctive social class, "lintheads" and "millbillies," in the vernacular.[55]

Leila Johnson and one of the field supervisors, B. S. Hill, showed Hickok the mill settlements ringing Greenville. The route led past block after block of rundown shacks. The "spare help," Johnson's caseload, lived hand to mouth in the tumbledown places or a bit farther out of town, where they could scratch out a garden on submarginal farms. "They've never had steady employment in the mills," Johnson explained. "They never will have steady employment. They are the people we are looking after now, on CWA or direct relief. What are we going to do with them?" The best of the workmen, those with steady employment, lived in sturdier company-owned housing nearer the mills. The bosses felt a sense of obligation toward these favored hands; they were the last to be laid off during slack times and the first to be rehired.[56]

Spare help or permanent, mill workers shared a distinctive and retrograde cast of mind, Cash suggested. However dire the realities, the typical linthead seemed blind to them. "He is not displeased with his

---

*The essay was the genesis for Cash's seminal study of southern culture. Published in early 1941 after a dozen years of excruciating labor, *The Mind of the South* won a Pulitzer Prize for Cash. He died in Mexico in mysterious circumstances in July 1941.

millshanty—for the reason that it is, at worst, a far better house than the cabins of his original mountain home," he explained. "And he has little real understanding that his wages are meagre. In his native hill society, money was an almost unknown commodity and the possession of ten dollars stamped a man as hog-rich; hence, privately and in the sub-conscious depths of him, he is inclined to regard a wage of that much a week as an affluence." His religion, too, enabled him to endure a tremendous amount of hardship: "It plainly becomes blasphemy for the mill-billy to complain. Did God desire him to live in a house with plumbing, did He wish him to have better wages, it is quite clear that He would have arranged it." According to Cash, southern individualism, southern Protestant Christianity, and an inborn easygoing indolence made adaptation to modernity a halting, painful process for most poor whites.[57]

Returning to Columbia with its wide avenues and green-domed capitol, the sole survivor along Main Street of Sherman's fiery passage in February 1865,* Hickok met with a presumably representative group of South Carolina farmers: planters, truck men, and, in Cash's phrase, "the one-gallus squires of the uplands." Long, the Clemson agriculturalist, Malcolm Miller, the state relief director, Leila Johnson, and, perhaps surprisingly, the South Carolinian novelist Julia Peterkin had organized the session. Hickok noted the incongruities of Peterkin's involvement. The burghers of Gaffney, South Carolina, had banned her Pulitzer Prize–winning Scarlet Sister Mary (1928) from the local library. She had written sympathetically about the Low Country's Gullah culture and held decidedly eccentric views about the laborers the assembled agrarians referred to as "our niggers." "You must understand, Miss Hickok," she said with an edge to her voice, "that down here Negroes are not people."[58]

Three of every four South Carolinians were still working in agriculture in 1934, and they would take in more cotton than their great-grandfathers had harvested in 1850. But eight million acres were so worn out as to be virtually barren. That said, the cotton planters were the most vociferous

---

*Confederates set fire to cotton stored in warehouses and stacked along the streets of Columbia to keep it from the Federals. Sherman's troops were indifferent or inept firefighters, and the blaze consumed most of the center city.

among the farmer delegation. They complained that CWA programs were luring hands out of the fields and spoiling them with living wages and decent treatment. "The CWA wage is buzzing in our Niggers' heads," they insisted, though as yet they had little cause for cavil, for it was winter still and the plowing had barely begun. Asparagus season would commence on March 1 in the sandy belt that ran through the middle of the state, and the truck farmers fretted. The peach growers complained that the black women who pruned their trees refused to work now that their husbands had CWA jobs. "The gentlemen did not have what you would call a social viewpoint," she told Hopkins. They counted on an endless labor surplus to keep wages down, and they reflexively opposed the CWA. She recorded this exchange:

Hickok: What will the hands do in the slack season?
Truck farmer: Oh, they can fish.[59]

Hickok struck south for Charleston later that afternoon. It had been a bitter winter, one of the coldest in memory, with temperatures falling to 8 degrees below zero as far south as Richmond, Virginia. North and south, some 20 million people, according to *Time* magazine, were left "with no means of obtaining fire or food, except from the public purse." During the second week of February a cold front brought sleet, freezing rain, and the first reported snow in South Carolina since 1915. The roads were treacherous. Fortunately Malcolm Miller had made her a present of a jug of South Carolina's celebrated corn liquor. "Arriving here pretty tired and a bit chilled tonight," she wrote Hopkins, "I took one drink of it—and wondered what had kicked me behind the ear!" The crooked cobblestone streets and the distinctive chimneypots of the old quarters—south of Broad Street, Charleston remained an eighteenth-century city—were picturesque, and the storm (the palmettos were sheathed in ice) kept her in town an extra night. The Automobile Club advised against traveling the next day, but by then the sky had cleared and the ice had melted away. She pushed on to Charlotte.[60]

North Carolina had experienced significant industrial development during the 1920s, primarily in textiles, furniture, and tobacco, with population growth approaching 60 percent in the manufacturing counties of Guilford, Durham, and Mecklenburg. But as Hickok discovered, country folk were pouring into the towns for reasons other than the prospect of work in the mills. As many as ten thousand tenants in the eastern part of the state were being displaced owing to the AAA's acreage reduction scheme and to farm consolidation and mechanization. "They've come because there's no place for them to live in the country," she observed. "Every abandoned shack is filled up." In Wilson, said to be the world's largest bright-leaf tobacco market, she found the relief office so crowded she could barely push her way inside for a meeting with the director. Virtually every empty dwelling in Wilson, every outbuilding, housed evicted tenant farmers. She had been told the refugees would break the locks off vacant houses and settle in.[61]

Hickok drove into the hinterlands on Valentine's Day to inspect three families of squatters. The first, of "obviously very low grade mentally," inhabited a ruined tenants' cabin, the equivalent, she judged, of a Dakota corn crib. So inept and even hexed was the head of the household that the landlord refused to allow him to plant a crop on his few ragged acres. A second family, with eight children and "of better grade mentally," lived in a shed, "a few old boards hanging together," for which a benevolent landlord charged 75 cents a week in rent. "He's walked this country over," the woman of the house said of her husband. "He can't git no place to crop." The third family, "distinctly high grade," lived in a tobacco barn. Like the first two families, this one would be forced to drift into Wilson soon, probably in a matter of weeks, in search of relief and a place to live. "Seems like we just keep goin' lower and lower," the cropper's sixteen-year-old daughter told her. Slight, fair, blue-eyed, and afflicted with a streaming cold, she was a picture of dejection. Pinned to her faded overalls, Hickok noticed, was a 1932 campaign button with a profile of FDR.[62]

Hickok had been traveling for nearly six weeks, logging five thousand miles in Bluette. Things went fairly smoothly, car and driver surviving without a scratch, until close to the end. A week in North Carolina and three mishaps, one after another: a milk truck clipped her in Fayetteville, crumpling the car's right bumper; in Chapel Hill she scraped the left front fender negotiating the curving, narrow entrance to a hotel; and a bus backed into the car in Durham, further damaging the front end and beating in one of the horns. "It looks as though it had been through the Argonne!" she wrote Kathryn Godwin.[63]

Her head cold persisted. And Hickok filed another complaint with Godwin, one that made her want to tinge the air blue with obscenities. In mid-February *Time* published a long paragraph about her in a cover story on Harry Hopkins, describing her as "a rotund lady with a husky voice, a peremptory manner and baggy clothes." The article implied that Hopkins had offered her the FERA job at Eleanor Roosevelt's behest. She admitted to the whiskey voice, to the shapeless clothes, and even to the bulk, but the reference to Mrs. Roosevelt stung. She took strong objection, too, to *Time*'s characterization of her manner: peremptory? Still, she was headed for home. "Unless I get wrecked altogether," she wrote Godwin, "I'll be back in Washington Tuesday afternoon sometime and shall report in Wednesday morning."[64]

EMPIRE OF MISERY

The Southwest and California, March–August 1934

The little Chevrolet convertible, patched, serviced, and fitted out for the long haul, had been a remarkably reliable means of transport for Lorena Hickok. Bluette had carried her safely over a rapidly improving federal road network in New York and New England and through virtually the entire Southeast, from Virginia to South Florida. Now Hickok set out from Washington on March 25, Sunday, on a long swing that would take her 2,500 miles west to Phoenix, Arizona. Driving into the amplitude of the southern spring, she reached Montgomery, Alabama, on Wednesday after stops in Roanoke, Virginia, and Athens, Georgia.

The relative ease and speed of the initial stages of Hickok's next-to-last major investigative trip for Harry Hopkins were a testament to the development of the U.S. highway system. In 1919, a U.S. Army truck convoy leaving Lafayette Square, Washington, on July 7 required sixty-two days to cover the 3,242 miles to the Presidio in San Francisco, an average of about fifty miles a day. West of the Missouri River the roads were dirt or sand, and few bridges could bear the convoy's weight. After years of negotiation, state and federal authorities agreed in 1926 to a final list of U.S.-designated (and federally funded) numbered national routes. By 1934 the system, though still a work in progress, was largely in place. Construction crews completed the network during the years of the Great Depression, rebuilding roads for high-speed travel: straightening rights-of-way, lengthening curves, building shoulders, installing guardrails, and surfacing with concrete or macadam. New Dealers sold the road projects as emergency jobs, made-work. But there were powerful economic arguments too. Car and truck registrations approached 26 million by 1931—one automobile for every 4.63 Americans—and the number of vehicles on the roads continued to increase during the Depression. The highway system moved people and goods with growing efficiency. By the end of the 1930s, trucks would carry nearly 10 percent of U.S. freight shipments along the national complex of trunk roads.[1]

During nearly a week in Alabama, Hickok investigated industrial and labor conditions, the status of white-collar city dwellers on relief, the impact of the termination of the Civil Works Administration, and the New Deal's nascent rehabilitation programs in the countryside. As usual, the newspapers reported improving conditions. Perhaps so, but she found the state's major industrialists pessimistic. "Business is better . . . than it was a year ago," she reported to Hopkins. "But it's not enough better." A number of sources attributed such improvements as there were to government "priming." A big Birmingham steel operator told her his first-quarter production increased 300 percent from the same three months in 1933. But three-quarters of the increase came from federal loans to railroads for rails and other track improvements. "Withdraw this Government aid," he told her, "and we'd be no better off than we were a year ago and perhaps much worse off." He fretted that business would collapse with the withdrawal of government support.[2]

The administration had been scaling back the CWA since midwinter, a skittish FDR settling finally on a March 31 end date. A temporary measure that aimed to see the most vulnerable Americans through what would go down as one of the harshest winters on record, the CWA achieved its purpose for 4 million hard-pressed families. "It was a grand thing," Hopkins told reporters on the last day of the CWA's life. "It seems to me that it did the trick." But costs were dramatic, far higher than New Dealers had anticipated. Hopkins spent $1 billion ($750 million of it on labor) over the 136-day life of the program. On March 22, the final CWA payday, 2,133,000 workers earned $29 million, down from a peak weekly payroll of $60 million in early January.[3]

Why did the president shut down the program? The British economist John Maynard Keynes had pressed for a far larger government jobs program than Hopkins delivered, one that would remain in place for the duration of the crisis. In a letter published in *The New York Times* on the last day of 1933, Keynes had urged the president to borrow as heavily as necessary to boost employment. "Nothing else counts in comparison with this," he wrote. Roosevelt should press Harold Ickes and the Public Works Administration to pick up the pace. "I do not blame Mr. Ickes for being cautious and careful," Keynes went on. "But the risks of less speed must be weighed against those of more haste. He must get across the crevasses before it is dark." Orthodox in fiscal matters, FDR ignored Keynes. He dreaded the run-up of budget deficits. Some of his aides warned, too, of the danger of creating a new class of Americans with permanent claims on the federal treasury, like war veterans. Charges of graft, waste, inefficiency, and political favoritism in the CWA also played a role. "Everyone wanted a chance at the grab bag," Florence Peterson wrote in *The Atlantic Monthly*. The program had inherent weaknesses, Peterson argued, among them higher wage rates than private industry would pay for similar work. Hickok had seen the benefits of the CWA firsthand. Yet she too had concluded that it was time for the program to end.[4]

FDR's decision to disassemble the CWA did not go unchallenged. As late as March 26, Eleanor Roosevelt suggested to Hickok that it might be extended to May 1. Likewise, the Socialist Norman Thomas lobbied aggressively for an extension. The president and Hopkins received sixty thousand telegrams and letters in support of the program. "There is practically no indication of recovery apart from the deliberately lifting measures taken by the administration itself," *The Raleigh* (N.C.) *News & Observer* asserted in February, when Hopkins accelerated the demobilization of the agency. "It was a bold government which embarked upon CWA. It will be a bolder government which ends it." *The Nation*, the liberal weekly magazine, called the decision a "Back-to-Hoover Movement" and possibly "the most ill-advised step [FDR] has taken since his inauguration." *The New Republic* censured FDR for practicing retrograde

economics and inept politics. "At one stroke," the magazine asserted, "the
Roosevelt administration has cut off much of the good will it had created
by setting up the CWA and putting so many of the unemployed at work."
According to American Federation of Labor returns, the jobless rate still
exceeded 20 percent, more than 11 million people, with no real prospect
of improvement in the offing.[5]

Hickok believed that *something* would have to replace the CWA. The
administration suggested that FERA work relief and local jobs programs
would absorb most of the surplus CWA workers. Still, millions likely
would return to unemployment. Few people anticipated a boost from
Ickes's PWA, which persisted in its plodding ways. In Alabama, Hickok
found, legal and bureaucratic entanglements caused additional delays for
the PWA. For the time being, FERA would have to pick up the slack.*
And there was a lot of slack. Some seventy-three thousand Alabamians
crowded the relief rolls as of March 31. With the demise of the CWA,
relief officials told Hickok, they expected an immediate rise to ninety
thousand. As a consequence, she encountered gloom, sometimes shad-
ing into doom. "I regret to say that nobody seems to have a banjo on
his knee," she reported from Birmingham. "They don't seem to feel like
playing on banjoes!"[6]

Hickok felt far from chipper herself, possibly on account of over-
work. "Darling, try not to get so tired," ER wrote her. "This is a long trip
with no breaks & if you go on as you have begun you will be worn out."
Over a couple of days Hickok interviewed fifteen white-collar workers,
one-time members of Birmingham's middle class, among them an ac-
countant, an insurance agent, a masseur, an architect, a pawn shop clerk,
and a musician. The sessions were exhausting and stressful, though the
interviewees accepted the fact that the CWA's days were over. "They
were very mild," she wrote Hopkins. "Had few kicks to make. Generally
I'd say they were dumb with misery." But they still hoped to be able to
work for whatever relief they would receive—to save their self-respect.[7]

These clients once had been proud and self-sufficient. Appearances

---

* It would be a full year before the New Deal's Works Progress Administration, Harry Hopkins, proprietor, emerged to offer fresh opportunity for the unemployed.

mattered, but the relief agencies couldn't be of much help there. "They want to cling to some semblance at least of their normal standards of living," Hickok saw. "We can provide overalls, but not tailored business suits. We can't keep those white collars laundered." Nor would they consider moving to a cheaper neighborhood. "Apparently they won't even let themselves be starved into it," she observed. To a man, they found it impossible to live decently on their relief benefits, which started at $4.80 a week. At first, a young musician told her, he, his wife, and their seven-month-old baby managed to rub along all right. But rent consumed $3 a week. "I do everything I can to pick up a little money to pay that rent," he said. "I've washed windows. I've even gone out and competed with Niggers to get jobs mowing lawns." He'd pawned everything of any value: his wife's engagement ring, his watch, most of his clothes, the musical instruments that once brought him a livelihood. In the weeks he couldn't earn enough through odd jobs to knock off part of the rent, he tried to make the best of the $1.80 weekly balance. "Most of the time we honestly don't have enough to eat," he said matter-of-factly. "We buy all the flour and bacon we can, what we call 'white meat' down here, cheaper than the bacon you'd ordinarily eat—and a few green vegetables. The first night we have a pretty good dinner, the second night not quite so good, and so on until the last two nights we're eating nothing but bread and flour gravy." His wife's teeth were falling out. He obtained a relief order for a doctor's visit; the doctor diagnosed an inadequate diet. All the same, she continued to nurse the baby. She had no choice. They couldn't afford to buy enough milk to keep her healthy.[8]

Not for the first time, Hickok witnessed how visits from the relief investigators eroded the clients' confidence and sense of self-worth. The calls were humiliating no matter who came to the door. But most demoralizing, it seemed to her, were visits from young, attractive, college-educated female social workers. Why not send a middle-aged man? "He's less conspicuous," a client told her. "At least we can kid ourselves into thinking the neighbors think he's a salesman of some sort." It was the wives, he said, who most resented the pretty young investigators. He continued: "Suppose you were my wife—and I'll bet you're thinking your lucky stars you're not—run down, without any decent clothes,

looking ten years older than you ought to look. How would you like
it if some smooth-faced—not a wrinkle anywhere—young girl, nicely
dressed, all made up, came into your house, sat down on the edge of
a chair and began to ask you a lot of personal questions. You'd want to
throw something at her, wouldn't you? The contrast is just too painful,
that's all."[9]

Hickok sped south out of Birmingham on U.S. 31 on the morning
of March 28 for two days in the Alabama Black Belt, so named for the
rich darkness of the soil and the skin color of a majority of the inhabitants. In the countryside west of Montgomery she met tenants and
croppers, planters, small-town merchants, county agricultural agents,
and relief workers. The reports were mixed. With the breakup of the
plantation system in the decades after the Civil War, the size of Alabama
farms had contracted steadily; by the early 1930s the average place covered sixty-eight acres. (Nationally, 60 percent of farms were a hundred
acres or fewer.) More than 70 percent of all Black Belt farm families
were tenants, and 88 percent of black farmers rented or cropped. Most
tenant families lived in more or less hopeless circumstances. The professional relief people Hickok interviewed pinned their hopes on the
government rehabilitation initiative, which sought to teach the country
people how to farm, tend the livestock, look after the house, keep the
accounts, and feed and care for themselves properly. The big landowners and the town merchants disparaged the improvement schemes. "It
is to them rather humorous that we should take all that trouble for 'jest
pore white trash an' niggers,'" Hickok observed. The social workers
assumed that, given a real chance, proper instruction, and adequate supervision, the dispossessed might actually be able to make better lives
for themselves.[10]

The large landowners baffled her. She wondered about their grasp
of reality, even when talk turned to their own places, some of them
baronial estates of upward of a thousand acres. As had been the case
in Georgia and South Carolina, few, if any, of the tenants had received
acreage reduction checks from the Agricultural Adjustment Administration. The money had gone to the planters, and they seemed to think the
taps would always flow. Then too, the planters appeared to be playing

the angles with Henry Wallace's agency. "Here's one for the Agriculture boys," she wrote Hopkins. "Farmers tell me that 75% of the land taken out of cotton production this year is going into corn! I wonder how they'll like that in Iowa." Still, she thought the planters might be cooperative in some ways. They seemed agreeable to waiving some tenant debts, for instance.[11]

Conversation in Black Belt country stores and plantation commissaries revolved around the merits of mules versus steers. A prime Alabama farm jack cost $100 to $150. A work ox—the country people called them steers—could be bought for $15 to $30. Naturally government agents insisted the farmers use oxen, but the farmers complained they were hard to break in and wouldn't work in the heat. "Let it get to be noon," one told Hickok, "and they jest lay right down—or wander off to the swamp." After a careful investigation, Hickok concluded that oxen, small animals actually, not much bigger than Shetland ponies, were mild, patient, and perfectly willing to pull their weight. A black tenant claimed he'd broken in one in only two days. (He'd named him Hustler.) Most of the men she spoke to, though, were ardent advocates of the immemorial mule. Said one, "Hell! This ain't no New Deal if we-all got to go back to plowin' steers!"[12]

Hickok prepared the Alabama reports in her room at the Monteleone Hotel in New Orleans, lamenting that she had been mewed up there with a typewriter for twenty-four hours over the weekend of April 7–8. "And in New Orleans of all places in the world," she wrote Kathryn Godwin. In fact she found time to indulge herself in the French Quarter, with dinner at Arnaud's: two gin fizzes, a shrimp dish, pompano baked in a paper bag, potatoes soufflé, a pint of Sauterne, crepes Suzette, black coffee. "You never tasted such food," she wrote ER; famously ascetic, the first lady probably hadn't. "What a town for a glutton!" Though the quality of the best restaurants remained high, the city's fortunes were at low ebb. "New Orleans is apparently, from the commercial standpoint, just a charming corpse," Hickok added. To Hopkins, she reported that the CWA effect was fading fast. A big coffee wholesaler told one of her sources that business fell off abruptly with the end of the program. The New Orleans relief caseload shot up, passing ten thousand in early April.[13]

She started for Texas at 5 in the morning of April 10, arriving in Houston by nightfall. If anything, she soon determined, conditions were worse in the Lone Star State than in Louisiana, "a godawful mess." Possibly her always changeable mood had veered south again. "At no time previously, since taking this job, have I been quite so discouraged as I am tonight," she wrote Hopkins from the Sam Houston Hotel on the 11th. The weekly food allowance for single women in Houston had been reduced to 39 cents. A toxic political dispute in Austin threatened a cutoff of relief funds to Houston and other cities. Houston's relief load reached 12,500 families and 2,700 single men and women in mid-April, with new applications pouring in at a rate of 1,100 a week.[14]

Hickok had dined that night with social workers assigned the cases of some five hundred unattached women: unemployables, those who could work if jobs became available, and itinerants. Hickok heard that one of the young male relief workers had borrowed a suit of old clothes and spent an evening among the transients to observe firsthand how they were getting along. He walked through a tough part of town, warding off one solicitation after another from the women of the streets.

"I can't," he told one of the women. "I haven't any money."

"Oh, that's alright. It only costs a dime."[15]

Hickok's encounters with Houston businessmen deepened her discouragement. Some industries, construction, for example, had basically collapsed. The city had overbuilt during the 1920s boom: "Their whole skyline is brand new. They won't be doing any building here for years." Still, parts of the new economy were comparatively healthy, with jobs available in the oil-drilling machinery field, for instance, though those companies hired only workers with specialized skills. The notion that the oil men would balk at taking on and training unskilled labor as a civic duty surprised and offended her. But this was Texas, after all. "Those babies are thinking in terms of 1929 profit," she wrote Hopkins. "Why, they'll let orders go, dammit, before they'll permit their cost of production to go up and cut into their profit. Now, if that's following the spirit of the New Deal, I'll eat my hat." Worse still, businesses large and small routinely flouted National Recovery Administration codes. They were out for whatever they could get, taking whatever advantage they could of government priming and widespread public confidence in the president.[16]

It would be an exaggeration to portray Hickok as an observer gifted with keen political insight. Even so, her account of a conversation over drinks with Houston's relief chairman, Lee Hager, would have struck a chill in Harry Hopkins. An admirer of Italy's Benito Mussolini, Hager had no faith in democratic processes. (As they talked, Hickok noticed that Hager kept the biggest pistol she'd ever seen behind his desk, within easy reach.) "What Roosevelt seems to be trying to do," he told her, "is to put over a Mussolini program in a democracy. It won't work. Businessmen won't follow any such program voluntarily. They're too selfish and too stupid." He proposed placing compulsory limits on profits and compulsory restraints on competition. "That's Fascism," Hager went on, "but it's the only thing that will do the trick. If Roosevelt were actually a dictator, we might get somewhere. This way it's hopeless." A couple of days' exposure to Texas's outsized problems seemed to undermine Hickok's faith in the New Deal. The obstacles to recovery began to look overwhelming, impossible to surmount through the ordinary operations of the political system. "If I were 20 years younger and weighed 75 pounds less, I think I'd start out to be the Joan of Arc of the Fascist movement of the United States," she proclaimed. "I've been out on this trip now for a little more than two weeks. In all that time I've hardly met a single person who seemed confident and cheerful. . . . Nobody seems to think any more that the thing is going to WORK."[17]

Leaving Houston on April 13, Hickok spent a couple of days touring the East Texas oilfields, where she discovered that, at full capacity, the industry could produce and refine a third of the gasoline used in the United States, "or maybe it's the world."* Howard W. Odum, the University of North Carolina sociologist, asserted that two hours of open flow from East Texas's nine thousand oil wells would supply all of Americans' daily consumption plus 50 percent. The United States produced two-thirds of

---

*A gallon of gasoline cost 10 cents in 1934.

the world's output of crude oil, according to Odum, and two-thirds of that came from fields in Texas and Oklahoma.

She pushed northeast into timber country on April 15 before doubling back across flat, dull prairie toward Austin. She fetched San Antonio two days later. Goats and the U.S. Army turned out to be key sectors of the San Antonio economy. "This town is feeling an improvement because of a pickup in the goat business," she reported, "furnishing mohair to the automobile manufacturers!" She learned, too, that San Antonio ranked among the U.S. leaders in the manufacture of baby clothes.[18]

Turning north again, Hickok covered the long dusty stretch to Dallas–Fort Worth. As a favor to Mrs. Roosevelt, she called on Elliott Roosevelt and his new wife, Ruth, then nearly to the end of her term with their first child and "big as a House." They served her lunch in their Fort Worth home. Hickok liked the rackety young Roosevelt's second wife, or so she told a fretful ER, and found Elliott "quieter, not so restless, *much* more mature." The couple lived quietly in an upper-middle-class neighborhood, with only a maid and a yard boy to look after them. If she intended to ease ER's worries about her son, her report seems to have achieved its purpose, anyway for the time being.[19]

"What an empire is this state of Texas!" Driving out of Fort Worth at sunrise on April 21, she swung west to Big Spring, 273 miles distant, crossing rangeland now intermittently broken by the plow, mostly cotton and grains. Oil too; prospectors had tapped the first reserves in 1928. Though the drive left her physically spent, she summoned the energy to write an after-dinner note to ER. The letter carried a tease, for she had read that the post office planned to issue a Mother's Day stamp commemorating the first lady: "God knows you're a mother alright, but . . . I always think of the Mother's Day mother as an old lady with a wistful expression and a cap and shawl." For a change she turned in early, dousing the light a few minutes past 10. She hoped to dream of ER; she hadn't done so on this trip. "The nearest I ever came was one night this week—I think it was the night I ate the Mexican dinner." She was up early on the 22nd, pushing west toward El Paso. In two weeks she would cover two thousand miles of Texas highways.[20]

Her reports were equivocal, offering a counterexample for every hopeful sign. The maritime industry, oil, cotton, and grains exported from the Port Arthur–Beaumont district, appeared to be in good shape. Conditions in timber country were dire. The cotton crop looked promising, but wheat, rice, and beef were suffering, mostly on account of low prices. In Dallas, the Lone Star Gas Company's sales climbed to a three-year high. Drought in the northern Panhandle would reduce the harvest there by 70 percent, and in the southern parts the rain had come too late, with most of the winter wheat seed carried away on the wind before it could sprout. The wool trade flourished in the West Texas sheep and goat country. In El Paso five banks had failed, and the silver and copper industries were slack. By midsummer Texas cowboys would be shooting a thousand cattle a day to spare them the torture of dying from hunger and thirst.[21]

Taking the good with the bad, she tentatively concluded, the New Deal recovery program appeared to be working in Texas. Yet relief caseloads kept rising: in San Antonio, with a population of about 280,000, 17,500 families—88,000 men, women, and children—were on the rolls. As in Atlanta and Birmingham, hundreds of Texas white-collar families were applying for relief for the first time. But Hickok sounded most concerned about the unemployables: the unskilled and undereducated, men forty and older and unattached women, especially ones approaching middle age. She ventured a rare prediction: "Before we get through with this business, we're going to have, not only stranded populations, but A WHOLE STRANDED GENERATION. What's the answer? Add that whole generation to the list of people who aren't going to get their jobs back because of technological advances, and—well, you've got something!" She wondered whether, in the end, she might turn out to be one of the strandees. "I'm over 40 myself. Suppose after this job is finished I couldn't ever get another? How would I like spending the rest of my life on relief—provided, as a single person, I could get relief?"[22]

Hickok toured New Mexico over four days in late April, reporting to Hopkins on April 27 from Socorro in the Rio Grande Valley seventy-five miles south of Albuquerque. U.S. 85 followed portions of the old Spanish

Camino Real through the fertile valley, farms alternating with grasslands. Beyond the little city's western horizon rose the Socorro Mountains, from which streams flowed toward the Rio Grande, replenishing the irrigation works that supported cotton, grains, fruit, and truck farming. Hickok forwarded basic data about the state: population 425,000, 60 percent Spanish American; the fourth largest of the 48 states in area, with 78 million acres but only 2 million of those arable; most of the state desert and mountains, good for little but light grazing.[23]

Hickok found the Spanish Americans, a mix of descendants of the European colonizers and immigrants from Mexico, more or less powerless, even though they had lived in the region far longer than the "Anglos" and regarded them as usurpers. "They've lost control of the land," she wrote. "They are now the laboring class, sheep herders, section hands, day laborers in the cities, small farmers." They composed 75 percent of New Mexico's relief caseload of twelve thousand families, a thousand transients and 1,750 single men and women. They lived in the country, mostly, and because of their low cost of living they drew a modest stipend of $8 to $10 a month. Their adobe houses looked sturdy, cheap, and comfortable. They raised a little food, but, like the rural Alabama poor, according to Hickok, they needed instruction and supervision: what to raise, how to raise it, and how to tend their stock.[24]

As for the unemployed Anglos, who were accustomed to a higher standard of living, there appeared to be no realistic prospect of recovery anytime soon. "Industry in New Mexico 'just ain't,'" Hickok asserted. The Santa Fe Railroad, the state's biggest employer, maintained a payroll of 7,500 in 1929. By 1933 the workforce had contracted to 3,200. One source told her the Santa Fe hadn't hired any new help for the Albuquerque maintenance shops since 1926. The shops' full-time workforce of 2,200 had fallen to 600 men working four days a week, and most of those let go had been skilled workers drawing good wages.[25]

New Mexico's mines were mostly idle too. Coal production slumped to a third of pre-Depression levels. The mines employed 3,500 men full time in 1929; in the spring of 1934, 2,200 short-time miners considered themselves fortunate to be able to work at all. Thus miners joined railroad workers on the state's relief rolls. The caseload included a significant number of dry farmers, though Hickok speculated they would "be alright if it ever rains again." The Albuquerque relief rolls topped one thousand; about 15 percent of the recipients were white-collar people. Those numbers were on the rise. A quarter of the city's fifty new cases a week came out of the broad middle class. Nor did Harold Ickes's slow-moving PWA offer much hope for the jobless. Hickok learned that only twenty-three men were working on PWA projects in Albuquerque. At its peak, the PWA would employ five hundred workers in the state.[26]

"Damn it," Hickok wrote Hopkins, "it's the same old story down here, wherever I go": two classes of people, whites and everyone else—blacks east of the Mississippi, blacks and Mexican Americans in Texas, Mexican Americans and Indians from Texas west. As matters stood, relief payments were insufficient to sustain a decent white standard of living, and with no jobs in sight whites were restive. For the second class (in New Mexico, mainly the Spanish Americans), benefits were adequate, even attractive. "Perfectly contented," she found the recipients. "Able, many of them, to get work, but at wages so low that they are better off on relief." Hickok had been told of ranchers offering herders wages as low as $7 a month. Landowners complained about not being able to find help because so many Mexican Americans subsisted on relief payments. She could understand why someone would take $8 or $10 a month in relief over $7 to tend another man's livestock. Maybe, she thought, the ranchers ought to consider raising wages a bit.[27]

Hickok exited New Mexico on April 29, heading into Arizona via the tourist center of Lordsburg. The highway traversed barren, empty country. West of the state line, between the towns of Douglas and Bisbee, the road suddenly deteriorated: loose gravel, poor grades, and sharp bends. It was, she would discover, a political football. Both towns had blocked repairs, on the grounds that an improved highway would divert traffic from one place or the other. "The result is about one wreck a week," she explained, "with a couple of fatalities every month or so." Hickok narrowly avoided becoming a fatality herself. She lost control of the car along a curve and it slewed wildly, overturned, and came to rest at the bottom of an embankment.

Shaken but unhurt, Hickok wired Mrs. Roosevelt at the White

House, prompting a flurry of responses: a phone call, a telegram, a letter. "Your wire [worried] me for fear you were worse hurt than you realized & the 'what might have happened aspect' I can't even face now," ER wrote. In a report to Hopkins, Hickok made light of the near-disaster. "I lost a day this week," she wrote him from Phoenix. "Since I had apparently carried most of the weight of the car on the back of my neck during the split-second while it was rolling over, the doctor seemed to think it might be a good idea for me to spend Monday in bed." As for Bluette, it was a total loss.[28]

"Feeling pretty sick about my car—it's a mess," she wrote Kathryn Godwin. "But I guess I'm lucky to be alive."[29]

Hickok traveled by rail to Denver for eight days in Colorado before pushing on to Los Angeles. With the destruction of Bluette she had lost the advantage of mobility, but there would be compensations: idle hours in the train that allowed her time to rest, recover from the exertions of the Colorado investigations, and compile a set of reports for Harry Hopkins. The train climbed the long grade toward Tennessee Pass through thick stands of pine. From the gap, at 10,400 feet, she could see Pike's Peak, with only a patch of snow at the summit. For the most part the upper slopes of the Front Range were bare, evidence of yet another dry winter. They should have been covered in white on the next to last Saturday in June 1934.[30]

Hickok had inspected the drought areas northeast of Denver on June 14 and 15, making her base in the town of Akron, a farm and railroad community of 1,500 bisected by the east–west line of U.S. 34. On the way her escort, a field engineer named Terry Owens, stopped the car a few miles east of Fort Morgan and announced, "You are now in the drouth area." Just then the clouds burst, releasing hail and heavy rain. Storms moved through the region on the afternoon of the 14th and blustered all night and into the next day, with lightning, hail, and torrential downpours. "They now consider the drouth broken in this part of the state," she wrote Mrs. Roosevelt. "Too late to save the small grains, but they think there will be good grazing and possibly some corn." Too late, too, for a rancher whose place lay athwart a broad swale. He had been watching his cattle slowly starve to death, foraging for dry, stunted buffalo grass and coming up mostly with sand. Floods of brown water roared down from the high places during the night, sweeping away his entire herd and submerging the house and barns.[31]

Drought-stricken northeastern Colorado farmers anticipated a wheat harvest about 5 percent of normal. In some places the plants poked up only a few inches from the cracked soil; in others there were no sprouts at all. Still, Hickok had seen worse in South Dakota the previous fall, and for that matter on the newsreels in a Denver movie house. But the cumulative effects were calamitous, for in Colorado the drought had entered its fifth year. "It's the same old story," she reported. "Farmers came in from Nebraska, Kansas, Missouri, homesteaded, and plowed up range country. For a few years they had phenomenal wheat crops. Then came the drouth." The AAA wheat allotment checks were the only income many farmers received in 1933.[32]

A day in the beet fields, June 15, gave Hickok her first glimpse of underage farm labor, children eight and ten years old in the open all day under a merciless sun. "It was not a nice picture," she wrote ER. She knew she should report to Hopkins that night, but she had been grinding her dentures incessantly for a couple of days, rubbing the roof of her mouth raw, and she felt awful. "So I think I'd better take said teeth out and go to bed," she went on. "If I don't I may not be able to wear them tomorrow." What she had seen that day would have increased the urge to gnash and grind. Most of the field hands, big and small, were Mexicans imported by the sugar companies, enduring the same sort of peonage she had witnessed in the Cotton South, only the sugar barons accomplished the exploitation more efficiently. Collectively, she discovered, the sugar companies were running a grift, "the most perfect system of gouging you ever heard of," bilking farmers, laborers, and the government alike. Hickok identified as archvillain the Great Western Sugar Company. "They've got themselves into a sweet spot where they have no responsibility whatever for anyone," she wrote. The company (and others) paid miserably for the crop. The farmers paid the hands starvation wages and still barely managed to survive. Meanwhile Great

Western harvested handsome profits and distributed generous dividends to stockholders.[33]

In January, *The Nation* reported that "the forces of justice and decency" were gathering to challenge Great Western. Growers' associations in Colorado and Nebraska demanded a more equitable share of sugar profits, threatening a year-long moratorium on beets if the conglomerate refused. And the United States Beet Sugar Association called for a ban on child labor in the fields. "Evidently the public clamor for common decency on the part of the sugar trust has begun to have results," the magazine suggested, "but it would be unwise to be too optimistic about the outcome yet." By June it was clear *The Nation*'s caution had been prudent. Hickok's inquiries showed Great Western's grip to be as vise-like as ever, and as painful to the growers as to the field hands.[34]

Hickok's sources told her that, on average, a Mexican migrant family could expect to earn less than $100 for a season's work in the beet fields. In some cases pay packets were withheld until December, because farmers delayed the harvest until as late in the fall as possible to allow for the maximum buildup of sugar in the root. Great Western's captive farmers needed labor from one season to the next, of course, so the company encouraged Mexican migrants to stay year-round. In the winter, the Mexicans—and a lot of the beet farmers too—went onto the relief rolls. According to Hickok, federal and state relief funds subsidized Great Western's peon labor force.[35]

She touched up the Colorado report as the train rattled down the western slope of Tennessee Pass over the Denver & Rio Grande Railroad's rough roadbed. Stupendous views flashed past Hickok's window: pine-clad flanks, jagged peaks, sheep grazing in the hillside meadows. The line dropped down to the floor of the Royal Gorge, the spectacularly stratified Grand Canyon of the Arkansas, the river rushing clear and green alongside the train. The scenery, the loveliest she'd seen, took some of the jolt out of the ride. "I'm feeling much, much better tonight than I have for a week or so," she wrote ER from the train. "I got terribly tired—more tired than I've ever been on any previous trip—and it was all so depressing. Sugar beets, drouth, abandoned coal camps." The ordeal of the Mexicans remained with her—thousands of men, women, and children bent double, hoeing and thinning the rows, weeding, lifting, and topping the plants. They filed into the fields at 6 in the morning and stayed at it, with a brief break for a meal in the blazing meridian, until 6 or 7 in the evening. The growers had assured her the work did no harm to children. Hickok spoke briefly with a man whose four daughters were working with him, the youngest age twelve. "Whether it's good for them or not," she wrote dryly, "I certainly did not enjoy seeing that 12-year-old—undersized, with a droop to her shoulders that no 12-year-old should have—working her way up those rows, alternately hoeing and stooping over to pull weeds." Another girl, "a bright little thing, with the keenest brown eyes," told her she had been working "in the beets" since she was eight.[36]

Hickok asked, "How do you thin beets? It must be hard on your back, stooping over that way all the time."

"It's better if you go on your knees."[37]

Hickok detected signs of recovery in Los Angeles. Her hotel, the eleven-year-old Biltmore on palm-shaded Pershing Square downtown, said to be the largest hotel west of Chicago, looked prosperous, and in fact receipts for the first four months of 1934 were up 35 percent from a year ago. The *Los Angeles Times* described southern California business activity as "relatively satisfactory" over the first six months of the year, noting that national surveys consistently identified the region as one of the economy's "white spots." Despite water shortages, agriculture appeared to be holding its own, as did the oil industry. Statewide, overall employment climbed 27 percent in May from the trough of a year before. Then too, Walt Disney had begun work on the Brothers Grimm's *Snow White*. "The film would be made all in color with cartoon characters," according to *The Times*. "It will not include the Big Bad Wolf, the Three Little Pigs or even Mickey Mouse." *Snow White and the Seven Dwarfs*, released in December 1937, would be Disney's first feature-length animated movie.[38]

But there were discouraging indicators too. From the relief angle, Hickok reported that Los Angeles was one of the black spots, with allegations of widespread graft and mismanagement in relief administration

and a bloated caseload of more than 110,000 clients. A survey of the city
and county concluded that the region contained many more people than
the economy could support, even in the most favorable circumstances.
(Los Angeles's population had doubled in every decade but one since
1870 and now exceeded 1 million.) Another complication: in mid-June
a U.S. District Court indicted the state's FERA and CWA administrator
and eight others on corruption charges involving hiring for the jobs program. Ray Branion and his codefendants insisted they were victims of a
frame-up for refusing to play politics in the allocation of CWA projects.
Hickok saw some justice in the claim, but perceived too that Branion had
run the jobs program with unerring incompetence.[39]

With the pressure of hard times, California politics had turned mean.
The conservative elites reviled Roosevelt and the New Deal, but, wary of
assailing a popular president, they instead attacked the first lady, Henry
Wallace, Rexford Tugwell, and Harry Hopkins. They played the Red card
shamelessly, accusing those closest to FDR of being dupes and probably
worse, and in every labor dispute they saw the hand of the Comintern.
Labor wars were brutal; the dominant economic and political class knew
no restraints of law or decency. Just now, in early summer, West Coast
longshoremen were on strike, and battered workers in the industrialized
agricultural regions of the San Joaquin and Imperial valleys—Mexicans,
Filipinos, blacks, and white refugees from the Dust Bowl—were sullen,
defeated, and plotting new outbreaks.

Hickok commuted to and from Los Angeles, Riverside, San Ber-
nardino, and the Imperial Valley for a week or so in late June and early
July, grueling slogs on city pavements and through dusty fields in intense
summer heat. "I'm so sleepy right now that I can hardly see the typewriter keys," she wrote Hopkins on June 27. A few days in the desert introduced her to what Carey McWilliams, writing in *The American Mercury*
in October, would dub California's "rural civil war." McWilliams asked
readers to visualize the Imperial Valley, "an enormous inner-valley sink,
reclaimed from desert and converted into a huge truck garden." Much
of the land lay below sea level, a desert hothouse ruled by a powerful
oligarchy of large farmers. Capital costs for irrigation works were heavy,
and inexorably the big operators absorbed the smallholdings. By 1934

fewer than a hundred individuals and companies controlled nearly all the cropland, producing cantaloupes, alfalfa, grapefruit, strawberries, grapes, peas, lettuce, barley, and dates on "industrialized plantations."[40]

The valley's migrant laborers, "fruit tramps" in the vernacular, worked for starvation wages. A federal labor commission survey of the pay of 204 pea pickers in early 1934 revealed that they earned an average of 56 cents a day, insufficient to meet even the most basic needs. With mass migration from the Great Plains and the Southwest (some 300,000 whites from these regions would pour into California during the Great Depression), field laborers lost what little leverage they once possessed. By midyear there were 142 workers for every 100 jobs in agriculture. Workers lived in primitive conditions, in makeshift colonies straggling along the irrigation ditches, through which flowed their only source of water. Cheap and available, the twenty thousand permanent Mexican inhabitants of the Imperial Valley made agriculture there both possible and profitable.[41]

As the Depression deepened, labor organizers moved in. The Valley overlords reacted with the familiar California pattern of red-baiting and the deployment of police power to crush the unions. The sheriffs and the deputies, the courts, American Legion vigilantes, and the newspapers all did the growers' bidding. In January 1934, after the Communist-led Cannery and Agricultural Workers Industrial Union launched a strike at pea and lettuce harvest time, police and vigilante groups used guns, tear gas, and clubs to break up meetings of workers. Police blocked the roads, denying food to the strikers, and county officials threatened mass deportations of Mexican and Filipino workers. Vigilantes kidnapped an American Civil Liberties Union investigating attorney, rolled his car off a bluff, and carried him away to San Diego. Two union organizers were sentenced to six months in jail for violating a law that gave the police chief authority to arrest people for talking in the street if he objected to what he thought they might be talking about. By late February the strike had been crushed.[42]

A National Labor Board investigation in early spring determined that Imperial Valley police and the courts had serially violated strikers' constitutional rights, including the rights of free speech and assembly.

They had carried out indiscriminate arrests that filled the jails, required excessive bail, and abused state vagrancy laws. A federally appointed labor conciliator, Brigadier General Pelham D. Glassford, concluded that "a group of growers have exploited a Communist hysteria for the advancement of their own interests; that they have welcomed labor agitation which they could brand as 'red,' as a means of sustaining the supremacy of mob rule, thereby preserving what is so essential to their profits— cheap labor." Glassford hinted that he had received a death threat for his trouble. Hickok passed along rumors that vigilantes had beaten him up before he left the Valley and, in a more imaginative act of political vandalism, had given him knockout drops in a cocktail.[43]

She felt the tension as soon as she arrived, for the aftershocks of war in the Imperial Valley lingered into midsummer. From her base at the Hotel Barbara Worth in El Centro, a little city of shaded patios and copiously watered flower gardens, Hickok made the rounds as best she could in the terrific heat and suffocating dust. Someone told her that the temperature the day before had reached 128 degrees. The glaring sun, the overpowering swelter, and the tightly sealed hotel room windows left her enervated and morose. "This valley is the damnedest place I ever saw—except Southern West Virginia and Eastern Kentucky," she wrote Mrs. Roosevelt. "There is the same suspicion and bitterness all through the place. An unreasoning, blind fear of 'Communist agitators.' If you don't agree with them, you are a Communist, of course." She returned to Los Angeles disoriented and dispirited, her impressions a blur: "heat, depression, bitterness, more heat, terrible poverty, heat again." Imperial County conditions were hellish. The smallholders up toward Riverside were in desperate straits. "What *are* we going to do with these people?" Hickok wondered.[44]

"As I look back on it all," she wrote Hopkins from the oasis of the Biltmore, "I am inclined to believe that everything I heard out there was affected by the heat and dust. Why in God's name anybody ever wants to live out there!"[45]

In Los Angeles big, bold headlines shouted news of an intensification of the West Coast dockworkers' strike, which had broken out in San Francisco in early May and spread north to Portland and Seattle and south to San Pedro, L.A.'s port. More than eleven thousand members of the International Longshoremen's Association and their sailor, cook, steward, stoker, and teamster allies had all but shut down seaborne commerce up and down the coast, although strikebreakers continued to move a trickle of goods in and out of San Pedro, a stronghold of the open shop. By the end of May, sixty-one heavily laden ships were swinging to anchor in San Francisco harbor. In June, offloads fell to less than half the depressed level of June 1933. As the strike wore on, consumer goods became increasingly scarce. The steamer *Iowan* landed twenty-seven tons of face powder at Pier 26, but it stayed under lock in the pier shed, leaving the cosmetics counters bare. The *Iowan*'s cargo of twelve tons of pickles likewise remained inaccessible, just as the Independence Day holiday loomed.[46]

By early July, *Time* magazine reported, eighty-nine deepwater vessels were marooned in the bay, and some $50 million worth of goods lay entombed along the three-and-a-half mile curve of the Embarcadero. Businesses estimated the strike's cost at $1 million a day. The maritime trade had built San Francisco, and in many ways the colorful, polyglot, sinful, and intermittently violent waterfront symbolized the city. Out of a population of 600,000, some 400,000 San Franciscans were male. Hundreds of lodging houses, seamen's shelters, cheap restaurants, taverns, pool halls, movie houses, tattoo parlors, and bordellos catered to their interests. Fully half the city's longshoremen were on relief. The employers, operating under the aegis of the Industrial Association of San Francisco,* "saw Red at every labor agitation," *Time* asserted. Two months into the strike, the two forces approached Independence Day in an attitude of belligerence. "Neither side is willing to concede anything," FDR's mediator, Assistant Labor Secretary Edward O'Grady, remarked.[47]

The longshoremen sought control of the hiring halls, a pay raise to $1 an hour, guarantees of a six-hour day and a thirty-hour week, and the closed shop. The employers countered with what sounded like a reasonable offer: union recognition but no closed shop, joint control of the halls, arbitration of wages and working conditions. They also agreed to end the

---

*Shippers, bankers, manufacturers, and railroad interests formed the Industrial Association in 1921 with the aim of forcing all the national unions off the waterfront.

hateful shape-up. Conservative union leaders accepted the proposal, and the newspapers trumpeted a settlement. But the ascendant radical leaders in the International Longshoremen's Association, among them the charismatic Australian Harry Bridges, branded the deal a sellout, and in a secret ballot the rank and file overwhelmingly rejected it.[48]

The shape-up worked this way: longshoremen turned up looking for cargo to unload at 6 o'clock every morning at the Ferry Building at the foot of Market Street. Because ships came and went irregularly, the demand for workers rose and fell. Hundreds of men would mill about until noon, only to learn that there might—*might*—be a few hours' work after 10 that night. Private contractors acting for the employers would select the men, often in exchange for kickbacks. Favoritism, nepotism, and graft were endemic. Union activists need not apply. The wharfingers' hourly wage, 85 cents, seemed adequate, but few had worked a full week since 1929; in 1933 longshoremen earned an average of $10.45 a week.[49]

The rising generation of ILA leaders determined to improve working conditions on the waterfront by seizing control of the hiring halls. San Francisco stevedores had earned a reputation as the fastest, most efficient movers of cargo on the West Coast. But it came at a price, according to Harry Bridges. They were driven like slaves; Bridges claimed to have seen men drop dead of exhaustion on the docks. The ILA and allied unions coalesced on June 18 as the Joint Maritime Strike Committee, choosing Bridges to lead what would become the greatest strike in San Francisco history.[50]

A lean, hawk-faced thirty-four-year-old, Bridges outmaneuvered the old flaccid leadership to emerge as the face, voice, and tactical genius of the ILA. After several years at sea, he had settled permanently on the San Francisco waterfront in 1922, and he wore the longshoremen's uniform—denim shirt, black canvas trousers, and flat white cap—with pride and defiance, his right arm distorted from years of wielding the longshoreman's claw. The Depression exacted a further toll on Bridges, as it had on all but the most favored of dockworkers, the thousand or so "star gang" members with connections among the employers and reputations for docility. In 1933–34 Bridges's clothes were threadbare, and he could barely pay the rent on the small apartment he and his wife shared in the working-class Mission District.[51]

Bridges offered no apology for the union's uncompromising stand. "It's because it's a militant strike that we've been successful so far," he told Evelyn Seeley of *The Nation* in June. "They can call them radical tactics but whatever they are they work. You get nowhere with all the good old legal tactics, all this reliance on injunctions, letting the scabs work, and so forth." Bridges and his lieutenants supervised a corps of a thousand pickets working twelve-hour shifts, Seeley reported, "just like the police." The union operated a soup kitchen and distributed strike relief. The rank and file admired and trusted Bridges as one of their own, for he slept in seamen's hotels, ate seamen's food, and spoke the seamen's language. In mid-June the ILA backed Bridges a second time, decisively rejecting a renewed employers' offer.[52]

Making no secret of its intention to run the union blockade, the Industrial Association raised money and recruited strikebreakers, including thirty or so college football players from Berkeley and a battalion of truck drivers from Los Angeles. The employers had a powerful ally in the San Francisco Police Department, which deployed seven hundred officers on July 3, the day chosen for the operation that would pry open the port. In the bright noonday sun, police carrying arms and wearing rubber helmets and gas masks advanced to clear the area in front of Pier 38. "Shotguns and revolvers roared, gas bombs were hurled into the midst of cursing longshoremen's pickets," *The San Francisco Chronicle* reported. Five trucks rolled away from the pier and down the Embarcadero under heavy police guard. In the initial assault, mounted police drove about three hundred pickets two blocks back from the waterfront to Second and Townsend streets. The strikers counterattacked with bricks, cobblestones, and railroad spikes. Some 2,500 longshoremen and their sympathizers milled along the edges of the smoke-shrouded zone of battle. By day's end the employers had moved eighteen truckloads of goods—birdseed, coffee, tires—from Pier 38 to a warehouse on King Street. Twenty-six strikers were hurt and one man died, thirty-four-year-old Argonne Riley, a strikebreaker, found sprawled in a gutter near the Seamen's Union headquarters, his skull fractured.[53]

The Industrial Association declared the port open the next day, July 4, but the opposing forces massed again the morning after, Thursday, this time with eight hundred police carrying heavier nightsticks and the noxious chemical agent DM confronting as many as five thousand strikers. Police opened with riot guns on a crowd of two thousand strikers along Steuart Street near the ILA headquarters. The assault forced the longshoremen off the Embarcadero, pushing them north as far as Pacific Street on the Barbary Coast. Retreating up the gentle slope of Rincon Hill, they knocked together a barricade and held off successive police assaults with improvised weapons, including a slingshot constructed out of lengths of lumber and rubber inner tubes that could hurl bricks at lethal velocity over a distance of four hundred feet. In a third attempt on Rincon Hill police advanced, revolvers drawn, through a curtain of smoke from the tear gas barrage and from grass fires started by sparks from spent gas canisters. When they cleared the barricade, the defenders had vanished.[54]

The battles of Bloody Thursday left two strikers dead and more than eighty injured, a third of them with gunshot wounds. Throughout the fighting the Industrial Association continued to shift goods off Pier 38, fifty truckloads by the end of the day. At around 5 in the afternoon 1,700 California National Guard troops marched in, two infantry regiments with a company of tanks in reserve, toylike vehicles but with skin tough enough to shrug off bricks and cobblestones. The soldiers took up positions along the Embarcadero and stared down the longshoremen from machine-gun posts set up on the roofs of the pier sheds.[55]

Three hundred miles to the south, Hickok followed the dock strike in the pages of *The Los Angeles Times*. For the most part, the big city press sided with the bosses. Conservative and implacably open shop, *The Times* made no effort to conceal its animus. "For nearly three months the greater part of the Pacific Coast has been standing with upraised arms at the mercy of the dock strikers and their Red supporters," declared a front-page editorial. "The strike passed from the control of organized labor into the hands of organized mobs. The Communists . . . control the situation." In San Francisco *The Chronicle* and *The Examiner* of William Randolph Hearst were equally strident. "Almost without exception," Evelyn Seeley wrote in *The New Republic*, "their news articles and the captions

[to] their pictures were used for anti-strike propaganda, brazen distortions and incitement to violence." *The Chronicle* played up alleged Red involvement. The *San Francisco Call-Bulletin*'s news coverage and page after full page of vivid photography stand the test of time pretty well; in editorial comment, the Hearst-owned evening newspaper called for law and order and settlement via arbitration, a spurious neutrality that tilted toward the employers.[56]

Along the Embarcadero, the troops enforced a tense, unhappy calm. Bridges called for the longshoremen to withdraw. "We can't stand up against police machine guns and National Guard bayonets," he said. Then he approached the San Francisco Labor Council with a proposal for a general strike of the city's forty-five thousand union workers.[57]

Eleanor Roosevelt's United Airlines flight from Chicago touched down at the Sacramento Airport on July 12, in time for the evening newspapers to file reports of her arrival. She would vacation in California with Lorena Hickok while FDR sailed to Hawaii in the cruiser USS *Houston*; she and the president were to meet in a couple of weeks when the warship reached Portland, Oregon. She had been planning the trip for weeks. "We'll go to Colfax and spend 5 or 6 quiet days," she had written Hickok in June. "Then we'll get the car, motor . . . over a lovely route thro' the Yosemite & in to San Francisco." Reporters mobbed the first lady the moment she stepped off the plane, and their editors treated her unannounced arrival in California as a subtle mystery. *The Call-Bulletin* speculated under a banner headline on page 1 that she had come as a "private emissary" of the president, with a brief to resolve the city's strike crisis.[58]

"She said she doesn't want any publicity on this trip," Althea McMasters, a stewardess on the United flight, told reporters at the airfield. But Mrs. Roosevelt couldn't wish the press away. For the first few hours, reporters and photographers tracked her every move, despite Hickok's low-comedy attempts to plead or deceive. "I used to be a newspaperman myself," she kept saying. Hickok tried a slapstick dodge, telling reporters crowding the lobby that Mrs. Roosevelt wanted to go to her room to freshen up before meeting them, then leading her through an alley door to the waiting Plymouth.* The car roared away from the hotel with the news hawks in hot pursuit. The chase reached a top speed of nearly eighty before Mrs. Roosevelt ordered the plainclothes state policeman at the wheel to pull over. Telling reporters she would reveal nothing about her plans, she sat calmly knitting in the shade alongside the road while they telephoned their editors for instructions. The standoff ended with Hickok and ER pushing on—alone—for Colfax in the Sierra Nevada foothills, where they spent a tranquil several days with Hickok's onetime flatmate Ella Morse and her husband.[59]

Then they moved on to Yosemite, where three days in the mountains exposed Hickok's inadequacies as an outdoorswoman. A heavy smoker, she tired easily at high altitudes. "I learned that nobody who smokes a great deal and whose heart is not strong should try to camp above 10,000 feet," Mrs. Roosevelt remembered. "She more or less panted throughout the days we were there." And Hickok had no aptitude for handling horses. Fortunately, a retinue of five park rangers accompanied the couple, serving as guides, cooks, and hostlers. They could not, however, save Hickok from a drenching when her mount, a playful beast, decided to roll over and spill her into a cold mountain stream. With ER showing little sympathy, the mishap left Hickok in a dangerous state of irritation. When a group of camera-carrying Yosemite tourists crowded too close to the party she lost her temper and, flailing her fleshy arms and feigning a charge, let loose a stream of obscenities, stunning the tourists and embarrassing the ever composed, always mannerly Mrs. Roosevelt. The outburst cast a pall over the rest of the vacation.[60]

As bad, perhaps, as the icy dip on the mountain was a glacial dinnertime encounter with Harold Ickes at the Ahwahnee Hotel in Yosemite Valley. Ickes and Hopkins long had been at bureaucratic odds over federally sponsored public works. Naturally Hickok sided with her boss, and in her reports she had sometimes derided the Public Works Administration and what she called Ickes's "trickle down method" of creating jobs:

---

*Mrs. Roosevelt had purchased the car, a gray convertible, for Hickok as a replacement for Bluette. She dubbed it "Stepchild."

big government orders for heavy equipment, on the theory that industry would hire more workers to manufacture it. Efficient and cost-effective, perhaps, but in Hickok's view the strategy failed to put sufficient
numbers of people to work. Mrs. Roosevelt stepped away from the table
briefly. "I've been reading your reports," Ickes told Hickok with a glance
meant to shrivel her into insignificance. "Interestin'." She thanked him,
then endured a seemingly interminable silence awaiting ER's return.[61]

In San Francisco in late July, Hickok arranged for what she hoped
would be a leisurely stay in one of her favorite places, the intimate Clift
Hotel in the shadow of the far-famed St. Francis. She intended to show
ER the sights of the city and take her to her favorite restaurants, but the
press quickly found her out. At breakfast one morning a photographer
rushed their table, dropped to one knee, and fired. In 1934 some photographers still used black powder for flash. "It would explode with a
deafening bang and a lot of smoke," Hickok recalled. When the fumes
cleared, they went off to attempt to enjoy the sights—Fishermen's Wharf,
the ferry ride to Sausalito, dinner at the Fairmont Hotel—with a queue
of newsmen astern.[62]

The travelers struck north in Hickok's new Plymouth, finding anonymity for a couple of days in pauses at Crater Lake and the Muir Woods
before spending the last night of the vacation in Bend, Oregon, where
celebrity once again overtook the first lady. Someone had spotted her.
Well-wishers packed into the hotel lobby, and the mayor himself stood at
the head of a long reception line. Here, finally, Mrs. Roosevelt seemed to
accept reality. No longer the mistress of her movements, she belonged to
the Americans wherever she went. Later, in their suite, she told Hickok,
"FDR said I'd never get away with it, and he was right. I can't." After a
pause, she went on: "From now on I shall travel as I'm supposed to travel,
as the President's wife, and try to do what is expected of me."[63]

The two-week trip ended in gloom and tension in Portland, where
Mrs. Roosevelt and the president were to rendezvous for the return journey to Washington. The first lady's hotel suite overflowed with flowers.
"All you need is a corpse," said Hickok, a quip that signaled the wreck
of her hopes for a life with ER. The relationship had peaked and would
never again approach the intensity of the first phase. Perhaps Hickok's

Yosemite tantrum had hastened the change. In any case, she returned to San Francisco, resuming work on August 5 in the aftermath of the city's four-day general strike, one of the great labor-capital confrontations of the era. The newspapers carried accounts of the home-bound first couple's stop at the Grand Coulee Dam in Washington, where FDR told a crowd of ten thousand that jobs-creating public works programs would go forward. *The San Francisco Chronicle* reported that divers searching the wreck of a treasure ship off Juneau, Alaska, had fought "furious battles with giant devil fish [octopus]" 365 feet below the surface of the sea. And in San Francisco twenty-nine jailed Reds were protesting their ordeal by refusing to eat or bathe. The wardens at the lockup threatened to turn fire hoses on them.[64]

The general strike continued to dominate the news. San Francisco's elites were still shaken from staring down Revolution, and now they sought to sweep the state clear of Reds. The mayor, Angelo Rossi, likening the waterfront crisis to the earthquake and fire of 1906 and blaming the troubles on the Communists, had declared a state of emergency on July 14, in spite of the powerful National Guard presence in the city, reinforced to nearly five thousand men and an additional armored unit. City and state officials appealed via wireless to President Roosevelt on the high seas. "A lot of people completely lost their heads," FDR would say later. "Everybody demanded that I sail into San Francisco Bay, all flags flying and guns double-shotted and end the strike." The president wisely left crisis management in the hands of his labor secretary, Frances Perkins, who remained calm, resisting calls to send federal troops and deport Harry Bridges.[65]

As general strikes go, San Francisco's proved to be remarkably gentlemanly, even though it graded as the largest labor uprising in the United States since 1919. Although Bridges and the rank and file had pressed for the strike, the conservative leaders of the Labor Council directed it, no matter what the newspapers were saying. The streets were eerily quiet on Sunday, July 15; there were no streetcars and only light motor traffic. There were no taxis abroad on Monday. Gas stations shut down. Office workers stayed home. The butchers were on strike. Milk and bread deliveries arrived sporadically. Only nineteen restaurants in the city were open. According to *Time*, 100,000 people evacuated San Francisco in the first twenty-four hours of the strike.[66]

The Strike Committee pursued limited aims, permitted food deliveries, and declined to cut the flow of water, gas, and electricity. Ships were moving in and out of the port, seventeen arrivals and twenty departures between July 14 and 16. And the general strike was short-lived. Over Bridges's objection, the committee voted on July 19 to end it and submit the issues to a federal arbitrator. The longshoremen, much weakened, held out for a week or so longer, then, in a referendum, voted overwhelmingly in favor of arbitration. They formally called off the dock strike on July 31, eighty-three days after it had begun. When the arbitrator's award came down in October, the ILA could claim a partial victory: there would be collective bargaining covering all West Coast ports; an end to the shape-up, with joint union-employer control of the hiring halls; a raise of 10 cents to 95 cents an hour; and a six-hour day.[67]

Time would say the newspapers' "bellowing" helped break the general strike, and *The New Republic* detected a conspiracy among Bay Area publishers to present the labor uprising as a Communist-led campaign to establish a San Francisco Soviet. The press cheered on a series of vigilante assaults on suspected radicals. But inflated news accounts and intemperate editorial commentary didn't fool Hickok. She wrote Hopkins, "Ever since the 'Vigilantes' went out and raided so-called 'Communist' headquarters, there have been big headlines in the San Francisco papers every day about ridding the state of Communists." Privately, her sources, among them Mayor Rossi, suggested that authentic Communists were rare and that the longshoremen's grievances had been urgent. Even so, right-wing mobs sacked the newsroom of the Communist *Western Worker*. Police invaded the headquarters of the Marine Workers' Industrial Union on Jackson Street, smashed the furniture, confiscated strike pamphlets, clubbed men in the hall, and arrested seventy-five seamen as alleged revolutionists. They then moved on to an ILA relief kitchen on the Embarcadero and netted another ten suspected Communists. A newly organized police Anti-Radical Squad staged a melee, reminiscent of Brownshirt provocations in Germany a few years before, in which police disguised as workers attacked Communists at the party's headquarters.[68]

"The workers looked very much like police dressed as workers," *The New Republic* suggested, "and it is harder for a cop to pass himself off as a worker than it is for a camel to get through the needle's eye."[69]

Hickok reached Topeka, the Kansas capital, on September 14, three weeks into a homeward stretch that included stops in Nevada, Utah, and Wyoming. Fittingly, she would bring her eighteen-month investigation into the human costs of the Great Depression to a close in the place where, in a way, it had begun two Septembers before, when she stood in fierce sunlight with thousands of wary farmers listening to commonplaces from Candidate Roosevelt. As president, Roosevelt had done much to ease the worst of the suffering for so many Americans, though perhaps not enough. Then too, as Hickok had been reporting for some time now, there were adumbrations of recovery, possibly owing to the New Deal. Moods were lighter. Pockets in Topeka, if not filled, at least were no longer empty of everything but lint.

Here too Hickok discovered an anomaly: drought had laid Kansas low, yet she detected an air of optimism and a glimmer of returning prosperity. Her route led through mile after mile of seared pasture and grain country in western Kansas, attenuated cattle, withered crops. "Here and there a cornfield that burned up before the stuff ever got much above knee high," she observed. "Fields of scant, ragged wheat stubble with pathetically little piles of straw. Russian thistle piled up for stock feed." In one southwestern county 1,036 of 1,800 families were on relief, with applications on the rise. Yet one of the relief workers told her that farmers had resisted the government's rural rehabilitation schemes. They didn't want to be rehabilitated, and they certainly didn't want to be moved off the land.

"All we need is a little rain," one of the farmers said.[70]

Plenty of misery still, but Hickok saw another side to the story when she toured the Kansas Free State Fair. On display were bumper crops of apples from northeastern Kansas, where wells that had flowed for sixty years went dry over the summer. Grains and hay were abundant at the exhibits, though she swore she had driven for two days earlier in the week without seeing a single haystack. Fair veterans said livestock compared favorably with other years. "Literally hundreds" of new Chevrolets sat bumper to bumper in the dusty fair parking lot. Inside the gate, Hickok pushed her way through surging crowds. Ten thousand people packed the grandstand for the night's show. "Hot dog sellers, peanut vendors, church supper pavilions—all doing a rushing business," she noted. A salesman told her he'd found buyers for ten natural gas- or kerosene-fueled refrigerators just that week, at prices ranging from $200 to $295. The downtown hotels reported a brisk business, especially among traveling salesmen. She wondered where the money was coming from. Wheat allotment benefits? Corn checks? Farmers with a crop to sell were getting better prices now. Perhaps people were buying on credit again. That struck her as a good sign, an expansion of the money supply—something Kansans had been demanding for decades. And finally, in a washroom in a Topeka office building, Hickok encountered something new in her experience: "A hot air drier for your hands, taking the place of towels, roller or paper. It operates like a hair drier in a shampoo parlor, by electricity."

Said Hickok's companion, "Wouldn't you just know they'd have it in Topeka, Kansas?"[71]

Epilogue

PROSPECTS

New York and Washington, January 1, 1935

The turn of the year 1935 brought tens of thousands of giddy New Yorkers into the streets in "one of the maddest and gayest celebrations this generation has ever seen," according to *The New York Times*. Thronging Times Square, they let out a shattering roar when the glowing white ball slid down the flagpole at the tolling of the midnight bell. They crowded into hotels, restaurants, and bars. They popped thousands of champagne corks. They packed theaters and movie houses. In the theater district, the liquor stores sold out of the best-selling brands by 9 o'clock and flashed rush orders to the warehouses. From the Hudson and the East River, ferryboats, ocean liners, merchant vessels, and small craft added their sirens and whistles to the din. After midnight light snow began to descend, the first snowfall of the winter.[1]

What were New Yorkers celebrating? "Reasons in plenty warrant the American people in entering the New Year cheerfully," an editorial in *The Times* asserted. The data on national income and gross domestic product seemed to suggest that economic recovery had gained momentum in 1934. "But what cannot be written into the statistics is something very different but most significant," *The Times* went on. "For the first time in five years the majority of the American people 'incline to hope rather than fear.'" Possibly a glance at the editors' selection of front-page stories for January 1 offered a partial explanation for the shift, though not much in the news gave cause for the claim of the lead story's headline: "City Greets the New Year in One of Gayest Moods." Other stories reported that Herbert Lehman had been sworn in for a second term as governor; that President Roosevelt strongly opposed early bonus payments to Great War veterans; that Hitler's Germany had decreed a program of conscript labor; that henceforth the Middle Eastern nation of Persia would be known as Iran. Aside from Hitler (and who could say whether he would be able to retain power?), gloom and doom hardly dominated the front page. Then too, there had been a thrilling rescue of four men whose Cleveland-bound American Airlines Curtiss Condor went down in the snowbound Adirondacks. Trees cushioned the impact of the crash, and all aboard the big biplane survived. The four were stranded for several days in two feet of snow and below-zero temperatures, but they would live. Rescuers hauled out the pilot, frostbitten and shaking with pneumonia, on a toboggan.[2]

At the White House, Lorena Hickok completed a cumulative report for Harry Hopkins on New Year's Day, equal parts retrospective analysis and forecast of the future. She had commuted between Washington and New York in November and December, dividing her time between Eleanor Roosevelt's quarters in the East Wing and her apartment on Mitchell Place in midtown Manhattan. The relationship had cooled considerably over the past few months, at least on ER's side. "I know you often have a feeling for me which for one reason or another I may not return in kind," she would write, "but I feel I love you just the same & so often we entirely satisfy each other that I feel there is a fundamental basis on which our relationship stands." Restless again, Hickok dreamed of returning to the Associated Press. Yet she would remain deskbound at the Federal Emergency Relief Administration through most of 1935, supervising Hopkins's agents in the field and collating their reports, responsibilities she alternated with brief investigative trips: to Missouri in June, to upstate New York in late July, to Indiana and Ohio in September, and to the Upper Peninsula of Michigan in icebound December. There would be brief returns, too, to West Virginia and the Dakotas, perhaps the most compelling of her 1933 forays into the depths of the Great Depression.[3]

The work, and perhaps the friendship with ER, had broadened and deepened Hickok in ways great and small. In Baltimore in the fall of 1934, she read of the first lady delivering a speech in New York City wearing a blue velvet dinner gown. "I'm feeling pretty 'red' tonight," Hickok wrote. "Contact with relief clients makes me that way. God damn it, none of us ought to be wearing velvet dinner gowns these days. Not when 4,000 Baltimore children couldn't go to school in September because they didn't have clothes. . . . The thought of you in a blue velvet dinner gown irritated me profoundly." ER responded patiently, perhaps mindful of the big picture as seen from 1600 Pennsylvania Avenue, with recovery under way and an imperative for the first lady to project an air of easy, confident affluence: "Darling, if we all stopped wearing velvet dresses there would be worse times than there are, if you have money you must spend it now, so I don't feel as guilty as you do, of course, if you could give it all where it would do the most good that would be grand but we can't always do that."[4]

In her January 1 report to Hopkins, Hickok stressed that relief would be essential in 1935, even if recovery proceeded on the president's timetable. Unemployment remained at a socially intolerable level of 20 percent in late 1934. "A little figuring from available data will show that it would require a boom exceeding that of 1929 for the millions at present out of work to be reabsorbed into employment," she wrote. These were the strandees, male and female, young, old, and middle-aged. They had been turned out of virtually every traditional industry: lumber, steel, mining, the building trades, agriculture. Increased productivity and mechanization would also work against the probability of job gains in 1935. A Keynesian without realizing it, she intended to suggest to Hopkins that government work programs would need to be extended, perhaps indefinitely, even permanently. When recovery happened, it would contain a paradox: increased industrial output without a corresponding reduction in unemployment. For one example, profit-making General Electric in Schenectady, New

York, added two thousand workers to the payroll in 1934, for a total of 11,500. It had employed 28,000 in 1929.[5]

The relief load, Hickok predicted, would rise through the winter months. New York and Chicago and the industrial cities of Pennsylvania, Ohio, and Indiana would see the rolls increase 10 to 15 percent. Many of these clients would be first-timers, men (and some women) who finally had exhausted the last of their savings, credit, and potential for assistance from family. Out of 252 new applicants for relief during one autumn month in Elmira, New York, forty-five were seeking assistance for the first time. Many had ridden out the crisis since 1931 or 1932. In Dallas, relief workers were sifting through applications from three hundred unemployed schoolteachers.

She wrote Hopkins, "So goes the nation's relief load—up, down a bit, up again perhaps higher than ever before—while the newspapers and the business leaders are filled with optimism, and the country, bored with relief, wonders why these people don't get back to work."[6]

Circumstances confirmed FDR in his leaning toward an expanded public works initiative for 1935–36, an instinct that would bring Hopkins's Works Progress Administration into existence. In New York City analysts reported no private-sector jobs in sight. In Providence, Rhode Island, a young man told one of the FERA investigators that he had worked a total of five months since 1930. "It's funny," he said. "A lot of times I get offered a drink. It seems people don't want to drink alone. But no one ever offers me a meal." In Chicago, the Pullman Company employed about 10 percent of its pre-Depression workforce. In Houston skilled workers were in demand, but nothing emerged for thousands of industrial innocents, farmhands and cowpunchers who had drifted in from the countryside. In Detroit social workers offered a class showing girls how to apply for work. Asked one girl, "How can you go up and apply for a job without crying?" In Scranton, Pennsylvania, hard-coal country, employment rose by 12 percent in 1934 while payrolls dropped by 22 percent. In Youngstown, Ohio, the steel mills reached 80 percent of capacity in the spring of 1936, roughly the level of 1929. But they employed ten thousand fewer men than they had in the year of the Crash.

"And so they go on," Hickok wrote, "the gaunt, ragged legion of the industrially damned."[7]

Hickok revisited West Virginia in October 1935. The lovely hills were aflame with color, masking the mining scars on the land and hard times in the coal patches. She met a homesteader at the Red House resettlement project near Charleston, a friend of Major Francis Turner, the state relief director who had shown her around Kanawha County two years earlier. An eleven-year-old boy introduced her to the family's white mongrel, Missy, and her litter of pups. They had nothing to feed her, she had gone dry, and the puppies were starving. Later, Hickok and Turner agreed to go halves on a case of dog food, in hopes the flow of Missy's milk would resume in time to save the pups.[8]

Turner drove her out to the site of the tent colony she had written Hopkins and Mrs. Roosevelt about in 1933: miners without work, sore-covered children splashing about in the polluted watercourse, women dressed in raveled shifts. The story had reached the president and at a word from him the colony vanished. "Those tents are all gone!" she wrote ER. "Every last horrible one of them! And only 15 of the 63 families remain there—living, not in tents, but in wooden houses they built for themselves, with the aid of the relief people! Gardens around them! Even flowers!" She reported that fifteen of the blacklisted miners were back to work—and in the mines that heretofore had locked them out.[9]

Nine months later, in July 1936, Hickok reprised her visit to drought-ravaged South Dakota. Conditions were worse even than in the parched summers of 1933 and 1934, with 100 million bushels of wheat destroyed in the Northern Plains and the Dakotas crop a total loss. The temperature reached 101 degrees. The roads were loose gravel, the winds incessant, the grasshoppers a biblical plague. "They sounded like drums, beating against the windshield," she wrote of the hoppers. She covered 329 miles on July 31. For mile after mile the fields were "as bare and brown and hot as griddle cakes." Nothing showed green. "God," she wrote ER, "this country looks awful. Not even the Russian thistles grew this year." Hopkins wondered aloud about a permanent "weather change" that might be turning the U.S. midsection into a desert.* He suggested that tens of thousands of farm families would have to be moved off the land permanently. As sometimes happened, Hickok felt her anxieties mounting, an attack of nerves in the offing. Part of the cause was political; she remained firm in her New Deal loyalties, and she felt real fear of the future should FDR lose the 1936 election. Part was personal. She gripped the wheel tightly, trying to ignore the wheeze of the engine, the dust and the clatter of gravel, and remember the nice things she'd had, the beautiful places she'd seen.

"But I'm having a hard time to keep from getting panicky, just the same," she wrote. "I hate being alone these days."[10]

Hickok reached Pierre the night of July 31 and checked into the St. Charles Hotel, where she had stayed in the fall of 1933. The hotel overlooked the bottomlands and, beyond, the broad Missouri. The railroad curved through the little capital and crossed the river by a massive iron bridge. Out of the glare of the sun and the roar of the wind, she achieved a degree of perspective. She understood that ER would not be inclined to mourn the loss should her husband be denied a second term. She knew too that pomp and power and adulation could isolate a man, distance him from the things that really mattered.

She wrote ER, "With all the faults—and the faults of some of the people around him—I still think he is a very great man. His defeat would be a terrible calamity for millions of people in this country."[11]

In November 1936 Roosevelt won reelection with 62 percent of the vote.

So the worst appeared to be over, and Americans sensed it. In its two-year life, FERA would deliver more than $2 billion in aid to the desperate. With the Works Progress Administration, Hopkins would institutionalize his great innovation: work relief rather than the dole. Hickok stayed on with Hopkins and for a year or two managed an expanded field in-

---

*Fifty years before, the geologist John Wesley Powell had warned that the Northern Plains, "the Great American Desert" of the early nineteenth century, were too dry for large-scale farming. (See chapter 6.)

vestigation program that sent journalists and writers into virtually every corner of the United States to follow up on her pioneering reports from 1933–34. She began casting about for new work after the 1936 election, applying (through Eleanor Roosevelt) for a public relations job on the staff planning the 1939 New York World's Fair. "I felt it would be a good thing for me to set an example by quitting, now the election is over," she wrote Grover Whalen, who headed the World's Fair committee. She won the job, but it was only a job. "Living—just going on living—simply doesn't mean a God damned thing to me, dear," she would write ER. "I'm being perfectly honest when I say I'll be relieved when it's over. I wish that it had happened when I had that automobile accident out in Arizona. I'd have died happy, as happy as I've ever been in my life." Later, the first lady helped Hickok land a position as executive secretary of the Women's Division of the Democratic National Committee. She continued to live in the White House until FDR's death in April 1945. Again with ER's assistance, Hickok pursued a writing career that included *Eleanor Roosevelt: Reluctant First Lady*, a study that focused on the years 1928–33, and a series of biographies (Helen Keller, FDR, Mrs. Roosevelt) for juvenile readers.[12]

ER remained loyal to Hickok and did what she could to soothe her friend's troubled spirit. "Hick dearest," she would write in August 1955, perhaps thinking of her own trials, "of course you will forget the sad times at the end and eventually think only of the pleasant memories. Life is like that, with ends that have to be forgotten."[13] Hickok moved into ER's Val-Kill Cottage on the Hyde Park estate after the war, and then in the late 1950s shifted to a small apartment in Hyde Park village. As her health deteriorated (from diabetes, along with ailments associated with heavy smoking and drinking), she became homebound and partially blind, unable to work for long stretches. She would end as she had begun, as one of America's strandees: the luckless, the marginalized, the victims of circumstance, the forgotten people. Up to her death in November 1962, ER helped her with cash handouts, gifts (a miniature English sheepdog, Jenny), and publishing contacts meant to advance her writing career.

Lorena Hickok died in May 1968. She had reached the age of seventy-five, a surprise, perhaps, given the way she had lived and the toll her turbulent emotions had exacted. The years 1933–34 remained professionally the most fulfilling and personally the happiest of her tumultuous but not inconsequential life. Hickok's historical legacy rests with her influence on Hopkins's welfare and jobs policies in a time when, for millions of ordinary people, a little help from the larger community meant the difference between hunger and subsistence, numb despair and a stirring of hope. Above all, it rests in the incomparable narrative record she left of America in the depths of the Great Depression.

NOTES

Preface

1. Lorena Hickok, "Introduction" (possibly for a study of the Works Progress Administration), unpublished typescript, Lorena A. Hickok Papers, Franklin Delano Roosevelt Presidential Library, Hyde Park, N.Y.; Lorena Hickok, *Eleanor Roosevelt: Reluctant First Lady* (New York: Dodd, Mead and Company, 1980 [1962]), 134.

2. Malcolm Cowley, *The Dream of the Golden Mountains: Remembering the 1930s* (New York: Viking Press, 1980), xi.

3. Alexander J. Field, *A Great Leap Forward: 1930s Depression and U.S. Economic Growth* (New Haven: Yale University Press, 2011), 23, 49; *The New York Times*, January 1, 1933, Section xx, 5.

4. Field, *A Great Leap Forward*, 277, 31, 37; "Lessons of the 1930s," *The Economist*, December 10, 2011, 76-77; David M. Kennedy, *Freedom from Fear: The American People in Depression and War, 1929–1945* (New York: Oxford University Press, 1999), 56.

Prologue

1. Lorena Hickok, *Eleanor Roosevelt: Reluctant First Lady* (1962; New York: Dodd, Mead, 1980), 14–15.

2. John P. Broderick, typescript profile of Lorena Hickok, Lorena A. Hickok Papers, Franklin Delano Roosevelt Presidential Library, Hyde Park, N.Y.; Ishbel Ross quoted in John F. Bauman and Thomas H. Coode, *In the Eye of the Great Depression* (DeKalb: University of Northern Illinois Press, 1981), 23.

3. Paul A. Dana as told to Lorena A. Hickok, "Drifted 22 Hours with Woman at Sea," *The New York Times*, November 15, 1928, 1.

4. Doris Faber, *Lorena Hickok* (New York: William Morrow, 1980), 71, 81, 84; Lorena Hickok, unfinished autobiography (typescript), Hickok Papers, FDR Library.

5. Quoted in Matthew Josephson, *Infidel in the Temple: A Memoir of the Nineteen Thirties* (New York: Knopf, 1967), 104.

6. Lorena Hickok, "Unfinished chapter," possibly to a projected study of the Works Progress Administration (by contents, 1937), Hickok Papers, FDR Library; Hickok, unfinished autobiography, 3, Hickok Papers, FDR Library.

7. *The New York Times*, January 1, 1933, 1, 15.

8. David Kennedy, *Freedom from Fear: The American People in Depression and War, 1929–1945* (New York: Oxford University Press, 1999), xiv.

9. Ibid., 87, 133; Bauman and Coode, *In the Eye of the Great Depression*, 3–4; Arthur M. Schlesinger Jr., *The Coming of the New Deal* (Boston: Houghton Mifflin, 1959), 87.

10. Kenneth S. Davis, *FDR: The New York Years* (New York: Random House, 1985), 312; Bauman and Coode, *In the Eye of the Great Depression*, 178, 5; Kenneth S. Davis, *FDR: The New Deal Years* (New York: Random House, 1986), 111; *The New York Times,* January 1, 1933, 12; Adam Cohen, *Nothing to Fear: FDR's Inner Circle and the Hundred Days That Created Modern America* (New York: Penguin Press, 2009), 150, 272, 75; Irving Bernstein, *Turbulent Years: A History of the American Worker, 1933–1941* (Boston: Houghton Mifflin, 1970), 22–23.

11. *The New York Times*, January 1, 1933, 1; Josephson, *Infidel in the Temple*, 74, 47–48.

12. Davis, *FDR: The New York Years*, 380, 381; Malcolm Cowley, *The Dream of Golden Mountains: Remembering the 1930s* (New York: Viking Press, 1980), 3; Cohen, *Nothing to Fear*, 279; *Time*, January 16, 1933, 12.

13. Kennedy, *Freedom from Fear*, 78–79, 107; Barry Eichengreen and Peter Temin, "The Gold Standard and the Great Depression," report, National Bureau of Economic Research, Cambridge, Mass., June 1997, 1, 6.

14. John Shover, *Cornbelt Rebellion: The Farmers' Holiday Association* (Urbana: University of Illinois Press, 1965), 12, 28; Bauman and Coode, *In the Eye of the Great Depression*, 3; Schlesinger, *Coming of the New Deal*, 11.

15. Josephson, *Infidel in the Temple*, 18–23.

16. Davis, *FDR: The New York Years*, 379; *The New York Times*, January 1, 1933, Real Estate section, 13; Josephson, *Infidel in the Temple*, 43.

17. Gerald W. Johnson, "The Average American and the Depression," *Current History* 35 (February 1932): 671–73; Davis, *FDR: The New Deal Years*, 101.

18. *The New York Times*, January 1, 1933.

1. View to a New Deal

1. John P. Broderick, typescript profile of Lorena Hickok, Lorena A. Hickok Papers, Franklin Delano Roosevelt Library, Hyde Park, N.Y.;

2. H. W. Brands, *Traitor to His Class: The Privileged Life and Radical Presidency of Franklin Delano Roosevelt* (New York: Doubleday, 2008), 242, 248.

3. Ibid., 241–42; Samuel I. Rosenman, ed., *The Public Papers and Addresses of Franklin Delano Roosevelt*, vol. 1: *The Genesis of the New Deal* (New York: Random House, 1938), 649–50.

4. *Time*, July 11, 1932, 9–10; Kenneth Davis, *FDR: The New York Years* (New York: Random House, 1985), 324–31; Eleanor Roosevelt, *This I Remember* (New York: Harper & Brothers, 1949), 66–67; Brands, *Traitor to His Class*, 246–47.

5. Lorena Hickok, *Eleanor Roosevelt: Reluctant First Lady* (1962; New York: Dodd, Mead, 1980), 32–33; Eleanor Roosevelt, *This I Remember*, 70; *Time*, July 11, 1932, 10; Davis, *FDR: The New York Years*, 335.

6. *The New York Times*, September 12, 1932, 2, and September 14, 1932, 1; *Time*, September 19, 1932, 11, and September 26, 1932, 10.

7. *Recent Social Trends in the United States,* report of the President's Research Committee on Social Trends (New York: Whittlesey House/McGraw Hill, 1934), 98, 505; Rosenman, *The Public Papers and Addresses of Franklin Delano Roosevelt*, vol. 1, 695–96; Hickok, *Eleanor Roosevelt*, 36; *Time*, September 26, 1932, 10; *The Nation*, September 28, 1932, 270.

8. John L. Shover, *Cornbelt Rebellion: The Farmers' Holiday Association* (Urbana: University of Illinois Press), 44; *Time*, September 5, 1932, 13; Josephine Herbst, "In the Grass Roots," *Scribner's Magazine*, January 1933, 47, 48–49.

9. Herbst, "In the Grass Roots," 47; *Time*, September 5, 1932, 13, and September 19, 1932, 4.

10. *The New York Times*, September 17 and 18, 1932, 1; *Time*, September 26, 1932, 10.

11. *Time*, October 3, 1932, 11; *The New York Times*, September 20, 1932, 1, 4, and September 21, 1932, 1; Davis, *FDR: The New York Years*, 368; *The New York Times*, September 24, 1932, 1.

12. Rosenman, *The Public Papers and Addresses of FDR,* vol. 1, 746–47, 750–51, 754; *The New York Times*, September 24, 1932, 1.

13. Rosenman, *The Public Papers and Addresses of FDR*, vol. 1, 751–52.

14. *The New York Times*, September 24, 1932, 1; Davis, *FDR: The New York Years*, 368.

15. *Time*, October 3, 1932, 11–12.

16. Hickok, *Eleanor Roosevelt*, 17, 37–38; *The New York Times*, September 26, 1932, 1.

17. *Time*, October 10, 1932, 9; Hickok, *Eleanor Roosevelt*, 39; *The New York Times*, October 1 and 2, 1932, 1.

18. *Time*, October 10, 1932, 9; Hickok, *Eleanor Roosevelt*, 39; *The Chicago Tribune*, October 1, 1932, 1.
19. Hickok, *Eleanor Roosevelt*, 43–44.
20. Lorena Hickok to Eleanor Roosevelt, n.d., Hickok Papers, FDR Library.
21. Hickok, *Eleanor Roosevelt*, 62, 45; Lorena Hickok, Associated Press report, October 30, 1932, Hickok Papers, FDR Library.
22. Hickok, *Eleanor Roosevelt*, 55.
23. Lorena Hickok, Associated Press typescript reports, November 9, 10, and 11, 1932, Hickok Papers, FDR Library.
24. *Time*, January 16, 1933, 14.
25. Ibid.; *Time*, February 6, 1933, 17.
26. *Time*, February 6, 1933, 17, and January 30, 1933, 15; Oswald Garrison Villard, "By Bus through the Middle West," *The Nation*, February 15, 1933, 224.
27. *Time*, March 27, 1933, 11–12; Villard, "By Bus through the Middle West," 224.
28. *Time*, February 13, 1933, 12–13, and February 6, 1933, 16–17; Adam Cohen, *Nothing to Fear: FDR's Inner Circle and the Hundred Days That Created Modern America* (New York: Penguin Press, 2009), 110; Jonathan Alter, *The Defining Moment: FDR's Hundred Days and the Triumph of Hope* (New York: Simon & Schuster, 2006), 2; Cohen, *Nothing to Fear*, 51; Malcolm Cowley, *The Dream of the Golden Mountains: Remembering the 1930s* (New York: Viking Press, 1980), 161.
29. Cohen, *Nothing to Fear*, 50; Davis, *FDR: The New York Years*, 440; Irving Bernstein, *Turbulent Years: A History of the American Worker, 1933–1941* (Boston: Houghton Mifflin, 1970), 7; Kenneth S. Davis, *FDR: The New Deal Years* (New York: Random House, 1986), 26.
30. Davis, *FDR: The New Deal Years*, 176–78; Doris Faber, *Lorena Hickok* (New York: William Morrow, 1980), 77; Rodger Streitmatter, ed., *Empty without You: The Intimate Letters of Eleanor Roosevelt and Lorena Hickok* (New York: Free Press, 1998), 9.
31. Streitmatter, *Empty without You*, 9; Hazel Rowley, *Franklin and Eleanor: An Extraordinary Marriage* (New York: Farrar, Straus and Giroux, 2010), 9–10.
32. Blanche Wiesen Cook, *Eleanor Roosevelt* (New York: Viking, 1992), vol. 2, 55.
33. Streitmatter, *Empty without You*, 9; Lorena Hickok, "The Making of an Introvert," autobiographical fragment, Hickok Papers, FDR Library.
34. Hickok, "The Making of an Introvert."
35. Ibid.
36. Ibid.
37. Ibid.; Faber, *Lorena Hickok*, 36.
38. Lorena Hickok, "The Making of an Introvert."
39. Ibid.
40. Hickok, *Eleanor Roosevelt*, 78–79; Davis, *FDR: The New York Years*, 431,

435; Davis, *FDR: The New Deal Years*, 176–78; Lorena Hickok, unfinished autobiography, 6–7, Hickok Papers, FDR Library; *The New York Times*, February 16, 1933, 1.

41. *The New York Times*, February 17, 1933, 5; Cook, *Eleanor Roosevelt*, vol. 2, 95; Davis, *FDR: The New Deal Years*, 179.

42. Lorena Hickok, memo, n.d. (by contents, February 1933), Hickok Papers, FDR Library.

43. Cook, *Eleanor Roosevelt*, vol. 2, 116; Lorena Hickok, AP dispatch, February 4, 1933, Hickok Papers, FDR Library.

44. Davis, *FDR: The New Deal Years*, 21, 24; Eleanor Roosevelt, *This I Remember*, 77.

45. Eleanor Roosevelt, *This I Remember*, 77; Barry Eichengreen and Peter Temin, "The Gold Standard and the Great Depression," report, National Bureau of Economic Research, Cambridge, Mass., June 1997, 1, 6.

46. Cowley, *The Dream of the Golden Mountains*, 109; *The Nation*, February 15, 1933; Alter, *The Defining Moment*, 5, 80; *The Nation*, March 1, 1933; *The New Republic*, March 1, 1933, 62, and March 8, 1933, 88.

47. Hickok, *Eleanor Roosevelt*, 95–96.

48. Samuel I. Rosenman, ed., *The Public Papers and Addresses of Franklin Delano Roosevelt*, vol. 2: *The Year of Crisis, 1933* (New York: Random House, 1938), 11, 15; *The New York Times*, March 5, 1933, 1.

49. Eleanor Roosevelt, *This I Remember*, 78; Faber, *Lorena Hickok*, 110; Hickok, *Eleanor Roosevelt*, 98–99.

50. Hickok, *Eleanor Roosevelt*, 103–5; Associated Press dispatch, *The New York Times*, March 5, 1933, 7.

51. Eleanor Roosevelt to Hickok, March 5, 1933, Hickok Papers, FDR Library.

52. Eleanor Roosevelt to Hickok, March 6, 1933, Hickok Papers, FDR Library.

53. Eleanor Roosevelt to Hickok, March 5, 7 and 11, 1933, Hickok Papers, FDR Library.

54. Hickok, unfinished autobiography, 3; Eleanor Roosevelt to Hickok, June 13, 1933, Hickok Papers, FDR Library.

55. *Time*, March 6, 1933, 47; W. W. Chapin to Hickok, n.d. (by contents, May 1933), Hickok Papers, FDR Library.

56. *The New York Times*, June 23, 1933, 1.

57. Eleanor Roosevelt to Hickok, June 13, 1933, Hickok Papers, FDR Library.

58. Robert Sherwood, *Roosevelt and Hopkins: An Intimate History* (New York: Harper, 1948), 45; *The New York Times*, May 23, 1933, 21; Davis, *FDR: The New Deal Years*, 80.

59. *The Washington Post*, May 23, 1933, 1.

60. "Relief: The Last Gasp of Private Charity," *The New Republic*, May 10, 1933, 355; Sherwood, *Roosevelt and Hopkins*, 45–46; Irving Bernstein, *A*

Caring Society: The New Deal, the Worker and the Great Depression (Boston: Houghton Mifflin, 1985), 30–31; *Time*, February 19, 1934, 13.

61. Sherwood, *Roosevelt and Hopkins*, 45.
62. Ibid., 5, 15; George McJimsey, *Harry Hopkins: Ally of the Poor and Defender of Democracy* (Cambridge, Mass.: Harvard University Press, 1987), 3.
63. Sherwood, *Roosevelt and Hopkins*, 29, 1; Bernstein, *A Caring Society*, 29; June Hopkins, *Harry Hopkins: Sudden Hero, Brash Reformer* (New York: St. Martin's Press, 1999), 167; *Time*, February 19, 1934, 13.
64. Alter, *The Defining Moment*, 279; Cohen, *Nothing to Fear*, 136; Matthew Josephson, *Infidel in the Temple: A Memoir of the Nineteen-Thirties* (New York: Knopf, 1967), 181. A pliant Congress passed the Emergency Banking Bill without actually reading it.
65. Alter, *The Defining Moment*, 279; Cohen, *Nothing to Fear*, 136.
66. *The New Republic*, March 1, 1933; *Time*, May 29, 1933, 7.
67. *Time*, May 22, 1933, 14 and April 17, 1933, 24.
68. *Time*, May 8, 1933, 14–15; Benjamin Roth, *The Great Depression: A Diary*, eds. James Ledbetter and Daniel B. Roth (New York: Public Affairs, 2009), 113; Arthur M. Schlesinger Jr., *The Coming of the New Deal* (Boston: Houghton Mifflin, 1959), 43.
69. *Time*, May 8, 1933, 14–15; Schlesinger, *Coming of the New Deal*, 43.
70. *Time*, May 15, 1933, 12–13; *The Washington Post*, May 23, 1933, 2.
71. Davis, *FDR: The New Deal Years*, 110; *The New York Times*, May 5, 1933, 11; *Time*, May 22, 1933, 17.
72. *The New York Times*, May 6, 1933, 4; *Time*, May 15, 1933, 15.
73. *Literary Digest*, August 19, 1933, 11; *Time*, May 15, 1933, 15.
74. *The New York Times*, May 11, 1933, 6; Paul Comly French, "Children on Strike," *The Nation*, May 31, 1933, 611–12; *The Wall Street Journal*, July 26, 1933, 7.
75. Hickok, *Eleanor Roosevelt*, 135; "Introductory Chapter," unpublished typescript, Hickok Papers, FDR Library.

2. Part of the Story

1. Lorena Hickok, itemized expenses, August 1933, Lorena A. Hickok Papers, Franklin Delano Roosevelt Presidential Library, Hyde Park, N.Y.; *The New York Times*, August 1, 1933.
2. Eleanor Roosevelt to Hickok, July 27, 1933, Hickok Papers, FDR Library.
3. Ruth A. Lerrigo, "Pennsylvania's Welfare Set-up," *The Survey*, May 1933, 188; Lorena Hickok to Harry Hopkins, field report, August 6, 1933, Harry L. Hopkins Papers, Franklin Delano Roosevelt Presidential Library, Hyde Park, N.Y.; Hickok, notes from Pennsylvania, August 1933, Hopkins Papers, FDR Library.

4. Lerrigo, "Pennsylvania's Welfare Set-up," 189; Hickok to Hopkins, field report, August 6, 1933, Hopkins Papers, FDR Library; Hickok, notes from Pennsylvania, August 1933, Hickok Papers, FDR Library; *The New Republic*, August 9, 1933, 320; *The Harrisburg Telegraph*, August 1, 1933, 13.

5. *Time*, August 7, 1933, 23.

6. Hickok to Eleanor Roosevelt, August 1933, Hickok Papers, FDR Library; Irving Bernstein, *Turbulent Years: A History of the American Worker, 1933–1941* (Boston: Houghton Mifflin, 1970), 174; *Time*, July 31, 1933, 13.

7. Hickok to Eleanor Roosevelt, August 1933, Hickok Papers, FDR Library; Hickok to Hopkins, field report, August 6, 1933, Hopkins Papers, FDR Library; Evan Clague, "When Relief Stops, What Do They Eat?," *The Survey*, November 15, 1932, 585.

8. Clague, "When Relief Stops," 583.

9. Ibid., 584–85.

10. Ibid.

11. Ibid., 584; Hickok, notes from Pennsylvania, August 1933, Hickok Papers, FDR Library.

12. Hickok to Hopkins, field report, August 6, 1933, Hopkins Papers, FDR Library.

13. Hickok to Eleanor Roosevelt, August 1933, Hickok Papers, FDR Library.

14. *The New Republic*, August 9, 1933, 330–31; *The Harrisburg Telegraph*, July 20, 1933, 1; Paul Comly French, "Children on Strike," *The Nation*, May 31, 1933, 611.

15. *The New Republic*, August 9, 1933, 331; French, "Children on Strike," 611–12.

16. French, "Children on Strike," 612; *Time*, July 31, 1933, 13.

17. French, "Children on Strike," 612.

18. Edmund Wilson, *The Thirties: From the Notebooks and Diaries of the Period*, ed. Leon Edel (New York: Farrar, Straus and Giroux, 1980), 399; Isidor Feinstein, "A Gentleman in Politics," *The American Mercury*, May 1933, 83.

19. Hickok to Hopkins, field report, August 6, 1933, and August 7–12, 1933, Hopkins Papers, FDR Library.

20. "Program of Relief" for Northampton County, Hopkins Papers, FDR Library; Hickok to Hopkins, field report, August 6, 1933, Hopkins Papers, FDR Library.

21. Hickok to Hopkins, field report, August 6, 1933, Hopkins Papers, FDR Library; Hickok to Eleanor Roosevelt, August 5 or 6, 1933, Hickok Papers, FDR Library.

22. Hickok to Kathryn Godwin, August 6, 1933, Hopkins Papers, FDR Library; Hickok to Hopkins, field report, August 6, 1933, Hopkins Papers, FDR Library.

23. Richard Lowitt and Maurine Beasley, eds., *One Third of a Nation: Lo-*

rena Hickok Reports on the Great Depression (Urbana: University of Illinois Press, 1981), xxv.

24. Eleanor Roosevelt to Hickok, August 5, 1933, Hickok Papers, FDR Library.

25. *Business Week*, August 19, 1933, 8, 20, and August 26, 1933, 18; Kenneth S. Davis, *FDR: The New Deal Years* (New York: Random House, 1986), 136–37, 239.

26. Federal Writers' Project, *Pennsylvania: A Guide to the Keystone State* (Philadelphia: University of Pennsylvania Press, 1940), 322; *The Scranton Times*, August 2, 1933, 3.

27. "Mining Anthracite," in *Stories from Pennsylvania History*, online, www .explorepahistory.com.

28. Hickok to Eleanor Roosevelt, August 1933, Hickok Papers, FDR Library; *The Scranton Times,* August 3, 1933, 3; *Time*, October 2, 1933, 12.

29. *The New Republic*, January 17, 1934, 282, and February 7, 1934, 349–50; *The Scranton Times*, August 3, 1933, 3.

30. Tom Tippett, "The Miners Fight Their Leaders," *The American Mercury*, June 1934, 131–32.

31. *The Scranton Times*, July 17, 1933, 3, and August 7, 1933, 3.

32. Hickok to Eleanor Roosevelt, August 1933, Hickok Papers, FDR Library; Hickok to Hopkins, field report, August 6, 1933, Hickok Papers, FDR Library.

33. *The Scranton Times*, August 4, 1933, 3; Hickok to Hopkins, field report, August 6, 1933, Hopkins Papers, FDR Library; "Mining Anthracite," in *Stories from Pennsylvania History*, online, www.explorepahistory .com.

34. Lorena Hickok, *Eleanor Roosevelt: Reluctant First Lady* (1962; New York, Dodd, Mead, 1980), 139, 136; "The Railroad in Pennsylvania," in *Stories from Pennsylvania History*, online, www.explorepahistory.com; *Recent Social Trends in the United States,* report of the President's Research Committee on Social Trends (New York: Whittlesey House/McGraw Hill, 1934), 80.

35. J. Horace McFarland, "Pennsylvania's Work Relief Roads," *Review of Reviews*, February 1933, 41–42; Feinstein, "A Gentleman in Politics," 85.

36. Hickok to Hopkins, field report, August 6, 1933, Hopkins Papers, FDR Library.

37. Hickok, *Eleanor Roosevelt*, 135; Hickok to Hopkins, field report, August 6, 1933, Hopkins Papers, FDR Library.

38. Hickok, *Eleanor Roosevelt*, 139, 136; Hickok to Eleanor Roosevelt, August 1933, Hickok Papers, FDR Library.

39. Hickok to Eleanor Roosevelt, August 1933, Hickok Papers, FDR Library.

40. *Business Week*, September 16, 1933, 8; Bernstein, *Turbulent Years*, 41–43.

41. Merle D. Vincent, "Chaotic Coal," *Survey Graphic*, November 1933, 544; Daniel Allen, "Mine War in Pennsylvania," *The Nation*, August 9, 1933,

176; *Time*, August 14, 1933, 11; *The New York Times*, August 1, 1933, 1, and August 2, 1933, 5.

42. Bernstein, *Turbulent Years*, 50–51; *Time*, August 21, 1933, 10, and August 7, 1933, 13; Allen, "Mine War in Pennsylvania," 177.
43. *Time*, August 7, 1933, 13; *The New Republic*, August 9, 1933.
44. *Time*, August 14, 1933, 11, and August 21, 1933, 10.
45. Allen, "Mine War in Pennsylvania," 206.
46. Daniel Allen, "Strike Truce in Pennsylvania," *The Nation*, August 23, 1933, 206; *Business Week*, August 12, 1933, 5; Bernstein, *Turbulent Years*, 57; Vincent, "Chaotic Coal," 539; *The New York Times*, September 13, 1933, 5.
47. Hickok to Hopkins, field report, August 7–12, 1933, Hopkins Papers, FDR Library; Hickok, *Eleanor Roosevelt*, 136.
48. Hickok to Hopkins, field report, August 7–12, 1933, Hopkins Papers, FDR Library.
49. Ibid.; Hickok, *Eleanor Roosevelt*, 136.
50. Hickok to Eleanor Roosevelt, August 1933, Hickok Papers, FDR Library; Hickok to Hopkins, field report, August 7–12, 1933, Hopkins Papers, FDR Library.
51. Hickok to Eleanor Roosevelt, August 1933, Hickok Papers, FDR Library.
52. Hickok to Hopkins, field report, August 7–12, 1933, Hopkins Papers, FDR Library; Unemployed Citizens League of Allegheny County, Pennsylvania, food prices, April–August 1933, Hopkins Papers, FDR Library.
53. *The New York Times*, August 14, 1933, 1.
54. Eleanor Roosevelt to Lorena Hickok, March 16, 1933, Hickok Papers, FDR Library; Blanche Wiesen Cook, *Eleanor Roosevelt* (New York: Viking, 1999), vol. 2, 47–48.
55. Eleanor Roosevelt, *This I Remember* (New York: Harper, 1949), 117; Eleanor Roosevelt to Hickok, March 16, 1933, Hickok Papers, FDR Library; Hickok, *Eleanor Roosevelt*, 148; Hazel Rowley, *Franklin and Eleanor: An Extraordinary Marriage* (New York: Farrar, Straus and Giroux, 2010), 192–93, 194.
56. Hickok, *Eleanor Roosevelt*, 136; Eleanor Roosevelt to Hickok, August 10, 1933, and August 25, 1933, Hickok Papers, FDR Library.

3. Coal Country

1. Dennis K. Scott, "Report on Coal Property," Scotts Run District, Monongalia County, West Virginia, June 10, 1933, West Virginia Collection, West Virginia University Library, Morgantown, 1–2; Phil Ross, "The Scotts Run Coalfield from the Great War to the Great Depression," *West Virginia History*, vol. 53, 1994, West Virginia Archives and History, www.wvculture.org, 21.

2. Scott, "Report on Coal Property," 19.

3. Behner Christopher Diaries, vol. 2, West Virginia Collection, West Virginia University Library, Morgantown, February 8, March 7 and 10, 1933.

4. Behner Christopher Diaries, vol. 2, April 3, 1933.

5. Behner Christopher Diaries, vol. 2, n.d. (January 1933).

6. Ibid.

7. Ibid.

8. *The Morgantown (W.Va.) Post*, August 15, 16, 19 and 21, 1933; *The Dominion News* (Morgantown, W.Va.), August 16, 1933.

9. Lorena Hickok, *Eleanor Roosevelt: Reluctant First Lady* (1962; New York, Dodd, Mead, 1980), 137.

10. *The Morgantown Post*, August 18, 1933, 1.

11. Ibid.; *The Dominion News*, August 18, 1933.

12. Eleanor Roosevelt, *This I Remember* (New York: Harper & Brothers, 1949), 127–29.

13. Hickok, *Eleanor Roosevelt*, 138–39; Hickok to Eleanor Roosevelt, August 23, 1933, Hickok Papers, FDR Library.

14. Hickok to Eleanor Roosevelt, August 23, 1933, Hickok Papers, FDR Library.

15. *Charleston (W.Va.) Daily Mail*, August 21–26, 1933; Edmund Wilson, *The American Jitters: A Year of the Slump* (1932; Garden City, N.Y.: Doubleday, 1958), 156.

16. Hickok to Eleanor Roosevelt, August 23, 1933, Hickok Papers, FDR Library; Lorena Hickok to Harry Hopkins, field report, West Virginia, August 16–26, 1933, Harry L. Hopkins Papers, Franklin Delano Roosevelt Presidential Library, Hyde Park, N.Y.

17. Hickok to Hopkins, field report, West Virginia, August 16–26, 1933, Hopkins Papers, FDR Library; Hickok to Eleanor Roosevelt, August 23, 1933, Hickok Papers, FDR Library.

18. Hickok to Eleanor Roosevelt, August 23, 1933, Hickok Papers, FDR Library.

19. *Logan (W.Va.) Banner*, August 8, 1933, 1; James D. Francis to J. E. Edgerton, July 10, 1934, Logan Coal Operators Association Papers, West Virginia State Library, Charleston; Hickok to Hopkins, field report, West Virginia, August 16–26, 1933, Hopkins Papers, FDR Library; Hickok to Eleanor Roosevelt, August 23, 1933, Hickok Papers, FDR Library.

20. Richard V. Lunt, *Law and Order versus the Miners, West Virginia, 1906–1933* (Charleston, W.Va.: Appalachian Editions, 1992), 155–56; Wilson, *American Jitters*, 159.

21. Hickok to Eleanor Roosevelt, August 23, 1933, Hickok Papers, FDR Library; Hickok to Hopkins, field report, West Virginia, August 16–26, 1933, Hopkins Papers, FDR Library.

22. Hickok to Hopkins, field report, West Virginia, August 16–26, 1933, Hopkins Papers, FDR Library.

23. Elmer Blankenship to William Blizzard, June 19, 1933, Blizzard Collec-

tion, West Virginia State Library, Charleston; *Logan Banner,* August 25, 1933, 1; Hickok to Hopkins, field report, West Virginia, August 16–26, 1933, Hopkins Papers, FDR Library.

24. R. L. Simms to William Blizzard, June 25, 1933, Blizzard Collection, West Virginia State Library; Hickok to Eleanor Roosevelt, August 23, 1933, Hickok Papers, FDR Library.

25. *Logan Banner,* June 16, 1933, 1; Hickok to Eleanor Roosevelt, August 23, 1933, Hickok Papers, FDR Library.

26. Hickok to Eleanor Roosevelt, August 23, 1933, Hickok Papers, FDR Library; Paul Salstrom interview with Woodrow Mosley, July 27, 1988, Oral History Project, Marshall University Foundation, transcript copy in the West Virginia Collection, West Virginia University Library; United Mine Workers questionnaire, n.d. (November–December 1933), Blizzard Collection, West Virginia State Library, Charleston; Wilson, *American Jitters,* 151.

27. Hickok to Eleanor Roosevelt, August 23, 1933, Hickok Papers, FDR Library.

28. J. W. Colley to T. B. Davis, March 8, 1933, Logan Coal Operators Association Papers, West Virginia State Library, Charleston; State of West Virginia, Unemployment Relief Administration Records, Department of Public Welfare, West Virginia State Library, Charleston.

29. Colley to Davis, March 8, 1933, Logan Coal Operators Association Papers, West Virginia State Library; Unemployment Relief Administration Records, West Virginia State Library.

30. Hickok to Eleanor Roosevelt, August 25, 1933, Hickok Papers, FDR Library.

31. Hickok to Hopkins, field report, West Virginia, August 16–26, 1933, Hopkins Papers, FDR Library; Hickok to Eleanor Roosevelt, August 23, 1933, Hickok Papers, FDR Library.

32. Hickok to Hopkins, field report, West Virginia, August 16–26, 1933, FDR Library.

33. Hickok to Eleanor Roosevelt, August 23, 1933, Hickok Papers, FDR Library.

34. Lorena Hickok, itineraries and expenses, Hickok Papers, FDR Library; *Recent Social Trends in the United States,* report of the President's Research Committee on Social Trends (New York: Whittlesey House/McGraw Hill, 1934), 184.

35. Salstrom interview with Mosley, July 27, 1988, Oral History Project, Marshall University Foundation; *The New York Times,* July 14, 2010, www.nytimes.com.

36. Hickok to Harry Hopkins, field report, Eastern Kentucky Coalfields, August 31–September 3, 1933, Hopkins Papers, FDR Library.

37. Oakley Johnson, "Starvation and the Reds in Kentucky," *The Nation,* February 3, 1932, 141; Herbert Abel, "Gun Rule in Kentucky," *The Nation,* September 23, 1931, 306.

38. Edmund Wilson, *The Thirties: From Notebooks and Diaries of the Period,* ed. Leon Edel (New York: Farrar, Straus and Giroux, 1980), 161, 168–69; J. C. Byars, "Harlan County: An Act of God?," *The Nation,* June 15, 1932, 673.

39. Johnson, "Starvation and the Reds in Kentucky," 142; Wilson, *The Thirties,* 169–70.

40. Wilson, *The Thirties,* 176–77; *The New York Times,* February 12, 1932, 44; Alan Trachtenberg, ed., *Memoirs of Waldo Frank* (Amherst: University of Massachusetts Press, 1973), 182.

41. Byars, "Harlan County," 673; *The Nation,* June 8, 1932, 651.

42. Byars, "Harlan County," 673.

43. Ibid.

44. Ibid., 674; Johnson, "Starvation and the Reds," 142.

45. Hickok to Hopkins, field report, Eastern Kentucky Coalfields, August 31–September 3, 1933, Hopkins Papers, FDR Library.

46. Ibid.

47. Ibid.

48. Ibid.

49. *The New Republic,* October 25, 1933, 291.

50. *The New York Times,* September 23, 1933, 5; Kenneth S. Davis, *FDR: The New Deal Years, 1933–1937* (New York: Random House, 1979), 257, 259; *Time,* October 2, 1933, 11.

51. *The Dominion News* (Morgantown, W.Va.), September 16, 1933, 1; *Logan Banner,* September 19, 1933, 1.

52. *Time,* September 25, 1933, 11; Salstrom interview with Mosley, July 27, 1988, Oral History Project, Marshall University Foundation; *The New Republic,* September 27, 1933, 170.

53. *The Morgantown Post,* September 23, 1933, 1; *The New Republic,* October 4, 1933, 197–98.

54. Eleanor Roosevelt to Hickok, September 28, 1933, Hickok Papers, FDR Library; *The New York Times,* October 4, 1933, 1, and October 9, 1933, 5; Hickok, *Eleanor Roosevelt,* 140.

55. Hickok, *Eleanor Roosevelt,* 140; *The New Republic,* December 6, 1933, 86; Behner Christopher Diaries, vol. 2.

56. Eleanor Roosevelt to Hickok, September 6, 1933, Hickok Papers, FDR Library; *The Literary Digest,* November 8, 1933, 12.

4. Strandees

1. Lorena Hickok to Harry L. Hopkins, field report, New York State, September 12–19, 1933, Harry L. Hopkins Papers, Franklin Delano Roosevelt Presidential Library, Hyde Park, N.Y.; Lorena Hickok to Eleanor Roosevelt, September 1933, Lorena Hickok Papers, Franklin Delano

Roosevelt Presidential Library, Hyde Park, N.Y.; Federal Writers' Project, *New York: A Guide to the Empire State* (New York: Oxford University Press, 1940), 389.

2. Hickok to Eleanor Roosevelt, September 1933, Hickok Papers, FDR Library.

3. Lorena Hickok, itinerary 1933–34, Hickok Papers, FDR Library; Doris Faber, *Lorena Hickok* (New York: William Morrow, 1980), 148.

4. Hickok to Hopkins, field report, New York State, September 12–19, 1933, Hopkins Papers, FDR Library; Hickok to Eleanor Roosevelt, September 1933, Hickok Papers, FDR Library.

5. E. O. Lundberg, "The New York State Temporary Emergency Relief Administration," *Social Service Review*, December 1932, 545; Kenneth S. Davis, *FDR: The New York Years, 1928–1933* (New York: Random House, 1979), 240–43; David Adie, "A State Handles Its Public Welfare Problems," *Social Service Review*, September 1933, 407.

6. Adie, "A State Handles Its Public Welfare Problems," 408, 418.

7. Hickok to Hopkins, field report, New York State, September 12–19, 1933, Hopkins Papers, FDR Library; H. Jackson Davis, "Where Relief Includes Medical Care," *Survey*, April 1933, 155.

8. Davis, "Where Relief Includes Medical Care," 155.

9. Hickok to Hopkins, field report, New York State, September 12–19, 1933, Hopkins Papers, FDR Library.

10. Ibid.

11. Hickok to Eleanor Roosevelt, September 1933, Hickok Papers, FDR Library.

12. Federal Writers' Project, *New York*, 287–90.

13. Ibid., 290; *The Rochester (N.Y.) Times-Union*, September 13, 1933, 1, and September 12, 1933, 1.

14. *The Rochester Times-Union*, September 13, 1933, 15, 23, and September 14, 1933, 24, 25, 35.

15. Federal Writers' Project, *New York*, 329–31, 333.

16. *The New York Times*, September 12, 1933, 3; Hickok to Hopkins, field report, New York State, September 12–19, 1933, Hopkins Papers, FDR Library.

17. Hickok to Hopkins, field report, New York State, September 12–19, 1933, Hopkins Papers, FDR Library.

18. *The Syracuse Journal*, September 12, 1933, 1, September 14, 1933, 3, and September 15, 1933, 2; Kenneth S. Davis, *FDR: The New Deal Years* (New York: Random House, 1986), 206.

19. *The Syracuse Journal*, September 15, 1933, 21.

20. *The Syracuse Journal*, September 16, 1933, 3; Hickok to Hopkins, field report, New York State, September 12–19, 1933, Hopkins Papers, FDR Library.

21. *The Rochester Times-Union*, September 5, 1933, 2; *The Watertown (N.Y.) Daily Times*, September 16, 1933, 2.

22. Benjamin H. Hibbard, "Who Gets the Milk Prices?," *The American Mercury*, June 1934, 158–60.

23. *The New Republic*, August 16, 1933, 2; Hibbard, "Who Gets the Milk Prices?," 162; Hickok to Hopkins, field report, New York State, September 12–19, 1933, Hopkins Papers, FDR Library.

24. Hickok to Eleanor Roosevelt, September 1933, Hickok Papers, FDR Library.

25. *The New York Times*, August 2, 1933, 2, and August 3, 1933, 3.

26. *The New York Times*, August 4, 1933, 4; *Time*, August 14, 1933, 13.

27. Edmund Wilson, "The Milk Strike," *The New Republic*, September 13, 1933, 122; Edmund Wilson, *The American Earthquake* (Garden City, N.Y.: Doubleday, 1958), 511.

28. Wilson, "The Milk Strike," 123–24; Wilson, *American Earthquake*, 513.

29. *The Ogdensburg (N.Y.) Journal*, August 8, 1933, 10.

30. *The New York Times*, August 6, 1933, 1, August 7, 1933, 1, and August 9, 1933, 1.

31. *The New York Times*, August 13, 1933, 1, and August 14, 1933, 1; *The Watertown Daily Times*, August 14, 1933, 5; Wilson, *American Earthquake*, 517.

32. Wilson, "The Milk Strike," 123–24; *The New York Times*, October 3, 1933, 23.

33. *The Watertown Daily Times*, August 14, 1933, 1, 4; Hickok to Hopkins, field report, New York State, September 12–19, 1933, Hopkins Papers, FDR Library.

34. Federal Writers' Project, *New York*, 533–34; *The Ogdensburg Journal*, September 20, 1933, 5, and September 21, 1933, 7. The St. Lawrence Seaway would not open until 1957.

35. *The Ogdensburg Journal*, September 18, 1933, 1, 5, September 19, 1933, 5, 9, and September 20, 1933, 10.

36. Hickok to Hopkins, field report, New York State, September 12–19, 1933, Hopkins Papers, FDR Library.

37. *The Plattsburgh (N.Y.) Daily Republican*, September 19, 1933, 1; *The Plattsburgh (N.Y.) Daily Press*, September 20, 1933, 5.

38. Hickok to Kathryn Godwin, September 23, 1933, Hopkins Papers, FDR Library.

39. Eleanor Roosevelt to Hickok, September 20 and 24, 1933, Hickok Papers, FDR Library; Hickok to Hopkins, field report, Maine, September 21–29, 1933, Hopkins Papers, FDR Library.

40. Hickok to Hopkins, field report, Maine, September 21–29, 1933, Hopkins Papers, FDR Library.

41. Ibid.; Hickok to Eleanor Roosevelt, September 1933, Hickok Papers, FDR Library.

42. Hickok to Hopkins, field report, Maine, September 21–29, 1933, Hopkins Papers, FDR Library; Hickok to Eleanor Roosevelt, September 1933, Hickok Papers, FDR Library.

43. *The Houlton (Me.) Pioneer-Times*, September 7, 1933, 2.

44. *The Eastport (Me.) Sentinel*, October 4, 1933, 1; Hickok to Hopkins, field report, Maine, September 21–29, 1933, Hopkins Papers, FDR Library.

45. Federal Writers' Project, *Maine: A Guide Down East* (Boston: Houghton Mifflin, 1937), 280; Hickok to Hopkins, field report, Maine, September 21–29, 1933, Hopkins Papers, FDR Library; Hickok to Eleanor Roosevelt, September 1933, Hickok Papers, FDR Library; *The Eastport Sentinel*, August 23, 1933, 1, September 20, 1933, 1, and September 27, 1933, 1, 4.

46. *The Eastport Sentinel*, August 30, 1933, 1.

47. *The Eastport Sentinel*, August 16, 1933, 1, 4, September 6, 1933, 5, and September 13, 1933, 1; Federal Writers' Project, *Maine*, 280.

48. Hickok to Hopkins, field report, Maine, September 21–29, 1933, Hopkins Papers, FDR Library; *The Eastport Sentinel*, September 13, 1933, 1; Federal Writers' Project, *Maine*, 280. In 1935 the federal government appropriated $7 million to begin work for the Passamaquoddy tidal project. Some worker housing and two dams were built before the government finally abandoned the on-again, off-again project in the 1970s.

49. Hickok to Hopkins, field report, Maine, September 21–29, 1933, Hopkins Papers, FDR Library.

50. Ibid.

51. Federal Writers' Project, *Maine*, 150, 152.

52. *The Houlton Pioneer-Times*, August 24, 1933, 1, and September 21, 1933, 1.

53. Hickok to Eleanor Roosevelt, September 1933, Hickok Papers, FDR Library; Hickok to Hopkins, field report, Maine, September 21–29, 1933, Hopkins Papers, FDR Library.

54. Hickok to Hopkins, field report, Maine, September 21–29, 1933, Hopkins Papers, FDR Library; Hickok to Eleanor Roosevelt, September 1933, Hickok Papers, FDR Library; *The Houlton Pioneer-Times*, August 31, 1933, and September 7, 14 and 28, 1933.

55. *The Houlton Pioneer-Times*, September 7, 1933, 1.

56. *The Houlton Pioneer-Times*, September 28, 1933, 1.

57. Hickok to Hopkins, field report, Maine, September 21–29, 1933, Hopkins Papers, FDR Library; *The Houlton Pioneer-Times*, August 31, 1933.

58. Hickok to Hopkins, field report, Maine, September 21–29, 1933, Hopkins Papers, FDR Library.

5. The Ghosts of Wall Street

1. Lorena Hickok to Harry Hopkins, field report, New York City, October 2–12, 1933, Harry L. Hopkins Papers, Franklin Delano Roosevelt Presidential Library, Hyde Park, N.Y.; "Relief Problems Vex New York," *The Christian Century*, October 11, 1933, 1277.

2. Hickok to Hopkins, field report, New York City, October 2–12, 1933, Hopkins Papers, FDR Library.

3. Hickok to Kathryn Godwin, October 10, 1933, Hopkins Papers, FDR Library.

4. Lorena Hickok to Eleanor Roosevelt, October 1933, Lorena A. Hickok Papers, Franklin Delano Roosevelt Presidential Library, Hyde Park, N.Y.

5. Eleanor Roosevelt to Hickok, October 7, 1933, Hickok Papers, FDR Library.

6. *New York World-Telegram*, July 24, 1933, 1.

7. Ibid.

8. Ibid.

9. Ibid.

10. Hickok to Hopkins, field report, New York City, October 2–12, 1933, Hopkins Papers, FDR Library; Hickok to Godwin, October 10, 1933, Hopkins Papers, FDR Library.

11. Matthew Josephson, "Relief: The Last Gasp of Private Charity," *The New Republic*, May 10, 1933, 354.

12. Ibid., 354–55; "Relief in New York City," *The Survey*, December 15, 1932, 696; Hickok to Hopkins, field report, New York City, October 2–12, 1933, Hopkins Papers, FDR Library; "The Poor Can Starve," *The Nation*, June 21, 1933, 684.

13. Hickok to Hopkins, field report, New York City, October 2–12, 1933, Hopkins Papers, FDR Library.

14. Matthew Josephson, *Infidel in the Temple: A Memoir of the Nineteen-Thirties* (New York: Knopf, 1967), 82–83; Matthew Josephson, "The Other Nation," *The New Republic*, May 17, 1933, 14–15; "The Poor Can Starve," 684.

15. Josephson, "The Other Nation," 14–15.

16. Ibid.

17. Hickok to Hopkins, field report, New York City, October 2–12, 1933, Hopkins Papers, FDR Library.

18. Ibid.

19. Ibid.

20. Ibid.; "The Poor Can Starve," 684.

21. Michael B. Scheler, "Relief That Does Not Relieve," *The Nation*, November 8, 1933, 539.

22. Josephson, "Relief," 355; *The New York Times*, October 1, 1933, 1; *The New Republic*, October 11, 1933, 239.

23. *The New York Times*, October 1, 1933, 1, and October 2, 1933, 3.

24. *The New York Times*, October 3, 1933, 26, and October 4, 1933, 25.

25. *The New York Times*, October 5, 1933, 1.

26. Malcolm Cowley, *The Dream of the Golden Mountains: Remembering the 1930s* (New York: Viking Press, 1980), 158; *The New York Times*, October 14, 1933, 6.

27. Hickok to Hopkins, field report, New York City, October 2–12, 1933, Hopkins Papers, FDR Library.

28. Ibid.; Marlise Johnston, "The Woman Out of Work," *Review of Reviews*, February 1933, 30.

29. Hickok to Hopkins, field report, New York City, October 2–12, 1933, Hopkins Papers, FDR Library.
30. Johnston, "The Woman Out of Work," 30.
31. Ibid., 30–31.
32. Cowley, *The Dream of the Golden Mountains*, 3–5.
33. Ibid.; Edmund Wilson, *The Thirties: From Notebooks and Diaries of the Period*, ed. Leon Edel (New York: Farrar, Straus and Giroux, 1980), 298.
34. Cowley, *The Dream of the Golden Mountains*, 3–5; John Dos Passos to Edmund Wilson, January 14 (?), 1931, in Townsend Ludington, ed., *The Fourteenth Chronicle: Letters and Diaries of John Dos Passos* (Boston: Gambit, 1973), 398.
35. Josephson, *Infidel in the Temple*, 315; William Soskin, "Rhapsodies in Red," *Forum*, December 1932, 353; Cowley, *The Dream of the Golden Mountains*, 35; Lewis M. Dabney, *Edmund Wilson: A Life in Literature* (New York: Farrar, Straus and Giroux, 2005), 133; Wilson, *The Thirties*, 407.
36. Cowley, *The Dream of the Golden Mountains*, 37, 42, 82.
37. Ludington, *The Fourteenth Chronicle*, 382–83; *The New Republic*, August 17, 1932, 6; Cowley, *The Dream of the Golden Mountains*, 42.
38. Cowley, *The Dream of the Golden Mountains*, 56–58.
39. *The New Republic*, August 17, 1932, 7; Cowley, *The Dream of the Golden Mountains*, 112, 153n; Dos Passos to Wilson, May 16, 1933, in Ludington, *The Fourteenth Chronicle*, 430; Wilson, *The Thirties*, 408, 352.
40. *The New Republic*, August 17, 1932, 6.
41. Wilson, *The Thirties*, 349.
42. See Hickok's field reports; Irving Bernstein, *A Caring Society: The New Deal, the Worker, and the Great Depression* (Boston: Houghton Mifflin, 1985), 31–32; *The New Republic*, October 18, 1933, 263.
43. Eleanor Roosevelt to Hickok, March 11, 1933, Hickok Papers, FDR Library; Hazel Rowley, *Eleanor and Franklin: An Extraordinary Marriage* (New York: Farrar, Straus and Giroux, 2010), 194; Kenneth S. Davis, *FDR: The New Deal Years* (New York: Random House, 1986), 181.
44. *The New York Times*, October 3, 1933, 4, and October 6, 1933, 4, and October 12, 1933, 1; *Time*, October 23, 1933, 12, and October 30, 1933, 9, 39; Cowley, *The Dream of the Golden Mountains*, 211.
45. *The New York Times*, October 11, 1933, 1.
46. *The New Republic*, October 25, 1933, 295.
47. Davis, *FDR: The New Deal Years*, 288, 268, 239, 245; Cowley, *The Dream of the Golden Mountains*, 208; George Soule, "Roosevelt Confronts Capitalism," *The New Republic*, October 13, 1933, 270–71.
48. *The New York Times*, October 9, 1933, 1, and October 10, 1933, 23; *The New Republic*, October 18, 1933, 263.
49. Soule, "Roosevelt Confronts Capitalism," 269.
50. Davis, *FDR: The New Deal Years*, 321–22; David M. Kennedy, *Freedom from Fear: The American People in Depression and War* (New York: Oxford University Press, 1999), 197.

51. *The New York Times*, December 31, 1933, section 8, 1.

52. Davis, *FDR: The New Deal Years*, 282–83, 293.

53. *The Nation*, June 21, 1933, 684; Bernstein, *A Caring Society*, 36; *The New York Times*, October 6, 1933, 7.

54. Bernstein, *A Caring Society*, 36–37; Cowley, *The Dream of the Golden Mountains*, 217.

55. Hickok itinerary, October–December 1933, Hopkins Papers, FDR Library; Hickok, "Introductory chapter," possibly for a projected study of the Works Progress Administration, Hickok Papers, FDR Library.

6. America's Siberia

1. Mary Heaton Vorse, "Rebellion in the Cornbelt," *Harper's Monthly Magazine*, December 1932, 1.

2. Ibid., 6; David M. Kennedy, *Freedom from Fear: The American People in Depression and War, 1929–1945* (New York: Oxford University Press, 1999), 197.

3. Lorena Hickok, itinerary, October–December 1933, Lorena A. Hickok Papers, Franklin Delano Roosevelt Presidential Library, Hyde Park, N.Y.; Lorena Hickok to Harry Hopkins, en route to Minneapolis, October 24, 1933, Harry L. Hopkins Papers, Franklin Delano Roosevelt Library, Hyde Park, N.Y.; Telegram, Hopkins to Hickok, October 26, 1933, Hopkins Papers, FDR Library; Telegram, Hickok to Hopkins, Minneapolis, October 27, 1933, Hopkins Papers, FDR Library; Federal Writers' Project, *Minnesota: A State Guide* (New York: Viking Press, 1938), 188.

4. Telegram, Hickok to Hopkins, Minneapolis, October 27, 1933, Hopkins Papers, FDR Library; Hickok to Hopkins, Minneapolis, October 28, 1933, Hopkins Papers, FDR Library; Lillian Symes, "Blunder on the Left," *Harper's Monthly Magazine*, December 1933, 91–92; *Time*, October 16, 1933, 13.

5. Hickok to Hopkins, Minneapolis, October 28, 1933, Hopkins Papers, FDR Library; *The Bismarck Tribune*, October 20, 1933, 1; *Time*, October 30, 1933, 11–12, and November 6, 1933, 17, 18.

6. Hickok to Hopkins, Minneapolis, October 28, 1933, Hopkins Papers, FDR Library.

7. Ibid.

8. *Time*, October 2, 1933, 12, and November 6, 1933, 17; *The Bismarck Tribune*, October 23, 1933, 4.

9. *Time*, November 6, 1933, 17–19, and November 13, 1933, 13; *The New York Times*, October 11, 1933, 33; *The Bismarck Tribune*, October 25, 1933, 1.

10. *Time*, November 6, 1933, 17, and November 13, 1933, 12–13; Kenneth S. Davis, *FDR: The New Deal Years* (New York: Random House, 1986), 289–90.

11. *Time*, November 13, 1933, 13.

12. Ibid.; *Business Week*, November 11, 1933, 8–9; Davis, *FDR: The New Deal Years*, 297.
13. Eleanor Roosevelt to Hickok, November 9, 1933, Hickok Papers, FDR Library.
14. Hickok to Hopkins, Winner, S.D., November 10, 1933, Hopkins Papers, FDR Library; Davis, *FDR: The New Deal Years*, 297.
15. Hickok to Hopkins, Dickinson, N.D., October 30, 1933, Hopkins Papers, FDR Library.
16. *The Bismarck Tribune*, October 30, 1933, 2; Hickok to Hopkins, Minot, N.D., November 1, 1933, Hopkins Papers, FDR Library.
17. Hickok to Hopkins, Dickinson, N.D., October 30, 1933, Hopkins Papers, FDR Library.
18. Ibid.
19. Ibid.
20. Federal Writers' Project, *North Dakota: A Guide to the Northern Prairie State* (New York: Oxford University Press, 1950), 250.
21. Hickok to Hopkins, Minot, N.D., November 1, 1933, Hopkins Papers, FDR Library.
22. Ibid.
23. Ibid.
24. Hickok to Eleanor Roosevelt, November 1, 1933, Hickok Papers, FDR Library; Hickok to Hopkins, Minot, N.D., November 1, 1933, Hopkins Papers, FDR Library; Telegram, Hickok to Hopkins, November 2, 1933, Hopkins Papers, FDR Library.
25. Hickok itinerary, October–December 1933, Hickok Papers, FDR Library; Alfred Klausler, "Brief Report from a Prairie Utopia," *The American Mercury*, June 1933, 197; Lorena Hickok to Kathryn Godwin, November 1, 1933, Hopkins Papers, FDR Library; Lorena Hickok to Eleanor Roosevelt, October 31, 1933, Hickok Papers, FDR Library.
26. *The Bottineau (N.D.) Courant*, October 25, 1933, 1; Hickok to Eleanor Roosevelt, October 31, 1933, Hickok Papers, FDR Library.
27. Hickok to Eleanor Roosevelt, October 31, 1933, Hickok Papers, FDR Library; Hickok to Hopkins, Bismarck, N.D., November 3, 1933, Hopkins Papers, FDR Library.
28. Hickok to Eleanor Roosevelt, October 31, 1933, Hickok Papers, FDR Library; Hickok to Hopkins, Bismarck, N.D., November 3, 1933, Hopkins Papers, FDR Library.
29. Hickok to Hopkins, Bismarck, N.D., November 3, 1933, Hopkins Papers, FDR Library.
30. Hickok to Eleanor Roosevelt, October 31, 1933, Hickok Papers, FDR Library.
31. Hickok to Hopkins, Bismarck, N.D., November 3, 1933, Hopkins Papers, FDR Library.
32. Minnie D. Craig, handwritten memoir, untitled, Minnie D. Craig Papers, State Historical Society of North Dakota, Bismarck, 17, 52.

33. Ibid., 18–19.

34. Ibid.

35. Eleanor Roosevelt to Hickok, November 7, 1933, Hickok Papers, FDR Library; Hickok to Hopkins, Bismarck, N.D., November 3, 1933, Hopkins Papers, FDR Library; Hickok to Hopkins, Ortonville, Minn., November 6, 1933, Hopkins Papers, FDR Library; Klausler, "Brief Report from a Prairie Utopia," 198.

36. Eleanor Roosevelt to Hickok, November 5 and 9, 1933, Hickok Papers, FDR Library.

37. Lorena Hickok, "The Making of an Introvert," autobiographical fragment, Hickok Papers, FDR Library.

38. Hickok to Hopkins, Pierre, S.D., November 9, 1933, Hopkins Papers, FDR Library.

39. *The Bowdle (S.D.) Pioneer*, November 2, 1933, 1, and November 9, 1933, 1.

40. Hickok to Hopkins, Aberdeen, S.D., November 7, 1933, Hopkins Papers; Federal Writers' Project, *South Dakota: Guide to the State* (New York: Hastings House, 1952), 94.

41. Hickok to Hopkins, Aberdeen, S.D., November 7, 1933, Hopkins Papers, FDR Library; Hickok to Hopkins, Ortonville, Minn., November 6, 1933, Hopkins Papers, FDR Library.

42. *Aberdeen (S.D.) Evening News*, November 6, 1933, 1; Hickok to Hopkins, Aberdeen, S.D., November 7, 1933, Hopkins Papers, FDR Library.

43. *Aberdeen Evening News*, November 3, 6, 7, 8, 9 and 10, 1933, 1; *Reporter and Farmer* (Webster, S.D.), November 2, 1933, 1.

44. *Aberdeen Evening News*, November 5, 1933, 1, November 8, 1933, 1, and November 9, 1933, 2.

45. Federal Writers' Project, *South Dakota*, 195; Hickok to Hopkins, Pierre, S.D., November 9, 1933, Hopkins Papers, FDR Library.

46. Hickok to Hopkins, Pierre, S.D., November 9, 1933, Hopkins Papers, FDR Library.

47. Ibid.

48. Hickok to Hopkins, Winner, S.D., November 10, 1933, Hopkins Papers, FDR Library.

49. Ibid.; Hickok to Eleanor Roosevelt, November 10, 1933, Hickok Papers, FDR Library; Federal Writers' Project, *South Dakota*, 303–4.

50. Hickok to Eleanor Roosevelt, November 10, 1933, Hickok Papers, FDR Library; Federal Writers' Project, *South Dakota*, 300–301.

51. Hickok to Eleanor Roosevelt, November 10, 1933, Hickok Papers, FDR Library.

52. Federal Writers' Project, *South Dakota*, 236; Hickok to Eleanor Roosevelt, November 11–12, 1933, Hickok Papers, FDR Library.

53. Hickok to Eleanor Roosevelt, November 11–12, 1933, Hickok Papers, FDR Library; Hickok to Hopkins, Lincoln, Neb., November 20, 1933, Hopkins Papers, FDR Library.

54. Hickok to Eleanor Roosevelt, November 11–12, 1933, Hickok Papers, FDR Library; *The Evening Huronite* (Huron, S.D.), November 12, 1933, 1; Hickok to Hopkins, Lincoln, Neb., November 20, 1933, Hopkins Papers, FDR Library; Federal Writers' Project, *South Dakota*, 236.

55. *The Evening Huronite*, November 12, 1933, 1.

56. Hickok to Hopkins, Lincoln, Neb., November 20, 1933, Hopkins Papers, FDR Library.

57. Hickok to Hopkins, Pierre, S.D., November 9, 1933, Hopkins Papers, FDR Library.

7. "The Richest Village in the World"

1. Lorena Hickok to Harry Hopkins, Omaha, November 20, 1933, Harry L. Hopkins Papers, Franklin Delano Roosevelt Presidential Library, Hyde Park, N.Y.; *The Omaha World-Herald*, November 19, 1933, 3; Lorena Hickok to Eleanor Roosevelt, November 20, 1933, Lorena A. Hickok Papers, Franklin Delano Roosevelt Presidential Library, Hyde Park, N.Y.

2. Hickok to Eleanor Roosevelt, November 21, 1933, Hickok Papers, FDR Library; *The Omaha World-Herald*, November 19, 1933, 3.

3. Hickok to Hopkins, Omaha, November 20, 1933, Hopkins Papers, FDR Library; *The Omaha World-Herald*, November 20, 1933, 3.

4. Hickok to Eleanor Roosevelt, November 21, 1933, Hickok Papers, FDR Library; *Time*, November 20, 1933, 16; *The Omaha World-Herald*, November 19, 1933, 1. Judd Gray had been a reluctant accomplice in Ruth Snyder's seven attempts on her husband's life. Rasputin-like, Albert Snyder survived each one—until the couple finally pulled off the murder using chloroform and a garrote.

5. Bruce Bliven, "Milo Reno and His Farmers," *The New Republic*, November 29, 1933, 63–64; Hickok to Eleanor Roosevelt, November 21, 1933, Hickok Papers, FDR Library.

6. Bliven, "Milo Reno and His Farmers," 64–65; Hickok to Hopkins, Omaha, November 20, 1933, Hopkins Papers, FDR Library; *The Omaha World-Herald*, November 22, 1933, 1.

7. Hickok to Hopkins, Omaha, November 20, 1933, Hopkins Papers, FDR Library; Hickok to Eleanor Roosevelt, November 21, 1933, Hickok Papers, FDR Library; Hickok to Hopkins, Lincoln, Neb., November 18, 1933, Hopkins Papers, FDR Library.

8. *The Omaha World-Herald*, November 20, 1933, 1; Hickok to Hopkins, Omaha, November 20, 1933, Hopkins Papers, FDR Library.

9. Hickok to Hopkins, Omaha, November 20, 1933, Hopkins Papers, FDR Library; Hickok to Eleanor Roosevelt, November 21, 1933, Hickok Papers, FDR Library; Hickok to Hopkins, Lincoln, Neb., November 18, 1933, Hopkins Papers, FDR Library.

10. *The Omaha World-Herald*, November 23, 1933, 1, 3.

11. Hickok to Hopkins, Lincoln, Neb., November 18, 1933, Hopkins Papers, FDR Library; Federal Writers' Project, *Iowa: A Guide to the Hawkeye State* (New York: Viking Press, 1938), 300, 311; Marcia Poole, *The Yards: A Way of Life* (Sioux City, Iowa: Lewis and Clark Interpretive Center, 2002), vol. 2, 94–95, 105; Scott Sorenson and Paul Chicone, *Sioux City: A Pictorial History* (Norfolk, Va.: Donning, 1982), 168.

12. Poole, *The Yards*, 151.

13. Sorenson and Chicone, *Sioux City*, 167.

14. *The Sioux City (Ia.) Tribune*, November 3, 4, 7 and 9, 1933, 1.

15. Hickok to Hopkins, Sioux City, Ia., November 23, 1933, Hopkins Papers, FDR Library.

16. Hickok to Hopkins, Des Moines, November 25, 1933, Hopkins Papers, FDR Library.

17. *The Sioux City Tribune*, November 20, 23, 27 and December 4, 1933, 1.

18. Transcript of Proceedings, Civil Works Administration Conference, Mayflower Hotel, Washington, D.C., November 15, 1933, 12, Hopkins Papers, FDR Library; Hickok to Hopkins, Des Moines, November 25, 1933, Hopkins Papers, FDR Library; *The Literary Digest*, November 18, 1933, 9.

19. Hickok to Hopkins, Des Moines, November 25, 1933, Hopkins Papers, FDR Library.

20. *The Sioux City Tribune*, November 25, 1933, 1; Hickok to Hopkins, Sioux City, Ia., November 23, 1933, Hopkins Papers, FDR Library.

21. Hickok to Hopkins, Des Moines, November 25, 1933, Hopkins Papers, FDR Library.

22. Hickok to Eleanor Roosevelt, Ottumwa, Ia., November 26, 1933, Hickok Papers, FDR Library.

23. Hickok to Kathryn Godwin, Des Moines, November 25, 1933, Hopkins Papers, FDR Library.

24. Hickok to Eleanor Roosevelt, Ottumwa, Ia., November 26, 1933, Hickok Papers, FDR Library.

25. Eleanor Roosevelt to Hickok, November 22, 1933, Hickok Papers, FDR Library.

26. Eleanor Roosevelt to Hickok, November 20, 1933, Hickok Papers, FDR Library; Hickok to Eleanor Roosevelt, November 26, 1933, Hickok Papers, FDR Library; Eleanor Roosevelt to Hickok, November 24, 1933, Hickok Papers, FDR Library.

27. Federal Writers' Project, *Iowa*, 374; *The Charles City (Ia.) Press*, November 29, 1933, 3; Hickok to Eleanor Roosevelt, November 28, 1933, Hickok Papers, FDR Library; *Recent Social Trends in the United States,* report of the President's Research Committee on Social Trends (New York: Whittlesey House/McGraw Hill, 1934), 506.

28. *The Charles City Press*, November 23, 1933, 1, and November 27, 1933, 6.

29. Hickok to Hopkins, Sioux City, Ia., December 4, 1933, Hopkins Papers, FDR Library.

30. Hickok to Hopkins, Fergus Falls, Minn., December 5, 1933, Hopkins Papers, FDR Library.

31. Hickok, "Making of an Introvert"; Doris Faber, *Lorena Hickok* (New York: William Morrow, 1980), 69–71; Rodger Streitmatter, *Empty without You: The Intimate Letters of Eleanor Roosevelt and Lorena Hickok* (New York: Free Press, 1998), xix; Lorena Hickok, foreword, unfinished autobiography, unpublished ms., Hickok Papers, FDR Library.

32. Eleanor Roosevelt to Hickok, November 29, 1933, Hickok Papers, FDR Library; T. S. Carskadon, "Hull House in the Hills," *The New Republic*, August 1, 1934, 312.

33. Hickok to Eleanor Roosevelt, November 28, 1933, Hickok Papers, FDR Library; Eleanor Roosevelt to Hickok, December 1, 1933, Hickok Papers, FDR Library.

34. Eleanor Roosevelt to Hickok, December 1, 1933, and November 27, 1933, Hickok Papers, FDR Library; *Time*, November 20, 1933, 12.

35. Eleanor Roosevelt to Hickok, November 18, 1933, Hickok Papers, FDR Library; *Time*, November 20, 1933, 13–14; *The Literary Digest*, November 18, 1933, 12.

36. Eleanor Roosevelt to Hickok, October 30, 1933, Hickok Papers, FDR Library; *Recent Social Trends*, 711–13; *The New York Times*, November 21, 1933, 1.

37. *The New York Times*, November 21, 1933, 1; Hickok to Hopkins, Sioux City, Ia., December 4, 1933, Hopkins Papers, FDR Library; Proceedings, Civil Works Administration Conference, 28, Hopkins Papers, FDR Library; Susan Ware, *Holding Their Own: American Women in the 1930s* (Boston: Twayne, 1982), 39.

38. Hickok to Hopkins, Sioux City, Ia., December 4, 1933, Hopkins Papers, FDR Library; Hickok to Hopkins, Fergus Falls, Minn., December 5, 1933, Hopkins Papers, FDR Library; Federal Writers' Project, *Minnesota: A State Guide* (New York: Viking Press, 1938), 417.

39. Federal Writers' Project, *Minnesota*, 381.

40. Hickok to Eleanor Roosevelt, December 5, 1933, Hickok Papers, FDR Library; Hickok to Hopkins, Brainerd, Minn., December 7, 1933, Hopkins Papers, FDR Library.

41. *Time*, April 24, 1933, 14; Hickok to Hopkins, Minneapolis, December 12, 1933, Hopkins Papers, FDR Library. Olson died of stomach cancer in August 1936.

42. Hickok to Eleanor Roosevelt, December 5, 1933, Hickok Papers, FDR Library.

43. Hickok to Hopkins, Brainerd, Minn., December 7, 1933, Hopkins Papers, FDR Library.

44. Hickok to Eleanor Roosevelt, December 5, 1933, Hickok Papers, FDR Library; Hickok to Hopkins, Brainerd, Minn., December 7, 1933, Hopkins Papers, FDR Library; *Recent Social Trends*, 105.

45. Hickok to Eleanor Roosevelt, December 5 (6), 1933, Hickok Papers, FDR Library.

46. Samuel I. Rosenman, ed., *The Public Papers and Addresses of Franklin Delano Roosevelt*, Vol. 2: *1933* (New York: Random House, 1938), 157–59; Hickok to Hopkins, Brainerd, Minn., December 7, 1933, Hopkins Papers.

47. Hickok to Hopkins, Brainerd, Minn., December 7, 1933, Hopkins Papers, FDR Library.

48. *Northland Times* (Bemidji, Minn.), November 24, 1933, 1, 13; *The Bemidji (Minn.) Daily Pioneer*, November 29, 1933, 1, December 2, 1933, 1, and December 6, 1933, 1; *Northland Times*, November 10, 1933, 1; Hickok to Hopkins, Brainerd, Minn., December 7, 1933, Hopkins Papers, FDR Library.

49. *Northland Times*, November 10, 1933, 12, December 8, 1933, 1, and December 15, 1933, 1.

50. Federal Writers' Project, *Minnesota*, 95; Hickok to Hopkins, Minneapolis, December 10, 1933, Hopkins Papers, FDR Library.

51. Federal Writers' Project, *Minnesota*, 323–24; Hickok to Eleanor Roosevelt, December 8, 1933, Hickok Papers, FDR Library; Hickok to Hopkins, Minneapolis, December 10, 1933, Hopkins Papers, FDR Library.

52. Hickok to Eleanor Roosevelt, December 8, 1933, Hickok Papers, FDR Library; Hickok to Hopkins, Minneapolis, December 10, 1933, Hopkins Papers, FDR Library.

53. Hickok to Hopkins, Minneapolis, December 10, 1933, Hopkins Papers, FDR Library; Hickok to Eleanor Roosevelt, December 8, 1933, Hickok Papers, FDR Library.

54. Hickok to Eleanor Roosevelt, December 8, 1933, Hickok Papers, FDR Library.

55. Ibid.

56. Hickok to Eleanor Roosevelt, December 10, 1933, Hickok Papers, FDR Library; Hickok, itinerary, December 1933, Hickok Papers, FDR Library.

57. Eleanor Roosevelt to Hickok, December 10, 12, and 23, 1933, Hickok Papers, FDR Library; *Time*, January 1, 1934, 5.

58. Hickok to Hopkins, New York City, December 29, 1933, Hopkins Papers, FDR Library.

59. Ibid.

60. Ibid.

8. The Stricken South

1. Howard W. Odum, *Southern Regions of the United States* (Chapel Hill: University of North Carolina Press, 1936), 563; Federal Writers' Project, *Georgia: A Guide to Its Towns and Countryside* (Atlanta: Tupper & Love, 1940, 1954), 19; Lorena Hickok to Harry Hopkins, Athens, Georgia,

January 11, 1934, Harry L. Hopkins Papers, Franklin Delano Roosevelt Presidential Library, Hyde Park, N.Y.

2. *The Atlanta Constitution*, January 1, 1934, 1; *The Atlanta Journal*, January 1, 1934, 4.

3. Eleanor Roosevelt to Lorena Hickok, January 9, 1934, Lorena A. Hickok Papers, Franklin Delano Roosevelt Library, Hyde Park, N.Y.; Aubrey Williams to Hickok, December 28, 1933, Hickok Papers, FDR Library; Expense account, Lorena Hickok, January–February 1934, Hickok Papers, FDR Library; *The Atlanta Journal*, January 1, 1933, 2; *The Atlanta Constitution*, January 1, 1934, 1.

4. Hickok to Hopkins, Athens, Ga., January 11, 1934, Hopkins Papers, FDR Library.

5. Ibid.

6. Eleanor Roosevelt to Hickok, January 9, 1934, Hickok Papers, FDR Library; Stephen Vincent Benét, *John Brown's Body* (New York: Heritage Press, 1948), vi, 416.

7. Hickok to Hopkins, Athens, Ga., January 11, 1934, Hopkins Papers, FDR Library; Hickok to Hopkins, Augusta, Ga., January 14, 1934, Hopkins Papers, FDR Library; Webster Powell and Addison T. Cutler, "Tightening the Cotton Belt," *Harper's Monthly Magazine*, February 1934, 311.

8. *Time*, January 15, 1934, 18; *The Atlanta Journal*, January 5, 1934, 1; Hickok to Hopkins, Athens, Ga., January 11, 1934, Hopkins Papers, FDR Library.

9. Augusta Unit, Federal Writers' Project, *Augusta* (Augusta, Ga.: City Council of Augusta, 1938), 34; Arthur Schlesinger Jr., *The Coming of the New Deal* (Boston: Houghton Mifflin, 1959), 59–60; *The Augusta Chronicle*, October 8, 1933, 1; *The Atlanta Journal*, January 1, 1934, 5; Powell and Cutler, "Tightening the Cotton Belt," 310–11.

10. Hickok to Hopkins, Athens, Ga., January 11, 1934, Hopkins Papers, FDR Library; A. Ray Rowland and Helen Callahan, *Yesterday's Augusta* (Miami: E. A. Seemann, 1976), 67; Federal Writers' Project, *Georgia*, 66; Odum, *Southern Regions of the United States*, 397.

11. Hickok to Hopkins, Augusta, Ga., January 14, 1934, Hopkins Papers, FDR Library.

12. Ibid.

13. Hickok to Hopkins, Athens, Ga., January 11, 1934, Hopkins Papers, FDR Library; Hickok to Hopkins, Augusta, Ga., January 14, 1934, Hopkins Papers, FDR Library; *Recent Social Trends in the United States,* report of the President's Research Committee on Social Trends (New York: Whittlesey House/McGraw Hill, 1934), 577.

14. Hickok to Hopkins, Augusta, Ga., January 14, 1934, Hopkins Papers, FDR Library.

15. Federal Writers' Project, *Augusta*, 92, 97; *The Augusta Chronicle*, November 28, 1934, 1.

16. Federal Writers' Project, *Georgia*, 73; Hickok to Hopkins, Augusta, Ga.,

January 14, 1934, Hopkins Papers, FDR Library; *The Augusta Chronicle*, October 12, 1933, 1, and January 14, 1934, 1.

17. Hickok to Hopkins, January 14, 1934, Hopkins Papers, FDR Library.

18. Ibid.; *Augusta Chronicle*, October 20, 21, 22, 24, and 27, 1933, 1.

19. *The Augusta Chronicle*, October 27 and 28 and November 2, 3, and 4, 1933, 1.

20. *The Augusta Chronicle*, January 14, 1934, 1.

21. Hickok to Hopkins, Jesup, Ga., January 16, 1934, Hopkins Papers, FDR Library; Federal Writers' Project, *Georgia*, 129; *The Savannah Evening Press*, January 15, 1934, 1.

22. Hickok to Hopkins, Jesup, Ga., January 16, 1934, Hopkins Papers, FDR Library; *The Savannah Morning News*, January 1 and 6, 1934, 1.

23. *The Savannah Morning News*, January 15, 1934, 1, 6.

24. Thomas Gamble, *Gamble's International Naval Stores Yearbook for 1932–1933* (Savannah, Ga.: N.p., 1932), 2, 11–12, 41, Savannah Public Library, Savannah, Georgia; "Commerce, Trade and Harbor Development, Savannah, Georgia," typescript, Savannah Public Library, Savannah, Georgia, 28–29.

25. "Commerce, Trade and Harbor Development," 29; Hickok to Hopkins, Moultrie, Ga., January 23, 1934, Hopkins Papers, FDR Library.

26. Hickok to Hopkins, Jesup, Ga., January 16, 1934, Hopkins Papers, FDR Library.

27. Ibid.

28. *The Savannah Evening Press*, January 8, 1934, 1; *The Atlanta Constitution*, January 10, 1934, 7; Hickok to Hopkins, Jesup, Ga., January 16, 1934, Hopkins Papers, FDR Library.

29. *The Atlanta Constitution*, January 18, 1934, 1; *The Atlanta Journal*, January 18, 1934, 1; Blanche Wiesen Cook, *Eleanor Roosevelt*, Vol. 2: *1933–1938* (New York: Viking, 1999), 154.

30. *The Atlanta Constitution*, January 20 and 21, 1934, 1; Cook, *Eleanor Roosevelt*, 155.

31. *The Atlanta Constitution*, January 22, 1934, 1; Eleanor Roosevelt to Hickok, January 23, 1934, Hickok Papers, FDR Library.

32. Hickok to Eleanor Roosevelt, January 22, 1934, Hickok Papers, FDR Library; Eleanor Roosevelt to Hickok, January 24, 1934, Hickok Papers, FDR Library.

33. Hickok to Eleanor Roosevelt, January 22, 1934, Hickok Papers, FDR Library; Hickok to Hopkins, Moultrie, Ga., January 23, 1934, Hopkins Papers, FDR Library; *The Atlanta Constitution*, January 19, 1934, 1.

34. Federal Writers' Project, *Georgia*, 272; Hickok to Eleanor Roosevelt, January 22, 1934, Hickok Papers, FDR Library.

35. Hickok to Eleanor Roosevelt, January 23, 1934, Hickok Papers, FDR Library.

36. *The Moultrie (Ga.) Observer*, January 23, 1934, 1; Hickok to Hopkins, Moultrie, Ga., January 23, 1934, Hopkins Papers, FDR Library.

37. *The Moultrie Observer*, January 2, 1934, 6, January 4, 10 and 11, 1934, 1, January 15, 1934, 1; Hickok to Hopkins, Tallahassee, Fla., January 24, 1934, Hopkins Papers, FDR Library.

38. Hickok to Hopkins, January 23, 1934, Moultrie, Ga., Hopkins Papers, FDR Library; Hickok to Eleanor Roosevelt, January 23, 1934, Hickok Papers, FDR Library.

39. Odum, *Southern Regions of the United States*, 486; Hickok to Eleanor Roosevelt, January 23, 1934, Hickok Papers, FDR Library; Powell and Cutler, "Tightening the Cotton Belt," 308–9; Hickok to Hopkins, Moultrie, Ga., January 23, 1934, Hopkins Papers, FDR Library.

40. Powell and Cutler, "Tightening the Cotton Belt," 308–9; Hickok to Eleanor Roosevelt, January 23, 1934, Hickok Papers, FDR Library.

41. Hickok to Hopkins, Tallahassee, Fla., January 24, 1934, Hopkins Papers, FDR Library.

42. Hickok to Hopkins, Moultrie, Ga., January 23, 1934, Hopkins Papers, FDR Library; Hickok to Hopkins, Tallahassee, Fla., January 24, 1934, Hopkins Papers, FDR Library.

43. Powell and Cutler, "Tightening the Cotton Belt," 316–18; *Recent Social Trends*, 110.

44. Eleanor Roosevelt to Hickok, January 15, 1934, and January 24, 1934, Hickok Papers, FDR Library.

45. Hickok to Hopkins, Moultrie, Ga., January 23, 1934, Hopkins Papers, FDR Library.

46. Ibid.

47. Hickok to Eleanor Roosevelt, January 26, 1934, Hickok Papers, FDR Library.

48. Hickok to Hopkins, Daytona Beach, Fla., January 31, 1934, Hopkins Papers, FDR Library.

49. Hickok to Hopkins, Miami, January 29, 1934, Hopkins Papers, FDR Library.

50. *Business Week*, February 17, 1934, 14; Hickok to Hopkins, Miami, January 29, 1934, Hopkins Papers, FDR Library.

51. Federal Writers' Project, *Florida: A Guide to the Southernmost State* (New York: Oxford University Press, 1939), 209; Bruce Bliven, "Warmth for Sale," *The New Republic*, March 7, 1934, 98–100; *Time*, February 19, 1934, 12.

52. Hickok to Hopkins, Columbia, S.C., February 5, 1934, Hopkins Papers, FDR Library.

53. Eleanor Roosevelt to Hickok, January 27, 1934, and February 8 and 9, 1934, Hickok Papers, FDR Library.

54. Hickok to Hopkins, Columbia, S.C., February 5, 1934, Hopkins Papers, FDR Library; Hickok to Hopkins, Greenville, S.C., February 7, 1934, Hopkins Papers, FDR Library; *Time*, February 19, 1934, 11–12; Hickok to Hopkins, Raleigh, N.C., February 14, 1934, Hopkins Papers, FDR Library.

55. Federal Writers' Project, *South Carolina: A Guide to the Palmetto State* (New York: Oxford University Press, 1939), 70–71, 242; W. J. Cash, "The Mind of the South," *The American Mercury*, October 1929, 188; Odum, *Southern Regions of the United States*, 493–94.

56. Hickok to Hopkins, Greenville, S.C., February 7, 1934, Hopkins Papers, FDR Library.

57. Cash, "The Mind of the South," 187, 189–90.

58. Hickok to Hopkins, Greenville, S.C., February 7, 1934, Hopkins Papers, FDR Library; Cash, "The Mind of the South," 191.

59. Federal Writers' Project, *South Carolina,* 60, 64, 67; Hickok to Hopkins, Greenville, S.C., February 7, 1934, Hopkins Papers, FDR Library; Hickok to Hopkins, Charleston, S.C., February 10, 1934, and February 8, 1934, Hopkins Papers, FDR Library.

60. *Time*, February 19, 1934, 11; Hickok to Hopkins, Charleston, S.C., February 10, 1934, Hopkins Papers, FDR Library.

61. Odum, *Southern Regions of the United States*, 563; Hickok to Hopkins, Raleigh, N.C., February 14, 1934, Hopkins Papers, FDR Library.

62. Hickok to Hopkins, Raleigh, N.C., February 14, 1934, Hopkins Papers, FDR Library.

63. Hickok to Kathryn Godwin, Greensboro, N.C., February 14, 1934, Hopkins Papers, FDR Library.

64. Hickok to Kathryn Godwin, Greensboro, N.C., February 18, 1934, Hopkins Papers, FDR Library; *Time*, February 19, 1934, 12.

9. Empire of Misery

1. Alexander J. Field, *A Great Leap Forward: 1930s Depression and U.S. Economic Growth* (New Haven: Yale University Press, 2011), 71–73; Frederic L. Paxson, "The Highway Movement, 1916–1935," *American Historical Review* 51, no. 2 (1946): 244; *Recent Social Trends in the United States,* report of the President's Research Committee on Social Trends (New York: Whittlesey House/McGraw Hill, 1934), 176, 172.

2. Lorena Hickok to Harry Hopkins, Birmingham, Ala., April 1, 1934, Harry L. Hopkins Papers, Franklin Delano Roosevelt Presidential Library, Hyde Park, N.Y.; Hickok to Hopkins, New Orleans, April 8, 1934, Hopkins Papers, FDR Library.

3. *The New York Times*, March 31, 1934, 3; Wayne T. Parrish, "CWA Ends after Brightening Up Nation," *The Literary Digest*, April 21, 1934, 9.

4. Kenneth S. Davis, *FDR: The New Deal Years, 1933–1937* (New York: Random House, 1986), 305; *The New York Times*, December 31, 1933, section 8, 2; Robert Skidelsky, *John Maynard Keynes, 1883–1946: Economist, Philosopher, Statesman* (New York: Penguin, 2003), 507; Florence Peterson, "CWA: A Candid Appraisal," *Atlantic Monthly*, May 1934, 587–88.

5. Eleanor Roosevelt to Lorena Hickok, March 26, 1934, Lorena Hickok Papers, Franklin Delano Roosevelt Presidential Library, Hyde Park, N.Y.; Davis, *FDR: The New Deal Years*, 312; Clipping, *The Raleigh News & Observer*, n.d. (February 1934), Hopkins Papers, FDR Library; *The Nation*, March 28, 1934, 346; *The New Republic*, April 4, 1934, 201.

6. Hickok to Hopkins, Birmingham, Ala., April 2, 1934, Hopkins Papers, FDR Library.

7. Eleanor Roosevelt to Hickok, April 1, 1934, Hickok Papers, FDR Library; Hickok to Hopkins, Birmingham, Ala., April 2, 1934, Hopkins Papers, FDR Library.

8. Hickok to Hopkins, Birmingham, Ala., April 2, 1934, Hopkins Papers, FDR Library.

9. Ibid.

10. Hickok to Hopkins, New Orleans, April 7, 1934, Hopkins Papers, FDR Library; Howard W. Odum, *Southern Regions of the United States* (Chapel Hill: University of North Carolina Press, 1936), 59–61; *Recent Social Trends*, 505.

11. Hickok to Hopkins, New Orleans, April 7, 1934, Hopkins Papers, FDR Library.

12. Ibid.

13. Hickok to Hopkins, Houston, April 13, 1934, Hopkins Papers, FDR Library; Hickok to Eleanor Roosevelt, April 9, 1934, Hickok Papers, FDR Library.

14. Hickok to Eleanor Roosevelt, April 11, 1934, Hickok Papers, FDR Library; Hickok to Hopkins, Houston, April 11, 1934, Hopkins Papers, FDR Library.

15. Hickok to Hopkins, Houston, April 13, 1934, Hopkins Papers, FDR Library.

16. Hickok to Hopkins, Houston, April 11, 1934, Hopkins Papers, FDR Library.

17. Ibid.

18. Hickok to Hopkins, San Antonio, April 17, 1934, Hopkins Papers, FDR Library; Odum, *Southern Regions of the United States*, 325, 184.

19. Hickok to Eleanor Roosevelt, April 19, 1934, Hickok Papers, FDR Library.

20. Hickok to Eleanor Roosevelt, April 20, 1934, Hickok Papers, FDR Library.

21. Hickok to Hopkins, San Antonio, April 17, 1934, Hopkins Papers, FDR Library; Hickok to Hopkins, Albuquerque, April 25, 1934, Hopkins Papers, FDR Library; *The San Francisco Chronicle*, July 27, 1934, 4.

22. Hickok to Hopkins, San Antonio, April 17, 1934, and Albuquerque, April 25, 1934, Hopkins Papers, FDR Library.

23. Federal Writers' Project, *New Mexico: A Guide to the Colorful State* (New York: Hastings House, 1940), 251–52; Hickok to Hopkins, Socorro, N.M., April 27, 1934, Hopkins Papers, FDR Library.

24. Hickok to Hopkins, Socorro, N.M., April 27, 1934, Hopkins Papers, FDR Library.

25. Ibid.

26. Ibid.; Hickok to Hopkins, May 8, 1934, Hopkins Papers, FDR Library.

27. Hickok to Hopkins, Socorro, N.M., April 27, 1934, Hopkins Papers, FDR Library.

28. Eleanor Roosevelt to Hickok, April 29, 1934, Hickok Papers, FDR Library; Hickok to Hopkins, Phoenix, May 4, 1933, Hopkins Papers, FDR Library; Telegram, Eleanor Roosevelt to Hickok, April 29, 1934, Hickok Papers, FDR Library.

29. Hickok to Hopkins, Phoenix, May 4, 1933, Hopkins Papers, FDR Library; Hickok to Kathryn Godwin, May 4, 1934, Hopkins Papers, FDR Library.

30. Hickok to Hopkins, Los Angeles, June 25, 1934, Hopkins Papers, FDR Library; Federal Writers' Project, *Colorado: A Guide to the Highest State* (New York: Hastings House, 1941), 230.

31. Hickok to Hopkins, Denver, June 17, 1934, Hopkins Papers, FDR Library; Hickok to Eleanor Roosevelt, June 15, 1934, Hickok Papers, FDR Library.

32. Hickok to Hopkins, Denver, June 17, 1934, Hopkins Papers, FDR Library.

33. Ibid.

34. *The Nation*, January 31, 1934, 115.

35. Hickok to Hopkins, Denver, June 17, 1934, Hopkins Papers, FDR Library; A. P. Peck, "Sweet Beets," *Scientific American*, May 1933, 281.

36. Hickok to Eleanor Roosevelt, June 23, 1934, Hickok Papers, FDR Library; Federal Writers' Project, *Colorado*, 301; Hickok to Hopkins, en route, Denver to Los Angeles, June 23, 1934, Hickok Papers, FDR Library; Peck, "Sweet Beets," 281.

37. Hickok to Hopkins, en route, Denver to Los Angeles, June 23, 1934, Hickok Papers, FDR Library.

38. *Los Angeles Times,* July 2, 1934, section 2, 1; July 4, 1934, 6, 8, and July 5, 1934, 12.

39. Hickok to Hopkins, Los Angeles, June 27, 1934, Hopkins Papers, FDR Library; Federal Writers' Project, *California: A Guide to the Golden State* (New York: Hastings House, 1939), 209; *Los Angeles Times*, July 2, 1934, section 2, 3.

40. Hickok to Hopkins, Los Angeles, June 27, 1934, Hopkins Papers, FDR Library; Carey McWilliams, "The Farmers Get Tough," *The American Mercury*, October 1934, 241–43; Kevin Starr, *Endangered Dreams: The Great Depression in California* (New York: Oxford University Press, 1996), 63.

41. Federal Writers' Project, *California*, 640; McWilliams, "The Farmers Get Tough," 241–43; Starr, *Endangered Dreams,* 67.

42. McWilliams, "The Farmers Get Tough," 241–42; *The New Republic*, January 24, 1934, 293; Starr, *Endangered Dreams,* 81.

43. McWilliams, "The Farmers Get Tough," 243; *The New Republic*, March 21, 1934; Hickok to Eleanor Roosevelt, July 3, 1934, Hickok Papers, FDR Library.

44. Hickok to Eleanor Roosevelt, July 3, 1934, Hickok Papers, FDR Library; Hickok to Hopkins, Los Angeles, July 1, 1934, Hopkins Papers, FDR Library; Hickok to Eleanor Roosevelt, August 15, 1934, Hickok Papers, FDR Library.

45. Hickok to Hopkins, Los Angeles, July 1, 1934, Hopkins Papers, FDR Library.

46. *The Nation*, June 13, 1934, 672; *San Francisco Call-Bulletin*, July 2, 1934, 2, 15.

47. *Time*, July 16, 1934, 13; Starr, *Endangered Dreams*, 84–87, 102; *San Francisco Call-Bulletin*, July 2, 1934, 1.

48. Evelyn Seeley, "San Francisco's Labor War," *The Nation*, June 13, 1934, 672–73; Starr, *Endangered Dreams*, 94–95; *The San Francisco Chronicle*, July 1, 1934, 1.

49. Seeley, "San Francisco's Labor War," 672–73; Starr, *Endangered Dreams*, 86.

50. Starr, *Endangered Dreams*, 93; Irving Bernstein, *Turbulent Years: A History of the American Worker, 1933–1941* (Boston: Houghton Mifflin, 1970), 256, 270.

51. Bernstein, *Turbulent Years*, 253, 260; Richard L. Neuberger, "Bad Man Bridges," *Forum*, April 1939, 195; Starr, *Endangered Dreams*, 93.

52. Seeley, "San Francisco's Labor War," 673; Starr, *Endangered Dreams*, 93; Neuberger, "Bad Man Bridges," 198.

53. *San Francisco Call-Bulletin*, July 2, 1934, 1, July 3, 1934, 1, and July 4, 1934, 1; *Time*, July 16, 1934, 13; *The San Francisco Chronicle*, July 4, 1934, 1; Bernstein, *Turbulent Years*, 272.

54. *Time*, July 16, 1934, 14; Starr, *Endangered Dreams*, 106; *Los Angeles Times*, July 6, 1934, 1; *San Francisco Call-Bulletin*, July 6, 1934, 1.

55. *San Francisco Call-Bulletin*, July 6, 1934, 1; Starr, *Endangered Dreams*, 108; "War on the West Coast," *The New Republic*, August 1, 1934, 308.

56. *Los Angeles Times*, July 1, 1934, 1; "Journalistic Strikebreakers," *The New Republic*, August 1, 1934, 310–11; *The San Francisco Chronicle*, July 5, 1934, 1.

57. *Time*, July 16, 1934, 14; Starr, *Endangered Dreams*, 109.

58. *San Francisco Call-Bulletin*, July 12, 1934, 1; Eleanor Roosevelt to Hickok, June 18, 1934, Hickok Papers, FDR Library; Lorena A. Hickok, *Eleanor Roosevelt: Reluctant First Lady* (New York: Dodd, Mead, 1962), 158; *The San Francisco Chronicle*, July 13, 1934, 1.

59. *San Francisco Call-Bulletin*, July 12, 1934, 1; Hickok, *Eleanor Roosevelt*, 158–59.

60. Blanche Wiesen Cook, *Eleanor Roosevelt* (New York: Viking, 1992), vol. 2, 204–6; Hickok, *Eleanor Roosevelt*, 166–67.

61. Hickok, *Eleanor Roosevelt*, 169–70.

62. Ibid., 173; Cook, *Eleanor Roosevelt*, 209–10.

63. Davis, *FDR: The New Deal Years*, 377. See Hickok, *Eleanor Roosevelt*, 172–76.

64. Hickok, *Eleanor Roosevelt*, 143; *The San Francisco Chronicle*, August 5, 1934, 1.

65. Hickok to Hopkins, Bakersfield, Calif., August 15, 1934, Hopkins Papers, FDR Library; Starr, *Endangered Dreams*, 113, 117; *San Francisco Call-Bulletin*, July 17, 1934, 1, 2; *Time*, July 23, 1934, 11.

66. *Time*, July 23, 1934, 10–11.

67. *Time*, July 30, 1934, 13; *San Francisco Call-Bulletin*, July 16, 1934, 2; Starr, *Endangered Dreams*, 117–18, 121; Hickok to Eleanor Roosevelt, August 8, 1934, Hickok Papers, FDR Library; Hickok to Hopkins, Bakersfield, Calif., August 15, 1934, Hopkins Papers, FDR Library.

68. *Time*, July 30, 1934, 13; "War on the West Coast," 309; Hickok to Hopkins, Bakersfield, Calif., August 15, 1934, Hopkins Papers, FDR Library; *San Francisco Call-Bulletin*, July 17, 1934, 1.

69. "War on the West Coast," 309.

70. Hickok to Hopkins, Topeka and Kansas City, Mo., September 15, 1934, Hopkins Papers, FDR Library; Hickok to Eleanor Roosevelt, September 14, 1934, Hickok Papers, FDR Library.

71. Hickok to Hopkins, Kansas City, Mo., September 15, 1934, Hopkins Papers, FDR Library.

Epilogue

1. *The New York Times*, January 1, 1935, 1.

2. *The New York Times*, January 1, 1935, 26, 1; Kenneth S. Davis, *FDR: The New Deal Years* (New York: Random House, 1986), 428.

3. Eleanor Roosevelt to Lorena Hickok, May 13, 1935, Lorena Hickok Papers, Franklin Delano Roosevelt Presidential Library, Hyde Park, N.Y.; Hickok to Eleanor Roosevelt, August 3, 1935, Hickok Papers, FDR Library.

4. Hickok to Eleanor Roosevelt, November 2, 1934, Hickok Papers, FDR Library; Eleanor Roosevelt to Hickok, November 3, 1934, Hickok Papers, FDR Library.

5. Lorena Hickok to Harry Hopkins, January 1, 1935, Harry Hopkins Papers, Franklin Delano Roosevelt Presidential Library, Hyde Park, N.Y.; Davis, *FDR: The New Deal Years*, 465; *Recent Social Trends in the United States,* report of the President's Research Committee on Social Trends (New York: Whittlesey House/McGraw Hill, 1934), 807.

6. Hickok to Hopkins, January 1, 1935, Hopkins Papers, FDR Library.

7. Davis, *FDR: The New Deal Years*, 465; Hickok to Hopkins, January 1, 1935, Hopkins Papers, FDR Library; Eleanor Roosevelt to Hickok, May 4, 1936, in Rodger Streitmatter, ed., *Empty without You: The Intimate Let-*

ters of Eleanor Roosevelt and Lorena Hickok (New York: Free Press, 1998), 184.

8. Hickok to Eleanor Roosevelt, October 19, 1935, Hickok Papers, FDR Library.

9. Ibid.

10. Hickok to Eleanor Roosevelt, July 31, 1936, Hickok Papers, FDR Library; *Time*, July 13, 1936, 13–14; *Business Week*, July 11, 1936, 13, and August 8, 1936, 11.

11. Hickok to Eleanor Roosevelt, July 31, 1936, Hickok Papers, FDR Library.

12. Hickok to Grover Whalen, n.d. (November 1936), Hickok Papers, FDR Library; Hickok to Eleanor Roosevelt, January 19, 1939, in Streitmatter, *Empty without You*, 215.

13. Eleanor Roosevelt to Hickok, August 9, 1955, in Streitmatter, *Empty without You*, 284.

INDEX

Abbott, Leon, 99–100
Aberdeen, S.Dak., 24, 166–68
Aberdeen Evening News, 167
Addams, Jane, 190
Adkins Shirt Company, 46
African Americans, 203, 204–6, 209,
   211–12, 216, 220, 225–26, 234
Agricultural Adjustment Act, 35, 37
Agricultural Adjustment Administration, 51, 97, 131, 132, 151, 156,
   165, 176, 204, 234
   crop reduction program of, 37, 150,
      153, 156, 177, 215, 216, 218, 227
   hog reduction program of, 35, 150,
      152, 156, 176–77
agricultural surplus, 145–46
Agricultural Workers Industrial
   Union, 247
agriculture, 12, 36–37, 51, 148–73,
   234–35
   pay in, 202–3
   prices in, 116, 145, 146, 148,
      150–52, 155n, 156, 165–66, 193,
      204, 210, 220–21, 223, 239
   size of farms and, 234
Agriculture Department, U.S., 85,
   151
aircraft, xv, 75, 81, 213
Alabama, 234–35, 240

Allen, Daniel, 59
Amalgamated Clothing Workers of
   America, 38
American Civil Liberties Union, 247
American Farm Bureau Federation,
   20
American Federation of Labor, 143,
   146, 183, 232
American Friends Service Commit-
   tee, 5–6, 42, 55, 67, 78–79
American Guide series, xiv
American Jitters (Wilson), 50, 135n
American Legion, 183, 247
American Mercury, 47–48, 53, 101, 159,
   164, 224, 246
Anderson, Sherwood, 83
Andersonville Prison, 208n
anthracite, 52, 55
Arizona, 241–42
Army, U.S., 238
arthritis, 76
Arthurdale, W.Va., 90, 97, 188
Artley, Will, 209, 211
assembly, freedom of, 247
Associated Press, xiii, 1, 2, 9, 11, 16,
   17n, 26, 29–30, 31–32, 38, 41, 79,
   104–5, 119, 215, 262
asthma, 76
Astor, Vincent, 21

Atlanta, Ga., 200–202, 217–20
Atlanta Constitution, 200, 212
Atlanta Journal, 200–201, 214
Atlantic Monthly, xiv, 231
Augusta, Ga., 206–8
Augusta Chronicle, 208
Augusta National Golf Course, 207
"Aunt Cora," 87
Axel's Castle (Wilson), 103

Bakers, 44
Bangor & Aroostook Railroad, 115
Bangor Daily News, 110
banks, banking crisis, 8, 14, 21,
    27–28, 35, 99, 148, 239
Battle Creek Journal, 25
beans, 62
Beasley, Maurine, 50
Beccaras, 44
Beech-Nut foods, 97
beef, prices of, 62, 97, 239
beets, 243–45
Behner, Mary, 67–69, 90
Bell County, Ky., 81–88
Beltrami County, Minn., 194–95
Bemidji, Minn., 194–95
Benét, Stephen Vincent, 202
Berkshire Knitting Mills, 42–43
Berle, A. A., 15
Berry, Tom, 152, 153, 154, 167, 169
Bethlehem Steel, 49
Bicknell, Lewis, 166
Biltmore Hotel, 15, 19
Bismarck, N.Dak., 20, 152, 154,
    156–57, 163
Bismarck Tribune, 150, 151, 154–55
Bittner, Mary, 102
Black Mountain Coal Company, 88
Blair, John Henry, 88
Bliven, Bruce, 176, 222
Blizzard, William, 76
Blue Eagle, 40, 43, 61, 82, 183, 212
Bluette (Hickok's car), 91–92, 109,
    201, 227, 229, 241–42, 254n

Boettinger, John, 16, 17, 26
Bogan, William J., 36
boll weevils, 204
Boone, Caroline, 82
Boonville, N.Y., 103–6
Borden, 102
Bowdle, S.Dak., 165–66
Bowdle Pioneer, 165
Boylan, John, 53
Boyle, Elwood P., 99
Bradley, Charles C., 36–37
Bradley, J. T., 85
Brain Trust, 9, 144
Branion, Ray, 246
Bridges, Harry, 250–51, 256
Brock, W. H., 88
Brooklyn-Manhattan Transit Company, 125
Brooks, J. M., 83, 85
Broun, Heywood, 122, 142–43
Brown, Charles S., 117
Bryan, Charles W., 150, 177
Bryan, William Jennings, 150, 177
Bryan, Wright, 214
Bureau of Industrial Relations, 47
Business Week, xiv, 221
"Buy Now" drive, 144
Byars, J. C., 83, 85–86
Byrd, Harry, 9

California, 4, 14–15, 229–30, 245–46,
    248
Calvert, Cleon, 83, 84
capitalism, failures of, 10, 15, 137,
    138, 140
Cash, W. J., 224–25
Castle Hotel, 174
Catholic Charities, 123
cattle, 16, 85, 102, 152, 155, 158, 167,
    169, 179, 180, 214, 220, 239, 243,
    258
Cedar Rapids Gazette, 152
Central Park, Hooverville in, 119
Cermak, Anton, 26

Chafin, Don, 75
Chamber of Commerce, 60, 99
Chapin, W. W., 17
Chapman, Francis J., 210
charities, 5, 66–67
Charles City Press, 186
Charleston, W.Va., 72–75, 79
Charleston Daily Mail, 72
Chicago, Ill., 4, 9–11, 17, 26, 36, 87,
    149, 158, 167, 184, 198, 264
Chicago Board of Trade, 21
Chicago Tribune, 16, 184
chickens, 85, 90, 155, 169
child labor, 35, 243–45
Christian Century, 128
Christianson, Adolph, 155, 162, 164
churches, 193–94
cigarette tax, 79
City Work Bureau, 124
Civilian Conservation Corps, 190
Civil War, U.S., 200, 202n, 206, 208,
    210, 225
Civil Works Administration (CWA),
    168, 177, 178, 194, 197, 201–2,
    214, 224
  African Americans and, 205, 211, 226
  Augusta levees repaired by, 206
  Bemidji relief of, 194–95
  farm pay of, 203
  graft investigation of, 215
  Iowa relief of, 180–83, 187
  New York relief of, 198–99
  pay rates of, 181, 216, 219, 223, 226
  popularity of, 180–81, 215–16, 219
  rats exterminated by, 216
  winding down of, 223, 230–32
Claff, Julian, 120–21
Claff, Ruby, 23, 120–21
Clague, Evan, 44
clothing, 41, 49, 79, 94, 114, 128, 131,
    156, 157, 158, 159, 160, 162, 164,
    175, 181, 194, 217, 222
coal, coal mining, 6, 51–55, 60–61,
    65–73, 74, 78–79, 81–82, 88–90,
    110, 136, 201, 240

coal code, 88–89, 108
coffee, 62, 87, 97, 121, 251
Colley, J. W., 78, 79
Colorado, 14, 242–45
Colquitt County, Ga., 215–18
Commerce Department, U.S., 36
Commodity Credit Corporation, *see*
    corn loan program
Commonwealth Club, 14–15
Communists, 36, 48–49, 82–84, 110,
    138, 166, 194, 248, 252, 256, 257
Community Council, 44
constitutional rights, 247
convict labor, 219–20
Cook, Blanche Wiesen, 22
Coolidge, Calvin, 119
Coon, Frank T., 36
Cooper, Kent, 31
copper industry, 239
corn, 13, 20, 35, 176, 177, 204
Corning, N.Y., 91–94
Corning Glass Works, 91
corn loan program, 146, 147, 150,
    152, 168, 176, 182, 184–85, 187
cornmeal, 87
Corn Palace, 179n
cotton, 20, 35, 154, 203–4, 210, 215,
    225–26, 239, 259
  price of, 204, 223
cotton gin, 204
cotton pickers, xv, 218
Country of the Pointed Firs, The (Jew-
    ett), 110
Cowley, Malcolm, xiv, 5, 28, 133,
    135, 136, 137–39, 146
  on Pineville mission, 83
cows, 101, 102, 106, 155, 158, 169,
    192
Coxey, Jacob, 2–3
Craig, Minnie D., 162–63
Cramp, Wallace, 20
cream, creameries, 157, 160, 166,
    167, 191
Creech, R. W., 86
Creech Coal Company, 86

Croly, Herbert, 135–36
crop reduction program, 37, 146, 150, 153, 156, 177, 215, 216, 218, 227
currency reflation, 152
Cutler, Addison, 218
Cuvillier, Louis A., 105

Dairymen's League, 102–3
Dall, Anna Roosevelt, 12, 16, 26, 64, 198
Dallas, Tex., 264
Dana, Paul, 2
D&D Shirt Company, 37–38, 46–47
Davis, Kenneth, 14
Davis, T. B., 78
deficit spending, 145
deflation, 6, 28
Democratic National Committee, 19, 267
Democratic National Convention, 1932, 9–11
dental care, 121
Denver, Colo., 14, 242–45
Denver & Rio Grande Railroad, 244
Des Moines Register and Leader, 176
Detroit, Mich., 264
diabetes, 96, 267
Dickens, Charles, 98
Dickinson, Roy, 25
Dillon, Clarissa, 187–88
Dillon, Thomas, 149, 187–88
diphtheria, 76
Dittoe, Beulah, 85
dollar devaluation, 209–10
Dominion News, 69, 71, 88
Dos Passos, John, 83, 135, 136, 138–39
Douglass, Frederick, 96
Dreiser, Theodore, 83, 139
Drexel & Co., 43
drought, 258–59, 265
Drowne, Ralph, 98, 100
Dust Bowl, 155, 246

dust storms, 147, 171–73
dysentery, 76

Eastman, George, 96
Eastport Sentinel, 111, 112
education, xv, 67, 130, 170, 196, 263, 264
eggs, 97, 167
Eichengreen, Barry, 28
Einstein, Albert, 218
Eleanor Roosevelt: Reluctant First Lady (Hickok), 267
electric bills, 128
electric power, 12, 45, 107, 113–14, 137, 257
Elmira, N.Y., 264
Embarcadero, 252–53
Emergency Committee on Unemployment, 5
Emergency Unemployment Relief Committee, 124
Emerson, Ralph Waldo, 113–14
Emery, Roscoe, 113
Engels, Friedrich, 136
Erie Canal, 96, 98
Etheridge, Ruth, 85
Evans, Herndon, 84
Evening Huronite (Huron, S.Dak.), 172
Exile's Return (Cowley), 136

Factors Row, 209, 210
Farley, James, 11
Farmer-Labor Party, 151
Farmers' Holiday Association (FHA), 37, 150, 151, 152, 166, 167, 176, 178, 179
Farmers' Loan Association, 157
Farmers Union, 175–76
farm prices, 6, 51
farm strike, 151–53, 176–82, 184
fascism, 143, 237
Fay, Elton, 11–12

Federal Council of Churches, 193
Federal Emergency Relief Admin-
    istration (FERA), xiii–xiv, 17*n*,
    32–34, 36, 41, 42, 56, 62, 69, 82,
    140–41, 155, 189, 190, 266
    assistance cut off by, 87–88
    CWA workers absorbed by, 232
    draft of, 35
    Hickok's acceptance of job with,
        38–39
    money granted by, 266
    New York relief of, 107, 108
    state relief programs mandated by,
        141
    see also Hickok, Lorena
federal loan programs, 163–64,
    184–85
Federal Power Commission, 113
Federal Reserve, 51
Federal Surplus Commodities Cor-
    poration, 131
Federal Writers' Project, xiv
Feinstein, Isidor, 48, 58
Ferber, Edna, 184
Fergus Falls, Minn., 191–92
Fernsler, David, 41–42
Field, Travis, 209
Fireside Chats, 35
First Congregational Church, 179
Fish, Hamilton S., Jr., 104
Five-Year Plan, 137
Fleming, Peter, 107
Florida, 220–23
Florida land bubble, 221
flour, 62, 79, 87, 95–96, 97, 216
Floyd County, Iowa, 187
Ford, Henry, 104, 135*n*
Forum, 137
Foster, William Z., 139
Fox, Charles, 46, 49
Fox Sisters, 96
Frank, Waldo, on Pineville mission,
    83, 84–85
freedom of speech, 247
Freeman, Douglas Southall, 202

Freeman, Richard, 154, 184, 191,
    192–93, 195
Frick combine, 57, 58–60, 89
fruit tramps, 247
Full Fashioned Hosiery Workers of
    America, 42

Gable, Clark, 108
Gamble, Thomas, 210, 211–12
Gandhi, Mohandas, 40
Garner, John Nance, 9, 11
gas bills, 128
Geer, B. E., 223
Georgia, 200–220, 234
Germany, 40*n*, 108, 218–19, 257, 262
Gibbons, Mary, 123
Gibson, Harvey D., 124*n*
glass, 91
Glassford, Pelham D., 248
Glen Alden Coal Company, 54
goats, in San Antonio economy, 238
Godwin, Kathryn, 50, 109, 120, 123,
    158–59, 173, 184, 228, 235, 242
Goldberg, Jacob, 34
gold standard, 6, 15, 28
Googe, George L., 208
Gorman, Eugene J., 46
Grady, Henry, 200
grains, 167, 239, 242
Grand Canyon, 244
Grand Coulee Dam, 146, 256
Grange, Red, 25
grasshoppers, 163, 171
Gray, Judd, 176
Great Crash, 6–8, 32, 119, 210, 215,
    264
Great Western Sugar Company,
    243–44
Guss, Hale A., 46–47

Hager, Lee, 237
Hagerty, James, 15, 17
Hall, Lee, 77

Hansel, John, 19
Hansmeier, Ralph, 166
Hanson, Helen, 114
Harlan County, Ky., 81–88
Harlan Miners Speak, 83, 139
Harlow, Jean, 108
Harpers, xiv
Harper's Monthly Magazine, 218
Harrisburg Telegraph, 42
Hart-Parr, 186n
Hatfields, 74, 79
Hayes, Patrick, 132
Hayes, W. D., 181, 187
H. C. Frick Coke Company, 56
Hearst, William Randolph, 1, 2, 26,
    99, 252, 253
Herbaugh, Frank, 158
Herbst, Josephine, 13
Herring, Clyde, 37, 151, 152–53, 184
Hibbard, Benjamin H., 101, 102
Hibbing, Minn., 195–96
Hickok, Addison, 23, 24
Hickok, Anna, 23, 24
Hickok, Lorena, xiii–xv, 11
    at Associated Press, xiii, 1, 2, 9, 26,
        29–30, 31–32
    car accident of, 241–42
    childhood of, 22–25
    Colorado trip of, 242–45
    Communists as viewed by, 180
    death of, 267–68
    drinking by, 2, 185, 226
    early journalism of, 25–26
    on FDR's western tour, 12, 16,
        17–18, 19
    FERA job accepted by, 38–39
    Florida trip of, 220–23
    follow-up for reports of, 267
    Georgia trip of, 200–220
    in Iowa, 147, 176–82
    Kentucky trip of, 86–88
    as Keynesian, 263–64
    Los Angeles trip of, 245–46,
        248–49
    Maine trip of, 110–18

Middle Border trip of, 148–73, 174
    in Minnesota, 191–98
    moods of, 109, 158–59, 160,
        184–87, 220, 232–33, 248
    New Mexico trip of, 239–41
    New Orleans trip of, 235–36
    New York trip of, 91–109, 119–40
    North Carolina trip of, 226–28
    Pennsylvania trip of, 40–64
    press coverage disdained by, 189
    racial views of, 211–12
    San Francisco trip of, 229–30,
        249–53, 256–57
    smoking by, 2, 254
    "State of Florida"survey of, 220–21
    Texas trip of, 236–39
    Time's criticism of, 228
    weight gain by, 197
    in West Virginia, 69–81
    World's Fair planned by, 267
Hickok, Lorena, Eleanor Roosevelt's
    friendship with, xiv, 21–22,
        30–31, 32, 39, 45, 49, 50–51,
        54–55, 57, 61, 62–64, 69, 70,
        71–72, 73, 75, 89, 92–93, 95, 96,
        102, 111, 116, 154–55, 158, 159,
        162, 163, 164, 170, 175, 183, 186,
        193, 197, 201, 267
    argument and reconciliation in,
        198, 202
    beginning of, 16, 17–18, 23
    ER's busy schedule and, 141–42
    ER's fancy clothing and, 263
    on Georgia trip, 212–13
    Hickok's article on ER in, 17–18, 19
    Hickok's bad moods and, 109, 160,
        185, 220, 232
    Hickok's car accident and, 241–42
    Hickok's commitment to, 187–89
    Hickok's interviews of ER in, 1,
        29–30
    Hickok's job offer and, 228
    Hickok's loyalty in, 26–27
    passion in, 22, 147, 197
    peak of, 255–56

racism and, 211–12
on western vacation, 253–56
Hickok, Myrtle, 23
Hickok, Ruby, 23
highway system, 229–30
Hill, B. S., 224
Hitler, Adolf, 28, 218–19, 262
Hodson, William, 35
hogs, 13, 20, 35, 150, 152, 155, 156, 158, 167, 176, 177
Hold Your Man (film), 108
Holiday movement, 179
homelessness, 5, 120, 125, 130, 206
Home Loan Corporation, 99
Home Relief Bureau, 123, 127
Hook, Sidney, 3
Hoover, Herbert, 5, 6, 8, 27–28, 29
Hoover, Herbert, Jr., 210
Hoovervilles, 119, 136, 196
Hopkins, Harry, xiii, xiv, 32, 38, 40, 41, 45, 49–50, 51, 62–63, 79, 80, 87, 106, 109, 127, 131–32, 140, 141, 146, 148, 155, 156, 159, 165, 166, 167, 169, 173, 177–78, 182, 189, 198, 200, 203, 205, 208, 214, 219, 220, 221, 223, 228, 229, 230, 232n, 237, 242, 257, 262
  background of, 32–33
  conservative attacks on, 246
  draft federal relief program submitted by, 35
  federal civil works program of, 153–54
  Ickes's disputes with, 254–55
  Keynesian plan of, 146–47
  put in charge of FERA, 32–34, 36
  on relief for women, 190
  as TERA director, 93
  weather change feared by, 265–66
  work relief institutionalized by, 266
Houlton, Maine, xiv, xvi, 114–18
Houlton (Maine) Pioneer-Times, 116–17
housing, 78, 112, 130–31, 188, 203, 224

Houston, USS, 253
Howe, Louis, 10, 17, 29, 64, 149
Hundred Days, xiii, 51
Hutchinson Coal Company, 76

Ickes, Harold, 108, 146, 147, 182, 183, 232, 241, 254–55
income, xv, 97, 101, 120, 144, 145, 243, 261
Independent Miners' Relief Committee, 83
Indiana, 262
Industrial Association of San Francisco, 249
industrial production, 4
inflation, 142, 145
Information Service, 123
infrastructure, xv
International Longshoremen's Association, 250–53, 257
Iowa, 6, 21, 147, 150, 176–78
Iowan, 249
iron, 54–55
Island Creek Coal Company, 78

Japan, 215
Jefferson, Thomas, 14
Jewett, Sarah Orne, 110
John Brown's Body (Benét), 202
John Reed Club, 133
Johnson, Gerald P., 7–8
Johnson, Hugh, 59, 88, 89, 99, 107, 143–44, 167, 183
Johnson, John A., 19–20
Johnson, Leila, 224, 225
Johnston, Marlise, 133, 134
Joint Maritime Strike Committee, 250
Jones, D. C. "Baby Face," 88
Josephson, Matthew, xiv, 5, 21, 33, 135, 136
  on New York relief, 123–24, 125–26
J. P. Morgan, 135

Kansas, 6, 16, 243, 258–59
Kansas Free State Fair, 258–59
Keeney, H. G., 175, 177
Kentucky, xiv, 6, 72, 81–88, 90, 92, 94, 104, 139, 140, 217, 248
Kentucky Relief Board, 82
Keynes, John Maynard, 145, 231
King, Wilbur, 117
Kings County Medical Society, 199
Klausler, Alfred, 159, 164
Knox County, Ky., 87
Kreisler, Fritz, 218
Kump, H. G., 69, 72

Labor Council, 256
Labor Department, U.S., 208
Lainson, Percy, 13–14
Langer, William, 150, 152–53
lard, 62, 87, 216
Lavelle, Michael J., 4
Law and Order League, 180
Lawrence, James E., 177, 178
Lee, Robert E., 210
LeHand, Missy, 64
Lehman, Herbert, 8, 18, 40, 94, 100, 103, 105, 262
Lenin, V. I., 136
Lewis, John L., 52–53, 57, 74
Lilly, Joseph, 122, 123, 128
Lincoln Tunnel, 146
Lippmann, Walter, 10, 28
Literary Digest, 90, 189
livestock reduction program, 35, 150, 152, 153, 156, 176–77
Logan (W.Va.) Banner, 77
Logan County, W.Va., 75–79, 81, 89
Logan County Coal Operators Association, 78
Lone Star Gas Company, 239
Long, W. W., 223
longshoremen strike, 246, 249–53, 256–57
Los Angeles, Calif., 245–46, 248–49
Los Angeles Times, 245, 252

Lowitt, Richard, 50
Lynch, Clay, 60

McCandless, Kenneth, 175–76
McConnell, Lincoln, 216–17
McCoys, 74, 79
McDonough, Clare, 60–61, 62
McGrady, Edward F., 59
Machado, Gerardo, 222
McIntire, Ross, 197
McIntyre, Marvin, 12
MacIntyres, 44
McMasters, Althea, 253
McWilliams, Carey, 246
Maine, xvi, 51, 91, 109, 110–18
Maine Emergency Relief Board, 117
Maloney, Tom, 53–54
Mann Act, 47
Marine Workers' Industrial Union, 257
maritime industry, 239
Martin, Herbert S., 19–20
Marx, Karl, 136
means tests, 56
mechanization, 227, 263–64
Mencken, H. L., 47–48
Mercer, Lucy, 17, 22
Methodist Church, 66, 68
Mexicans, 244–45
Miami, Fla., 26, 118, 201, 221–23
Michigan, 21, 24–25, 262–63
Middle Border, 6, 147, 148–73, 174
migrant laborers, 247
milk, 35, 101–6, 136
Millay, Edna St. Vincent, 110
Miller, Malcolm J., 202, 203, 225, 226
mill villages, 224–25
Milwaukee Sentinel, 25
Mind of the South, The (Cash), 224
mines, xv, 6, 52–54, 57–59, 66, 72, 73, 76–78, 81, 82, 88, 89, 110
    in Minnesota, 196–97
minimum wage, 38, 89

Minneapolis Tribune, 149, 164
Minnesota, 6, 147, 191–98
Mississippi River, 12, 185, 241
Missouri, 243, 262
Missouri River, 168, 169, 170, 174, 179, 229, 266
Mitchell, Charles E., 32
Mobridge, S.Dak., 168
Modern Quarterly, 140
Moley, Raymond, 12, 15
money supply, 4, 145
Morgantown Post, 70, 89
Morgenthau, Henry, 149, 178
Mormon Tabernacle, 14
Morris Freezer shirt factory, 38
mortgages, 21, 44–45, 99, 116, 152, 156
    farm, 37
Moses, Tom, 58, 89
Mosley, Woodrow, 78, 81
Moultrie, Ga., xvi, 215–18
Moultrie (Ga.) *Observer,* 215
movies, 42, 64, 68, 185, 243, 245
mules, 203, 208, 212, 235
Mullock, F. W., 181
Mussolini, Benito, 237

Nation, xiv, 12, 20, 28–29, 46, 59, 83, 85, 128–29, 231, 244, 251
National City Bank, 32
National Conference of Catholic Charities, 132
National Cornhusking Championship, 176
National Dairy Products, 102
National Farmers Union, 20, 35, 174
National Farmers Union Convention, 174, 175–78, 190
National Guard, Calif., 53, 252, 256
National Guard, N.Dak., 150
National Guard, S.C., 208
National Guard, W.Va., 79
National Industrial Recovery Act, 35, 43, 57, 73, 146
National Labor Board, 142, 247–48

National Labor Relations Board, 207
National Miners Union, 82, 86
National Recovery Administration (NRA), 40, 59, 63, 72–73, 74, 76, 88, 89, 96–97, 100, 107, 110, 115, 121, 133, 142, 143–44, 150, 151, 152, 208
    minimum wage of, 205
    unpopularity of, 183–84
    wage increases of, 201
    working hours restricted by, 201
National Women's Press Association, 31
natural gas, 52
Nazism, 108, 218–19
Nebraska, 6, 13, 16, 147, 148, 150, 173, 174–778, 182, 243, 244
Neediest Cases Fund, 5
Newburg Cash Store, 161
Newburg Mercantile, 161
New Deal:
    Communist attack on, 143
    corporate greed as threat to, 143–44
    Hickok as witness to results of, 39, 48–49, 54, 68, 88, 147
    outlined in FDR's speeches, 28
    radicals' view of, 133, 139
    rural insurrection feared in, 148
    skepticism about, 48
    "theorists" of, 150
    see also specific individuals and programs
New Mexico, 239–41
New Orleans, La., 235–36
New Republic, xiv, 29, 33, 36, 41, 58–59, 83, 89, 102, 104, 123, 135, 136, 139, 143–44, 176, 231–32, 252–53, 257–58
Newspaper Guild of New York, 143
New York, N.Y., 21–22, 25–26, 30, 32, 40, 47, 64, 83, 92, 96, 103, 106, 110, 119–40
    relief programs in, 93, 120, 121–26, 198–99
    unemployment in, 3–4

New York Central Railroad, 98
New York *Daily Mirror,* 1, 26
New York Evening Telegram, 121
New York Life Insurance, 20
New York State, 33, 91–109
New York Stock Exchange, 21
New York Times, 2, 4, 15, 17, 40, 88, 117*n*, 144, 145, 190, 231, 261–62
New York Tribune, 25
New York World-Telegram, 120, 121–23, 128, 142–43, 199
Nonpartisan League, 164*n*
Norfolk & Western Railroad, 79
Northampton County Unemployed League, 49
North Carolina, 213, 223, 226–28
North Dakota, xiv, xvi, 6, 20, 147, 148, 150, 153, 155, 217
North Dakota Corn Show, 152
Northland (Minn.) *Times,* 194, 195
North Star, 96
Nourmahal (yacht), 21
nurses, 94

O'Brien, John, 132
Odum, Howard W., 204, 223, 237–38
Ogdensburg, N.Y., 102–7
Ogdensburg (N.Y.) *Journal,* 107
Oglethorpe University, 10
O'Grady, Edward, 249
Ohio, 262
oil, 52, 237–38, 239
Oklahoma, 238
Olson, Floyd, 151, 152–53, 191–92
Omaha, Nebr., 190
Omaha World-Herald, 175
O'Neal, Edward A., III, 20
Open Shop, W.Va., 72–76
Oriskany, N.Y., 105
Otter Tail County, Minn., 191–92
overproduction, 6, 176
Owens, Terry, 242
oxen, 235

Parnall, Christopher, 94–95
Passamaquoddy Bay, 111–14
Passamaquoddy Tidal Power Development Project, 113
Payne, Helen, 186
Pecora, Ferdinand, 32
Peek, George, 178
pellagra, 217, 218
Pennsylvania, 6, 40–64, 110, 137, 140, 141, 142, 170, 205, 264
Pennsylvania Emergency Relief Board, 60
Pennsylvania Railroad, 55, 221
Perkins, Frances, 35, 63–64, 256
Peterkin, Julia, 225
Peterson, Florence, 231
Philadelphia Community Council, 44
Philadelphia Daily Record, 42
Philadelphia Quakers, 66–67
Pickett, Clarence, 55, 60, 64, 66, 69, 78–79
pig slaughter, 131
Pinchot, Cornelia Bryce, 38, 47, 48
Pinchot, Gifford, 38, 46, 47–48, 55–56, 58
Pinchot Roads, 55, 60
Pineville, Ky., 83–88
Pineville (Ky.) *Sun,* 84
Pioneer (FDR's railroad car), 12
Piscek, Stanley, 106
Plattsburgh, N.Y., 108
Plattsburgh (N.Y.) *Daily Press,* 108, 109–10
Plattsburgh (N.Y.) *Daily Republican,* 108
poor boards, 33
pork, 131, 132, 165, 216
Porter, John, 15–16
potatoes, 44, 62, 70, 115–16, 117
poultry, 167, 170
Powell, John Wesley, 155, 266*n*
Powell, Webster, 218
Presbyterian Church, 66, 68
prices, 62, 121, 125, 201, 212

agricultural, 116, 145, 146, 148,
150–52, 155*n*, 156, 165–66, 193,
204, 210, 220–21, 223, 239
commodity, 145
consumer, 125, 144, 183, 221, 259
factory, 145
fixing of, 143, 150, 176
minimum, 150
stock, 136
productivity, xv, 263–64
industrial, 4
Program for Relief, 49
Progressivism, 135
Prohibition, 10, 35, 97, 168
Prudential Insurance Company, 21
Public Works Administration (PWA),
108, 114, 146, 151, 182, 183, 205,
231, 232, 241
African Americans and, 205
graft investigation of, 215
"trickle down method" of, 254–55
Public Works Board, 178
Pulitzer, Joseph, 121, 122
Pullins, Harry, 68
Pullman Company, 264
Pursglove family, 89
Pursglove Mining Company, 67
Pyrex, 91

Quakers, 79, 90

racism, 211
railroads, 6, 11, 12, 14, 55, 98, 148,
150, 230
Raleigh News & Observer, 231
Ramsaye, John G., 49
Raushenbush, Stephen, 47
Reconstruction Finance Corporation,
8, 76
Red Cross, 45, 55, 78, 79, 114, 161,
203
Reichstag fire, 108
relief agents, 80

Reno, Milo, 150, 152, 175–76
Reporter and Farmer, 167
Review of Reviews, 134
rice, 35, 62
Richberg, Donald, 40
Ricker, A. W., 178
Riley, Argonne, 251
Rinaldo, Charles, 100
Robideau, Frank, 101
Rochester, N.Y., 96–97
Rochester (N.Y.) *Times-Union,* 96, 97
Rockland, Maine, 110–12
Rockne, Knute, 25
Roosevelt, Eleanor, 8, 11, 40–41, 69, 114
allegations of corruption against,
187–88
Arthurdale project of, 90, 97, 188
asceticism of, 235
busy schedule of, 30–31, 141–42, 198
"Buy Now" campaign promoted
by, 144
celebrities entertained by, 218
childhood of, 22
conference on women held by,
177, 190
conservative attacks on, 246
Georgia visited by, 212–13
Hickok's friendship with *see*
Hickok, Lorena, Eleanor Roosevelt's friendship with
Hoover as viewed by, 27
pig killing protested by, 131*n*
press coverage of, 16, 17–18, 189,
253–54
racial views of, 212, 213
Scotts Run visited by, 70–71, 89–90
wedding of, 16
on western tour, 16–18, 19
Roosevelt, Elliott, 22, 238
Roosevelt, Franklin Delano, xiii
agrarian revolution feared by, 148
assassination attempt on, 26
on church and state, 193–94
coal code signed by, 88, 108
CWA disassembled by, 231

Roosevelt, Franklin Delano *(cont.)*
  CWA program announced by, 168
  and Democratic National Convention, 9–11
  elected New York governor, 1
  in election of 1936, 266
  expectations for, 28–29
  faith of people in, 61, 68, 195, 211, 227
  Grand Coulee Dam speech of, 256
  Hawaii trip of, 253
  Hickok's letters and reports read by, 51
  Hoover's desire to work with, 27–28, 29
  inauguration of, 29–30
  Keynesian public works program approved by, 146–47
  last day as New York governor, 8
  in meeting with Middle Border governors, 153
  movies enjoyed by, 64
  New York relief program of, 93
  polio of, 213*n*
  radicals' view of, 139
  Topeka speech of, 258
  on tour of western states, 11–19
  vacations of, 112
Roosevelt, James, 12, 16
Roosevelt, Ruth, 238
Roosevelt, Theodore, 23, 38, 47, 133
Ross, Ishbel, 2
Rossi, Angelo, 256
Royal Gorge, 244
Rudich, Mark, 125
Rugan, George, 117
Russian Revolution, 7, 25
Russian thistle, 147, 155, 165, 265
Ryan, Martin, 59

Sacco, Nicola, 137
Salvation Army, 79, 123, 134
San Francisco, Calif., 14–15, 209, 223, 229–30, 248, 249–53, 255–57

San Francisco Call-Bulletin, 253
San Francisco Chronicle, 251, 253, 256
San Francisco Examiner, 252
San Pedro, Calif., 249
Santa Fe Railroad, 240
Savannah, Ga., 209–12
Savannah Evening Press, 209–10
Scarlet Sister Mary (Peterkin), 225
Schick, David, 42, 43
Schmedeman, Albert, 152–53, 154
Schuyler, Montgomery, 7
Scott, Dennis K., 66
Scotts Run, 65–72, 88, 89–90
Scotts Run Settlement House, 67
Scranton, Pa., 50, 52–55, 62
Scranton Coal Company, 52
Scranton Times, 53
Scribner's Magazine, 13
Scripps-Howard, 121–22
Secret Service, 30
Seeley, Evelyn, 251, 252–53
Senate, U.S.:
  Agriculture Committee of, 20, 35
  Banking and Currency Committee of, 32
Shays's Rebellion, 36
sheep, 155, 239, 240, 244
Shelley (mines manager), 56
Shepperson, Gay, 203, 214, 215
Sherman, William Tecumseh, 200, 206, 208, 210*n*, 225
Sherwood, Robert, 34
shoes, 45, 79, 161, 215, 217
Short, Wallace, 179
silver, 175, 180, 239
Simkhovitch, Mary, 133–35
Simpson, John A., 20, 35, 175
Sioux City, Iowa, 13–14, 151–52, 176–82
Sioux City Journal, 179
Sioux City Tribune, 179, 180
Sioux Indians, 170
Siplon, Joe, 186
Smith, Al, 9, 11
Smith, Frederick, 206

Smith, George Otis, 113–14
Smith, H. E., 77
Smith, Walter B., 84
Snow White (film), 245
soldier preference law, 183
Soule, George, 144–45
South Carolina, 142, 202, 204, 207,
 208, 210, 222, 223–26, 234
South Dakota, 6, 147, 148, 155,
 169–71, 243, 265
Soviet Union, 7, 137, 209–10
sows, 169
speech, freedom of, 247
Stalin, Joseph, 137–38
Stalp, Ben, 176
Star, 177–78
State Relief Board, 78
steam shovels, xv
steel, 62, 69, 89, 137, 142, 230, 263
stocks, 6–7, 51, 136
Stockyards National Bank, 158
Straight, Willard, 135
strandees, xv, 93–94, 133–35
strikes, 61, 136
 in Iowa, 151–53, 176–82, 184
 Johnson's denunciation of, 143
 longshoremen, 246, 249–53,
  256–57
 steelworker, 142
 textile, 207–8
strip mining, 81
Strom, O. T., 161
Strout, E. A., 7
sugar, 243–44
Sullivan, Jesse, 77
Sumnick, Gus, 17
Survey, 44
Sutherland, Mabel, 76
Symes, Lillian, 149–50
Syracuse, N.Y., 97–99
Syracuse Journal, 99, 100

Talmadge, Eugene, 203, 207
Tammany Hall, 120, 121, 122, 123

tariffs, 6
Taub, Allan, 85
taxes, 6, 12, 19, 32, 69, 102, 110, 116,
 117, 145, 150, 151
 cigarette, 79
 in New York, 93
 poll, 42
tax warrants, 36
Taylor, F. B., 13
Taylor, Frank, 123, 127
technology, xv, 213
television, xv
Temin, Peter, 28
Temporary Emergency Relief Administration (TERA), 93, 98,
 102, 107, 128
Tennessee, 72
Tennessee Pass, 242, 244
Tennessee River Valley, 113
Texas, 236–39
textiles, 6, 136, 142, 215, 216, 226
textile strike, 207–8
Thomas, Norman, 231
Time, xiv, 12, 13, 16, 19, 33, 36, 38,
 43, 53, 58, 151, 176, 189–90, 203,
 226, 228, 249, 257
Times Square, 4, 5, 261
Tippett, Tom, 53
tobacco, 35, 79, 226
Topeka, Kans., 12–13, 258–59
To the Finland Station (Wilson), 136
Townley, A. C., 164*n*
truck drivers, 180
trucks, xv, 230
tuberculosis, 76, 113, 218
Tug Fork River, 79
Tugwell, Rexford, 146, 150, 246
Turner, Francis, 79–80, 81

Unemployed Councils, 133
Unemployed League, 56
unemployment, xv, 4, 36, 51, 125,
 263–64
 in New York, 3–4

unions, 35, 86, 89, 96, 100, 179, 183, 247
  textile, 207–8
  see also specific unions
Union Square, 132–33, 175
United Mine Workers of America,
  52–54, 57–59, 66, 72, 73, 77–78,
  81, 82, 88, 89
United States, post-World War II
  boom in, xv
United States Beet Sugar Association,
  244
USA (Dos Passos), 136
U.S. Steel Corporation, 4, 58, 196

Vanderbilt, Commodore, 98
Vanzetti, Bartolomeo, 137
Veblen, Thorstein, 7
Vestris, 2
Villard, Oswald Garrison, 20–21
Virginia, 72, 84–85, 86, 185, 188, 202,
  229
Vorse, Mary Heaton, 148

wages, 35, 38, 46, 212
  of miners, 73
Wagner, Robert F., 142
Wallace, Henry A., 101, 150, 153,
  167, 177, 235, 246
Wall Coal Company, 212
Walsh, Thomas J., 31
Warm Springs, Ga., 21, 28, 188,
  212–13, 217
Warner, John A., 103
Warner Club, 26
Warren, George F., 145

Washington Post, 33
Weather Bureau, 171–72
West Virginia, xvi, 5, 6, 64, 65–81,
  89–90, 92, 110, 136n, 140, 217,
  248, 263, 265
Whalen, Grover, 267
wheat, 6, 20, 35, 51, 150, 155n, 156,
  157, 176, 243, 259
Whitney, Eli, 204
Whitney, Travis, 199
William Sisters, 175
Wilson, Edmund, xiv, 47, 50, 73, 135,
  136, 137, 138–39, 140
  on milk strike, 103–4, 105, 106
  on Pineville mission, 83
Wilson, M. L., 97
Wilson, Woodrow, 135
Wisconsin, 148, 150, 152
Wolman, Leo, 140
women, 6, 133–35, 177, 190
Women's Home Missionary Society, 67
Woodhead, Albert, 106
wool, 239
Work, Glenn, 70
Work, Mrs., 71
working hours, 35
Works Progress Administration, xiv,
  141, 264
World's Fair, 267

YMCA, 123
Young, Henrietta, 108
Youngstown, Ohio, 264

Zangara, Giuseppe, 26

ABOUT THE AUTHOR

Michael Golay has taught history at Phillips Exeter Academy in New Hampshire since 2000. He worked as a daily journalist for many years. As an independent scholar, he published three books on aspects of nineteenth-century American history and coauthored a comprehensive reference work on the life, work, and times of William Faulkner. Golay's *A Ruined Land: The End of the Civil War* (1999) was a finalist for the prestigious Lincoln Prize in American History in 2000. He is also the author of *To Gettysburg and Beyond: The Parallel Lives of Joshua Lawrence Chamberlain and Edward Porter Alexander* (1994) and *The Tide of Empire: America's March to the Pacific* (2003). The revised edition of *A Critical Companion to William Faulkner* appeared in 2008.